THE HUDSON
THROUGH THE YEARS

THE HUDSON
THROUGH THE YEARS

Third Edition

Arthur G. Adams

FORDHAM UNIVERSITY PRESS
New York

Second printing, with corrections, 1997
Third printing, with corrections, 1998
Fourth printing, revised, 2000

First edition published by Lind Publications, 1983

Library of Congress Cataloging-in-Publication Data

Adams, Arthur G.
The Hudson through the years / by Arthur G. Adams. — 34d ed.
p.   cm.
Includes bibliographical references and index.
ISBN 0-8232-1676-4 (hardcover); ISBN 0-8232-1677-2 (paperback)
1. Hudson River (N.Y. and N.J.)—History.   2. Hudson River Valley
(N.Y. and N.J.)—History.   3. Hudson River (N.Y. and N.J.)—
Navigation—History.   4. Inland navigation—Hudson River (N.Y. and
N.J.)—History.   I. Title.
F127.H8A225   1996
974.7'3—dc20   96-1737
                                                                          CIP

Printed in the United States of America

To Daryl

Contents

Acknowledgments

A work of this scope is not completed without the encouragement and help of a great many people. It would be impossible to name all those who have been of assistance, but I would like to particularly thank the following: Mrs. Frances Reese of Scenic Hudson Preservation Conference and Mr. Charles T. Keppel for their early encouragement and many practical suggestions; Mr. Peter Stanford of the National Maritime Historical Society for his enthusiastic endorsement of a "Maritime View" history of the Hudson; Messrs. Alfred Van Santvoord Olcott and George Van Winkle Kelly for their information about the old Hudson River Day Line, and Captains Lynn Bottum and the late George Clancy of the *M. V. Dayliner* for sharing their knowledge of the river and knowledge of earlier days on the Hudson; Captain William O. Benson of Sleightsburg, New York for his information about early twentieth century steamboating and activities on Rondout Creek; Messrs. John Novi and Charles Cullen for sharing their knowledge of the Delaware & Hudson Canal; Mr. Jack Campbell for sharing his knowledge of the Morris Canal, the Keansburg Steamboat Company, and the Patten Line; Mr. Graham T. Wilson, Mr. Raymond J. Baxter, and Mr. Harry Cotterrell for help on the Hudson River ferries; Rev. John Finn for information on the Revolution in Bergen County, and Mr. Gardiner T. Watts for similar information about Rockland County. I would also like to thank Mr. Raymond J. Baxter, Mr. William Ewen, Jr., Mr. John F. Matthews, Mr. Frank Wilson, the Port Authority of New York and New Jersey, the Triborough Bridge and Tunnel Authority, the New York Convention and Visitor's Bureau and Railroad Magazine for the use of illustrative material.

Finally I wish to thank my family for their great patience and understanding during the years it has taken to prepare this manuscript.

Arthur G. Adams

Introduction and Reminiscences

The reader may wonder what has motivated the writing of still another book about the Hudson, and I think it fair to give some explanation. In the first place, no really complete history of the River has been published in this century. In recent years many facets of life along the Hudson have disappeared entirely and are being rapidly forgotten. Circumstances have brought me into close contact with the River since early childhood, and over the years I have acquired materials on many diverse aspects of the River, which are rarely found in any single collection. While another writer would have to spend considerable time and money traveling in order to collate the necessary material for such a book, I have it right at hand.

Although born as late as 1935, I have to some measure experienced the fullness of the River—the last days of the steamboat and railroad eras, and have vivid recollections of many things now long-gone from the River. While the dry statistics will remain in various libraries and archives for future researchers and writers, they will not be able to interpret them in the light of first hand experience. Although some still have the memories, many do not have access to the necessary data, or are too old or feeble, to undertake a task of this magnitude. Therefore, if this data is to be collated and interpreted in the light of first hand experience, it is expedient that I make the effort.

From early childhood my father took me on the Hudson River ferries. One of my earliest memories is of the old steam ferries between Edgewater and 125th Street Manhattan. I also remember seeing the Night Line steamers pass on their way upriver in the early evening. They stopped running in 1939 and it is easy to see, from looking at pictures of them, how impressive they must have been to a four year old child. The large Day Boats such as the *Hendrick Hudson* also made strong impressions.

It used to be my parents' habit to take a ride in the early evening to the Englewood Yacht Basin, where we would walk along the water's edge to see the passing steamers and watch the comings and goings of the Dyckman Street Ferry—which still used walking beam paddle-wheelers. A similar boat called the *F. R. Pierson* ran on the Alpine-Yonkers route which we used occasionally. Later this was replaced by the oval-shaped, virtually cabinless, diesel-powered *John J. Walsh*. While I was still very young we made extensive use of the West Shore Railroad ferries from Weehawken to 42nd and Cortlandt Streets. This latter trip was a much prized treat, with its 4 mile trip down the busy river, dodging the many tugs, lighters, and car floats, and passing the many ocean liners, troop ships, and freighters—not to mention all the other ferry boats and river steamers. It is incredible how *empty* the river looks today compared with what I remember. Another popular route was the Electric Ferry from Weehawken to West 23rd Street, where the United States Lines passenger liners used to dock. I vividly recall seeing the French Line's great *Normandie,* with its burned out hull, heeled over at its pier. During World War II there was gas rationing and my father used every possible short cut to save gas. This brought me onto many other long-gone ferry lines, such as the Pennsylvania Railroad route from Cortlandt Street to Exchange Place in Jersey City—the ancient Paulus Hook Ferry; the Jersey Central Communipaw Ferry; and the Erie's Pavonia Ferry; not to mention the lines of the Lackawanna's Hoboken Ferry Company to Christopher and Barclay Streets. We also used all the ferries between Staten Island and Brooklyn, Manhattan, Perth Amboy, Elizabeth, and Bayonne. Later in life I continued to use these as long as they continued to operate in preference to tunnels and bridges. Upriver I crossed many times on the Kingston-Rhinecliff and Newburgh-Beacon Lines. While I remember seeing the Nyack Ferry, I never traveled on it nor on the Highland-Poughkeepsie route.

For a number of years I commuted on the Weehawken-Cortlandt Street route. The boats had no radar, ship to shore radios, or phones. During dense fog they blew their whistles and listened for echoes, fog horns, and bells mounted on the docks. I crossed many times in dense fog, both day and night. This is a frightening feeling in a busy harbor. One foggy morning in 1958 I was going to work on the 8:30 AM boat from Weehawken, sitting in the upper cabin reading a book, when our boat, the *Albany,* collided with another West Shore ferryboat, the *Stony Point.* Although heading in opposite directions the collision was not fully head-on. The strong rounded bows absorbed the impact and caused them to rebound and lurch. It gave the passengers an awful fright and we literally crept the rest of the way down to our slip at Cortlandt Street, hugging the ends of the many piers to keep our bearings. On one occasion we headed into the wrong slip and had to back out. Fortunately damage to both boats was minimal.

Another episode in 1959 was not so fortunate. At that time I was working for a reinsurance company as a Direct Excess Casualty Insurance Underwriter. Among their accounts was the Lackawanna Railroad and its subsidiary Hoboken Ferry Company. We had just renewed their insurance policy when, one morning, their ferryboat *Chatham,* heavily loaded with commuters, attempted a race with a coastal freighter and lost. The freighter cut into the starboard passenger cabin causing much damage and injury to passengers. Fortunately they were able to get her to her Manhattan slip at Barclay Street before sinking. About a half-hour after the accident a newspaper reporter noticed a man walking down Broadway with a large white life preserver around his waist with *Chatham* lettered on it. The man was so shocked that he didn't realize what he was doing. The reporter asked him if he was nervous and he said—"Not in the least." Later that morning my boss came into the office. When I told him that the *Chatham* had been hit by a freighter I thought he would have a heart attack. He remarked that "We never should have renewed the policy on that old tub." From that time forward the insurance companies gave the railroads a hard time and raised the insurance costs—thus helping to drive the ferries from the river. They also disliked company outings on excursion boats because, if a disaster occurred, too many people under the same group policy would be killed or injured. This hastened the decline of the excursion business.

I only remember two bad times concerning rough weather. Late one afternoon in 1958 I took the Cortlandt Street ferry from Weehawken. The river was running high choppy waves of a rather peculiar type not often encountered on the Hudson. The decks were awash for the entire trip and the headwind was so strong that we took twice our usual time for the crossing. On another occasion (I was not on this trip), the West Shore ferryboat *Rochester* had its top deck ripped off by a miniature cyclone between 42nd Street and Weehawken.

I can remember seeing five or six ferryboats lined up in their slips at Weehawken or Hoboken on weekends when they were not all in service, and as many as twelve or thirteen boats at a time crossing in the lower river.

The upriver lines also left some memories. The *George Clinton* of the Kingston-Rhinecliff line used to sail down Rondout Creek and pass the lighthouse. There was an old man who sold warm flat birch beer at the Rhinecliff landing because "carbonated and cold drinks are not good for you." I think people patronized him because he was such a pathetic character. The ferries were very socializing and humanizing. You saw other people, talked to them, and shared an experience with them in every crossing, whereas today people travel in the capsulized isolation of their automobiles. They also brought you in daily contact with the River—the tides, the winds, the rain, the waves, the fog, and the beautiful effects of light on the water.

The Newburgh-Beacon boats were impressive for their very black smoke and smell of burning soft coal. I particularly remember crossing from Beacon to Newburgh about 11:00 AM one bright sunny winter morning when there was a crust of skim ice on Newburgh Bay. I stood on the forward deck in the keen air and listened to the tinkle of the bow cutting through the ice and watching the ice chips tossed up and glittering in the sunlight. Other winter crossings through heavy ice flows on the lower river come to mind. Large chunks of ice would thud against the hull and there was a continuous crunching sound.

I can remember returning home from the theater or opera on the midnight boat from 42nd Street and standing on the rear deck, playbill in hand, watching the lights of Manhattan, and enjoying the cool breeze. On mellow sunlit afternoons you could see the motes of thick dust in the golden light in the cavernous gangways, silent passenger cabins, and vehicle teamways. I remember the raising and lowering of the landing bridges and upper deck gangplanks and the peculiar chain rattle as the dockman turned the winch wheels, and how the boat would push against the dock until made fast. Coming into the slip it would reverse its engines to slow down. In crossing the river account was taken of the tides and current. The pilot would aim either slightly up or down stream from the opposite landing so that the tide would carry him to the right spot—except at slack water when he aimed straight across. During the busy days you often had to maneuver between barges, lighters, seagoing ships, and other ferries.

Gradually the ferry lines faded away. For brief periods I commuted on the Erie and Lackawanna boats and was on the final trips of both lines, as I had been some years before at the demise of the West Shore routes. I sadly realized that a way of life was passing.

The ferries were a great way to see the ocean liners. During the 2nd World War they were all painted gray. The *Queen Mary* was particularly impressive in this livery. After the War they all sported bright new paint jobs and looked very smart. Usually the scheduled North Atlantic liners were painted with black hulls and white super-structures with red stacks . . . . Those on southern routes or cruise services were painted all white with buff color or yellow stacks. There were still some three stackers operating in my time. The *Queen Mary* was one as were the *Brittania* and the *Queen of Bermuda.* This last one had a gray hull, white super-structure and three big bright red stacks with black bands. She used to sail out on Friday afternoons as I was coming home from work on the Cortlandt Street boat, and was a very grand and impressive sight. I can also remember seeing the tugboats assist the great liners into their berths. Captain Nigel Kingscote, Port Captain for the Cunard Line, was a fellow commuter with me to West Englewood on the West Shore Railroad. He was responsible for the safe docking of the Queens.

On occasion as many as a dozen large liners would be tied up next to each other in the Hudson at Manhattan. You can imagine what a thrill it was to stand on the deck when I sailed on one myself. Today only a few cruise ships call at New York. The whole busy scene has vanished—ships and docks and all the ceaseless activity—and it now all seems like a dream.

I remember my first steamboat trip—from 42nd Street to Bear Mountain. We went upriver on the *Alexander Hamilton* and came home on the *Robert Fulton.* This must have been prior to 1940 for I remember being impressed not only by the giant inclined piston engines, but also by the carpets, wicker furniture, potted palms, and paintings and my father's complaint about the high price of a roast beef dinner in the dining room, which was then quite elegant. In later years it broke my heart to see this room degraded to a vulgar cafeteria. I well remember subsequent trips on the *Hendrick Hudson* and *Peter Stuyvesant*. Another great water travel event was when my father took me to Boston on the Eastern Steamship Lines, *St. John* overnight through Long Island Sound and the Cape Cod Canal. This was just before German submarine attacks on coastal shipping put a stop to this service. It is sad for me to think that I am probably one of the youngest persons alive to have traveled from the North River on ocean liners, coastal liners, river steamers, and sound steamers. In another year it would have become impossible to have traveled on all four types of ship.

In my teens I took advantage of cheap excursions from Jersey City to Bridgeport, Connecticut and to Atlantic Highlands via the Battery and Brooklyn—not to mention cruises around Manhattan on the Circle Line.

I have been fortunate in traveling to and from Albany on the *Hendrick Hudson, Alexander Hamilton, Peter Stuyvesant,* and *Robert Fulton* of the Day Line on quite a few occasions, and as recently as 1977 on a special excursion of the sound steamer *Martha's Vineyard*. This last trip gave me a rare opportunity to introduce my own two children to the upper Hudson. I particularly remember returning home from Chicago with my father on the old New York Central *Water Level Limited* and getting off at Albany to take the *Hendrick Hudson* down to Bear Mountain, from which point we took the West Shore Railroad to our home in North Jersey. What was interesting is that he used his regular through Chicago to New York Pullman tickets on both the steamer and the West Shore. This must have been about 1947—and possibly we were among the last passengers to ever use this particular alternate routing privilege. Our Pullman tickets entitled us to a day parlor on the steamer, and I can remember a white jacketed black steward, bringing drinks and sandwiches from the dining room to my father at a little table on our private deck. In later years, after discontinuance of the regular Albany boat, my wife and I took Labor Day Weekend three day excursions each year to Albany from 1958 until 1962, when they were discontinued. Usually the sidewheeler *Alexander Hamilton* was used, but in 1960 the propeller *Peter Stuyvesant* was operated. My diary records that there was a terrific lightning storm as we were passing New Baltimore. I also remember the most beautiful rainbow after this storm as we approached Albany. That same evening we took a Pullman to Buffalo and visited Niagara Falls, returning on the Pullman to Albany the next night to take the boat home. The last trip from Albany was not particularly sad. My diary entry reads as follows: "Monday-Labor Day, September 3, 1962—left 10:00 AM Str. *Alexander Hamilton*—Madison Street wharf. Capt. DeWitt Robinson. Fine day's trip to New York. Supper at home. Slight headwind and unusual number of small craft."

Little did anyone know that this would be the last sidewheel steamer ever to leave Albany. Usually on these trips we took a "trip on the trip," meaning that while staying at the old Ten Eyck Hotel in Albany, we would take a one day excursion on the Delaware & Hudson train either to Lake George for a boat trip or to Saratoga Springs. One year we took the Boston & Albany Railroad across the Berkshires to visit a friend in Springfield, Massachusetts. My only regret is that we did not then have any children so that another generation could have this experience. These trips were most enjoyable because the boat was not as crowded as on regular trips on the lower river. Much baggage was brought on board and the porters used the old human-chain method of passing baggage to load the dollys. I can remember the entire space around the Purser's Office piled to the ceiling with baggage. Dinner was a slow affair, but the food served on these special trips was good, especially the roast beef and fried Butterfly Shrimp. Luncheon on one crowded trip lasted from West Point to Kingston! On another trip, I think it was 1959, the beautiful Miss Rheingold Girls were all on board. Still another time Guy Lombardo's Orchestra, with Guy himself conducting, played on the downstream voyage from Albany to Poughkeepsie. Even though it was actually a Monday, they kept playing "Cruising Down the River on a Sunday Afternoon." We had seats outside on the main deck forward, just off the dance floor. It was a beautiful sunny day and the banks of the River were lined with people who had come down to see the steamer pass—which was then a rare sight on the upper Hudson. It was altogether delightful and probably as close as you could get to the great old steamboat days.

There used to be an evening cruise on Saturday night, which we took each year except the time we went to Niagara Falls. It left Albany at about 8:00 PM and cruised down to near New Baltimore or Coxsackie. Usually there was a moon, but one dark year they had the devil of a time turning the ship around in pitch darkness near Schodack Island and we nearly ran aground. On the *Peter Stuyvesant* trip in 1960 on the moonlight cruise we hit a powerboat near Castleton and demolished it and killed its driver and his passenger. I can remember the music and engines stopping and a couple of youths running toward the stern and jumping overboard in an attempt to save the people in the powerboat. On Monday morning we saw them still dragging the river. These moonlight sails were great fun and never rowdy, as was often the case on trips out of New York City. The Kenwood Generating Station of the Niagara Mohawk Power Co., with its great smokestacks belching smoke, would be all lit up and was most impressive. The raising of the Dunn Memorial Lift Bridge was also very interesting, as was turning around the ship by winches at the Madison Street Wharf (actually a concrete quay.) I remember that on one trip they forgot to cast off all the lines and we were picking up speed when the ship came to a shuddering halt and all its joints creaked. I thought the super-structure was going to keep on going down the river while the hull stopped. On yet another trip the tide was so low at Albany that we had to unload from the upper deck, as the gangplank would have been at too steep an angle to climb from the main deck. On one trip downriver the ship rolled on a wave and upset an upright piano on top of a man and injured him so badly that he had to be taken off at an unscheduled stop at Yonkers. On still another northbound trip a man had gotten on board to see his family off at Manhattan. He failed to get off on time and we all thought he would have to go to Albany as no stops were scheduled. At Bear Mountain we came in close to the dock although no stop was scheduled. The man jumped to the dock in order to take a bus or train back to New York and made it safely!

On regular excursions to Poughkeepsie I can remember the boats running quite late into the autumn and one particular night coming back in a black driving rain aboard the *Peter Stuyvesant*. We huddled around the steam radiators. Captain Brinkman was in charge and had a difficult time docking us in the dark, rain, and high wind at Pier 81. He was yelling at the deckhands . . . an unusual breech of decorum. On another trip, in perfectly good weather, the *Stuyvesant* ran aground on the mud near the Dutton Lumber Company dock at Poughkeepsie.

A rather frightening experience occurred on Saturday, August 28th, 1965. We had just returned from a lengthy European trip on which we had sailed up the Rhine from Rotterdam to Basle. My diary entry reads:

> Trip up Hudson with Bob and Linda Clark on Hudson River Day Line to Poughkeepsie to compare with Rhine—on *S.S. Alexander Hamilton,* Capt. Edward Grady. Very fast trip until, 2 miles south of Yonkers on return, log rams and jams port wheel. Drift onto mud at Mt. St. Vincent and towed back to pier 81 by tugs *Carol Moran* and *Nancy Moran* - very frightening—site of *Henry Clay* disaster in 1848.

I was standing on the main deck forward, near the capstan, when we hit the log. It felt as though the entire ship "hit a bump." We were going about 18 knots at the time and the wind was broadside from the Palisades. It was a nice clear day, but the river was running whitecaps. This was about 5:00 PM. We had noticed a great deal of large driftwood earlier that day, but we never thought it would bother the ship. What had happened was that it got caught in the feathering wheel mechanism and, jamming against the inside of the paddle box, had partially unseated the paddle shaft bearings so that the engine could not turn. We were powerless. The wind from the west pushed us up onto the mud about 20 feet from the stone embankment of the New York Central Railroad. We were stuck on there a long time before help arrived from New York and it was a painfully slow tow back to the City. However, the damage could not have been severe, as we learned that the *Hamilton* made its regular run the next day. The only other thing like this was on an Albany trip on the *Hamilton* when we hit the wave of the incoming tide meeting a strong down current near Glasco while heading south one morning. This was near a place known as the Maelstrom. It gave us quite a lurch.

My father would take us on the steamers to the football games at West Point. During the days of gas rationing he would use the boats for business travel between Newburgh, Poughkeepsie, and Kingston. The point I wish to make is that, as the years passed use of the boats ''for transportation'' gradually gave way to ''Use for pleasure excursions.'' Thus I have known river travel under both aspects.

Two sad trips involved my elderly grandfather who was in a nursing home in the 1960s, and my father during his final illness a few years later. Coincidentally, the last ''outing'' that both of them ever took was a short cruise from Bear Mountain to Poughkeepsie and return on the *Alexander Hamilton.*

My grandfather was in his late eighties. Born in England, he lived in New York City from the time he was ten years old. As a boy he would frighten his mother to death in the following manner. He was always an excellent and powerful swimmer. He and his friends would go swimming in the Hudson off West 125th Street. They would swim out into the middle of the river. There was much driftwood in those days and they would get a big log and try to maneuver into the double wake of a paddle steamer. Where the two wakes crossed a wave was formed which would ''pull'' the log for many miles. They would sometimes go far upriver behind a steamer and then get the wake of a boat going downriver to go home. He knew all the famous steamboats around the turn of the century and claimed that he could tell them by their distinctive whistles. In later years he went into the coal business in New York and had a dock and yard near 125th Street.

My wife's grandfather, Archibald Hart, was General Counsel and a Director of the Hudson Navigation Company that ran the Night Line. We still have many stock certificates of this company. Her father claimed that if they were still good we would have majority control. He used to tell of trips on the night steamers as a boy with his father on ''Directors' Outings'' to a club in the Adirondacks. He tells how he was allowed to operate the great searchlight mounted on the ship. He also used to recount his father's tales about the late C. W. Morse who he considered a ''great scoundrel,'' and after whom one of the largest steamers was named.

The saddest trip of all, however, was on September 6th, 1971, when my wife and I and our two children were on board the last trip of the *Alexander Hamilton* between Bear Mountain and Poughkeepsie. We knew that an era was coming to an end. After getting off at Bear Mountain, we raced the ship south along the river by automobile in the hope of getting some good photographs. However, it turned very misty, and my last sight of active sidewheel steam operation on the Hudson was at Englewood Yacht Club, where I had first known the steamers. The *Hamilton* sailed into the mist just off the Cloisters. It literally faded away and gave a mournful salute on the whistle to some people on the dock at Dyckman Street.

For a number of years in the 1960s, I had written letters to influential preservation institutions and museums in an attempt to awaken them to the significance of the *Alexander Hamilton* as the last of the great sidewheelers. However, nothing developed from my efforts.

I was cheered by word that the South Street Seaport Museum would take the *Hamilton* for preservation. They did keep it for a while, but betrayed their trust. It was sold for use as a floating restaurant at Atlantic Highlands, far from its old territory. The restaurant plan fell through and she was subject to exposed conditions and began to deteriorate. I visited her there and saw her very battered. In 1978 she was purchased and moved to the Navy Pier at Leonardo in Sandy Hook Bay. This also is a very exposed location. Here she was swamped and sunk in a violent storm. Attempts are now being made to raise funds to raise her and tow her to the Hudson where she would be restored as a permanent exhibit and memorial to the steamboat age. I have also visited the *Peter Stuyvesant* moored at Anthony's Pier 4 Restaurant in Boston Harbor. They did a beautiful job of restoring her—both inside and out. She was fit up as a cocktail lounge and gift ship, and although the restoration was not fully accurate, it was obviously done with loving care. Unfortunately she was flooded and sunk in the great storm of 1978 and it is now planned to scrap her.*

Ironically, the one Dayliner that I didn't know as a child, the *Chauncey M. Depew,* is now moored in the Hackensack River at Secaucus. It has been turned into a restaurant and beautifully restored. She suffered many vicissitudes, including service as a troop transport, tugboat, harbor tender, and excursion boat at Bermuda and Boston, and sinking in Chesapeake Bay. In 1977 I finally made her acquaintance.

A very cheering trip was when my wife and children accompanied me on the maiden voyage of the new *M. V. Dayliner* on Saturday, June 10th, 1972—New York to Poughkeepsie and return—Captain Edward Grady. It was heartening to see the tradition of service continued but it was not the same. Nothing will ever replace the old steamers.

I'm not sure if all the foregoing is of interest to anyone. However, I do know that I find descriptions of scenes in the nineteenth century of great interest, and feel I should record some of these twilight scenes of the steamboat age on the Hudson so that future generations will know what it was like.

I suppose you might say that I am pretty well steeped in the "brine of Hudson's wave," but I have other memories of the shore and the railroads that ran down both sides of the River.

My first train ride was from Weehawken to Bear Mountain on the West Shore Railroad. The train was pulled by a large Pacific type steam locomotive and was very crowded, as was the terminal. The old coaches had polished rose-wood panelling and green plush push-over seats. I was particularly impressed when the train ran along the water's edge from Stony Point to Iona Island. Arriving at Bear Mountain, we walked up a steep covered ramp to the top of a bluff overlooking the Hudson, and then over a less steep ramp across the old bear pits and Route 9W. The ramps have now been removed.

In following years I rode on the West Shore many times and frequently used it on my visits to New York City, and then commuted on it for about a year and a half until passenger service was discontinued and it was relegated to freight service only. In fact, for the last few months, I was the sole remaining daily passenger on my regular train, which consisted of a locomotive and eight cars. The reason for this was that the connecting ferry had been discontinued first and only a few people found an alternate way to get to the West Shore trains. I had figured out a way of taking the Susquehanna Railroad from Jersey City to Ridgefield Park, where the two lines shared a common station. The empty West Shore train would arrive from Weehawken, and I would ride to West Englewood in solitary and dismal splendor on my "private train." Naturally, this ridiculous situation did not last long and the railroad ultimately got court permission to discontinue all the remaining passenger trains. I used to kid the crew that if they did not stop at exactly the right place at the West Englewood platform I would abscond to the bus and leave them with no passengers—it was gallows humor.

---

*Has been scrapped at time of publication.

In previous years I had frequently used the trains to Kingston and Albany. I made it a point to ride on both the last passenger train from Albany and on the last commuter run. For several years I had worked with commuter groups trying to save the service, which had 10,000 daily riders and over twenty daily trains at the time the New York Central petitioned to discontinue all passenger service. They did everything possible to get rid of the trains and drive away people. Their ultimate success served to awaken the public to the plight of commuter services in general. Possibly some day service will be restored on the West Shore.

I also travelled on the trains of the New York, Ontario & Western Railway, which utilized West Shore tracks between Weekhawken and Cornwall. These were among the first dieselized trains in the United States. The West Shore retained steam until quite a late date. The big freight locomotives were of the Niagara, and the Mohawk class, and Pacifics were used for passenger trains.

West Shore trains pulled into the old Union Station at Albany. This certainly was a busy place with trains of five lines coming and going (West Shore, Delaware & Hudson, New York Central, Rutland Railway, Boston & Albany) to such points as Binghamton, Chicago, St. Louis, Cincinnati, Toronto, Montreal, and Boston. I don't know how many times I passed through or changed trains here on trips using all the different lines.

Particularly impressive was the ride along the Hudson on the New York Central's westbound *Twentieth Century Limited,* with the sun setting over the Hudson and the distant Catskill Mountains. The train itself was superb. I remember the frozen upper river late one winter afternoon about 1960 with the Coast Guard ice breaker cutting a channel near Stuyvesant Station. I also remember the West Shore's last "name train" leaving Albany with a big indicator board reading *Storm King Limited.* The names *Commodore Vanderbilt, Laurentian, Mount Royal, Green Mountain, Cayuga, Empire State Express, Water Level Limited, Ohio State Limited, New England States,* and many more all evoke memories of pleasant and exciting trips—often to such distant places as Seattle or Los Angeles. The Hudson Valley was the grand gateway to the West. On a more humble level I remember taking a trip on the now abandoned Northern Railroad of New Jersey line up along the side of Clausland Mountain between Piermont and Nyack. It was a pleasant Saturday afternoon with all the sailboats out on the Tappan Zee. I have also travelled along the shores of Raritan Bay on the way to and from the Jersey Shore on the New York & Long Branch Railroad.

The trolley lines also stick in my memory. The big yellow cars of the Public Service Railroad came down the Palisades to Edgewater Ferry from Palisade Junction and to Weehawken Ferry from 48th Street up on the cliffs. This last line was thrilling, as it rode between Pershing Avenue and a steep cliff and had a considerable (25%) grade with a sharp turn 2/3rds of the way down. There was a "safety switch" permanently set into a sand pit here in case of runaway cars. On every downbound trip the motorman had to get out and set the switch back onto the main track. After the car passed the switch it would automatically snap back into the sand pit position. I also remember the open sided cars on 42nd Street and 125th Street, Manhattan. I understand that the city now wants to put streetcars back on these routes.

Palisades Amusement Park with its great ferris wheel and Bob Sled roller coaster atop the Palisades was a favorite place to visit. Before the great fire there were three roller coasters—the gentle "Scenic Railway," the wilder "Sky Rocket," and the unusual "Bob Sled." This last ride hoisted cars up 150 feet inside an enclosed incline and then sent them down a trackless roller coaster. The cars were equipped with caster wheels and ran through polished wooden troughs rather than on tracks. There were many loops and dips. The site is now occupied by the Winston Tower Apartment Development.

Many of these recollections are children's recollections, as I was only a child when they still existed. In the later twilight years my enjoyment was poignant as I realized I was watching the end of not only a technology but a way of life. Whenever possible I documented these things with camera and kept a journal or diary of my use of these vanishing modes of transport. They were the life of the Hudson River. Today the Hudson is largely lifeless and ignored. It is our loss. I hope that the information contained in this work will inspire future generations to return, to use, and to enjoy the Hudson, which has given me, and millions before me, so much solid enjoyment in the leisurely appreciation of grand scenery and good company.

The reader will find that I do not intrude my personality into the remainder of this work. However, before saying farewell, I would like to share some recollections and perceptions—written in what is perhaps a very unsophisticated attempt to convey the poetic essence of the moment:

> Among the many happy days spent among the Catskills and on the Hudson, certain moments shine out with pellucid clarity—epiphanies—emanations of the spiritus loci.

> A sultry mist hangs over the Kaaterskill Clove. White banners of dust over the cement mills at Alsen and the distant Berkshires appearing in a landscape by Claude. Lunch served on the terrace of the Ledge End Inn. Cool crisp salad. Sparkling tableware, deft, white jacketed waiters. Cicadas. Murmuring of flowing water. I am living a Mary Roberts Rhinehart novel or a scene from a Winslow Homer sketch—August 1958.

> The train moves softly through the golden late afternoon, the distant Catskills silhouetted against the declining sun. Motes of golden dust and the faint aroma of hot oil and coal smoke. The genial crew chat with the few traveling salesmen, women, children, and college students. The conductor, a jovial round faced Dutchman, informs one and all that he is also an itinerant licensed barber in his off hours. It is hot. The brakeman, a strapping young fellow, invites me back into the baggage car where we can enjoy the air blowing in through the open door and watch the distant Catskills. He surreptitiously offers me a can of cold beer. We drink in silence, drinking in also the golden glory of the afternoon. The spell is broken as we rumble across the high trestle north of Catskill—station stop. June 1954—Train #2 of the West Shore Railroad—*The Storm King*.

> An unbroken sea of white cotton—endless billows. A slight chill in the air. We are in another world. Sealed off from humanity. Time. Eternity. Glory. My son huddles against me in awe. July 1973—4:00 AM—Sunrise—Prospect Rock—North Mountain.

> My passengers go "ou, ow, ah, ugh" with every bump. Sunlight filters through cool green branches of hemlock and fir as we splatter the puddles from the recent rain. Dewlike drops of water sparkle in the sun on the evergreen boughs. The smell of the forest is acrid and clean. We bounce along beside the swollen brook, through the mud and the puddles.—A late afternoon about 1950 on the Frost Valley Road.

> Clacking along through the hills of Sullivan County. Cows on the hillsides. The air is dusty and hot. Drowsiness covers the land. We sit silently in our camp chairs on the observation platform. Isolated from the world. We are alone. The only passengers on the train for a 130 mile trip. Idyllic—Ferndale, Fallsburgh, Mountaindale, Summitville, Mamakating, Middletown—Cornwall—the Hudson burnished silver in the late afternoon sun. June 1952—The O&W *Mountaineer* southbound midweek.

> Cool spray. Damp rocks and moss. Ferns—lichen—a nymph's haunted grotto. Not a mortal soul around, but many spirits dwell here. A slanting shaft of golden sunlight and glorious music of the broken rill. Pristine essence. Mid-afternoon—July 1950. Kaaterskill Falls as first seen at a time when it was almost entirely forgotten by many.

> Eight lathered horses nudge their way to the trough of cool, clear water. The four drivers pull at the reins in an attempt at maintaining order. The young ladies in frilly cotton and their escorts in poplin suits and boaters descend to stretch their legs. Flies buzz in the hot afternoon sunlight and worry the horses. Flip goes the whip! Back again. Flip again! Got em! Sunlight dapples the fern covered forest floor. Pungent aroma of essentially moist woodland in hot sun. Gentle laughter. The road between Hotel Kaaterskill and Catskill Mountain House in 1880? No. Monday, June 13, 1960 midway between Lake Mohonk and Lake Minnewaska Mountain Houses.

> Arcady? Yoknapatawpha County? St. Charles Parish? Bullfinch? William Faulkner? George Washington Cable? Late afternoon sun gilds the Doric columns and pediment as we emerge from the woods onto the rough grass sward. Ruined drives and columns askew. A tall gaunt dead tree. Tara? Sherman's Desolation? The Course of Empire: Desolation? July 1958—About 5:00 PM. First view of ruins of Catskill Mountain House—from the West.

Chunk, Chunk, Chunk—dum-da-da-daa-daa, dum-da-da-daa-daa. The telegraph jangles. Hiss, whiss, hiss, whiss. Clunk, Clunk, Clunk—Silence—swish, Thump. Jangle, Jangle. Chug, Chug, Chug. Engines in reverse. Violent hissing of water. Jangle, Jangle, Jangle. Engines halt. Thumper, thumper, thumper of compressors. Smell of hot oil and grease. Clunk goes the gang plank. Creaking of ropes. Thud of feet on the gangplank. Jangle, Jangle—Full speed ahead. Funky smell of churned up riverbottom. Hiss whish, hiss whish. Clunker, clunker, clunker. A Hudson River landing as observed from near the engine room on the main deck of a sidewheeler. Unforgettable.

That was the essence of a bygone age as I have known it, having had the good fortune to observe it in its final Gotterdammerung. The preceding paragraphs tell the discerning spirit more about the true Romantic essence of the Catskill-Hudson Region than all the "facts" in the following volume. Perhaps, however, it is impossible to capture such ethereal things as aromas, a certain slant of light, a mood, a sense of brooding yet grand melancholy, or pure exhilaration spirit.

Vale!

Arthur G. Adams
Mahwah, NJ
February 3, 1979

Preface to Revised Third Edition

Since *The Hudson Through The Years* was first published in 1983 there has developed a real need to update the book. Various minor refinements and corrections were made in the second printing. However, subsequent research has clarified many obscure points. Also, many of my readers have contacted me to share information and reminiscences. Hearing from my readers is always a great pleasure and I have made it a point to incorporate the new information into the revised text . . . and several "historical mysteries" have now been solved.

1 Indian Period

It is difficult to pinpoint the date when aboriginal man first visited the Hudson Valley. The New York State Archeological Association owns a site near Athens where it is believed that prehistoric man mined flint stones 12,000 years ago. Other archeological findings in New Jersey date back about 8000 years. It is possible that the area served as a hunting ground during inter-glacial periods. The entire record is very sketchy.

Recorded history begins about the year 1300 AD. Most of the records are only legends, but these legends seem to provide consistent internal evidence. According to the *Walam Olum* or *Red Score* of the Lenni Lenape Indians, they first reached the Atlantic Seaboard only a few hundred years before the period of white discovery c1400 AD. According to this Indian epic, the Lenni-Lenape or "original people" had migrated from a very cold region in the North via the Middle West, in their search for a "river that flowed two ways." (Possibly the tidal Hudson.)

The Lenni-Lenape Indians occupied most of New Jersey and the upper reaches of the Delaware River and the lower west bank of the Hudson. They were sometimes called the Delaware Indians and were an Algonkian speaking nation. They lived in round houses and had stone implements. Corn, squash, pumpkin, and beans were cultivated and they used fish as fertilizer. Their pottery was of high quality and indeed their general level of culture was higher than that of the New England Indians.

There were several distinct groupings. The Unalachtigo lived in Southern New Jersey. The Minsi or Monsey centered in the Port Jervis area and more properly belong to the Catskill and Ramapo regions. The Unami lived largely in the Northern and Central parts of New Jersey, and their territory reached from the Raritan Valley to Saugerties on the Hudson.

Some were also settled on Staten, Wards, Coney, Welfare, and Governors Islands as well as in Brooklyn. They included the Canarsee Tribe, of which Sessys was the Sachem. Other tribes of the Unami were the Hackensacks, Pomptons, Raritans, Saulrickans, and Tappans, living in the areas still bearing their names. It was Unami Indians who first greeted Henry Hudson on September 3, 1609 at Communipaw, New Jersey. They were generally friendly to the white men except when unduly provoked as at the time of the Pavonia Massacre. It is interesting to note that every bit of land in New Jersey was fairly purchased from the Indians—a claim that no other State can make. During the French & Indian War the Delawares sided with the English, and they later adhered to the English during the American Revolution. The aforementioned Pavonia Massacre occurred in 1647 under the administration of Willem Kieft on the Patent of Michael Pauw in present day Jersey City. The dispute was

The Fort New Amsterdam on Manhattan. Plate in *Beschrivjvingke Van Virginia, Nieuw Nederland,* published by Joost Hartgers, Amsterdam, 1651. View is looking west.

later settled by Peter Stuyvesant. There was an earlier Indian Uprising in 1643. At that time a peace was negotiated with Oratam (sometimes called Oritani) of the Hackensack Indians. Sporadic uprisings occurred until 1658 when Peter Stuyvesant repurchased an area on the west shore of the Hudson near the great Clip or Chip above Weehawken. In 1662 Chief Oratam was authorized to arrest anyone selling brandy in Indian territory. In 1618 the Lenni-Lenape numbered about 10,000 in New Jersey. By the time of the American Revolution there were almost none left. Eventually most of them moved to Indiana, Ontario, Kansas, and Oklahoma.

The Wappinger Confederation were alligned with the Mahicans or Mohicans. Their territory included most of Long Island, the East Bank of the Hudson, and the West Bank from Catskill north to the edge of the Mohawk Territory above Albany. On Long Island they were divided into subtribes of the Montauk Confederation. The Wappinger Confederation consisted of the Wappinger or Wappingi Tribe, who were concentrated around Poughkeepsie and in Western Connecticut; the Nochpeem; Kitchawank; Sintsink (near Ossining or Sing-Sing); the Pachami, near Beacon; the Wecquaesgeek; Siwanoy and Manhattans. The Wappingers were also called the Waubun (=east) Acki (=land). Their war chiefs were Wapperonk and Aepjen, who participated in the Dutch and Indian Wars of 1643 and 1663.

Manhattan Island was occupied by three groups of the Manhattan Indians. Manhattan is a corruption of Menohanet, or "people of the islands," in the Mohican language. The Werpoes occupied lower Manhattan. Meijeterma was their Sachem. The Rechewanis occupied the Middle East side. Their name means "little sand stream," and Rechewac was their Sachem. The Inwood section of Upper Manhattan was occupied by the Weckquaesgeeks. In 1715 the Freeholders of New Harlem, by special tax, raised a fund with which Col. Stephen Van Cortlandt made a final settlement with the Manhattan Indians. The original Indian Purchase had been made by Peter Minuit in 1626 for $24.00 worth of hardware, kettles, and rum. The original Werpoe settlement was on the site of present day Foley Square.

A subtribe of the Minsi, known as the Waoranecks or Waranawankongs, lived in the Esopus or Kingston area on the West Bank of the Hudson. They were corn raising Indians and dwelt along the Esopus Creek where there were good bottom lands. The Indian word for river or large creek is Seepus, and therefore this group was sometimes known as the Esopus Indians from their habitat.

The Mohicans or Mahicans, who dwelt mainly on the East Bank of the Hudson, had their Council Fire on Schodack Island across from Coeymans. They were in continual conflict with the Mohawks, who in 1664 forced them to move their Council Fire from Schodack to the neighborhood of Stockbridge, Massachusetts. It is ironic that the name Schodack derives from Scoti-ack or "place of the *ever-burning* council fire." In 1680 "King Aepgin of the Mahicans sold to the Van Rensselaers all that tract of country on the west side of the Hudson, extending from Beeren Island up to Smacks Island and in breadth two days journey."

By about 1750 a decisive battle had been fought between the Mohawks and Mahicans at Rodgers Island near Catskill, and the Mahicans were badly beaten and their power broken. Finally the Mahicans drifted back eastward to join their relations, the Mohegans of Connecticut. The remnants of the tribe now live around New London. James Fenimore Cooper, in his *Last of the Mohicans,* set in 1757 during the French & Indian War, describes the exploits of one of the Mahican Chiefs after the dispersal of his tribe. Several exciting episodes are set around Glens Falls. The Mahicans and Delawares fared rather poorly between the upper and nether millstones of the Iroquois and White infiltration and disappeared from the Hudson Valley.

It is generally agreed that the people who later comprised the Iroquois Nations occupied upper New York State about 1300 AD. There was considerable ferment between various tribes of the Iroquois at the time of white discovery. Earliest white penetration pre-dates some very important events in Indian history. There were sporadic visitations by French Traders from the St. Lawrence into the Upper Hudson Valley from 1525 until 1609. It is believed that French traders built a stockade on Castle Island near Albany around 1540. During the 1560s the Iroquois Nations were threatened by powerful tribes from the Middle West. These western aggressors had been beating the New York tribes singly in battle for some time when a visionary leader named Haya-watha, or Hiawatha, appeared. He was a follower of the Prophet Deganawidah. According to legend, he was meditating on an island in the Susquehanna River when he had a vision. He was shown five arrows tied together—they could not be broken. Haya-watha then summoned a great council of the five New York tribes to meet at the island. Haya-watha, a Mohawk, was respected for his visions and mystical powers, and he gained a sympathetic audience from the representatives of the beleaguered tribes. This meeting, at which the Iroquois Confederation was formed, was in 1570.

The original five tribes were the Mohawks, Oneidas, Onandagas, Cayugas, and Senecas. Later, about 1722, some Tuscaroras were adopted by the Oneida Tribe. The Oneidas were the only tribe to side with the Colonists during the Revolution, the rest of the Iroquois joining with the British. The few surviving Oneidas now live in Wisconsin.

The five Iroquois tribes called themselves the Ogwanonhsioni or "long house builders," after the type of homes they constructed. They conceived of their Confederation as a great "Long House" extending across the State of New York. The Mohawks were fond of calling themselves the "guardians of the eastern door of the Long House." The name Iroquois is really a Delaware one; and a derogatory one at that. It means "real snakes" or "adders." The Mohawks called themselves the Kanyengehaga, or "people of the place of flint," referring to the area around Cohoes. Mohawk is a corruption of the Delaware word Maquaas, which means "those who eat people." This deprecatory term arose from their cannibalistic practice of eating some of the flesh of their victims in order to attain some of their prowess in battle. Possibly it also could have arisen from their aggressive warlike behavior. In any event, the Iroquois became an important power until after the American Revolution. The newfound "strength in unity" inspired Benjamin Franklin in his conception of a Confederation of the English Colonies. A rather less beneficial result was that the Iroquois became bullies to their neighbors the Mahicans and the Delawares. The powerful Huron and Algonquin Tribes of Canada feared them and their raids on the annual western fur caravans to Montreal. They had good reason for such fear, as they were friends of the French, and the French were mortal enemies of the Iroquois. This situation had come about in the following manner.

In July of 1609, while on an exploring expedition accompanied by Hurons, Samuel Champlain opened gun fire on some Iroquois near the southern end of Lake Champlain. As the Iroquois were unfamiliar with firearms, and the Hurons were operating outside of their own territory, this action was considered unfair and was much resented by the Iroquois. They become implacable enemies of the French and did much to help the English win Canada from France in 1763. They remained faithful to the English during the American Revolution, much to their detriment.

Two famous Seneca chiefs, Cornplanter (c1740-1836), son of an Indian woman and an Albany Trader, and Red Jacket (c1758-1830) were active during the American Revolution and the War of 1812.

The Cayugas, like the Senecas and Onandagas, gave their name to a major upstate lake and later emigrated to Ontario. Remnants of all the Iroquois tribes remain in New York State, and the great Mohawk River takes its name from the notable tribe who once dwelt along it banks. An interesting event concerning the Mohawks was the capture of the French Jesuit priest, Isaac Jogues, in 1643. He was taken to their settlements and tortured. In 1644 he escaped through Albany in a Dutch ship. In 1646 he returned to Canada from France and proceeded to Auriesville, New York, to negotiate peace between the French and the Iroquois. After a third visit to the Iroquois he was seized, tortured and beheaded—but not before winning some converts whose influence continues even today. He was the first American Martyr and there is a shrine to him at Auriesville.

Generally speaking, the Hudson Valley was not an area of major Indian fights. The abundant food from the river and rich bottom lands provided enough for all. As the settlers purchased the land, the Indians gradually withdrew from the valley.

2 Period of Discovery

After the early explorations of America by Christopher Columbus in 1492 and John Cabot in 1498, the Hudson River enters History in 1524 with Giovanni da Verrazano, a Florentine sailing in the service of Francis I of France. He explored the North American coastline from North Carolina to Maine in his ship the *Delfina*, and was probably the first European to enter New York Harbor. He called the Hudson the "Grand River," or "River of the Steep Hills." The next visitor was a Portuguese, Estevan Gomez, in 1525. He was sailing for Spain to explore the region between Rhode Island and Maryland. This area came to be called the "Tierra de Estevan Gomez" on early charts. The Hudson was recognized by many names, such as the "Rio de Gomez," "Rio de Guamas," and Rio San Antonio." In 1569 it appears on several charts as the Norumbega River." Between 1525 and 1609 there was considerable French visitation of New York Bay.

In 1534 Jacques Cartier penetrated the St. Lawrence for France. Shortly after this French traders began filtering down into the Adirondacks and as far as the Albany area where it is suspected they erected a trading post on Castle Island around 1540. In 1581 a Walloon named Adrian Van Loon arrived in Canada, and by 1598 he was trading actively throughout the Adirondacks. Years later his descendants were to migrate to the area of Athens in Greene County and purchase the Loonenburg Patent. They later changed the spelling of their name to Van Loan.

About 1598 several Dutch captains visited New York Bay. The first well documented visit was that by Henry Hudson, an Englishman sailing in the employ of the Dutch East India Company in 1609. He had explored the Atlantic coastline from Nova Scotia to the Chesapeake, and entered New York Bay on retracing his way back northward on September 3rd of that year. He had sailed from Texel in Holland with a crew of 18 or 20 men in an 80 ton vessel called the *Half Moon*. A complete journal of the voyage was kept by his mate, Robert Juet, which gives a very interesting and picturesque description of the river. Wallace Bruce capsulizes Juet's description as follows:

> Reaching Cape Cod August 6th, and Chesapeake Bay August 28th, he coasted north to Sandy Hook. He entered the Bay of New York September 3rd, passed through the Narrows, and anchored in what is now called Newark Bay; on the 12th resumed his voyage, and, drifting with the tide, remained overnight on the 13th about three miles above the northern end of Manhattan Island; on the 14th sailed through what is now known as Tappan Zee and Haverstraw Bay, entering the Highlands and anchored for the night near the present dock at West Point.

On the morning of the 15th beheld Newburgh Bay, reached Catskill on the 16th, Athens on the 17th, Castleton and Albany on the 18th, and then sent out an exploring boat as far as Waterford.[1]

Actually his ship did not get above the Overslaugh Bar and only a small party proceeded twenty miles further upstream to the mouth of the Mohawk River. The furthest point reached, on September 22nd, was near Waterford. Returning to the ship, they set sail downriver on the 23rd. On October 1st they were opposite Stony Point; and 2nd at Manhattan; the 3rd at Hoboken and on the 4th passed out to sea through the Narrows. There were numerous encounters with the Indians. On September 6th John Colman was shot through the throat by an Indian arrow while rowing through the Kill Van Kull on taking soundings—the first white man to be killed by an Indian in the Hudson Valley. He was later buried on Sandy Hook—also called Colman's Point. The reader is urged to obtain a copy of Juet's journal. It is readily available in Roland Van Zandt's excellent book *Chronicles of the Hudson,* Rutgers University Press, New Brunswick, 1971. Mr. Van Zandt has done an excellent job of annotation, relating the action to modern place names.

Although Hudson, an Englishman, was working for the Dutch; earlier, in 1606, James I of England had laid claim to the entire Atlantic Seaboard under the Charter of Virginia. However, this did not stop the Dutch, in 1610, from establishing a trading post at Pavonia, which is present day Jersey City, or the Dutch Captains, Adriaen Block (after whom is named Block Island), Cornelius Jacobsen May (after whom is named Cape May), and Hendrick Christaensen from trading in the area between 1611 and 1613. Nor did it stop the Dutch from giving the "Merchants of North Holland Chartered To Trade" a four voyage monopoly for trading in the Hudson River in 1614. In 1616 Captain May's ship *Tiger* burned at Manhattan. His crew built a new ship (the first to be built along the Hudson) and called it the *Onrest* or *Restless.* That same year another trading post was established at Bergen, also in present day Jersey City.

This did not go unnoticed and, in 1617 and 1618, Sir Samuel Argal raided the primitive settlements at New Netherlands in an attempt to assert English sovereignty. A minor disaster occurred in 1617 when Fort Nassau, near present day Albany, was destroyed by a flood, but apparently trading continued, because, in 1619, the Governor of the Plymouth Colony, who also claimed the Hudson Valley, agreed to "protect Dutch trading on the River," whereas, in 1620, the Dutch refused Puritans the right to settle along the Hudson.

As early as 1614 the Dutch had a trading post at Rondout. Fort Nassau at Albany was established this same year on Castle Island, under the command of Hendrick Christaensen. In 1615 Champlain again invaded Iroquois territory and was defeated near Oneida Lake. The big attraction was furs—especially Beaver Fur. The Iroquois welcomed the opportunity to trade furs for firearms from the Dutch, with which to fight the French. Trade flourished, whereas agriculture did not take too readily. It was easier to trade than to clear and cultivate the land, and much more profitable.

---

[1]Wallace Bruce *The Hudson By Daylight.*

3 Period of Settlement and Patroonships

We have seen the settlement of Bergen in 1616. The naming of this locality has proven an interesting point to historians. Some claim that there were some Norwegians among the Dutch and that they named it after Bergen in Norway. This seems unlikely as Jersey City bears little physical resemblance to Bergen in Norway, with its high mountains. Others claim it was named after Bergen-op-zoom in Holland, which is in a marshy area and a more likely comparison. It is likely that the name was derived from the features of the countryside, as "Bergen" denotes a ridge between two marshlands, that is, those of the Hudson and Hackensack Rivers. The name survives in Bergen County, New Jersey, which once embraced this area prior to the secession of Hudson County in 1840.

We have noted that in 1618 Sir Samuel Argal, on his way from Virginia to Nova Scotia, insulted the Dutch and destroyed their plantations. To guard against further molestations the Dutch settlers secured a license from King James I of England to build cottages and to plant for traffic as well as subsistence, pretending it was only for the convenience of their ships touching there for fresh water and provisions on their voyage to Brazil. This was open recognition of English claims. In 1621 James I claimed sovereignty over New Netherlands "by right of occupation." Also, in 1621 the Dutch government chartered the Dutch West India Company to take over the areas of New Jersey, New York, and Connecticut, explored by the predecessor Dutch East India Company. This led James I to complain to The Hague. The complaint did not prevent the Dutch West India Company from sending out thirty Walloon families to settle in the Albany area in 1623, and from building the four-bastioned Fort Aurania (Orange) in 1624. This superseded Fort Nassau on Castle Island. Here, in 1624, the first white child along the Hudson was born. Also in 1624, Cornelius Jacobsen May, first Director of the New Netherlands Company, arrived in Manhattan in the ship *New Netherland* with thirty families of colonists pursuant to a grant given by the West India Company in 1623. Other ships bringing traders and settlers were the *Mackerel* in 1623 and *Oranje Boom* in 1625.

Some authorities claim May purchased some land from the Indians for 60 Guilders, or $24.00, two years before the Indians made an identical deal with Peter Minuit! In fairness to the Indians, they frequently did not understand just exactly what they were selling. They often thought they were selling only some particular rights such as fishing, hunting, planting, housebuilding, and so forth. In 1623 a similar charter had been granted to Captain Cornelius Jacobs of Hoorn (Van Horne). Things were now moving rather fast. The French did not abandon their claim either, and in 1624 the Dutch chased some Frenchmen who were attempting to erect their Arms of France. In 1625 Master Kryn Fredericke, an engineer, staked out a Dutch fort on Manhetes (Manhattan) Island, near the present Battery. The French continued to settle on Staten Island—mainly Huguenots. They were accepted by the Dutch so long as they did not attempt to exert French sovereignty.

Many of the early settlers of New Amsterdam were seeking religious freedom. Holland was very tolerant for the times and the supposition was that this same freedom would prevail in the settlements. The early settlers consisted not only of Dutchmen, but Walloons, Huguenots, English Dissenters, Scotch Presbyterians, Quakers, Jews, Catholics, Poles, and Norwegians. Polish settlers were quite dominant on the West Bank of the Hudson as is attested by such names as Zabriskie. Albert Saboreweski acquired the 2000 acre New Paramus Patent in 1662 from the Indians, and this was officially confirmed to Jacob Zaborowski in 1713.

The French Huguenot, David des Marest, was another prominent early settler who soon moved to the Hackensack River Valley in protest against having to support the established Dutch Reformed Church. To a large extent the Poles and French rapidly intermarried with the Dutch, and Dutch culture and language prevailed in the lower Hudson Valley. In the Mid-Hudson region the Huguenots retained their identity for a much longer time. Manhattan was always the greatest melting pot, and English influence spread from there. However, pockets of Huguenot influence remained in New Rochelle, Brooklyn, Staten Island, and along the Raritan River.

In 1626 Peter Minuit made the famous purchase of Manhattan Island for $24.00.

THE PATROONSHIPS

To foster settlement, as well as trade, the Dutch West India Company established a form of the Manorial System known as the Patroon System. Under this semi-feudal system large grants of land were given to entrepreneurs who undertook to build a Manor House (often a rough cabin), and bring over settlers and commence agricultural development. The settlers became tenant farmers, owing rent to the landlord or Patroon. The Patroon usually refused to sell land in *fee simple* and the preferred method of tenure was by *Three Life Leases*. Generally speaking the Patroon System was not a success. Settlers preferred to own their own land and it was not long until grants or patents were being given to individuals or groups of associates for smaller holdings. Patroonship grants were made in 1630 to Michael Pauw (Pavonia Patent including much of Hudson County and Staten Island), and to Myndert Myndertsen Van der Horst in 1641 (Bergen County area). They did not prosper.

The Dutch West India Company tried a new method to attract settlers. They offered 200 acres to anyone who would bring with him five men to till the ground in 1640. In 1650 they improved the offer by placing on the land stock and implements for which the settlers were permitted to pay rent. At the end of six years the settlers were obliged to purchase the stock. There was a temporary interruption in 1643 during an Indian uprising, but from this period on settlement went on apace in the lower Hudson Valley—Hudson, Rockland, Bergen, and Richmond Counties. Settlement of Manhattan Island was also rapid, as is attested by the fact that bears and wolves were extinct on the island by 1686.

On the Upper River the Large Grant or Patent was the order of the day, both under Dutch, and later on under English rule. It would be exceedingly difficult to draw up a comprehensive list of patents in the Hudson Valley and Northern New Jersey, and such is not the province of this short history.[1] Often they were called "Manors" by the English.

---

[1] Many are described in detal under the appropriate location heading in the author's *The Hudson: A Guidebook to the River*.

The first Large Grant was made in 1629 to Killaen Van Rensselaer, a pearl and diamond merchant, and uncle of Wouter Van Twiller, a director of the Dutch West India Company and later the third Governor of the New Netherlands. The tract centered on Fort Aurania and was on both sides of the Hudson River. It covered an area measuring 24 by 48 miles. Van Rensselaer himself did not venture to the new world, but sent out his relative Roelf Janssen as overseer. The tenants had to buy all supplies from the commissary and have their grain ground at the Patroon's mill. By 1637 the Patent covered 700 square miles. This was the only one of six major Dutch Patroonships to survive under later English domination; in 1685 Killaen's grandson being confirmed in his rights to the Manor of Rensselaerwyck by the English. Indeed, the Manor remained intact even after the American Revolution, at which time it embraced all of Albany and Rensselaer and a large part of Columbia Counties. In 1838 there were between 60,000 and 100,000 tenant farmers on the Manor according to whose estimate you accept. At that time Stephen Van Rensselaer III, later known as "The Good Patroon," was 6th Lord of the Manor at five years of age. This clearly was an anoma-

View of Battery area of Manhattan early Dutch period, prior to construction of fort.

ly in the new Republican nation. By the mid-nineteenth century, the large estates were finally abolished by a Constitutional Act.

On April 8, 1680 Van Rensselaer had purchased from King Aepgin of the Mahicans "all that tract of country on the west side of the Hudson, extending from Bearn Island up to Smack's Island, and in breadth two day's journey." In 1642 the Van Rensselaers built Fort Crailo "at the ferry at Crawlier over against Albany" at Greenbush, and now known as Rensselaer. It has been restored and is still standing. Fort Crailo served as the Upper Manor. It was enlarged in 1740 by Col. Johannis Van Rensselaer to its present size and was occupied by Van Rensselaers until 1871. In 1758 it served as the Headquarters of General James Abercromby on his way to Ticonderoga during the French and Indian Wars. Here an army surgeon, Dr. Richard Shuckburgh, sitting on the edge of a well near the Fort, wrote the poem Yankee Doodle, inspired by the bizzare appearance of the colonial troops.

A Lower Manor named Claverack (Clover Reach or Pasture) was built by Hendrick Van Rensselaer in 1685. A third house called DeVlackte, or The Flats, was built on the West Bank south of Watervliet, opposite Breaker Island, by Richard Van Rensselaer (c1664-1670). This last homestead was later sold to Philip Pietersen Schuyler.

By the time of the Governorship of Peter Stuyvesant (1647-1664), Killaen Van Rensselaer thought himself so powerful that he instructed his henchman Nicholas Koorn to build a fort on Barren Island and demand tribute tolls from passing vessels by "wapen recht!" We were to have the Rhenish Robber Barons on the Hudson.[2]

The power of the Van Rensselaers was becoming intolerable to the Company and the Director General (Governor) Peter Stuyvesant ordered the laying out of the town of Beverwyck adjacent to Fort Aurania. This was considered "Company Property" and was placed under the jurisdiction of three magistrates and was completely independent of the Manor of Rensselaerwyck, which surrounded it for miles on all sides. This was the nucleus of the present City of Albany.

Adriaen Van der Donck was given a tract in the neighborhood of Yonkers in 1646. Brandt Van Schlechtenhorst purchased a tract on Catskill Creek in 1649 and in 1661 Pieter Bronck settled in the neighborhood of Coxsackie. In 1665 an Indian Chief named Caniskeek sold a large tract of land near Athens, which was later resold to Jan Van Loan and was known as the Loonenburgh Patent. In 1652 Thomas Chambers settled at Esopus and in 1658 the area of Kingston was settled.

As this is not a political history of the New Netherlands, we will not concern ourselves with all the various developments at New Amsterdam. For reference purposes a list of Dutch and English Colonial Governors is appended to this volume, along with a tabulation of pertinent facts concerning the Counties in the Hudson Valley.

---

[2]For an entertaining description of this episode as told by Washington Irving in his "Knickerbocker History of New York," see the author's *The Hudson River in Literature—An Anthology.*

4 Dutch and English Colonial Periods

DUTCH COLONIAL PERIOD

During this period there was conflict between the patroons and the agents of the Dutch West India Company. The English kept asserting their claims to the area. There were various troubles with the Indians, claims of mismanagement on the part of the Governors, and frequent changes in command. The principal activity was still in the fur trade and pelts were being brought in to Albany from as far west as Saskatchewan. This acerbated the French in Canada and was one of the contributing causes of the various French and Indian wars, along with the long-standing feud between the Hurons in Canada and the Iroquois in New York. In effect Albany and Montreal became competing centers of an important trade extending west to the Rocky Mountains. When the English ousted the Dutch from New Netherlands, they then came into conflict with the French for this trade.

An important point should be kept in mind with respect to the Indians. Maize or corn agriculture was important to certain tribes—especially to those along the Esopus Creek near Kingston and along the Wallkill River. When settlers began to encroach on their corn lands, serious resistance began. As early as 1655 there was a general Indian Uprising on both sides of the Hudson, which was quickly suppressed. However, in 1659, shortly after the settlement of Wiltwyck (Kingston), the First Esopus War broke out. Up until this time the settlers had spread out in individual homesteads. During the War they took refuge in the village, leaving their farms subject to the depredations of the savages. In fact Wiltwyck had been built at the order of Peter Stuyvesant after the 1655 Uprising. Stuyvesant advocated the grouping of settlers in fortified towns. However, the settlers preferred to remain on their own homesteads, and between hostilities there was considerable fraternization with the Indians. Construction of fortifications gave the Indians the idea of constructing their own "forts" or "castles," which they soon did near Bruynswyck and Kerhonkson in the Wallkill and Shawangunk areas. The First Esopus War was quickly ended in 1660 when the settlers successfully attacked these Indian castles and freed prisoners. This quelled the uprising, but they made one very bad mistake. They sold a captive Indian chief into slavery on the Dutch plantations at Curacoa in the Caribbean. Later he escaped and made his way home and told of his bad treatment. This was greatly resented by the proud Indians and led to the Second Esopus War in 1663.

On June 7th, 1663 two hundred Indians attacked Wiltwyck and Hurley, massacring many of the inhabitants. Troops were levied and a full scale summer campaign was undertaken wherein the strength of the Indians was effectively broken once and for all. Except when working in concert with the English during the American Revolution, they were never again a factor in the Hudson Valley.

ENGLISH RULE

In 1664 a small British fleet under the command of Sir Robert Carr and Richard Nicolls sailed into New York Harbor and captured New Amsterdam after an abortive resistance under Peter Stuyvesant. The fortifications were in a state of dilapidation and the populace showed no desire to fight. King Charles II of England gave the former Dutch colony to his brother, the Duke of Albany and York, later to become King James II. The colony was renamed New York, as was the town on Manhattan Island. Fort Aurania became Fort Orange and the town of Beverwyck was renamed Albany in honor of the Duke's other title. Wiltwyck became Kingston. Few changes were made in the way of life and the Dutch Language still remained in common usage. The settlers were treated well by their new masters and the powers to control taxes, make laws, regulate trade, and grant land were transferred from the Dutch West India Company to the Duke. Richard Nicolls was appointed Governor from 1664 to 1668, and Francis Lovelace from 1668 to 1673. Governor Nicolls established the first Counties in New York State. The Duke handed New Jersey over to John, Lord Berkeley, and Sir George Carteret, who drew up a constitution in 1665 entitled "The Concession and Agreement of the Lords Proprietors of the Province of New Caesarea or New Jersey." This established civil government and bound the proprietors to levy taxes only with the consent of the legislature and not otherwise. Despite this, proprietary rule again threatened to revive the worst features of the patroon system. As elsewhere in the Hudson Valley, settlers who held land under Indian deeds, and confirmed by Governor Nicolls, objected to the proprietors' demands for rents. Stiff resistance developed. In 1670 Carteret and his Council confirmed the land rights of the Dutch charter of 1658. The document also provided for the support of the church and a free school and establishment of a court.

Shortly after the English occupation some troops were sent to Esopus under the command of a Captain Brodhead. The troops were uncouth and quarrelsome and picked fights with the equally pugnacious Dutchmen. The Huguenots soon joined in with the Dutchmen and the entire situation seems to have degenerated into a general brawl. There is great difficulty in attempting to ascertain which side was more at fault. Finally Governor Nicolls sent up two privy counsellors and the entire matter degenerated into a court contest, with many charges and counter charges. The public soon lost interest and finally, after taking much evidence, four of the Dutch Burgomasters were taken to New York City for sentencing. It is not recorded what, if any sentence was inflicted. This episode came to be called the Esopus Mutiny.

About 1670 several Christian Iroquois villages had been formed and the initial English-Dutch War had been settled by the Treaty of Breda in 1667. New York was formally ceded to the English. In 1668 a tract of 160,000 acres on the east bank of the Hudson was given to Robert L. Livingston, a Scotchman. Livingston Manor was formally given full Manor Status in 1686 and subsequently large tracts were acquired west of the Hudson as well.

RETURN OF DUTCH RULE

In 1673, on August 9th, the Dutch, who were again at war with the English, captured New York. The name was changed back to Nieuw Amsterdam, and the colony was put under the

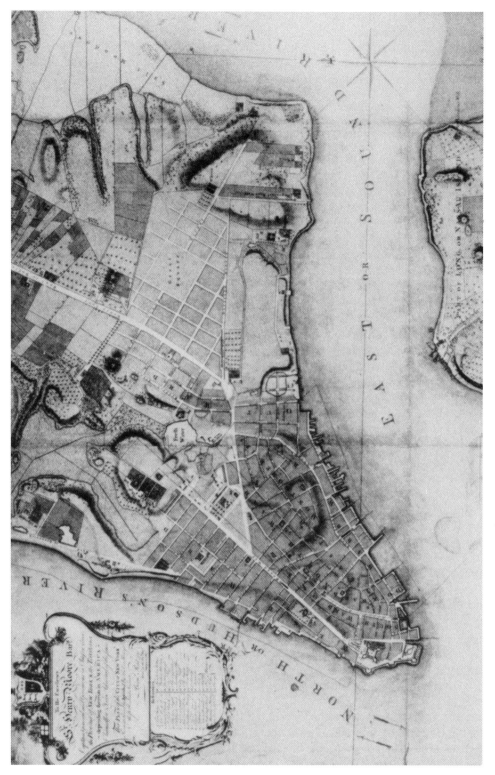

Plan of the City of New York during English Period drawn by Bernard Ratzen.

command of Cornelis Evertsen and a Council of War. Shortly thereafter Anthony Colve was appointed Governor General.

Dutch rule did not last for long however, as the Treaty of Westminster in 1674 confirmed the earlier Treaty of Breda and the English were returned control of New York. Edmund Andros was appointed Governor.

RETURN TO ENGLISH RULE

After the return of English rule the Crown regranted the eastern half of New Jersey to Sir George Carteret. In 1680, upon the death of Sir George Carteret, all of East Jersey was sold, in accordance with the terms of his will, to pay his debts. The purchasers were William Penn and eleven associates. Control of East Jersey soon spread into other hands as the original owners sold half-interests, creating Twenty-Four Proprietors by 1682. Many of these, in turn, sold fractional shares. In 1684 the owners organized the Board of Proprietors of the Eastern Division of New Jersey, with offices in Perth Amboy. This corporation is still in existence and still owns some lands.

The year 1683 is notable in that Governor Thomas Dongan called the first elected Representative Assembly in the colony and on July 22nd granted a "Charter of Liberties." Ten counties were then erected in New York and East Jersey. Under the new Charter, the elected representatives had the power to approve or reject all taxes. This put the colonists almost on a par with the people in England under Parliament. In 1686 New York and New England were consolidated into the Dominion of New England, and in the same year, the City of Albany was incorporated with Peter Schuyler as the first Mayor.

In 1685 the Duke of York became King James II and the colony became the property of the Crown. James II was a Catholic, and he was unpopular at home because of his attempts to abrogate the powers of Parliament. He was overthrown in the "Glorious Revolution" of 1688, and the Protestant William of Orange and Queen Mary were set upon the English throne.

In 1688 King William's War with the French broke out and the Canadian border became an area of skirmishing, while in 1689 the Union of New York and New England was dissolved with the democratic "rebel" Jacob Leisler seizing control of the government in New York, until he was deposed by Richard Ingoldesby and Governor Henry Sloughter in 1691 and Leisler was hanged. In 1690 the settlement of Schenectady was massacred by French and Indians. The First Continental Congress was called at New York City in 1690 to discuss ways to prosecute the war with the French, and in 1691 a popular assembly was also called and liberal laws promulgated. Peter Schuyler and Dutchmen from Albany conducted an expedition and defeated the French at La Prairie in Canada in 1691. Finally in 1697 peace was concluded.

The year 1702 saw the outbreak of Queen Anne's War, the American manifestation of the War of the Spanish Succession. Few incidents of this war impinged upon the colony of New York, and at its end in 1713 the Treaty of Utrecht recognized that the Iroquois were subject to British sovereignty. An expedition against Canada in 1711 from New York had been unsuccessful.

Meanwhile, in 1708, Governor Lord Cornbury had granted a patent of almost two million acres in the Catskills to Johannis Hardenbergh and six other grantees, who were merely "front men." This tract covered most of the present day Greene, Sullivan, and Ulster counties and also large portions of Delaware. There was some vagueness about the western boundary, and it was not fully surveyed until 1749, after which there was much litigation. This patient hung like a cloud over the Catskills for almost a hundred years and did much to hamper settlement. Eventually the Livingstons bought into the Hardenbergh Patent.

View of Fort George with the City of New York (1731-36). Known as the Carwitham View. Looking eastward.

About 1670 Samuel Edsall and Nicholas Varlet purchased from the Indians 1,872 acres of wasteland and meadow extending two miles north of the Town of Bergen; and shortly thereafter an additional tract between the Hudson River and Overpeck Creek (an arm of the Hackensack River) was patented to John Berry. This area embraced that part of Jersey City along the Hudson River and the present towns of Hoboken, Weehawken, and Guttenberg. In 1683 the Provincial Assembly had passed an act creating the counties of Bergen, Essex, Middlesex, and Monmouth in East Jersey. The boundaries of Bergen were set between the Hudson and Hackensack Rivers, from Newark Bay to the New York Province Line, and consisted of approximately 60,000 acres. This included all of the present Hudson County, which was separated in 1840.

In 1731 the French built a fort at Crown Point near the southern end of Lake Champlain, and in 1744 hostilities broke out again in King George's War, which was the American equivalent of the War of the Austrian Succession. In 1745 the settlement of Saratoga was destroyed by the French and Indians and in 1746 William Johnson was made head of the Indian Department. He called a great Indian Council at Albany in 1748 and generally gained their trust and respect. He took the sister of the half-breed Joseph Brant as his mistress and closely allied himself with the Iroquois.

5 Colonial Architecture of the Hudson

The earliest settlers in the New Netherlands spent their first few years in dugouts. These were in use on Manhattan Island until well after 1650. Generally they were six or seven feet deep, and of varying lengths and widths. The walls were lined with timbers and the bark of trees to keep the walls from caving in, and they had plank flooring. The roofs were composed of spars and were covered with bark or green sods. They were sometimes divided by partitions. Generally the new settlers lived in these accommodations for four or five years before constructing a more substantial dwelling.

Other early settlers built log or board cabins, as timber was quite plentiful. We know little about their construction or appearance, as few survived even into the nineteenth century. Quite probably they were similar to those built in our West, as conditions and available building materials were similar.

When the time came to build a permanent home, stone was the Dutchman's favorite building material. It was usually undressed at the earlier dates. The interstices were filled up with a mixture of clay or mud, and chopped straw or horsehair. Later shell lime, from the coastal oyster beds, was used, and before long, the limestone ridges along the Hudson were excavated for making calcined lime mortar. Upriver, the field stone was commonly used. But nearer Manhattan, and especially in the Rockland County area and New Jersey, sandstone was more common, as it was readily available and easily worked to a finer finish. Through the years the general quality of stonework finish improved substantially throughout the Hudson Valley. Typically the settler would first construct a small one or two room house. Later, as he became more affluent, he would build a much larger story-and-a-half (two story homes were not common) structure immediately adjacent, and joined to the original building, which was thenceforth used either as a kitchen or store room. The larger additions usually had a center hallway and one or two rooms on either side. The fireplaces, which were used for both heating and cooking, were located at the gable ends. Most of the houses had a cellar and a large storage attic with granary doors in the gable ends. These were used for storage of grain as well as of household implements. The doors were either of batten or panel type and cut horizontally in the middle to make the typical Dutch-Door. This was convenient for keeping children in and animals out, while providing ventilation. There were generally few windows, and these were usually heavily shuttered. Straight slope gable roofs were common in the upper Hudson Valley, but in New Jersey, Staten Island, Brooklyn, and parts of Westchester, it was common for the roof line to be carried out over a shallow piazza, or portico, running along the length of the front of the house. This roof had a gentle upward curve

Samuel Demarest House, New Milford, N.J. Typical of early type of stone construction used by the Dutch. Lines tend to be straight. Only rudimentary roof overhang above portico.
(New Jersey Historic Building Survey)

which was characteristic of the Dutch Colonial style, still often used today because of its pleasing appearance.

Straight gambrel roofs were common throughout the valley. In the Albany area steep sloping roofs were common, so that the deep snows would fall off easily.

Hardware was made of wrought iron, and frequently very well designed and quite artistic. Wood trim was rather limited until just prior to the Revolution. These early homes were snug and well suited to the region. They were functional, as well as picturesque. Very often the houses had to serve as fortresses against Indian attacks, and stout construction was imperative. Fort Crailo at Rensselaer is a good example of a fortress-manor house. Some of the earliest homes, especially at the Communipaw settlement, had thatched roofs but, as these could easily be set afire by attackers or sparks from the chimney, they soon gave way to wooden or slate shingles.

Brick was used along the river, where water transport and clay were readily available. Brick began to be used at an early date and brickmaking was one of the earliest industries in the Hudson Valley. Brick was the most common building material at Albany and in Manhattan. Cooper, in his novel *Satanstoe,* which has its action taking place in 1757, has this comment to make about buildings in Albany:

Near the head of this street stood the fort, and we saw a brigade paraded in the open ground near it, wheeling and marching about. The spires of two churches were visible, one, the oldest, being seated on the low land, in the heart of the place, and the other on the height at no great distance from the fort,—or about half-way up the acclivity, which forms the barrier to the inner country, on the side of the river. Both these buildings were of stone, of course, *shingle tenements being of very rare occurrence in the colony of New York,* though common enough further east. [p. 161][1]

Nearly all the houses were built with their gables to the streets, and each had heavy wooden Dutch stoops, with seats, at its door. A few had small court-yards in front, and here and there was a building of somewhat more pretension than usual. I do not think however, there were fifty houses in the place that were built with their gables off the line of the streets. [p. 167][2]

It was the custom for the citizens to sit out on the stoops in the early evenings during fair weather.

In his novel *The Water-Witch,* set during the Revolution, Cooper gives a description of townhouse architecture in Manhattan:

Here he soon stopped before the door of a house which, in that provincial town, had altogether the air of a patrician dwelling.

Two false gables, each of which was surmounted by an iron weathercock, intersected the roof of this building, and the high and narrow stoop was built of the red freestone of the country. The material of the edifice was, as usual, the small, hard brick of Holland, painted a delicate cream color.

A single blow of the massive glittering knocker brought a servant to the door.....[p. 15][3]

Let it be understood that Holland Brick is not brick imported from Holland, but rather a local brick molded to the standard Dutch size, rather than to the somewhat larger English standard.

Zabriskie-Christie House, Dumont, N.J. The small wing was the original house. Dormer window is much later addition. (Historic American Building Survey)

---

[1]James Fenimore Cooper, *Satanstoe,* Leather-Stocking Edition in Thirty-two volumes.
[2]Ibid.
[3]James Fenimore Cooper, *The Water-Witch.*

Vreeland House, Leonia, N.J. The stone wing was the original house. Use of wooden construction was a later development. Note fully developed portico and graceful gambrel roof.
(New Jersey Historic Building Survey)

The English, coming later, preferred wooden construction, using simplified copies of the Georgian or Palladian styles, then popular at home in England. This, in turn, was a greatly simplified neoclassical style. In story-and-a-half homes there were frequently low, wide windows facing the front and rear on the upper floor. These were known as "lie on your belly" or simply "belly" windows, as it was necessary to do just that in order to see out of them owing to the slope of the roof. Dormers did not come into general use until after the Revolution.

In the Mid-Hudson area, particularly in Ulster, Greene, and Columbia counties, stone remained popular until the mid-nineteenth century. The Huguenots, as well as the Dutch, showed a preference for stone, and this can be seen on Staten Island and in New Rochelle, as well as at New Paltz. With the Revolution, the Federal Style—the American version of Georgian—became popular, and ultimately gave way to the Greek Revival.

There are many well preserved houses of all the styles described above except the dugouts and Dutch townhouses. Many of these homes are undergoing authentic restoration. The classic Dutch Colonial, with the front portico and curving roof line, represents a genre unique to the lower Hudson River Valley and New Jersey and has a great amount of grace and charm. Altogether, the settlers in the Hudson Valley lived rather more comfortably than is usual for new settlers in a wilderness, and many early homes are still providing comfortable and gracious shelter to descendants of the original settlers.

6 French and Indian War

The French and Indian War, and its predecessors, King William's, Queen Anne's and King George's Wars were direct precursors of the American Revolution, in that the cost of these wars was one of the principal bones of contention between the colonies and the mother country. The colonists claimed that these wars were merely extensions of European conflicts and that they had contributed more than their fair share in men and arms in protecting British interests on the North American Continent. The English took the view that they had made large expenditures to protect the Colonies from the French and Indians. A large war debt had been incurred and someone would have to pay more taxes to cover the debt. England imposed such taxes on the colonies despite their protest—and this "taxation without representation" became one of the principal causes for the Revolution. Perhaps New York did not contribute as spectacularly as New England in the prosecution of the war, but its northern borders were an arena of much bloody fighting, although hardly any formal action took place in the lower Hudson Valley.

Before reviewing the principal events of this war, let us note an event which took place between the years 1710 and 1713. Queen Anne had been largely dependent on Scandinavian sources for such naval stores as tar, pitch, and turpentine. An influx of refugees from the German Palantinate was posing problems in England and the thought arose that possibly these people could be settled on the banks of the Hudson and put to work making turpentine. Little thought was given to the facts that these people were completely untrained for such work nor that the type and quantity of pine trees in the neighborhood were poorly suited for the production of such items. Nevertheless these people were transported to the Hudson, north of present day Saugerties, and settled on either side of the river in what are still known as East Camp and West Camp. Robert Livingston contracted to supply them with food and supplies on a very meager basis. Governor Robert Hunter at New York was given the thankless charge of the entire project. To make a long story short, the project did not work out, and the people were left to their own means. They felt deeply cheated as they had been promised land and a start on their own in the new world—and now they were left to shift for themselves at the start of what turned out to be a long and hard winter. Fortunately many of them were skilled at hand crafts, and these gradually drifted to the towns while others who knew something of farming moved to the Schoharie Valley, where they found good farming land, and to the vicinity of Newburgh. Ultimately many of these original Newburgh settlers moved on into Pennsylvania to join their compatriots. A relative few remained along the Hudson, although the terms of tenancy on the Manor lands were not particularly attractive.

Hostilities commenced in 1754 and a meeting was held at Albany to form a Plan of Union. Benjamin Franklin was a delegate to this conference and here he gained some of the expertise he was later to use in conjunction with the American Revolution. Military action during 1754 and 1755 consisted primarily of attacks against French forts in the West and Canada. The attempt to capture Fort Duquesne, under Braddock's leadership, was a costly failure, as were attempts on forts Frontenac, Niagara, Ticonderoga, and Crown Point. It was during this period that George Washington gained his first active military experience on the Duquesne Expedition. The tide turned in 1758 when Lord Jeffrey Amherst took Louisburg on Cape Breton Island. However, in that same year, Montcalm repulsed Abercromby at Ticonderoga in a particularly bloody engagement. This expedition is described in James Kirke Paulding's novel *The Dutchman's Fireside*. In 1759 Amherst succeeded in capturing Ticonderoga. Sir William Johnson and his Iroquois allies secured northern New York and the war became a contest for control of the St. Lawrence, and thus of the entire North American Continent. In 1759 the English under General Wolfe defeated the French under Montcalm on the Plains of Abraham at Quebec. Both brave commanders fell in the battle. A subsequent battle at Montreal gave the British full control and France had lost out entirely in North America. The fortunes of battle were formally recognized by the Treaty of Paris in 1763.

During the course of the war there was an important meeting of colonial governors at New York in 1755, and Fort Edward was erected that same year. There was also a victory known as the Battle of Lake George. In 1756 the French took the forts at Ontario and Oswego, and in 1757 the British surrendered Fort William Henry, at the southern end of Lake George, to the French and Indians. This surrender was followed by the Indian massacre which is described in the opening scenes of Cooper's *Last of the Mohicans*. Starting with Amherst's success at Ticonderoga in 1759, all French held posts were back in British hands in New York State by the end of that year. It was during this period that the British started the practice of paying Indians for enemy scalps.

Frontier life was hard and often lonely. The original forest cover of the region was dense with large hemlocks and other evergreens predominating over large areas. The forests were dark and gloomy and harbored such animals as wolves, mountain lions, and panthers. It was a far cry from today when principal forest cover is composed of such hardwoods as birch, beech, maple, oak, and chestnut, and the most dangerous animals are bobcats, Canadian Lynx, and bear. The new settler had to first find a spring or other source of drinking water, start to clear the land for planting, and then he would erect a crude lean-to type of shelter. We are told that the first settlers on Manhattan Island used dugouts as homes. Eventually these primitive accommodations were replaced with log cabins and then with sturdy stone homes, or, by the clapboard favored by the British. The settler made no attempt to clear the stumps but planted between them, and it was often many years before they rotted or he got around to pulling them. The initial crops were usually for the farmer's own consumption as there were no facilities at first to take the grain for milling, except along the Hudson itself. The pioneer farms had an unkempt appearance. Often the pioneer depended largely on hunting and fishing and some minor trading with the Indians to supplement his meager living. Often the Indians were friendly and helpful, but they could be treacherous, and it was most difficult to tell when you had aroused their superstitious fears, anger, or cupidity. However, during this pioneer period many a white child made friends with the Indians and was adopted into the neighboring Indian tribes. The early settlers thus became expert woodsmen and learned many of the Indian skills. Buckskin clothing was common. Early roads all led to the landings along the Hudson, which were served by sloops trading on the river.

Prior to the Revolution there was considerable exploration of Upstate New York. In 1757 Indians led British troops to the Great Sulphur Spring at present day Richfield Springs. The valley of the Schoharie had been settled as early as 1724 and Cherry Valley in 1740. Saratoga was settled in 1773.

7 The American Revolution

As stated before, the cost of the French and Indian Wars was a bone of contention between England and the colonies. In 1765 Parliament passed the Stamp Act, and in that same year the Sons of Liberty were formed and the Stamp Act Congress met to resist this method of raising revenue. As early as 1764 the New York Assembly had protested any taxation without representation. By 1766 resistance was so strong that Parliament rescinded the Stamp Act but also suspended the power of the Assembly. Subsequently excise taxes were imposed on many articles, which in 1768 led to formal boycotts. Things reached an impasse, and in 1770 the duties were repealed on everything except tea. In 1772 American forces attacked a British warship, the *Gaspe,* in Narragansett Bay. By December of 1773 things had reached such a fever pitch that colonial patriots dared destroying tea at the Boston Tea Party. The immediate results were Parliament's passing of the Boston Port Bill, closing that port, and revocation of the Massachusetts Charter in 1774.

On September 5th of that year the First Continental Congress met in Philadelphia, and on October 14th passed the Declaration of Rights of the Colonies. In February of 1775 the Congress sent a final petition to the King for redress of grievances, which went unheeded.

On April 19th a small determined group of patriots resisted British troops at Lexington, Massachusetts, and the war began.

On May 10th the Second Continental Congress met in Philadelphia, and on June 5th George Washington was appointed Commander in Chief. On June 7th Israel Putnam successfully defended Breeds Hill in the Battle of Bunker Hill. This raised the colonists' spirits, and on July 6th Congress issued a "Manifesto." Earlier, on May 17th, two-hundred and twenty five men had gathered in the house of Leendert Bronck in Coxsackie.

Bronck was a member of the Committee of Correspondence and Safety. They signed what is called the "Coxsackie Declaration," wherein they proclaimed that "Americans would not consent to be ruled, save by themselves," and "never to become slaves," and to oppose the "arbitrary and oppressive Acts of the British Parliament."

Later in 1775 Ethan Allen and Benedict Arnold captured Fort Ticonderoga and Crown Point, and General Richard Montgomery led an ill-fated expedition against the Province of Quebec and was killed during the attack on Quebec City, after successfully capturing Montreal. The expedition was a failure.

In February 1776 the British engaged Hessian mercenaries, but on March 17th they found it expedient to evacuate Boston. On April 1st the British fleet appeared off Sandy Hook, and Generals Charles Lee and Washington were sent to prepare the defense of New York City. In

24

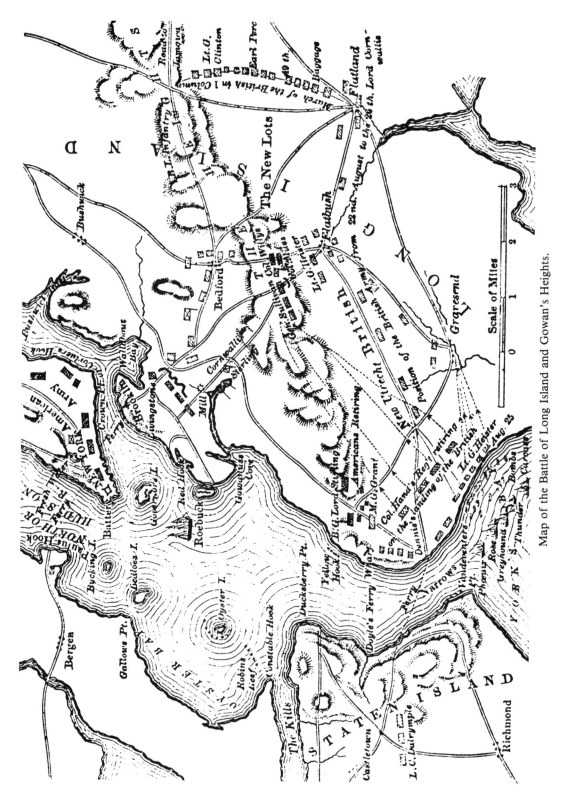

Map of the Battle of Long Island and Gowan's Heights.

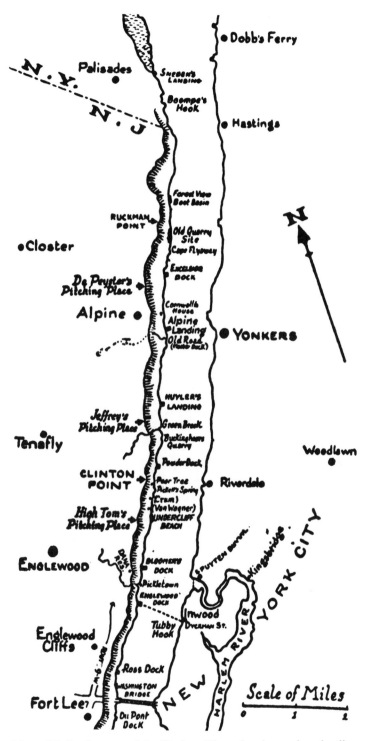

Map of Palisades area of the Hudson River showing various landings.

June British troops landed in Charleston, South Carolina, and General William Howe and his elder brother, Admiral Richard Howe arrived with Governor William Tryon off Sandy Hook and made an initial landing on Staten Island.

On July 4, 1776 Congress, assembled in Philadelphia, issued the Declaration of Independence, and it was soon promulgated throughout the colonies.

On August 27th the British, under Generals Grant, Cornwallis, Percy, and Henry Clinton, accompanied by Hessians under General De Hiester, landed on Brooklyn. The Americans under Generals Putnam, Sullivan, and Lord Stirling put up a noble defense, amidst which the heroic action of the Maryland Brigade was particularly notable. However, the fortunes of battle went against the Americans and, on August 29th, 9000 men, under the command of General Knox, made a strategic retreat to Manhattan under cover of early morning dark and fog.

The British Fleet Forcing the Hudson River Passage, 1776. Painting by Dominic Serres, the elder. (U.S. Naval Academy Museum)

Manhattan also proved untenable, and after notable engagements at Kipps Bay and Fort Washington, Washington ordered a retreat to White Plains. By September 15th Manhattan was entirely in British hands. The British retained control until after completion of the peace treaty in November 1783.

A major engagement was fought at White Plains on October 28th. The entire situation around New York City proved so untenable that on November 18th Washington ordered abandonment of Fort Lee. On December 12th he retreated to the Delaware. On December 13th the British occupied Newport, Rhode Island and had virtual control of all New Jersey. However, on Christmas Day, Washington conducted a surprise attack back across the Delaware and beat the British and Hessians at Trenton and Princeton. This ended action for the year.

The year 1777 saw American fortunes at a low ebb. The British gained control of Philadelphia after the American defeat at Brandywine Creek on September 11th. Earlier, on April 20th, the government of the State of New York was established at Kingston, and the first Constitution was issued. George Clinton was elected Governor on July 30th. During this period there was a great split of the population between Loyalists and Patriots. Many of the Patriots joined the New York Rangers who operated in guerilla fashion in the Hudson Highlands under Washington's general direction. The Loyalists rallied together under the Johnsons and Butlers with the Iroquois as allies. Most of the freehold farmers in the Hudson Valley and the large landowners were on the Patriot side. However, as they felt they would have little to gain by an American victory, many of the tenant farmers were loyal to the Crown.

Cornwallis's Headquarters at Alpine Landing. (Photo: Alfred Marks)

It was the grand strategy of the English to gain control of the Hudson Valley between Canada and New York City, and thus split the New England colonies from those further south. To resist this Washington determined to hold the Highlands of the Hudson and the Upper Hudson Valley at all costs. In the great British campaign of 1777 the chief strategy was for General John Burgoyne to march down from Canada via Lake Champlain and hook up with Sir William Howe and Sir Henry Clinton, who were to move up from New York, and with Barry St. Leger, who was to march from the west via Oswego and the Mohawk Valley. Burgoyne was halted at the Battle of Saratoga and St. Leger at the Battle of Oriskany. For reasons that have not yet been determined, Howe and Clinton failed to move north from New York City on schedule. Thus the campaign was abortive and the American victories were a turning point. These victories brought the French to the American side and the British never did succeed in splitting the colonies and controlling the Hudson Valley.

Vindictiveness on the part of the British over the defeat of the Saratoga Campaign led Sir John Vaughan to lead a marauding expedition up the Hudson after the capture of Forts Clinton and Montgomery in the Hudson Highlands by Sir Henry Clinton. He sailed up the Hudson with a fleet of thirty ships, eight of them square rigged, shooting at Staatsburg and landing and firing *Clermont,* the Livingston estate. On October 13th he set Kingston to the torch with great damage. This expedition had little military value for the British, except to vent their frustration.

28

Benedict Arnold Monument, Saratoga Battlefield Historical Park. Arnold was injured in his foot. (Author's collection)

Saratoga Battle Monument near Schuylerville, N.Y. (Author's collection)

View north from West Point, c1870. (Harry Fenn)

(left)

Kosciusko's Garden, West Point c1870 (Harry Fenn). The famous general was almost killed by a cannonball from a British warship while relaxing at this site.

Washington spent the winter of 1777-1778 at Valley forge amidst great want and suffering—but French aid was coming.

1778 saw General Clinton withdraw his British troops from Philadelphia back towards the Jerseys. Washington inflicted some punishment on him at the Battle of Monmouth near Freehold, New Jersey. On August 9th the French fleet, under D'Estaing, failed to recapture Newport. There was much maneuvering across the Jerseys during the summer. On November 11th the Indians and British made a bloody raid on Cherry Valley, New York. There was another great massacre in the Wyoming Valley of Pennsylvania, near present day Wilkes-Barre.

Washington Parting with his Guard at Headquarters, June 7, 1783. This is at the Hasbrouck House in Newburgh. Storm King Mountain is seen in the background.

In 1779 General Anthony Wayne led a brilliant attack upon Stony Point on the Hudson and recaptured it for the Americans. However, as it had little real strategic value and was difficult to hold, he again abandoned it, but the victory had a great value in boosting morale. In August Generals John Sullivan and James Clinton (brother of Governor George Clinton) led an expedition down the Susquehanna River to avenge the Cherry Valley and Wyoming massacres. On August 29th they defeated the British and Iroquois at Newtown, near Elmira. On October 22nd the property of Tory Loyalists was declared forfeit.

The year 1780 saw much maneuvering of the armies and Indian and Tory raids in the Mohawk and Schoharie Valleys. Benedict Arnold's treason plot to betray West Point was uncovered and the British spy Major Andre captured, tried and hanged. Although belonging to the enemy camp there was much sympathy for him as he was a very amiable young man and it was not part of his premeditated plan to go behind enemy lines out of uniform.

Action moved to the South during 1780 and 1781. On October 25th, 1781 the French and Americans beat the British near Yorktown, Virginia, in the last major battle of the war. Washington withdrew his army to Newburgh to defend the Hudson Highlands during the

Map showing Winter Cantonment of the American Army in 1783.

winter of 1781-1782. He remained there for the rest of the year while negotiations were being conducted in Paris.

While at Newburgh in 1783 Washington received the infamous Nicola letters and refused the crown with noble simplicity and expressing sorrow that anyone would have believed him capable of subverting the revolution he had just led. The Treaty of Paris was signed on January 20th and cessation of arms was announced on April 11th. Details of the Treaty were cleared up by September 3rd, and on November 25th the British, under Sir Guy Carleton, evacuated New York.

Washington bid farewell to his officers at Frauncis Tavern in New York City on December 4th and went to Philadelphia to resign his Commission on December 23rd. On December 13th Congress ratified the Treaty of Paris.

Note: The above account of the revolution has, of necessity, been merely an outline of major events. Detailed and circumstantial descriptions of military actions in the Hudson Valley are given in the author's *The Hudson: A Guidebook to the River.* Important material is contained under the headings: Brooklyn (Battle of Long Island); Paulus Hook; Bull's Ferry; Fort Washington; Fort Lee; Fort Tryon; Berrian Neck; Hastings; Sneden's Landing; Tappan; Croton Point; Waldberg Landing; Treason Hill; Tarrytown; Kings Ferry; Stony Point; Verplanck Point; Doodletown; Fort Clinton; Peekskill; Fort Montgomery; West Point; Bear Mountain; Hessian Lake; Plum Point; New Windsor; Newburgh; Fishkill; Beacon; Kingston; Bemis Heights; Saratoga; Schuylverville; and Fort Edward.

8 Peace and a New Nation

In 1784 the Continental Congress moved to New York City, as did the New York State Legislature. For the next three years the various states were busy setting up their governments and there was a great deal of discussion about the possible form a Federal Government might take. In 1787 the Constitutional Convention met in Philadelphia and drew up the Federal Constitution. Shortly thereafter John Jay, Alexander Hamilton, and James Madison issued the *Federalist Papers,* explaining the benefits of the new Constitution. It now became necessary for the various states to ratify the Constitution. This same year the Act Disenfranchising Tories was repealed. The wounds of the war were slowly beginning to heal; but many confiscated properties had changed hands, and the great Phillipse Patent had been broken up.

In 1788 the New York Legislature, meeting at Poughkeepsie, ratified the Federal Constitution and elected representatives to Congress. On April 30th, 1789 (the year of the French Revolution), George Washington was inaugurated on the steps of Federal Hall in Manhattan as first President of the United States. This same year Congress met in New York City, which, although it was not the largest city in the nation, was declared the Capital of the United States. Later, in 1790, the Capital was moved to Philadelphia, then the largest city, pending construction of a new Federal Capital in the District of Columbia.

At the end of the Revolution the Hudson Valley was primarily an agricultural area. Farming was concentrated along the river and creek beds in the bottom lands. It was an old saying that the Dutch knew how to "smell out" good fertile bottom lands, and they had ensconced themselves along the Hudson, Mohawk, Schoharie, Wallkill, Esopus, Fishkill, Passaic, Hackensack, and Raritan rivers. Consequently, the early settlers had grabbed off all the more desirable lands and new arrivals had to look further west.

The Catskills were more difficult to farm, with an ungrateful rocky soil, offering little inducement to settlers. The Indians had raised maize and during colonial times agriculture was the backbone of the Hudson Valley economy. The Central Hudson Valley was colonial America's "Bread Basket," with wheat and other grains being the major crops. Other important produce included maple syrup, hops, vegetables, tobacco, milk, butter, eggs, honey, wool, and livestock. The tenant farmers still found themselves under the odious three-life lease system, and chaffed under it while new arrivals shunned the area and went west to settle in Otsego and Montgomery counties.

The Whiskey Excise Act of 1791 created a great furor. Many frontier farmers had no way to get the grain crops to market economically. On-site distilling added value to their crop while decreasing bulk, and the finished liquor could be transported to market more easily than bulk grain. These farmers greatly resented the new excise tax and the Whiskey Rebellion was underway. Although it was not as virulent in the Hudson Valley as elsewhere, there was a general community of interest among all farmers. Enforcement of this law was the first real test of the powers of the new Federal Government. Eventually Federal power was recognized and the question of coinage became paramount next.

For a time, around 1790, whaling became an important Hudson Valley industry. Hudson, in Columbia County, was settled in 1783 by Quakers from Nantucket and Providence. They brought with them their whaling traditions, and by 1790 twenty-five schooners showed Hudson as their registered home port. Newburgh also participated in this activity.

In 1795 John Jay was elected Governor of New York, and John Fitch's steamboat was demonstrated in New York. In 1797 Albany was made the permanent State Capital.

During this period lumbering became a major industry. The first center of this activity was at Saugerties where the Livingston Family had sawmills and large tracts of timberlands in the Catskills. However the major activity soon centered above Albany. Vast stands of lumber were cut down in Washington County just after the Revolution. In his novel *The Chainbearer,* James Fenimore Cooper describes this feverish activity with its bootlegging of both timber, cut lumber, and rafts which were floated down to Albany, and in some instances, all the way to New York City. Tall straight trees were in particular demand for ship masts. Later, with the coming of the steamboat, the Hudson Highlands were heavily logged over to provide fuel for the boats, and to make charcoal for the rising iron industry. Many of the old skidways can still be seen on the side of Anthony's Nose near Bear Mountain.

A small-scale, but interesting, lumbering operation took place atop the Palisades in New Jersey. Trees would be cut atop the cliffs and then "pitched" down to the waterfront where they would be loaded into boats for shipment to New York. Most of this wood was used as heating fuel and the woodlots were owned by wealthy New Yorkers. The lumberjacks lived in small communities at the base of the Palisades, or "Under the Cliff." The name "Undercliff" is retained to this day in certain neighborhoods of Edgewater, Fort Lee, and Englewood.

Transportation was of great importance. The Hudson provided the principal highway during the period of open navigation. However, in winter almost all travel came to a halt. Most of the existing roads came down to the river landings. Only two major roads, one on either side, connected New York and Albany, and both ran considerably inland from the Hudson for long stretches to avoid having to cross the wide estuaries of streams tributary to the Hudson.

The eastern road was known as the Albany Post Road. During the French and Indian Wars, Lord Loundoun had broadened an old Indian trail between the Wading Place, at the northern tip of Manhattan Island, and "the ferry at Crawlier, over against Albany." In 1698 William and Mary had granted to Frederick Philipse authority to build a bridge across the Harlem River, near its junction with Spuyten Duyvil Creek. This former ford, or wading place, was thenceforth known as Kingsbridge, which remains in use as the name of a neighborhood to this day. Kingsbridge was reached from the Battery by Broadway, which ran as far north as Bloomingdale, near the present day Columbus Circle; thence by the Bloomingdale—Manhattanville, and Manhattanville—Kingsbridge roads. Manhattanville was located near present day 125th Street and the shore of the Hudson River. This exact same route is followed to this day by Broadway.

After the French and Indian War, Lord Loudon's military road was widened under Royal Authority to the width of four rods, English measurement, at the least. In 1703, the New York Provincial Assembly authorized improvements of the Kings Highway from Kingsbridge to Albany. Today the route can still be travelled—usually under the present names of Broadway, Kings Highway, Albany Post Road, or Route 9, depending on the section under consideration. After the Revolution this road was used a great deal by cattle drovers. In his novel *Satanstoe,* Cooper describes a trip over this road.

The roads along the western shore are somewhat more complex. From earliest times the Old Richmond Road ran along the eastern side of Staten Island from Ward's Point, across from Perth Amboy to Stapleton, where the ferry left for Manhattan and Brooklyn. A branch of this road ran northward to a point opposite Bergen Point, where there was a ferry across the Kill Van Kull, to present day Bayonne. From there the King's Highway ran northward to Paulus Hook, in present day Jersey City, which was the terminal of a ferry from Manhattan. Between Paulus Hook and Albany the King's Highway, or Albany Post Road, followed a devious route, often far inland from the Hudson. It first went west to the settlement of Bergen and then turned north, through the Bergen Woods atop the Palisades, to the Three Pidgeons Tavern, west of Hoboken. From there it dropped down the western slope of the Palisades Ridge to the edge of the Hackensack Meadows. It then ran north, along the present route of Grand Avenue, to English Neighborhood (Englewood), Tenafly, Demarest, Tappan, Blauvelt, Clarkstown, and Haverstraw, to West Haverstraw. Here it turned inland to the northwest, over the Ramapo Mountains to present day Harriman. North of Harriman there were two alternate routes. One went up Smith's Clove to Newburgh and then west to Montgomery, on the Wallkill River. The other route went west to Chester and Goshen, thence north to Montgomery. The highway then crossed the Wallkill River at Montgomery and ran north along its west side, beneath the Shawangunk Ridge, to Tuttletown, Butterville, Tilson Flats, and thence across and along the Rondout Creek to Eddyville and Kingston. From Kingston it ran north to Lake Katrine, Katsbaan, and Cauterskill, where it crossed a ford over Catskill Creek to Jefferson Heights, or Old Catskill. From there it ran to Athens, on the Hudson, and thence north to Coxsackie, New Baltimore, Coeymans, Glenmont, and Albany. Obviously, very good time could not be made over such a route, and the east side highway was more popular for through travel.

After the Revolution attention began to be given to lateral roads into the interior. Among the first to be incorporated was the Cherry Valley Turnpike in 1799. It ran west from Albany to Cherry Valley and Otsego County. Another important early turnpike was the Dutchess, Ulster & Delaware Turnpike (D.U.D.—which gave a new word to the English language after it failed to ever pay a dividend). It ran from the Connecticut town of Salisbury to Margaretville, on the East Branch of the Delaware, via Rhinebeck, Kingston, and Phoenicia, crossing the Hudson by ferry at Rhinecliff. It was an important route of western migration from Connecticut. The Susquehanna Turnpike went from Catskill to Wattle's Ferry on the Susquehanna River near Unadilla. Other major turnpikes were the Schoharie Turnpike from Athens to Schoharie; the Newburgh & Cochecton Turnpike from the Hudson River at Newburgh to Cochecton, on the Delaware, by way of Orange County and the Southern Catskill region; and the Orange Turnpike from Suffern and Sloatsburgh to Goshen.

Although these roads served as routes for western migration, their main purpose was to carry the produce of the interior to the Hudson for trans-shipment to New York City by water. Athens, Catskill, Kingston, Poughkeepsie, and Newburgh became important market centers and ferries were established at these points. The turnpikes were originally privately built and tolls were collected. However, many of them were financially unsuccessful, despite their great importance in opening up the area. The fact was that the interior did not provide sufficient agricultural produce to cover the heavy expense of roadbuilding in the mountains. Ultimately they were taken over by the towns, counties, and State as public highways, although tolls lingered long in the Catskill region.

Before the steamboat, most travel on the river was by sloop. These graceful and efficient sailing vessels had considerable carrying capacity and travelled between points on an irregular schedule. The captains were usually the owners, and were important and respected people in their home communities. Often they were charged with the care of children and elderly or infirm passengers and with commissions to make purchases in the city, or to sell the produce of upriver shippers in the City. Clearly their's was a position of great trust and responsibility. It is interesting that not a few were free negroes. These sloops remained in use many years after the advent of the steamboat. The well known re-creation, the *Clearwater,* is a fine typical example.

In October 1776 Congress appointed a committee to prepare plans for a military school. Shortly after the Revolution, in 1783, Washington suggested West Point as a possible site for a military academy. In his annual message in 1793 Washington again recommended West Point as a location. In 1794 Congress organized a corps of artillerists to be stationed at West Point, with thirty-two cadets attached. In 1798 the number was increased to fifty-six cadets. On March 16, 1802 Congress formally authorized the founding of a Military Academy at West Point, which opened on July 4th of that year with ten cadets.

The year 1804 saw the tragic duel between Alexander Hamilton and Aaron Burr, on the shores of the Hudson, at Weehawken, New Jersey—ending two brilliant political careers and Hamilton's life.

The year 1807 saw the first successful trip of Robert Fulton's *Clermont.* This event, and developments leading up to it, are described in a subsequent chapter. In 1817 the construction of the Erie Canal, to connect Lake Erie with the Hudson River, was authorized. This canal was to make New York *the* great seaport for the interior of the new nation. It was finally opened in 1825, and is also described in detail in a subsequent chapter.

9 The Early Ferries

The first ferries were simple canoes, dugouts, and rafts, manned by Indian traders. They accommodated foot passengers in a casual manner, but never made ferrying their principal business. The first organized ferry operated by a white man was that of Cornelius Dirckman, in 1642, across the East River. It was a flat-bottomed row boat. He placed a loud horn at both landings and performed service upon the "trumpet's clarion call." This soon proved to be a profitable business and Governor Peter Stuyvesant considered the possibility of government regulation. Some authorities say that the original Brooklyn Ferry was operated by Cornelius Hooglandt, in 1642. However, it is certain that in 1661 the New Netherland Council granted authority to William Jansen to operate a ferry to Communipaw for one year. It is not recorded whether or not the franchise was renewed.

Before the first steam ferryboats were put in operation on the Hudson in 1811, the trip across the Hudson might take anywhere from fifteen minutes to well over three hours, depending on the winds and tide, and in the winter, the blocks of ice that were moved about by the currents. Even on the shorter East River crossing to Brooklyn, there could be considerable danger. On one crossing in 1784 seven passengers were forced to abandon a ferryboat that was crushed by the ice and to climb upon the floating floe of ice, which carried them down as far as the Narrows before a rescue party could reach them. The eighth passenger was drowned. Sometimes passengers had to wait for days for favorable conditions to cross the rivers. The steam ferry wrought great changes. Only a few years later, in 1821, Timothy Dwight stated that he thought the passage by steam ferry more pleasant and safer than if there had been a bridge.

The following extract from James Fenimore Cooper's novel of 1845, *Satanstoe,* with a time setting of 1757, demonstrates the tremendous change in attitudes brought about by the introduction of the steam ferry:

> "I should have sent Evans to Yale, had it not been for the miserable manner of speaking English they have in New England," resumed my grandfather; "and I had no wish to have a son who might pass for a Cornishman. We shall have to send this boy to Newark, in New Jersey. The distance is not so great, and we shall be certain he will not get any of your Roundhead notions of religion, too. Colonel "Brom," you Dutch are not altogether free from these distressing follies."

> "Debble a pit!" growled the colonel, through his pipe; for no devotee of liberalism and latitudinarianism in religion could be more averse to extra-piety than he. The colonel, however, was not of the Dutch Reformed branch of the Follocks. He was an Episcopalian, like ourselves,

his mother having brought this branch into the church; and, consequently he entered into all our feelings on the subject of religion, heart and hand. Perhaps Mr. Worden was a greater favorite with no member of the four parishes over which he presided, than with Colonel Abraham Von Valkenburgh.

"I should think less of sending Corny to Newark," added my mother, "was it not for crossing the water."

"Crossing the water!" repeated Mr. Worden. "The Newark we mean, Madam Littlepage, is not at home (England); the Jersey of which we speak is the adjoining colony of that name."

"I am aware of that, Mr. Worden; but it is not possible to get to Newark (from the southern part of the Bronx), without making that terrible voyage between New York and Powles' Hook. No, sir, it is impossible and every time the child comes home, that risk will have to be run. It would cause me many a sleepless night!"

"He can go by Tobb's Ferry (Dobbs' Ferry), Matam Littlepage," quietly observed the colonel.

"Dobb's Ferry can be very little better than that at Powles' Hook," rejoined the tender mother. "A ferry is a ferry; and the Hudson will be the Hudson, from Albany to New York. So water is water."

As these were all self-evident propositions, they produced a pause in the discourse; for men do not deal with new ideas as freely as they deal with the old.

"Dere is a way, Evans, as you and I know py experience," resumed the colonel, winking again at my father, "to go rount the Hudson altoget'er. To pe sure, it is a long way, and a pit in the woods; but petter to undertake dat, than to haf the poy lose his l'arnin'. Ter journey might be made in two mont's, and he none the wuss for ter exercise. Ter major and I were never heartier dan when we were operating on the he't waters of the Hutson. I will tell Corny the roat."

..........As for the Powles' Hook Ferry, it was an unpleasant place, I will allow; though by the time I was junior I thought nothing of it. My mother, however, was glad when it was passed for the last time. I remember the very first words that escaped her, after she had kissed me on my final return from college, were, "Well, Heaven be praised, Corny! you will never again have any occasion to cross that frightful ferry, now college is completely done with!" My poor mother little knew how much greater dangers I was subsequently called on to encounter, in another direction. Nor was she minutely accurate in her anticipations, since I have crossed the ferry in question, several times in later life, the distances not appearing to be as great of late years, as they certainly seemed to be in my youth."[1]

In 1664 William Merritt was granted a franchise by the English Government for a term of twenty years to operate a ferry from Manhattan to Brooklyn. He paid an annual rent of £20 for this privilege, and contracted to build ferry houses on either side of the river and furnish two boats for the transport of cattle and horses at the rate of 6 pence per head, and two boats for the transport of passengers, at the rate of a penny apiece. The boats were flat-bottomed scows, made of broad planks, and with no keel. These boats were often propelled by negro slaves, and sometimes the oars were supplemented by a sail when conditions were favorable.

A similar franchise was granted to Johannes Verveelen for a ferry across the Harlem River to Bronckside in 1667.

Under the administration of Richard Coote, First Earl of Bellomont, in 1700, a charter was granted to Samuel Bayard for a ferry to Weehawken and in 1712, under Governor Robert Hunter, a franchise was granted for a ferry to Staten Island. This franchise was confirmed by the New York City Council in 1755.

Three major franchises were granted under King George II. In 1733 a charter was granted to Archibald Kennedy, for a ferry to Pavonia. In 1743 one was granted to Alexander Colden of Quassaick (Newburgh) to operate a line to Fishkill, and in 1752 a ferry was chartered to

---

[1] James Fenimore Cooper, *Satanstoe,* Complete Works of J. Fenimore Cooper.

connect the Ulster & Salisbury Pike on the east shore with the Ulster & Delaware Turnpike on the west shore at Long Dock near Rhinecliff.

Aside from the rowboats, sailing vessels were used on the longer runs. They were known as piraguas, or periaugers, and were flat-bottomed and carried two masts. This type of boat remained in operation, largely unchanged, up until the advent of steam ferries. We can get some idea of the size of these boats from the records of three operated between 1816 and 1818 by Cornelius Vanderbilt. He first went into business at the age of sixteen in 1810, operating a piragua from his home in Stapleton on Staten Island to Manhattan. His first boat cost him $100, which he borrowed from his mother and repaid by plowing, harrowing, and planting a field of corn. The size of the boats in question were:

"Dread" - 1816 - 49' x 14' x 4'4"
"Governor Wolcott" - 1817 - 49' x 13' x 4'
"General Armstrong" - 1818 - 50' x 13' x 4'6"

In 1767 Cornelius Van Voorst established a ferry from Manhattan to Powles Hook in Jersey City, although there are indications that there may have been a previous ferry on this route since 1764. A charter for a ferry to Horsimus or Hoboken was granted in 1774, and assumed by Hermanus Talman. These connected with a line of stages run by Andrew Van Buskirk to New Bridge, near Hackensack. The ferry was operated by sailboats and rowboats.

Other early routes were from Manhattan to Bulls Ferry north of Weehawken and from Dobbs Ferry to Sneden's Landing, then known as Paramus. There were two Kings Ferries. The better known one was from just north of Stony Point to Verplanck's Point below Peekskill. The other was between Hampton Point above New Hamburg to Cedarcliff, below Marlboro, which was then known as Hampton. Also there was the ferry from Albany to Crawlier.

John H. Morrison, in his *History of American Steam Navigation,* gives us an interesting picture of Hudson River ferry navigation just prior to the introduction of steam navigation:

In 1810 there were propositions before the Legislature for improvements in the ferries, which required the owners of ferry boats to have their names painted with white letters on the stern of the boat, and the words "Ferry Boat", on the inside of the stern. It was furthermore proposed that the owners of ferry boats should at all times in the months of May, June, July, August, and September, have their boats ready for passage from half an hour before sunrise until 9 o'clock in the evening, and in all other months from sunrise until 8 o'clock in the evening; and that no passenger should be detained more than five minutes. It was proposed that a sufficient number of barges for passengers should be kept at all of the ferries, upon which barges no baggage or lumber should be carried. Four men were to be employed to row every barge, and in every horse boat two men. The passenger barges should not be less than 22 feet long and 7 feet wide, and no more than fourteen passengers should be ferried in them at one time.[2]

The stage was now set for the dramatic improvements to be brought about by steam power.

---

[2]John Harrison Morrison, *History of American Steam Navigation.*

10 The Coming of the Steamboat

It can truly be said that commercial steam navigation had its birth on the Hudson River. Robert Fulton's *North River Steamboat of Clermont,* which made its first successful commercial trip from New York to Albany on September 4th, 1807, can be said to be the start of the steamship industry. However, prior to this time Fulton and others had done considerable experimentation with steamboats—some of it in local waters.

The earliest record of an attempt at steam navigation can be credited to Blasco de Garay, a Spanish Naval Officer under Charles V, who in 1543 constructed a paddle-wheel vessel to be moved by steam. It is not recorded whether he had any success with his experiments. In 1630 an English patent was granted to David Ramseye, "to make shippes and barges goe against strong wind and tide." In France a similar patent was granted to Denys Papin of Blois, in 1690, and he constructed a boat in 1707, which had some limited success. However, nothing more came of these early attempts, for steam engine development was not yet far enough along. In the early 18th Century, Thomas Newcomen, John Smeaton, and James Watt made important contributions to steam engine design and construction. In 1769 James Watt joined Matthew Bolton in a steam engine manufactory in Soho, a suburb of Birmingham, England. They specialized in pumping engines. Benjamin Franklin visited the Bolton works and contributed some improvements of his own. The time was now ripe for further nautical development.

In 1764, William Henry, of Lancaster, Pennsylvania, operated a small steam vessel on the Conestoga River. This experiment was known at first hand by John Fitch and Robert Fulton. In 1774, Perier Freres built a small steamboat for operation on the Seine, and in 1783 the Marquis de Jouffray operated one on the Rhone at Lyons. In 1786, James Rumsey built a small steamboat operated by hydraulic jets at Shepherdstown, West Virginia, on the Potomac River. Much of this early experimentation was desultory and was made without knowledge of similar experimentation going on elsewhere.

The first individual to make serious sustained efforts towards the development of a steamboat in America was John Fitch (1743-1798). Fitch was born in Windsor, Connecticut, served as apprentice to a clockmaker, and eventually set up a brass shop. He served briefly in the Continental Army and as a sutler selling tobacco and beer. After the War he took his profits and purchased land grants along the Ohio River. These proved to be valueless, and he drifted back to Pennsylvania, where he became interested in steamboat development. He obtained exclusive steam navigational rights from the States of New Jersey and Pennsylvania for the years 1786-1787, and in the later year successfully operated a steamboat on the Delaware River at a speed of 3 to 4 mph. This was followed by other boats, in 1788 and 1790, which made 7 mph and operated regularly for a time between Trenton, Bordentown, Bristol and Burlington. Despite his rapid advance, Fitch's backers were timid and did not support his further efforts, which suffered a great set back when a fourth vessel was wrecked by a storm. He experimented further with miniature vessels on Collect Pont on Manhattan Island, and with a screw propeller in 1796. Fitch's first steamboats were propelled by oars hanging from a horizontal framework, not by a conventional paddle wheel. He always seemed just on the verge of commercial success, but lacked the proper backing. Ultimately he became despondent, took to drink and drifted back west to Bardstown, Kentucky, where he committed suicide in 1798.

Another early steamboat builder was Samuel Morey, who operated a boat on the Connecticut River in 1790. He built another paddle-wheel boat in 1793, and in 1794 made a voyage in it from Hartford to New York City. In 1797 he had a side wheeler operating between Philadelphia and Bordentown on the Delaware River, in which travelled Chancellor Livingston, Robert Fulton, and Col. John Stevens. Morey's main contributions were in the design of stern and side type paddle wheels.

In 1791, Nathan Read developed the vertical, multiple-tube, firebox boiler which best suited early steamboat designs. In 1792, Elijah Ormsbee operated a small steamboat on Narragansett Bay. The reason that nothing much came of these early experiments seems to have been lack of capital, rather than of inventive genius. Meanwhile, much practical knowledge was being gained.

Back in England, Patrick Miller, James Taylor, and William Symmington were doing much experimentation around 1788, and there was much interest in applying steam propulsion on the extensive network of canals. The British, with much good reason, claim that the first successful commercial steamboat was William Symmington's *Charlotte Dundas,* which was successfully tried on the Forth & Clyde Canal in 1801. She had paddle wheels and a Watt built engine and pulled two 70-ton barges. Henry Bell, an associate of Symmington's, built a successful oceangoing steamboat, *The Comet* in 1812, which had two paddle wheels on each side! But we are anticipating.

Back at home in America, these experiments were being closely observed by some wealthy capitalists. Chancellor Robert R. Livingston (1746-1813), of the great Hudson River patent holding family founded by Robert Livingston (1654-1728), was particularly interested in the possibilities of steamboats. He resided at his estate *Clermont,* opposite Saugerties. He attended Kings College (now Columbia University), was admitted to the bar, and became a partner of John Jay. He was a member of the Continental Congress and served on the committee to draft the Declaration of Independence. In 1781, he was appointed the first secretary of the Department of Foreign Affairs (Secretary of State). From 1777 to 1801 he was the first Chancellor of New York State and administered the oath of office as President to George Washington. In 1801, Thomas Jefferson appointed him Minister to France, where he conducted the negotiations leading to the Louisiana Purchase.

Prior to leaving for France, Livingston travelled in Samuel Morey's Delaware River steamboat, in 1797, and in 1798 he participated with Col. John Stevens, John Stoudinger, and Nicholas J. Roosevelt in the construction and operation of a small steamboat, the *Polacca,* on the Passaic River at Belleville, New Jersey, and is reputed to have made a trip in it from there to New York City.

While in France Chancellor Livingston met the man who was to bring his steamboat interests to fruition. Robert Fulton (1765-1815) was born at Little Britain, Pennsylvania. He first learned the trade of gunsmith, and was accomplished in this business at the time of the American Revolution. He next turned to landscape and portrait painting, and in 1786 went to England to study with Benjamin West. Little Britain is near Lancaster, and it is likely that as a boy Fulton knew of William Henry's steamboat experiments on the Conestoga. In 1794 Fulton's interests turned to engineering, and he was engaged by the Duke of Bridgewater as engineer on his system of private canals and particularly on a project to replace locks with inclined planes. In 1796, he was invited to Paris by the American merchant, poet, and diplomat, Joel Barlow (1754-1812), who was interested in steamboat development and had brought the plans of the *Polacca* to France with him. He resided with Barlow for seven years, during which time he occupied himself developing submarines and other destructive naval weaponry for the French and British governments. It was during this time that he became acquainted with Chancellor Livingston.

In 1803 Fulton, Barlow, and Livingston pooled their talents and resources to build a steamboat for operation on the Seine. This successful experimental vessel was 86 ft. long and 8 ft. wide. As Livingston held a monopoly from the New York State Legislature for steamboat operations in that State, the success of the experiment led him to contract with Fulton to build a steamboat for operation on the Hudson River. Before returning to America they ordered a steam engine from Boulton & Watt, to be sent to New York in 1806; and upon returning home they ordered a hull to be built by Charles Browne, of New York City, whose yard was on the East River.

Before continuing with the story of Robert Fulton, it is useful to consider the work of the Stevens Family also of this period, as it was soon to come into conflict with the Fulton-Livingston combination.

This illustrious engineering dynasty was founded by Colonel John Stevens. He studied law at Kings College, and shortly thereafter, joined his father, a wealthy landowner, in Jersey politics. During the Revolution he served as Treasurer of the State of New Jersey, and from 1782 to 1783 was Surveyor General of that State. In 1784 he purchased extensive tracts at Hoboken. Upon his father's death in 1792 he inherited a vast estate. For the moment we will ignore his steamboat activities to note that from 1810 on he became interested in railroad development and, in 1815, he received from the State of New Jersey the first railroad charter in the United States for construction of the Camden & Amboy Railroad. In 1825 he operated a small steam locomotive on a circular track on his Hoboken estate. This little locomotive had a vertical steam boiler which activated a cog wheel that engaged a ratchet rail between the running rails—as in the Mt. Washington Cog Railroad.

His son, Robert Livingston Stevens (1787-1856) carried on his father's interests. He became Chief Engineer for the Camden & Amboy, and imported the early steam locomotive *John Bull* from England for operation on that line, and invented the famous Stevens, or American Type steel rail, which came into general use in railroad construction. In the marine field, he invented the spring piling used in ferry slip and steamboat wharf construction, and made the following important contributions to steamship development: He invented the high pressure boiler; tabulated the laws of variance of resistance of water to vessels at various speeds, and developed the graceful "hollow water line," which was later used on Clipper Ships. This was known as the "wave line" form of vessels. He anticipated Ericson with the "feathering" paddle wheel, and developed the sponson or strut guards used on sidewheel ships. He was a pioneer in the use of anthracite as fuel, and first to mount boilers on the guards. He developed the "skeleton" style of walking beam; two-part wheel floats; hog frames; artificial blast for furnaces; spring bearings under paddle shafts; double poppet valves; metallic packing rings, and the "Stevens Cutoff" valve gear. Anticipating future events, he also drew up plans for a vehicular tunnel under the Hudson River!

A nephew, Francis B. Stevens, worked with Robert L. Stevens in developing the "Stevens Cutoff." Another brother, Edwin Augustus Stevens (1775–1868), worked closely with his father and brother in all their enterprises. Edwin initiated the construction of the first railroad from New York to Philadelphia; was a pioneer builder of ironclad warships; and invented the "Stevens Plow." He was also founder of the Stevens Institute of Technology in 1871, which was created as a bequest in his will.

Returning to the marine activity of Colonel John Stevens, let us note that he owned the Hoboken Ferry franchise from 1789 to 1794. In 1794 he became President of the Bergen Turnpike Company, and again, in 1811, reacquired franchise for the Hoboken Ferry; at that time undertaking to furnish a steam ferry to Vesey Street, (later to Barclay Street), Manhattan, from Hoboken. This was the world's first franchised steam ferry route, and operated continuously until November 22nd, 1967—156 years. Colonel Stevens could undertake this ambitious commitment because he had sufficient experience in steamboat construction. In 1804 he had built a small boat called the *Little Juliana*. She measured 25 ft. x 5 ft., had two four-bladed propellers and carried steam at 50 lbs. per sq. inch, generated in a sectional high pressure boiler. The engine had a cylinder of 10" diameter with a 24" stroke.

In 1807, he built the *Phoenix,* a paddle wheel vessel for the Hoboken to New Brunswick run. However, this ran into trouble with the Fulton-Livingston monopoly, and she was brought around by sea to operate on the Delaware River in 1808. This was the first open sea voyage by any steamboat. Captain E. S. Bunker was in command. Captain Bunker had very advanced ideas and had previously operated a high class line of passenger-only sloops on the Hudson. This sea voyage was completed successfully despite encountering a strong gale. The *Savannah* made her ephocal transatlantic voyage in 1818.[1]

In 1811 Colonel Stevens introduced the new *Juliana,* with side paddle wheels, on the Hoboken Ferry. The last steam ferry to close out service in 1967 was the *Elmira,*[2] which was still equipped with reciprocating steam engines and burned anthracite.

Before turning to the ephocal voyage of the *North River Steamboat of Clermont,* let us finally note a few later Stevens vessels: *Philadelphia,* of 1813; *Passaic,* also of 1813—first steamboat to burn coal; *Hoboken*—first with skeleton walking-beam; *Trenton*—first with boilers on guards; *North America* and *Pioneer,* all of 1822; and the *Pioneer,* of 1823. These ships were all important in the development of the standard ship types that were to handle the bulk of traffic for almost a century.

Despite all the important engineering developments of the Stevens Family, popular interest was first strongly caught by the endeavors of Chancellor Livingston and Robert Fulton. In 1807 their ship, originally called simply *North River Steamboat,* was launched at Charles Browne's shipyard near Corlears Hook on the East River. Later she was also known simply as the *Clermont,* after Chancellor Livingston's Hudson River estate. There is a persistent, and erroneous, story that she was built at North Bay, near Clermont. This is incorrect. In her second season of operation she was registered under the name: *North River Steamboat of Clermont,* which might be how the error arose. Clermont was simply her home port, or port of registry—but the name *Clermont* stuck, although it never was her official name.

The engines were built by Boulton & Watt of Birmingham, England. As originally built, the *North River Steamboat* measured 130 ft. x 16 ft. x 7 ft. deep. She had a square stern, as

---

[1]It is of interest to note that the last passenger liner equipped with reciprocating steam engines to sail from New York Harbor was the *Stavangerfjord* of the Norwegian American Line, in November 1964.

[2]The *Elmira* was 188 ft. long, 43 ft. breadth, and was built in Newport News, Virginia, in 1905. The other surviving vessel was the *Lackawanna,* built in Newburgh, N. Y. in 1891. She measured 219 ft. x 40 ft., but had been dieselized and made into the flagship of the Lackawanna Railroad Ferry fleet, successor to the Hoboken Ferry franchise. George Eastland, Public Relations Officer of the Erie-Lackawanna Railway, which then owned the Hoboken Ferry Company, said that fewer than 3000 passengers were still using the ferries daily, compared with 100,000 daily at the turn of the Century. Let it be noted that the railroad had contrived this development largely through service cutbacks to avoid operating the boats which were expensive to run.

was common with all the early Fulton-Livingston steamboats, and carried masts and sails. She had two paddle-wheels—one on each side—15 feet in diameter, and of the radial type. They were unenclosed in any housing. The cylinder was 24'' diameter, with a 4 ft. stroke. She was equipped with a low pressure boiler twenty feet long by seven feet deep and eight feet broad.

There was much cynicism about the claims made for the new ship, and she was called "Fulton's Folly." On Monday, August 17, 1807 she sailed for Albany from the foot of Cortlandt Street Manhattan, with a list of invited guests, and without using sails against the slight headwind. She arrived at Albany on Wednesday, August 19th, after an elapsed sailing time of thirty-two hours, including no landings. There was a twenty hour layover at Clermont—not included in the thirty-two hours. Her return trip to New York took thirty hours, with no stops whatever, and again without any use of sail. This first experimental trip was a complete success. Morrison gives us the following interesting information:

> She excited the astonishment of the inhabitants of the shores of the Hudson, many of whom had not heard of an engine, much less of a steamboat. There were many descriptions of the effects of her appearance upon the people on the banks of the river: some of these were ridiculous, but some of them were of such a character as nothing but an object of real grandeur could have excited. She was described by some who had indistinctly seen her passing in the night, to those who had not had a view of her, as a monster moving on the waters, defying the wind and tide, and breathing flames and smoke.
>
> She had the most terrific appearance from other vessels which were navigating the river when she was making her passage. The first steamboats, as other do yet, used dry pine wood for fuel, which sends forth a column of ignited vapor many feet above the flue, and whenever the fire is stirred, a galaxy of sparks flies off, and in the night have a very brilliant and beautiful appearance. This uncommon light first attracted the attention of the crews of other vessels. Notwithstanding the wind and tide were adverse to its approach, they saw with astonishment that it was rapidly coming towards them: and when it came so near that the noise of the machinery and paddles were heard, the crews—if what was said in the newspapers of the time be true—in some instances shrunk beneath the decks from the terrific sight, and left their vessels to go on shore, while others prostrated themselves and besought Providence to protect them from the approaches of the horrible monster which was marching on the tides and lighting up its path by the fires which it vomited.[3]

The experimental trip was such a success that Fulton and Livingston ventured to advertise in the New York papers on September 2nd, 1807 as follows:

> The North River Steamboat will leave Paulus Hook Ferry on Friday, 4th of September, at 6 in the morning, and arrive at Albany on Saturday in the afternoon. Provisions, good berths, and accommodations are provided. The charge to each passenger as follows:

To Newburgh	3	Dolls. -- Time,	14 hours
To Poughkeepsie	4	Dolls. -- Time,	17 hours
To Esopus	4½	Dolls. -- Time,	20 hours
To Hudson	5	Dolls. -- Time,	30 hours
To Albany	7	Dolls. -- Time,	36 hours

> For places, apply to Wm. Vandervoort, No. 48 Courtland Street, on the corner of Greenwich Street.[4]

---

[3]John Harrison Morrison, *History of American Steam Navigation,* p. 22.
[4]Ibid, p. 24.

Robert Fulton's *North River Steamboat* of Clermont (early).

She left on her first commercial trip with 12 Albany and 3 way passengers. Another advertisement from this same year gives the additional interesting information:

STEAMBOAT
For the information of the Public
The Steamboat will leave New York for Albany every Saturday afternoon exactly at 6 o'clock and will pass

West Point.........	about	4 o'clock Sunday Morning
Newburg...........	about	7 o'clock Sunday morning
Poughkeepsie.......	about	11 o'clock Sunday morning
Esopus............	about	2 o'clock in the afternoon
Red Hook.........	about	4 o'clock in the afternoon
Catskill...........	about	7 o'clock in the evening
Hudson............	about	9 o'clock in the evening

She will leave Albany for New York every Wednesday morning exactly 8 o'clock, and pass

Hudson............	about	3 o'clock in the afternoon
Esopus............	about	8 o'clock in the afternoon
Poughkeepsie.......	about	12 o'clock at night
Newburg...........	about	4 o'clock Thursday morning
West Point.........	about	7 o'clock Thursday morning

As the time at which the boat may arrive at the different places above mentioned may vary an hour more or less, according to the advantage or disadvantage of wind and tide, those who wish to come on board will see the necessity of being on the spot an hour before the time. Persons wishing to come onboard from any other landing than those here specified, can calculate the time the boat will pass, and be ready on her arrival.

Innkeepers or boatmen, who bring passengers on board, or take them ashore from any part of the river, will be allowed one shilling[5] for each person.

---

[5]Shilling equals 12½ᶜ.

Price of the passage—from New York

To West Point $2.50
  " Newburg 3.00
  " Poughkeepsie 3.50
  " Esopus 4.00
  " Red Hook 4.50
  " Hudson 5.00
  " Albany 7.00

From Albany

To Hudson $2.00
  " Red Hook 3.00
  " Esopus 3.50
  " Poughkeepsie 4.00
  " Newburg . . . . and West Point 4.50
  " New York 7.00

All passengers are to pay at the rate of $1.00 for every twenty miles, and half a dollar for every meal they may take.

Children from 1 to 5 years of age to pay half price, provided they sleep, two in a berth, and whole price for each one who requests to occupy a whole berth.

Servants, who pay two-thirds price, are entitled to a berth; they pay half price if they do not have a berth.

Every passenger paying full price is allowed 60 pounds of baggage; if less than whole price, 40 pounds. They are to pay at the rate of 3 cents per pound for surplus baggage. Storekeepers, who wish to carry light and valuable merchandise, can be accommodated on paying 3 cents a pound.

Passengers will breakfast before they come aboard. Dinner will be served up exactly at 1 o'clock; tea, with meats, which is also supper at 8 o'clock in the evening; and breakfast at 9 o'clock in the morning. No one has a claim on the steward for victuals at any other time.

Captain Samuel Jenkins-Master; David Mandeville-Pilot

Robert Fulton's *North River Steamboat of Clermont* as later modified with paddle enclosures.

We can see that Fulton and Livingston had a well organized line in operation in very short order. During the winter the steamboat was lengthened to 150 feet and her paddles were enclosed in a housing to prevent their being rammed and injured by envious sailboatmen, and to prevent splashing the passengers on deck. Her name was officially changed to simply

North River on the official rolls for 1808. Operating speed was 5 mph.

Business was good from the start and Fulton and Livingston were protected in their monopoly on New York State waters. The Stevens interests had to either limit their operations to New Jersey and Pennsylvania waters, or pay a licensing fee to Fulton and Livingston. Refinements in machinery and improvements in speed were now made in rapid succession. By 1817 the Stevens steamers could make 15 mph, and 20 mph, was usual by 1846. Thereafter very little improvement in speed was made.

After establishing the *North River* on the Hudson run, Fulton provided two steam ferries, the *Jersey* for the Paulus Hook route in 1812, and the *Nassau* for the East River crossing to Brooklyn in 1813.

Additional Regular Fulton-Livingston steamboats were: *Raritan* and *Car of Neptune,* in 1809; *Paragon* in 1811; *Fire-Fly* and *Hope* in 1812; *Lady Richmond* in 1813; *Olive Branch* in 1815; and *Chancellor Livingston* that same year—the year of Fulton's death. Also in 1815, Fulton built the *Demologos* or *Fulton the First,* a naval ship of 2,475 tons which carried a "formidable battery." That was the first steamship of the U. S. Navy. During this period Fulton established his own engine works in the Soho section of Hoboken, and his home in Jersey City. In 1815 he took James P. Allaire, the New Jersey iron master, as partner. Allaire succeeded to the works upon Fulton's death, and his firm built many famous boats in later years.

11 The War of 1812

Most present day Americans are rather unclear about the causes of the War of 1812. They thnk of it as a sort of "Second Round" of the American Revolution inflicted upon us by the British. Actually the United States declared the war. American merchants felt that the British were hampering American trade. British "Orders In Council" forbade neutral trade with France during the Napoleonic Wars. We thought it our right to continue trade with France. American seamen were impressed at sea by British warships and the British were generally making it unpleasant for those who sought to break their Continental Blockade and trade with France.

American Frontiersmen, seeking new lands in the West and Northwest, claimed that the British in Canada were stirring up the Indians and arming them—and this is probably true. Soon a movement developed to "take Canada." New England merchants, whose trade was suffering from the Continental Blockade, formed a political faction known as the War Hawks. They persuaded James Madison to declare war on Britain in 1812.

It soon became apparent that America was not ready for such a major undertaking. We could not "take Canada at a blow." An attack upon Detroit by General William Hull was unsuccessful and surrendered to a smaller force under Isaac Brock.

The United States did better at sea that year. The *Constitution* under Isaac Hull captured the British man of war *Guerriere,* and the *United States* under Stephen Decatur captured the *Macedonian.* Our privateers carried the action to the very shores of Britain and one such action is described in Cooper's novel *The Pilot.* On the other hand, a land attack on Queenstown Heights, on the Niagara Frontier, was beaten back.

In 1813 the tide turned strongly against the United States. The *Shannon* defeated the U. S. ship *Chesapeake* under Captain James ("Don't give up the ship!") Lawrence. American forces were beaten at the Battle of the Raisin River near Detroit. The Americans, under James Wilkinson, were unsuccessful along the St. Lawrence and the British captured Ogdensburg and also burned Buffalo and Black Rock on the Niagara Frontier. However, we beat the British at the Battle of Plattsburg.

Our luck was better on Lake Erie. In September of 1813 Captain Oliver Hazard Perry won a decisive battle near Presque Isle, at which he uttered the memorable aphorism "We have not yet begun to fight." Under his protection American forces under General William Henry Harrison succeeded in capturing Detroit—the British forces burning it upon their retreat to Canada.

In 1814 things looked bad for the U. S. The British landed and captured Bladensburg,

Fortifications at Fort Wadsworth Staten Island built for the War of 1812.
(Drawing c1870 by Harry Fenn)

Maryland and Washington, and controlled Chesapeake Bay. They burned the Capitol Building and the White House. Their advance was checked at Fort McHenry on the Patapsco River near Baltimore. It was during this battle that Francis Scott Key wrote the poem "The Star Spangled Banner" while prisoner upon a British warship. This action took place in August. Earlier in the year American forces had crossed the Niagara River and won engagements at Chippewa and Lundy's Lane (Ontario), under the command of General Jacob Brown.

On the other hand, the British captured Fort Ontario at Oswego and invaded northern New York. The war was becoming unpopular in New England, whose extensive shipping interests were idled and a Convention was called at Hartford where possible secession was considered. The culminating action of the year was in September, when Sir George Prevost led a force down the west side of Lake Champlain towards the Hudson Valley. This campaign was checked on the water by Captain Thomas MacDonough, who defeated the British fleet at the Battle of Plattsburg, sometimes called the Battle of Lake Champlain, near Valcour Island.

By this time things were at a stalemate and John Quincy Adams, Henry Clay and Albert Gallatin were dispatched to Ghent where negotiations took place, culminating in the Treaty of Ghent on December 24, 1814. One major action, the Battle of New Orleans, took place after the signing of the Peace Treaty when Andrew Jackson won a decisive victory on January 8th, 1815. This was the end of hostilities. The War of 1812 served to strengthen the Union and a feeling of Nationalism was engendered. It also helped to open up the West and set the stage for full scale expansion of the New Nation and the State of New York. America become isolationist as it turned its attention to internal development.

12 Early Steam Ferries and Horseboats

Among the most important internal improvements of the early nineteenth century was the new steam ferryboat. We will recall from Chapter 10 that Colonel John Stevens of Hoboken owned the Hoboken Ferry Franchise from 1789 to 1791, and in 1811 he re-acquired this franchise. Stevens was interested in the development of steamboats and in 1804 had built an experimental steam ferry named the *Little Juliana*. The boat was named after his daughter. In that year he was not operating the Hoboken Ferry. The *Little Juliana* measured 86 ft. x 14 ft. and had two four-bladed propellers of five feet diameter. She carried steam at 50 lbs. pressure per square inch, generated in a sectional high pressure boiler. The engine had a cylinder of 10" diameter with a 24" stroke. Colonel Stevens also built the steamboat *Phoenix,* a sidewheeler, in 1807.

Robert Fulton's *North River Steamboat* made its first trip in 1807, and thus secured the New York State monopoly for himself and Chancellor Livingston.

Nonetheless, Colonel Stevens introduced his *New Juliana,* a steam ferry boat, on the Hoboken Ferry in 1811. That same year the lease on the Powles Hook ferry expired, and a consortium including Robert Fulton, Elisha Boudinot, of Newark, and Nicholas Roosevelt, of New York, made application. Steven's boat made its first trip in October 1811—the first steam ferry to operate anywhere in the world. However, Fulton did not get his boat, the *Jersey,* into operation on the Powles Hook route until July 1812. The *Jersey* took 15 minutes for the trip and operated on a half-hourly schedule. Fulton had a complete system of landing bridges worked out as well, which we shall discuss shortly. The Paulus Hook Ferry Company was re-incorporated as the York & Jersey Steamboat Ferry Co. in March 1814.

Also, in 1814, Robert Fulton, and his brother-in-law, William Cutting, established the New York & Brooklyn Steamboat Ferry Association to operate from Beekman's Slip Manhattan (now the foot of Fulton Street) to Brooklyn. The first boat on this run was the *Nassau.* The *Jersey* had meanwhile been joined by the *York* on the Powles Hook line. Fare for foot passengers on the Brooklyn Ferry was established at 4ᶜ—twice the rate in row or sail ferries.

Fulton's activity soon led Colonel Stevens to discontinue use of the steam ferry on the Hoboken line, and in 1814 he reverted to use of a horseboat invented by Moses Rodgers. Rodgers's first horseboat had been used on the East River, and his second one on the Hoboken run.

These first horseboats consisted of three hulls of equal length and breadth, placed parallel

Hoboken Ferry *Team Boat* Circa 1800. (Author's collection)

and firmly connected at a sufficient distance apart so as to leave room on either side of the middle hull for paddle wheels. A circular platform was constructed in the center hull, which had cleats to give the horses traction. This treadmill was connected by a gear mechanism to the paddle wheels. The boat used 2, 4, or 8 horses or mules. The first boat was single ended, but inconvenience in docking led to building the second one with double ends—a contrivance followed by Fulton in his own first boats, and used on the Hudson ever since. Horseboats are known to have been used on the East River, Hoboken Ferry, and at Newburgh. The Newburgh boat, the *Moses Rodgers,* was launched in 1816. It was capable of carrying a load of "one coach and horses, a wagon and horse, seventeen chaises and horses, one additional horse, and fifty passengers." These equine monstrosities were soon superseded by steam. Another horseboat at Newburgh, *The Dutchess,* was converted to steam and renamed the *Jack Downing.* They could not compete after the breakup of the Fulton-Livingston monopoly when steamboating was open to all. Stevens must have come to some royalty understanding with the Monopoly, as on November 3, 1821, he incorporated The Hoboken Steamboat Ferry Company, and on April 22, 1822, placed the steam ferryboat *Hoboken* on the Hoboken to Barclay Street run. This service ran continuously until the *S. S. Elmira* closed out service at 5:45 PM on November 22, 1967—145 years! At that time it was the last steam ferry on the Hudson—as it was the first line of steam ferries if the pioneer *New Juliana* is considered the first steam ferry, and the horseboat hiatus is ignored.

The first steam ferries were somewhat similar to the horseboats in design, but consisted of only two hulls. Here is how Fulton himself described them in a letter to Dr. David Hosack in 1812:

First. She is built of two boats, each 10 feet beam, 80 feet long and 5 feet deep in the hold, which boats are distant from each other 10 feet, confined with strong transverse beams, knees and diagonal braces, forming a deck 30 feet wide and 80 feet long....Reflecting on a steam ferry for Hudson River, the waves usually running up or down, I found a great breadth of beam absolutely necessary to prevent the boat rolling in the trough of the sea. This is attained by two boats and one space, giving 30 feet beam.

Second. By placing the propelling water wheel between the boats, it is guarded from injury by ice or shocks on approaching the wharf, or entering the docks, which operation being performed twenty-four times in the twelve hours, allows no time for fending off with boat hooks. To give dispatch and convenience, it is necessary the boat should arrive at the bridge without the possibility of any injury; hence all important parts of the machinery should be carefully guarded, particularly the propelling wheel.

Third. The whole of the machinery being placed between the two boats, on the beams over the open space, leaves 10 feet wide on one side on the deck of the boat for carriages, horses, cattle, etc., the other having neat benches and covered with an awning, is for passengers. On the latter side, there is a passage and stairs to a neat cabin, which is 50 feet long and 5 feet clear from the floor to the beams, and furnished with benches for passengers in rainy or bad weather. In the winter there will be a stove in this cabin, which will add much to the comfort of the passengers while navigating through the ice.

Fourth. Although the two boats and space between them give 30 feet beam and proportionate stability, yet they present sharp bows to the water, and have only the resistance in water of one boat of 20 feet beam, which diminution of resistance gives speed in crossing.

Fifth. The space from stem to stern is 20 feet wide, which gives ample room at each end for carriages or persons to enter or go out of the boat.

Sixth. Both ends being alike, and each having a rudder, she never puts about. At New York the horses and carriages enter at one end of the boat, the horses' heads towards Jersey. On arriving, they go out at the manner at the other end of the boat without changing the line of direction; in like manner, when coming from Jersey to New York. Thus the shortest possible and quickest movement of all that is to pass is made to save time and secure convenience. Her rudders are equipollent—the iron shaft which serves as a rudder-post standing in the middle of each, equal on each side of the centre, it can go either end foremost. With yokes and parallel bars, the movements of the rudders are carried to the helms, the only position where the helmsman can have a full view of all around the boat, and see how to steer her into the dock.[1]

Early view of Brooklyn Ferry from Portfolio of Views for *American Scenery* by William Bartlett.

---

[1]John Harrison Morrison, *History of American Steam Navigation,* pp. 518-520.

The double hulls were dispensed with in 1836. A double-ended ferry is only practical when terminal facilities permit of running into special slipways out of the sweep of current. Such terminal facilities are expensive and are only possible where large traffic exists. All subsequent vessels were of the sidewheel, wooden hull type with beam engines. These old ships had reverse sheer and a very large camber to the top of a superstructure covering the main deck and having a circular wheel house at either end. The main driveways for vehicles were in the center and the familiar cabins labeled MEN and WOMEN on either side of the driveway—a custom which has survived to the present day. Traditionally the men's cabin was on the downstream side. Usually there were two vehicle gangways, separated by a casing containing the smoke stack and the vertical connecting rods to the walking beam. As the paddle shaft was usually somewhat above the level of the strength deck, there was usually a hump in midship in both vehicle gangways, and in the passenger cabins. A legacy of the old sidewheel days is to be found in the majority of modern screw propelled ferryboats in the overhanging main deck. It is still customary to speak of the breadth of the ship as the "breadth over guards," meaning breadth over the paddle guards.

13 Further Developments of Ferryboat Technology

Steel hulls are used today, but light-weight wooden superstructures survived until quite recent times. Longitudinal strength is a factor of great importance on account of the heavy deck loads caused by the vehicular traffic—alternately of a static and a rolling nature. For this reason, frame and reverse frame construction is used in conjunction with truss girders spaced at varying distances from the centerline of the ship in accordance with the size. Other important features of modern Hudson River ferryboats were double hulls, with compartmentalized sections and watertight bulkheads, and provision for direct passenger loading to the second deck.

Many ferries on the Hudson, in addition to the side passenger cabins, had a large passenger saloon on the upper deck. Interior stairways, often of elaborately carved and paneled rare woods, connected the two decks amidships, or at each end of both sides, in the MEN and WOMEN cabins. These stairways were plentifully bespattered with signs warning passengers not to descend when the boat is entering her slip—a wise precaution, because the inevitable bump as the ship hits the side stakes of the slipway is more than likely to precipitate passengers to the bottom of the stairway with more speed than dignity. As a matter of fact, these stairways were not much used when top deck loading arrangements are provided at terminals; but they were desirable for ready access from deck to deck in the event of fire or collision. Hudson River ferries usually provided seating accommodations, lavatories, and wash places. Coffee and buns were available on the Hoboken boats, and there are snack bars on the present day Staten Island boats.

Proper metacentric height must always be provided to insure a "stiff ship" under all conditions of loading, heeling, and trim. It must be remembered that human freight, when transported in bulk, either in ferryboats or excursion ships, has all the bad characteristics of a bulk cargo such as grain or coal, in addition to the danger of panic. A mad rush of passengers from one side of a ferryboat to the other may easily put the deck under water. For this reason, the flared section has much to recommend it, since the heeling would gradually increase the load water-plane area. As a specific example, it may be mentioned that a ferry with a 48.5 ft. extreme breadth has a metacentric height of 11 feet.

When approaching the slips at the termination of a trip, passengers naturally crowd to the unloading end of the ship, and tend to put her down by the head. Trimming tanks are not usually operated to counteract this because the trim by the head so caused is comparatively of a temporary nature.

The ends of the main deck were usually rounded and fit conveniently into concave recesses in the landing gangways, the ferry being held in place by ropes or pins on each side. During the railroad mergers of the 1950s it became apparent that the radius of the bows of the ships of the different railroads were not the same, and they had to be modified to fit into slips belonging to another line. There was no single standard configuration.

Upper deck loading was first perfected in 1905 and put into use on the Hoboken Ferry. It was also used on the Pennsylvania Railroad, Jersey Central, and Staten Island lines, where it is still in use today.

Approaches to the slips are marked and protected from the current by wooden upright "spring" pilings lashed and bolted together, and having plenty of "give" so that, in the last few yards of her journey, the vessel is practically hemmed in sideways. The "spring" piling was developed by John Stevens. The face boards of the piles are coated with thick grease to minimize the force of glancing blows. In their heyday, the tops of the face boards and pilings were painted white, and contrasted smartly with the black grease. Often fog-bells, with large round sound deflectors, were mounted at the ends of the bulkheads to guide the ferries into dock in fog and at night. Each dock had its own interval of bell stroke. A few lines also used fog horns. By keeping her engines turning slightly ahead, the ferries, when berthed, could keep their nose hard up to the dock. This could be a dangerous practice if the deckhands and dockmen were too lazy to fasten the lines as well. On several occasions boats drifted out from the dock while loading, dumping vehicles and passengers into the water with fatal results. I remember seeing such an accident as a child at the Edgewater ferry terminal, in which several lives were lost. This particular incident led to strict enforcement of proper berthing rules in subsequent years. Often a strong tide or wind would bring the ferry into the slip partially sideways, and the ship would bounce back and forth from side to side several times—often quite roughly. Good pilots could minimize this, however.

Propulsion was by screw propellers on modern ferryboats, the paddle wheel rapidly disappearing since the 1920s. The last sidewheel ferry on the Hudson was the *F. R. Pierson x Musconetcong,* which operated on the Yonkers-Alpine line. She was formerly an old Lackawanna Railroad, Hoboken Ferry boat, and had a walking beam engine. Also lasting until the 1940s was the *Brinkerhoff,* operating as a "relief boat" on the Dyckman Street-Englewood Line. She was originally from the Highland-Poughkeepsie Line.

In direct-steam-powered screw propelled boats, a compound or triple expansion reciprocating engine was arranged with the usual auxiliaries in an engine room adjacent to a boiler room, from which it was separated by a watertight bulkhead. The thrust-shaft ran the length of the ship, under the boilers for part of the length. The two thrust blocks were at either end of the engine. Reversal of the engine obviously meant reversal in direction of motion of the ship, because of the opposite turning wheels. Control was on the engine and was carried out by bell orders from the pilot house. Steam-turbine-electric, or diesel-electric ships sometimes had direct control from the pilot house. Reciprocating engines remained popular up until the end, because of their powerful and fast reversal properties, useful in frequent docking.

In the 1920s diesel-electric boats, called "Electric Ferries," made their appearance on the Hudson. The last ones remaining in service were on the Governor's Island and Liberty Street-Jersey Central Routes. They had originally been used on the Staten Island to 69th Street Brooklyn Line, which specialized in vehicular, rather than passenger traffic. On the primarily passenger lines, the traditional steamboats proved more suitable. A typical steam ferry, such as was used on the railroad owned routes, might have engines developing 1100 h.p. at 125 rpm, and driving two four-bladed cast steel propellers, eight feet diameter by twelve feet pitch. There were usually two steering engines, one at each end at engine room level, rod controlled from the bridge.

An important requirement of a ferryboat was that it have longitudinal stability to resist burying its nose; and that it not draw more than twelve feet of water. Also, it had to have good maneuvering power when forereaching with engines stopped, and it had to be able to fight ice and steer well when trimmed by the head. In many innovations the Hoboken Ferry was the leader. In 1823 it had the first steamboat ferry with a "ladies cabin" below decks, that was carpeted and had fire places and large mirrors. In 1856 it operated the first night service, and in 1876, used the first screw propellers. In 1879 it had the first double deck boats, and in 1905 developed upper deck loading.

Boats of the different lines had distinctive paint schemes. In the early days white was the most popular color on all lines, and remained popular on the upriver lines for many years. Downriver, it remained longest in use on the Hoboken Ferry; where in later years it was superseded by a light buff with white pilot houses and gold-leaf lettering. The Newburgh boats were first painted red, and later green under the ownership of the New York Bridge Authority. The Fort Lee and Edgewater ferries were red; West Shore Railroad used mustard buff, with gold and red trim; Erie used green with white pilot houses and black trim; Pennsylvania Railroad used Tuscan Red with gold trim; whereas the Central Railroad of New Jersey favored a two-tone green scheme with white pilot houses and trim. The Staten Island ferries are painted a rust-red with white trim. The various lines of electric ferries favored a dark or dull green, with black and gold trim. Gilded lanterns sat atop the pilot houses on almost all lines, usually with a gilded ball as finial. Stacks were almost always painted black, with the insignia of the operator displayed thereon.

Let us conclude our technical descriptions with a quotation from *Efficient Railway Operation,* by Henry S. Haines:

> A distinctive feature of some of these ferry terminals is the location of the waiting-rooms and accessory conveniences for passengers in the second story of the building to afford easy communication with the upper-deck cabins of the ferry boats. The terminal buildings of recent construction (1919) have steel frames sheathed with copper. They rest on piling, and the roof projects over the slips sufficiently to protect the passage to and from the boats. Buffer platforms are placed in the floor at the head of the slips to diminish the shock to the terminal structures from impact. As the ferries are also used for local street-traffic, driveways to the boats and passenger accommodations are necessarily required on the ground floor, separated from the railroad terminal. A large suburban traffic is to be provided for, in addition to the long-distance travel; also the terminal is necessarily duplicated on the city side.[1]

Undoubtedly Mr. Haines had the new Delaware, Lackawanna & Western terminal at Hoboken, of 1905, and the new Central Railroad of New Jersey Terminal at Communipaw, of 1914, in mind. Similar construction was used on the Staten Island Ferry terminals at Whitehall Street Manhattan and St. George, Staten Island, and by the Pennsylvania Railroad at Exchange Place, Jersey City. Smaller scale versions were at 23rd Street, Barclay Street, Cortlandt Street, and Liberty Street, in Manhattan. Several Manhattan terminals had footbridges across West Street, prior to construction of the West Side Elevated Highway.

The Whitehall Street Terminal of the Staten Island Ferry had direct access to elevated trains on the upper level. In later years, Fulton's float bridge technology for lower deck loading was superseded by using truss or girder bridges, hinged on the wharf side, that could be raised or lowered to accommodate the varying tides. They were suspended by chains or strong steel cables, and were raised or lowered by either ratchet wheels or electric motors, and were counterweighted. The arch-truss type of bridge predominated, and for some strange reason, were almost universally painted red, and were made of wood. The girder type construction was used at the West Shore Railroad's Weehawken Terminal. The vehicle gangways were usually cavernous and dark, but provided capacious protection from the elements.

---

[1] Henry S. Haines, *Efficient Railway Operation,* p. 292.

14 Early Nineteenth Century Developments

In 1832 a Hudson Valley man, Martin Van Buren of Kinderhook, was Vice President of the United States. He had married a lady from Catskill, and was active in the politics of the Albany Regency. In 1837 he was elected eighth President of the United States.

During this period, long before the advent of the automobile, leather had great importance for making saddles and harnesses, in addition to its traditional role as a material for footware. Tannin, obtained from the bark of the Hemlock tree (*Tsuga Canadensis*), was the major source of tannin used in leather manufacture. A great deal of this hemlock bark was required to obtain a small quantity of tannin. Consequently it was cheaper to carry raw hides to the forests where the hemlock grew for tanning than to carry the bark to the hides. Thus many large tanneries grew up in the Catskills. Great wagons, loaded with hides, would be pulled up into the mountains by straining horses over the primitive roads and turnpikes leading from the river. These hides often came from as far away as the Argentine, and the finished leather was exported all over the world. Vast tanneries were established near Palenville in Kaaterskill Clove, Tannersville, Hunter, Prattsville, Phoenicia, Samsonville, and Claryville. Millions of large hemlock trees were cut down only for their bark, the bleached timbers being left to dry and eventually rot, or serve as fuel for great forest fires. The tanneries moved to follow the hemlock supply. Later, when the hemlocks were virtually depleted, the tanners turned to oak, and the industry gradually moved southwestward, out of the Hudson region. There was a great boom in tanning during the Civil War, but the industry was pretty much dead by the turn of the century.

Abundant water power along the many streams flowing into the Hudson led to development of industry at an early date. Grist mills, sawmills, fulling mills, paper mills, iron works, carding works, and woolen factories sprang up. The valley of the Catskill Creek was particularly heavily industrialized very early. In 1836 the Port of Catskill shipped "substantial quantities" of butter, tallow, hay, potash, and shingles—and also 3,000,000 board feet of lumber and 250,000 sides of sole leather from the tanneries.

Although the early Patroons had established grist and saw mills on the Neperhan and Pocantico Rivers, these operations were tiny compared with subsequent development along the Casper Kill, Esopus Creek, Fall Kill, and particularly the Landsman Kill, near Rhinebeck, which must have held some kind of record, supporting the following industries within six short miles, with relatively little actual fall: 4 grist mills; 4 saw mills; 2 paper mills; 1 tannery; 1 carding mill; and 1 plaster mill. This last mill ground up gypsum, brought from Nova Scotia as ships ballast to the Long Dock, into fertilizer for local use. The way in which the thirteen mills obtained sufficient head of water from the limited flow was by building mill dams and ponds. The mills would actually work only ten hours out of each twenty-four, with the water replenishing the levels of the mill ponds during the other fourteen hours. There may be a lesson in all this for the energy-hungry twentieth century. The stream was named for Casper Landsman, the first miller on the stream.

This was not too unusual an occurrence. The Maune Kill, near Marlboro, was originally known as Jews Creek, after the mills of Gonsalez the Jew, an important early developer. The name of Saugerties, is a corruption of "Da Zaagertijis," or "the saw mills," which congregated along the Esopus Creek and Sawyers Kill.

Other early industries included barrel making, hoop shaving, dying, and shipbuilding. Glassmaking was conducted at Shady, near Woodstock, at the foot of the Catskill Mountains, where there was the right kind of sand and abundant charcoal. The glass was carried to the Hudson over the Glasco Turnpike, which terminated at Glasco Landing, below Saugerties.

The Hudson Valley was the cradle of the American iron industry. Before the Revolution iron was being mined in the Ramapo Mountains and Highlands of the Hudson at Ringwood, Sterling Furnace, Southfields, Forest of Dean, Forest of Arden, and along Montgomery Creek, now known as Popolopen Creek. The entire area now covered by Harriman Interstate Park, and behind West Point, was full of small furnaces and forges. Much of the ammunition used in the Revolution was made at these back-woods establishments, inside the American lines of defense. America's first great arsenal, the West Point Foundry, was established just below Cold Spring in 1817, and operated until 1884. During the War of 1812 President James Madison ordered the creation of four foundries in different parts of the country. Cold Spring was chosen as one, as it could be protected by the fortifications at West Point. At this time James Kirke Paulding, the writer and native of the Hudson Valley, was serving as Secretary of the Board of Naval Commissioners, and he appointed Gouverneur Kemble as the Director of the new foundry. This foundry was a pioneer in much technology and built America's first iron ship, the revenue cutter, *Spencer*. Its greatest fame came from the Parrott gun, which was later used in the Civil War, and was invented by Robert P. Parrott, who was one of the directors. For many years the foundry operated a fleet of seven sloops plying between Cold Spring and New York City.

Their *Victorine* was supposedly the fastest sloop on the river. The foundry ultimately closed down because it could not compete with more modern plants. Some of the iron used was mined behind Mt. Taurus.

At Fort Montgomery, between 1746, when the first mining operations began in the Forest of Dean, and 1934, when the last mine shut down, roughly 2,000,000 tons of high grade ore was taken from the area. It was a pinkish calcite with crystalized magnetite, which produced between 60 and 61 percent iron, with a low sulphur content, which was excellent for pre-Bessemer production.

The Hudson Iron Works, located at South Bay, just below Hudson, converted much of the crude ore from the Fort Montgomery area into "pigs," ready for the manufacturer's use. In 1860 they produced 16,000 tons of "pig iron." They also utilized hematite from mines at West Stockbridge, Massachusetts. Other iron works were located at Ancram.

Another of the Arsenals established in 1813 was at Watervliet. This one is government owned and still in operation, and was enlarged as recently as 1942.

Troy developed as an iron and steel center at an early date. The iron plates for the *Monitor* were manufactured here. Horatio Winslow's Troy Iron Works were the first in the United States to use the Bessemer Process. Troy remained the iron and steel capital of the country until Andrew Carnegie opened his mills near Pittsburgh in 1873. The Troy Furnace of Republic Steel is still in operation.

The first bridge across the Hudson River was built between Troy and Green Island in 1835 by the Rensselaer & Saratoga Railroad.

15 The Fulton-Livingston Steamboat Monopoly

The Fulton-Livingston steamboat monopoly granted by the New York State Legislature served to dampen further development of the steamboat on the Hudson, and few steamboats were built by others. Exceptions were the *Philadelphia,* the *Pennsylvania,* and the *Aetna,* which perished in a spectacular explosion in New York Harbor in 1824 with loss of life. Other developers hesitated to make the investment and take the necessary risks if they had to pay royalties to the Monopoly.

Other entrepreneurs were now itching to get in on the lucrative business without paying tribute, and there were now enough capable engineers and machinists to supply their needs. There was much hasseling about interstate routes, such as from New York to Staten Island, Elizabethport, Amboy, Newark, Raritan River points, and Monmouth County. The State of New Jersey began to consider the New York Fulton-Livingston Monopoly Law an infringement on her own rights, and soon each state had diametrically conflicting laws. Matters came to a head in the famous case *Gibbons vs. Ogden.* The story is neatly told by Fred Erving Dayton in his book *Steamboat Days.*

It was in 1820 that efforts were made to break down the Fulton-Livingston grant. The endorsement of the bill *Gibbons vs. Ogden* offered no suggestion of the many important propositions of Constitutional Law which immediately came forward, the suit being skillfully handled by Daniel Webster. The result of the suit was to establish the authority of the Federal Government to regulate navigation and other interstate relations.

The opposition's first move was to inspire the New Jersey legislature to pass an act providing that if any of its citizens should be 'enjoined or restrained by any writ of injunction, or order by the Court of Chancery of the State of New York, by virtue, or under color of any act of the Legislature of that State, from navigating any boat or vessel moved by steam or fire, belonging in part, or in whole, to him, on the waters between the ancient shores of the State of New Jersey and New York, the plaintiff or plaintiffs in such writ or order shall be liable to the person or persons aggrieved for all damages, expenses and charges occasioned thereby, to be recovered with triple costs,' etc.

A situation was created where two sovereign States had passed laws in direct conflict. The Fulton-Livingston interests sued out their injunctions against two boats, *Bellona* and *Stoudinger,* (later known as *Mouse-in-the-Mountain*), owned by Gibbons and operated as a ferry from the Battery in New York, across the bay and Kill von Kull to Elizabethtown, New Jersey.

Thomas Gibbons, owner, was principal in the suit brought by Aaron Ogden in behalf of Fulton and Livingston. Ogden had been Governor of New Jersey, and was owner of a similar ferry service between New York and Elizabethtown. He had first opposed the Monopoly in 1814, in an effort to upset Fulton claims, and himself claiming to be the proprietor of "an ancient and accustomed ferry," and he sought to further strengthen his position by securing a coasting license from the United States Government, and by assignment to himself, from the Fitch heirs, of the original patent granted to Fitch, and all national and State rights of every sort in connection with it.

Having fortified his demand, Ogden presented a statement to the New York Legislature, asserting his right to maintain a steam ferry...

"The Committee (of the New York State Legislature) reported that the steamboat had been patented by Fitch... that the exclusive legislation in favor of Fulton and Livingston was unconstitutional and oppressive. The committee's report was rejected by the New York Senate and Ogden was denied the privilege he asked. Ogden next brought the matter before the New Jersey Legislature; but here too, he was defeated; and so powerful were the influences marshalled against him that New Jersey repealed its former measures denying New York steamboats to use New Jersey waters. Beaten at home and in New York, Governor Ogden made peace with the Fulton-Livingston interests, and a compromise was effected, the quarrel being kept out of the courts, and a decision avoided.

Ogden, who had fought and been beaten by the monopoly, was ten years later, placed in position of complainant for the Fulton interests. He obtained an injunction against Thomas Gibbons' ferry, on the ground that his own rights had been invaded, and the Court of Errors sustained him because the case, in its opinion, presented no conflict between State and national laws and jurisdiction.

The case in New Jersey came before the Supreme Court of the State in 1822 and Chief Justice Kirkpatrick held, after discussing States' rights and constitutional privileges, that New York had attempted to interfere with the ancient shores of New Jersey, and that Gibbons was entitled to damages and triple costs under the enactment of that State. The Chief Justice advised however, that the question ought to be brought before the United States Supreme Court, Gibbons appearing as the appellant from the decree of the New York Court.....

Every precaution was taken to make the case one of which the Supreme Court would have to take cognizance, the Gibbons boats having secured a license under the act of Congress 1793, governing vessels employed in coastwise trade, and with which license the injunction orders of New York State courts unwarrantably interfered, as was claimed. The case came to trial in February 1824....."

We need not concern ourselves with the various arguments pro and con. Continuing from Dayton, we find that;

Mr. Chief Justice Marshall[1] handed down his memorable decision, for the length of which he apologized. He had added another important opinion to the number which he had given to establish the legal foundation of the new nation, and to make its new and untested constitution workable and respected organic law. He held that Congress, in being given the power to regulate commerce, was given the power to regulate navigation. It was as expressly granted as if the term "navigation" had been added to the word "commerce" already in the Constitution.

But, said the opinion, "the power to regulate commerce does not look to the principle by which boats are moved. That power was left to individual discretion. The act demonstrates the opinion of Congress that steamboats may be enrolled and licensed in common with vessels using sails. They are entitled to the same privileges and can no more be restrained from navigating waters and entering ports which are free to such vessels than if they were wafted on their voyage by the winds instead of being propelled by the agency of fire. The one element may be as legitimately used as the other, for every commercial purpose authorized by the laws of the river, and the act of a State inhibiting the use of either to any vessel, having a license under the act of Congress, comes, we think, in direct collision with that act.....

---

[1]John Marshall (1755-1835) Fourth Chief Justice of the United States.

The death-knell of the Fulton-Livingston monopoly was rung and the decree which the United States Supreme Court issued declared "the several laws of the State of New York which prohibit vessels, licensed according to the laws of the United States, from navigating the waters of the State of New York, by means of fire or steam, repugnant to the Constitution and void."[2]

With the death of the monopoly, other investors soon jumped into the ring. Prominent among them were "Commodore" Cornelius Vanderbilt, of Staten Island, Daniel Drew, Isaac Newton, and "Live Oak" George Law. At a later date William C. Redfield, Thomas B. Cornell, Jacob Tremper, Absalom Anderson, and Alfred Van Santvoord became powerful steamboat operators. Initially these men had primary interest in steamboats, but eventually some of them developed strong interests in the new railroads: the Stevenses with the Pennsylvania Railroad; Vanderbilt with the New York & Harlem and New York Central railroads; Daniel Drew with the Erie; William Redfield with the Hudson River Railroad; and Thomas Cornell with the Ulster & Delaware. As time went on, the steamboats began to be supplanted by rail services, and competition grew up between the two modes, except in the case of railroad owned ferry services.

---

[2]Fred Erving Dayton, *Steamboat Days,* pp. 22, 27, 30, 31.

16 The Erie and Champlain Canals

Five major canals poured their commerce into the Hudson River and New York Harbor—The Champlain, Erie, Delaware & Hudson, Morris, and Delaware & Raritan. The first two handled general cargo and the last three specialized in coal and iron ore. Today only the Erie and Champlain canals, metamorphosized into the New York State Barge Canal, remain in operation.

The importance of the Erie Canal in the development of New York City, and in Hudson River shipping, cannot be overemphasized. The other three remained important as long as coal remained a major heating fuel, and until the railroads gained full efficiency. About the turn of the century their importance began to fade. The Delaware & Raritan retained some importance as part of the Intra-Coastal Waterway, but was superseded by newer routes along the Jersey shore.

Early in the nineteenth century there was an outbreak of "Canal Fever." The colonies had long been largely dependent on water transport, and the original settlements were largely along the seaboard and tidal rivers. With acquisition of vast tracts of land in the interior, a need for more adequate transportation than the poor roads of the time provided became obvious and pressing. The acquisition of vast tracts west of the Appalachians made direct communication with the Atlantic seaboard imperative. Prior to the Louisiana Purchase in 1803, the produce of the Old Northwest Territory moved mainly down the Mississippi to New Orleans, which was then French territory and this was unsatisfactory. The alternate way of shipping to the sea was via the Great Lakes and St. Lawrence River. However, this was through Canadian territory, and, as the War of 1812 proved, was also unsatisfactory. George Washington favored the building of a canal west along the Potomac, but it was not built until 1828, as the Chesapeake & Ohio Canal, which never got west of Cumberland, Maryland. Its westward extension, the National Road, our first Federal Highway, was not built until 1815. This road extended the route from Cumberland to St. Louis.

New York State interests were not behind in foresight, and from an early date, sought to improve the Hudson-Mohawk route to the Great Lakes. As early as 1792, the Inland Lock Navigation Company, under the direction of General Philip Schuyler, was chartered to build a canal around the falls of the Mohawk at Little Falls. This canal utilized the relatively easy north side of the river and was almost completed by 1793. However, work was suspended owing to engineering and financial difficulties. In the early 1800s it cost as much to move a ton of merchandise thirty miles by land as moving it from England to America by sea. Thus, the need for a canal remained imperative. So long as it cost a dollar to send a bushel of wheat to New York, which could be raised for fifty cents in Illinois, most of the grain, pork, whiskey, and other goods from the West, continued to float down the Mississippi. Every enterprising Atlantic Coast seaport wanted to tap this wealth.

Proposals for a canal from the Hudson River to either Lake Ontario or Lake Erie began to be bruited about. In 1810 DeWitt Clinton lent his political support in the New York Legislature to this concept, and a Study Commission was formed including himself, Gouverneur Morris, Stephen Van Rensselaer, and Thomas Eddy. In 1811 this Commission recommended the Lake Erie, rather than the Lake Ontario canal.

The War of 1812 stilled the issue, but served further to confirm the need. In 1815 a public meeting was held in New York City with DeWitt Clinton as Chairman. He drew up an Erie Canal proposal, known as the *New York Memorial,* and obtained signatures to a petition presented to the Legislature for the canal's authorization. The matter was debated during 1816 and 1817, with the Lake Ontario interests opposing. Veto on a National Waterways project at this time forced the entire financial burden of any canal upon the State of New York. Nonetheless, the Canal Bill passed the Legislature in April of 1817; a Canal Fund was established; special taxes were levied; and work began on the Fourth of July in 1817. This same year DeWitt Clinton was elected Governor for his first term, which lasted until 1823. He was later to serve another term from 1825 to 1828. The canal was to run 363 miles from Albany to Buffalo.

The route followed the west bank of the Hudson River from Albany to Cohoes, and then cut across and around the Cohoes Falls, to the Mohawk Valley at Crescent. It then followed the Mohawk River Valley to Rome, where it cut south of Lake Oneida to Syracuse. It then went west to Rochester and Lockport. From Lockport west, it followed the valleys of Torenanta and Tonawanda Creeks to Tonawanda, on the Niagara River. From there, ten miles north of Buffalo, it followed the east shore of the Niagara River south to Black Rock, and thence to the mouth of Buffalo Creek, sometimes called the Buffalo River.

There was a small harbor at Black Rock, and an Erie Basin at Buffalo. By 1906 the Buffalo terminal complex had grown to include a stone breakwater and lighthouse at the north end of Buffalo Harbor, plus the adjacent Hamburg Canal and City Ship Canal. At the far opposite end, in Brooklyn, an Erie Basin of sixty acres was built to afford harborage to canal boats pulled down the Hudson by tow boats from Albany.

Wild "bog trotters," from the West of Ireland, were set to work pulling stumps along the route. Conventional tools, such as pick and shovel, could not be used in many places, and the workers could wear only a slouch hat and flannel shirt owing to the soggy, boggy ground. Work progressed again, however, and the first section from Utica to Albany, was opened in 1823, and from Salina to Buffalo in 1825. All told, construction took eight years. During this period of construction the derisive name of "Clinton's Big Ditch" was applied but it soon came to be referred to as the "Grand Canal." President Thomas Jefferson had said, "talk of making a canal 350 miles long through a wilderness is little short of madness." The final breakthrough was at Lockport, and Jefferson was proven wrong.

Upon completion, a great Celebration was held. It began at Buffalo on October 26, 1825, where cannons were fired in salute. The signal was given by cannon fire all along the route as far as Sandy Hook, New Jersey. Governor Clinton, and other dignitaries, were on hand for a cruise starting at Buffalo and continuing all the way to New York Harbor. There was rejoicing and banqueting all along the line. The first boats through were the passenger packets, *Seneca Chief, Superior,* and *Commodore Perry,* followed by the *Buffalo,* out of Erie, Pennsylvania. These were joined at Rochester by the *Young Lion of the West.* On November 4th, 1825, there was a great celebration when the boats were towed into New York Harbor. Twenty two steamboats, (a great number for that time), accompanied the canal boats out into the Lower New York Bay where Governor Clinton poured a keg of Lake Erie water into the Atlantic—"The Marriage of the Waters." This was reminiscent of the Doge of Venice throwing a golden ring into the waters of the Adriatic. One of the kegs is now in the collection of the New York Historical Society.

Principal physical features of the canal were as follows: At Albany there were extensive basins, and at Watervliet there was a lateral outlet to the Hudson, which aided connectivity with the Champlain Canal. The usual course of the canal was 4 ft. deep, 28 ft. wide at the bottom and 40 ft. wide at water level. There were 83 locks, built of massive stone. The chambers were 90 ft. x 15 ft., and they accommodated boats of over 100 tons burden. A stone aqueduct still in use today as a highway bridge, carried the canal across the Mohawk River at Rexford. At Little Falls the canal ran through the rocky and hilly region just south of the river, and ran through a two mile cut in solid rock, and descended 50 ft. through five locks. This section was built in only eighty days—a great engineering achievement for the times. At Rochester, there was a great aqueduct 750 feet long across the Genesee River, just above the Falls. This had twelve piers and eleven arches and offered spectacular views. At Lockport the canal traversed a ridge of flint and limestone. Here there was a great staircase of five parallel ascending and descending locks—ten in all. There was a total rise of seventy-five feet. Also at Lockport, thirty miles from Buffalo, was a seven mile long rock-cut twenty feet deep. These locks were a favorite subject of engravings for many years. Indeed, the public enthusiasm was so great that the Opening Celebration in New York was painted by the noted artist, Anthony Imbert. This now hangs in the Museum of the City of New York.

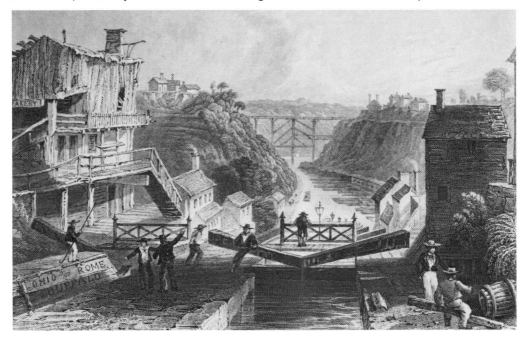

Lockport on the Erie Canal, by William Bartlett.

The financial success was immediate. The tolls from the canal exceeded the interest on the State's debt even before completion. The tolls in the opening year exceeded $750,000. Total cost of the basic canal, before construction of feeders and improvements made between 1884-1894, was $7,600,000. Total tolls by 1882, when tolls were abolished, came to $78,000,000. The canal had shown large profits from the start.

The first major feeder was the Oswego Branch, from Syracuse to Lake Ontario in 1828.

Other major feeders are listed at the end of the chapter. Some further improvements were made between 1884 and 1894, but basic inadequate navigability and fraudulent administration by "The Canal Ring," brought plans for basic improvements and conversion into the New York State Barge Canal of today.

The effects of the new canal were immediate and stupendous. During the first decades of the nineteenth century the cost of transporting Midwest crops to the East alone was higher than the cost of growing them on less productive eastern farms with poor, overworked soil. The Erie Canal cut costs to a fraction and wool, wheat, pork, and whiskey came east at prices New England farmers could not match. Westbound freight consisted of salt, furniture, and general merchandise. In 1826 over 19,000 boats passed one small town on the route. The freight rate from Columbus, Ohio to New York, via the Canal was cut to $2.50 per 100wt, and the trip took only twenty days. Packet boats charged passengers 1½ᶜ per mile, and travelled at 1½ mph. It was not unusual to see up to seventy boats waiting to go through a lock. By 1847 the Albany trade was greater than that at New Orleans from the entire Mississippi River system. By 1883, 28,000 men and boys, and 16,000 horses and mules worked on the canal, and during the busy season, an average of 150 boats per day reached tidewater. By 1888 Harper's School Geography had this to say:

> Three great water routes to sea, and many lines of railway, are the principal channels of domestic commerce. The second of these water routes, by the Great Lakes, the Erie Canal, and the Hudson River to New York is the principal commercial route of the continent.[1]

Scene on the Erie Canal, c1830 by John W. Hill.

By 1835 great flour mills had been built on the upper falls of the Genesee at Rochester, and the Genesee Valley had become the Nation's great wheat growing area. This was only made possible by the canal.

---

[1]*Harper's School Geography,* author(s) name (s) not given, pp. 33, 34.

In 1812 Rochester was a wilderness. By 1830 it had a population of 20,000 and boasted the most modern large hotel in America. It shipped 202,900 barrels of flour in 1826. Lockport grew from two houses in 1821 into a city by 1826. Buffalo had one house in 1814. By 1839 it had a population of 25,000, a stone pier, and a lighthouse, and magnificent steamboats. The first Lake Erie steamboat was the *Walk-in-the-Water* of 1818. In fact, the Great Lakes became the western extension of the Erie Canal, as the Hudson was the eastern extension. The entire commerce of the West flowed through Buffalo. A single shipment of fur pelts in 1826 was valued at $100,000.

The Erie Canal also spurred the growth of New York City and its financial development as a center of shipping, banking, and insurance. It opened eastern markets to the farm products of the Great Lakes region, fostered immigration to the Old Northwest, and helped create numerous large cities. However, it was not without its counter effects, as described by James Kirke Paulding in his ''New Mirror'' of 1828:

"Without a doubt,'' observes our old fashioned friend, Alderman Janson, whom we quote as the great apostle of antediluvian notions, "without doubt canals and locks are good things in moderation; but some how or other, I think I have a prejudice in favour of rivers, where they are to be had, and where they are not, people may as well make up their minds to do without them. In sober truth, it is my firm opinion, and I don't care whether any body agrees with me or not, that the great operation of a canal is, merely to concentrate on its line, and within its immediate in-fluence, that wealth, population, and business, which if let alone, would diffuse themselves naturally, equally, and beneficially through every vein and artery of the country. The benefits of a canal are confined to a certain distance, while all beyond is actually injured, although all pay their proportion of the expenses of its construction.''

"I once was,'' continues the alderman, "a little mad myself in the canal way, like most people, and actually made a pilgrimage in a canal boat all the way to Buffalo. I found every body along the sides of the canal delighted with the vast public benefits of these contrivances; they could sell the product of their lands, and the lands themselves for twice or thrice as much as formerly. I rub-bed my hands with great satisfaction, and was more in love with canals than ever. Returning, I diverged from the line of the canal, into some of the more remote counties, and found all the people scratching their heads. "What is the matter, good people all, of every sort, what can you want now the great canal is finished?'' "The damned canal. The devil take the great canal,'' cried all with one voice: "every body is mad to go and settle on the canal.'' "To be sure they are, my good friends and fellow citizens, and that is the beauty of a canal; it raises the price of land within a certain distance to double what it was before.'' "Yes, and it lowers the price of land not within a certain distance in an equal if not greater proportion; it is robbing Peter to pay Paul. Nobody thinks of coming here to settle now—they are all for the canal.'' O ho, thought I, then a canal has two sides, as well as two ends.''[2]

In 1849 Nathaniel Parker Willis lodged another complaint against the canal (and the new railroad) on more aesthetic grounds in his article, *The Four Rivers*:

We fed our eyes on the slumbering and broad valley of the Mohawk. How startled must be the Naiad of this lively river to find her willowy form embraced between railroad and canal—one in-truder on either side of the bed so sacredly overshaded! Pity but there were a new knight of La Mancha to avenge the hamadryads and water-nymphs of their wrongs and injuries from wood-cutters and contractors! Where sleep Pan and vengeful Oread, when a Yankee settler hews me down twenty wood-nymphs of a morning? There lie their bodies, limbless trunks, on the banks of the Mohawk, yet no Dutchman stands sprouting into leaves near by, nor woollen jacket turn-ing into bark, as in the retributive olden time. We are abandoned of these gods of Arcady! They like not the smoke of steam funnels.....

Either run your railroads away from the river-courses, gentlemen contractors, or find some other place than your passengers' eyes to bestow your waste ashes!.....

---

[2] James Kirke Paulding, *New Mirror for Travellers and Guide to the Springs,* pp. 215, 216.

There is a drowsy beauty in these German flats (near Little Falls), that seem strangely profaned by a smoky monster whisking along twenty miles in the hour. The gentle canal-boat was more homogeneous to the scene. The hills lay off the river in easy and sleepy curves, and the amber Mohawk creeps down over its shallow gravel with a deliberateness altogether and abominably out of tune with the iron rails. Perhaps it is the rails out of tune with the river—but any way there is a discord. I am content to see the Mohawk, canal, and railroad inclusive, but once a year.[3]

By the 1850s the railroads had destroyed the canal's long haul advantages. In order to speed up traffic, thought was given to recourse to steam navigation. However, the wash from paddles or propellers undermined the banks and justled barges in the crowded basins. There was need for a special type of steamboat for canal navigation that would overcome these problems; and the Canal Commissioners offered a prize for its invention. In 1873 William Baxter demonstrated a steam canal boat that travelled at the moderate speed of 3 9/10 mph on only 14 82/100 lbs. of coal per mile—twice the speed at half the cost of horse power. Implementation was hindered however, by the narrow locks and shallow bed.

In 1903 the New York Legislature authorized a thorough overhauling and reconstruction of the Erie Canal, Champlain Canal, and associated feeders into the New York State Barge Canal. This was confirmed by public referendum. The total system is 525 miles long, is twelve feet deep, has 310 ft. long electrically operated locks to accommodate 2000 ton vessels, and cost over $175,000,000. Construction began in 1905 and was completed by 1918. The main canal now runs from Troy to Tonawanda via the following route, which deviates quite a bit from the old Erie Canal:

Troy to Waterford via the Hudson River; up a flight of locks to the canalized Mohawk River at Waterford; to Crescent, Vischer Ferry, Rexford, Schenectady/Scotia, Rotterdam, Amsterdam, Fort Johnson, Tribes Hill/Fort Hunter, Auriesville, Fultonville/Fonda, Sprakers, Canajoharie/Palatine Bridge, Fort Plain/Nelliston, St. Johnsville, Little Falls, Herkimer/Mohawk, Frankfort, East Schuyler, Utica, Yorkville, Whitesboro, Oriskany and Rome. Here it leaves the Mohawk and cuts across to Lake Oneida, at Sylvan Beach, following Wood Creek. From the west end of Oneida Lake it goes to Brewerton and Three River Point, where there is a junction with the Oswego Canal. This is near Syracuse. Next farther west is Thomas, where there is a junction with the Cayuga and Seneca Canals. Following west we come to Clyde, Lyons, Newark, Palmyra, Fairport, Rochester, Spencerport, Brockport, Albion, Medina, Lockport, and Tonawanda. It utilizes the Niagara River to Buffalo.

The canal is toll free. The Mohawk Valley route remains important in domestic commerce. In 1947 the canal handled a total cargo of 4,000,000 tons. The adjacent railroad in that same year handled an average of 300 daily freight and passenger trains.

In 1956 one hundred tugboats moved 4,500,000 tons of freight—98% of which was petroleum products. Commenting upon the importance of this trade route in 1956, Governor Averell Harriman gave the following eulogy:

"Trade came our way. Trade begot merchants, shippers, bankers, brokers, insurance men, manufacturers. We were able to provide services to the rest of the United States and the world—services that we have been developing over the years. We attracted skilled labor from all over the world. One skill, of course, generates another. Ingenuity grows out of opportunity. Perhaps more so than most States, we are an authentic cross section of American life. Business ranges from small farms to industries that are among the country's largest. Our

---

[3]Nathaniel Parker Willis, *The Four Rivers,* pp. 201, 202.

Tug and oil barge on Champlain Canal near Schuylerville. (Photo Arthur G. Adams)

people come from all religions and racial backgrounds. As a melting pot, we've had the advantage of immigrants' enthusiasm and vigor.'' He then went on to say that this was brought about first by the Erie Canal, then the New York Central Railroad, and in the present day by the New York State Thruway.

The other major segment of the New York State Barge Canal system, the Champlain Canal, connects Troy with Whitehall (formerly known as Skenesborough), at the far southern tip of Lake Champlain; thus, with the lake and the Richelieu River, forming a through water route to the St. Lawrence River in Canada. This canal is 66 miles long and utilizes canalized sections of the Hudson River between the Federal Lock at Troy (Lock No. 1), and Fort Edward. There it leaves the Hudson and follows Wood Creek to Whitehall, by way of Dunhams Basin, Smiths Basin, Fort Ann and Comstock. Originally the canal branched off from the Erie Canal at Cohoes, crossed the Mohawk River on an aquaduct, and followed the west shore of the Hudson past Mechanicville, Stillwater, Bemis Heights, and Coveville to Schuylerville. (This section is now filled-in and sections are utilized by U. S. Route 4.) At Schuylerville the canal begins following the east shore of the Hudson through Thomson, Fort Miller, and Fort Edward. From Fort Edward, where it leaves the Hudson, to Whitehall, it is paralleled by the Delaware & Hudson Railroad, and from Fort Ann to Whitehall, by U. S. Route 4. Today there are 12 locks. The bridges over the canal are all low with only fifteen feet clearance, and they are fixed in place. Some barges like the *Sheila Moran,* of the Moran Towing & Transportation Company, have retractable wheelhouses that sink into an elevator shaft when going under a bridge. Sailboats must unstep their masts. This canal was first built in 1819 as the Champlain & Hudson Canal, and improved and incorporated into the New York State Barge Canal in 1918. Traffic consists largely of petroleum and paper barges and pleasure craft.

EXACT ROUTE OF ORIGINAL ERIE CANAL

Through the years the route of the Erie Canal has been changed from time to time, and substantially at the time of inauguration of the New York State Barge Canal System. The original route was substantially the same as shown on Crams Superior Map of New York of 1906, and ran as follows:

Albany, Menands, Cohoes, Crescent, Visher Ferry, Rexford, (Aqueduct over Mohawk River), Schenectady, Rotterdam, Patterson, Fort Hunter, Fultonville, Auriesville, Randall, Downing, Sprakers, Canajoharie, Fort Plain, St. Johnsville, Mindenville, Indian Castle, Little Falls, Jacksonburgh, Mohawk, Ilion, Frankfort, Harbor, Utica, Whitesborough, Oriskany, Rome, New London, Stasy Basin, Higginsville, State Bridge, Wampsville, Canastota, Sullivan, Kirkville, Manlius Center, Desono, Syracuse, Camillus, Belle Isle, Memphis, Weedsport, Port Byron, Montezuma, Clyde, Lock Berlin, Lyons, Newark, Port Gibson, Palmyra, Wayneport, Bushnell Basin, Pittsford, Brighton, Rochester, (Aqueduct over Genessee River), Otis, Greece, Spencerport, Adams Basin, Brockport, Holley, Hulbertson, Hindsburg, Albion, Eagle Harbor, Shelby Basin, Reynals Basin, Orangeport, Lockport, (Torenanta Creek), Hodgeville, Pendleton, Wendelville, Tonawanda, Black Rock, Buffalo.

FEEDERS TO THE ERIE CANAL

Black River — Rome and Lyons Falls	35 miles
Cayuga & Seneca — Montezuma and Geneva	21 miles
Champlain & Hudson — West Troy and Whitehall	66 miles
Genesee Valley — Rochester and Mill Grove	113 miles
Oswego — Syracuse and Oswego	38 miles
Oneida River Improvement — Oswego Canal and Oneida Lake	20 miles

17 The Iron and Anthracite Canals

The Delaware & Hudson Canal, completed in 1828, was the brainchild of two brothers, Maurice and William Wurts, who owned extensive anthracite fields in northeastern Pennsylvania. At that time anthracite was not generally recognized as a feasible fuel. The Wurts brothers demonstrated its clean burning qualities to a group of investors in New York City in 1823, and immediately gained backing for construction of a canal from the coal fields to tidewater at Rondout Creek—a total of 108 miles. There were to be 109 locks, fifteen aqueducts, and fourteen boat basins. The canal was to be 4 feet deep and 20 feet wide at the bottom and 36 feet wide at water level. The bed was to be lined with clay to prevent seepage and care was to be taken that this would not be undermined by otters, beavers, muskrats, moles, or other aquatic animals. The line was to be paralleled by the new telegraph and this was to be used for dispatching.

Philip Hone, soon to become Mayor of New York City, was elected the first President of the Canal Company in 1825. He was a personal friend of Washington Irving's and a close observer of contemporary life. His famous diary is a valuable source of information on the period. The new town at the coalfield end of the canal was named Honesdale in his honor. This engineering marvel was worked upon by such famous engineers as John Bloomfield Jervis, Horatio Allen, America's first locomotive engineer, Benjamin Wright, a famous surveyor, and John Roebling, developer of the suspension bridge and builder of Brooklyn Bridge.

Honesdale was connected with the mine area by a gravity railroad, whereon the loaded cars rolled down to the canal by gravity. The empty cars were hauled by a combination of cables and winches on inclined planes in the steep sections, and by one of the first steam locomotives used in the United States, the *Stourbridge Lion,* in the less steep sections. The locomotive was built in England. Horatio Allen, the first locomotive engineer, was also a practical mechanical engineer—not merely an engine driver. He later made many practical improvements in locomotive design, starting a tradition on the Delaware & Hudson. On August 8, 1829, he drove the first steam powered train to move in America.[1]

From Honesdale the canal followed along Lackawaxen Creek to Hawley and Lackawaxen, on the Delaware. Here it crossed the river and followed the north bank of the Delaware

---

[1] The author's grandfather was associated for many years with the Delaware & Hudson Railroad and the Hudson Coal Company . On April 28th and 29th, 1979, he and his family participated in the Sesquicentennial Celebration of the D & H Company, part of which consisted of a steam train excursion from Albany to Montreal and return.

(Left) William Wurts, (Right) Maurice Wurts, the founders of the Delaware & Hudson Canal.
(Courtesy of D&H Railroad)

downstream to Port Jervis, along the foot of the towering Hawks Nest Cliffs. A right of way had to be blasted out of sheer rock faces, and the hard-drinking Irish construction workers had numerous bloody fights with the raftsmen on the Delaware, who resented the canal as an obstruction to navigation. From Port Jervis the canal followed the Neversink River, Basher Kill, Homowack, Sandburg, and Rondout Creeks to Eddyville, near Kingston. At Rondout was located the famous Island Dock where the coal was unloaded from the canal boats and was stored prior to trans-shipment via coastal schooners and river barges, pulled by tow boats, such as the old sidewheeler *Norwich*. This made Rondout the major port on the mid-Hudson, and home base of the famous Cornell line of towboats.

The canal followed the northwestern foot of the Shawangunk Mountains for many miles. Many remains can be seen in the form of old locks, earthworks, and bridge abutments. However, there are very few water-filled sections left. It is largely paralleled by Routes 97, 209 and 213, although it would be necessary to often use secondary roads to follow the route more closely. The old Canal House Tavern at High Falls has been restored and reopened as a restaurant, and the Delaware & Hudson Canal Society operates an interesting museum at High Falls.

Eventually the dam which had been built across the Delaware River at Lackawaxen, to provide slack water in the river upon which the canal boats could be ferried across, proved too much of a hindrance to river navigation and too expensive to maintain, and was replaced by a suspension bridge that carried a water-filled trough. This aqueduct was completed in 1848. It was designed by John Roebling and consisted of four spans varying in length from 132 ft. to 142 ft. It is still in use today as a vehicular bridge, the water trough having been removed, and has been designated a National Historic Landmark. A toll is charged.

Other Roebling suspension bridges were at Lackawaxen Creek (1848-228 feet in two spans), Cuddebackville, across the Neversink River (1850-170 ft. in one span), and across the Rondout Creek at High Falls, where remains of the stone foundations of the viaduct and several old locks may be seen. From Lackawaxen, the route was as follows: Barryville, Pond Eddy, Mongaup, Port Jervis, Huguenot, Godeffroy, Roses Point, Cuddebackville, Westbrookville, Haven, Wurtsboro, Summitville (formerly Beatysburg), Phillipsport, Ellenville, Napanoch, Wawarsing, Kerhonkson, (formerly Middleport), Alligerville, High Falls, Bruceville, Lawrenceville, Rosendale, Creeklocks, and Eddyville. The highest point between the Hudson and the Delaware was at Summitville. The first through shipment of coal was received at Kingston on December 5, 1828. In 1842 the canal depth was increased to 5 feet, enabling the boats to carry an additional 10 tons. In 1847 the depth was again increased to 6 feet.

Boats were hauled by mules as the bow wave from a steamboat would damage the banks and barges tied up in the basins. The only steam vessel was the paymaster's launch *Minnie*. The captain and his family lived on board the canalboat in a cabin measuring 12 feet square. The trip from end to end took a week, and the canal was closed on Sundays. Whole families grew up, lived and died, on the canal. The "canallers" were a rough and tumble lot, and hard drinking was the norm, with many taverns along the line. They were also a musical lot, singing at their work. Popular songs included, *As I Went Down to Port Jervis, Haul On The Bowline,* and the comic *Mule Song,* with its concluding verse—"Never take the hind-shoe from a Mule."

Always essentially a single commodity canal, traffic began to dwindle with improvements in the parallel railroads, which could operate year around. In November 1898 the Delaware & Hudson Canal Company sent the last load of coal through, and in 1899 reincorporated as

Island Dock coal transfer terminal at outlet of Delaware & Hudson Canal on Rondout Creek, Rondout, N.Y. c1896 (Lionel DeLisser).

Towboats tied up for winter at Rondout Creek, c1896 (Courtesy John F. Matthews collection).

the Delaware & Hudson Railroad. They sold the canal to S. D. Coykendall of Kingston, who operated towboats on the Hudson and was a leading developer of the Wallkill Valley Railroad and the Ulster & Delaware Railroad. He operated the canal between Rondout and Ellenville until 1904 for the transport of Rosendale cement and general merchandise. The canal was totally abandoned in 1904.

The 106.69 mile long Morris Canal, between Phillipsburg on the Delaware and the Hudson at Paulus Hook in Jersey City, was originally chartered in 1824 to try to help reinvigorate New Jersey's iron industry; it was completed in 1836. The timber, long used as fuel, was running out, and it was necessary to bring in Pennsylvania coal for the industry around Paterson, Newark, and Jersey City. Hilly country was traversed, with a maximum elevation of 913 feet above sea level at Lake Hopatcong. Use was made of 11 inclined planes and 16 locks.[2] On the inclined planes the entire canal boat was lifted up out of the water on cradles. The canal succeeded in restoring prosperity to the iron industry, and so stimulated Newark's business that the city's population doubled between 1830 and 1835. Other iron furnaces were located at Dover. The inclined planes were from 500 feet to 1,500 feet long, and on occasion the chain would break, letting laden barges thunder down the ways and back into the water at the bottom. There is an old legend that, one day, a captain's wife was below decks in her cabin doing her laundry when the elevator chain broke and the barge went streaking down the ways. There was a large splash when it hit the bottom, whereupon the good wife stuck her head out the hatch, remarking that, ''the boys seem to be working a might fast today.''

The route left Phillipsburg on the Delaware and first ran a short distance east to Port Warren, Stewartsville, and Willow Grove, before turning northeast and following the Pohatcong Creek past Broadway, Brass Castel, Washington, and Port Colden. There it crossed over to the valley of the Musconetcong River at Port Murray, and continued along the northwest base of Schooley's Mountain to Hackettstown, Saxton Falls, Waterloo, and Stanhope (now called Netcong). Here there was a basin and plane into Lake Musconetcong. Adjacent Great

---

[2]Originally 23 smaller inclined planes and 23 locks.

The Strand at Rondout, c1896. (Lionel DeLisser)

Pond, to the north, now called Lake Hopatcong, was dammed to raise its level and provide a constant source of water for the canal. Continuing northeast from Stanhope, the next points reached were Port Morris and Shippenport. Here the canal crossed a ridge and dropped down into the valley of the Rockaway River at Wharton, an early iron milling town. From there it continued northeast through Dover, Rockaway, Denville, and Booton, where there was another plane. Here the canal left the Rockaway River and cut overland through Montville and Towaco to the Passaic Valley at Lincoln Park, where it crossed the Pequannock River, just above its confluence with the Passaic. Turning southeast, it crossed the Passaic River at Little Falls, where it again turned northeast to run along the northwestern base of Garret Mountain, and then continued south through Clifton, Richfield, Bloomfield, and Belleville to Newark. This section was roughly parallel to the Garden State Parkway and Market Street in Newark. From Newark it headed east along the present route of the New York & Newark Railroad, across the Passaic and Hackensack Rivers to Jersey City, where it ran south to a low point at the southern end of the Bergen Ridge near the Bayonne city line. Here it turned abruptly east, and then immediately north along the eastern side of the Bergen Ridge through Greenville and Claremont to the Communipaw section of Jersey City. Here it entered the Hudson and Tidewater or Morris Canal Basin, just north of Johnston Avenue and the Jersey Central Railroad terminal and south of Powles Hook, opposite, appropriately enough, Morris Street in downtown Manhattan. The canal was abandoned and drained in 1924, only the Morris Canal Basin still open to navigation.

In its heyday the Delaware & Raritan Canal carried a greater tonnage than the Erie Canal. In 1866 it handled over 2,500,000 tons of cargo and the canal was a major factor in the development of the Ports of New York and Philadelphia. Prior to its construction in 1834, it sometimes took sailing trips of two weeks to go around Cape May between Philadelphia and New York. This was often treacherous ocean sailing and the canal provided an all-weather inland route.

Hundreds of Irish immigrants who dug the canal are buried along its route, victims of a cholera epidemic. The canal was 44 miles long and had ten locks. It began with a dam across the Delaware River at Raven Rock, just above Stockton, New Jersey. This diverted water into what was called the ''feeder,'' which ran along the east shore of the Delaware, south through Stockton, Lambertville, Washington Crossing, Trenton, and Bordentown. This feeder collected barges of coal coming off the Lehigh Canal from the southern Pennsylvania anthracite fields north of Reading and near Mauch Chunk. The main canal left the Delaware at Trenton and headed northeast along what is now Feeder Street to Assunpink Creek, and along this creek to Bakersville, where it followed Shipetaukin Creek to Port Mercer. Here it crossed over to the valley of Stony Brook, a tributary of the Millstone River. Next came Princeton, where it followed the present line of the artificial Lake Carnegie into the Millstone River proper. It continued northeast through Kingston, Rocky Hill, Griggstown, Blackwells Mills, and South Bound Brook, where it turned east by southeast to follow the south shore of the Raritan River to Somerset and New Brunswick, where a lock let it down to tidewater. The canal was open to commercial traffic until 1932. Today large stretches are open for recreational boating, but you cannot get a large boat all the way through, as parts of it around Trenton and Bordentown are filled in and the locks are all inoperative.

Most of the traffic coming off these canals found its way to the Hudson River and New York Harbor. Today the role of the canals in building up the Port of New York is often forgotten, but all five canals played an important part in Hudson River commerce.

THE ERIE CANAL SONG

I had a mule; her name was Sal
  Fifteen miles on the Erie Canal,
She was a good old worker, and a good old pal,
  Fifteen miles on the Erie Canal,
We pulled some barges in our day,
Filled with lumber, coal and hay,
And she knew every inch of the way,
  From Albany to Buffalo.

Low Bridge! Everybody down!
Low Bridge! For we're comin' to a town,
You'll always know your neighbor,
You'll always know your pal,
If you've ever navigated,
ON THE ERIE CANAL.

THE E-R-I-E

We were forty miles from Albany,
Forget it I never shall,
What a terrible storm we had one night
On the E-ri-e Canal.

Oh the E-ri-e was a-rising,
The gin was getting low;
And I scarcely think we'll get a drink
Till we get to Buffalo.

We were loaded down with barley,
We were chuck up full of rye;
And the Captain he looked down at me
With his goddam wicked eye.

Two days out from Syracuse,
The vessel struck a shoal,
And we like to all been foundered
On a chunk o'Lackawanna coal.

We hollered to the captain
On the towpath, treadin' dirt;
He jumped on board and stopped the leak
With his old red flannel shirt.

The cook she was a kind old soul,
She had a ragged dress;
We hoisted her upon a pole
As a signal of distress.

The winds begin to whistle
And the waves begin to roll
And we had to reef our royals
On the raging Canawl.

When we got to Syracuse,
The off-mule he was dead,
The nigh mule got blind staggers,
And we cracked him on the head.

The captain, he got married,
The cook, she went to jail,
And I'm the only son-of-a-gun
That's left to tell the tale.

(Alternate Verse)

Oh the girls are in the Police Gazette,
The crew are all in jail;
I'm the only living sea-cook's son
That's left to tell the tale.

CHORUS

O the E-RI-E was a-risin'
And the gin was a-gittin' low,
And I scarcely think we'll git a drink
Till we get to Buffa-lo-o-o,
Till we get to Buffalo.

MORRIS CANAL BALLAD

Old Bill Miller,
Ridin' on the tiller
Steering round the Browertown Bend;
Old Davy Ross,
With a ten dollar hoss
Comin' up the Pompton Plane.

18 Art in the Hudson Valley

Not all early nineteenth century development was in the fields of technology and commerce. The Hudson River and its mountainous surroundings gained the attention of artists at a fairly early date. In 1820 there appeared a volume of engravings executed by J. R. Smith and John Hill entitled *"Hudson River Portfolio."* The engravings were taken from the work of William Guy Wall (1792-1864), who was born in Ireland and came to America in 1818. His works provide important documentation of the river shortly after 1800 and provide views of such localities as New York Bay, Governors Island, Brooklyn Heights, Fort Montgomery, Newburgh Bay, Esopus Creek, the Catskills, Cohoes, and Bakers Falls.

This engraving tradition was continued by William James Bennett, J. C. Bentley, and J. R. Smith, who engraved the drawings of William H. Bartlett (1809-1854) for use in Nathaniel Parker Willis's travel book of 1840, *American Scenery: Of Land, Lake, and River: Illustrations of Transatlantic Nature,* published in London by George Virtue and R. Martin & Co. of New York. There are thirty-seven views of Hudson River area scenery and towns. Typical views include those of the Colonnade of Congress Hall at Saratoga Springs, West Point, the Narrows, Ballston Spa, Stony Point Lighthouse, Undercliff, The Seat of General Morris, Sing-Sing Prison, Albany, Troy, Catterskill Falls, and the Catskill Mountain House. Thus, besides delineating the scenery, they provide important social and architectural documentation.

Harry Fenn (1838-1911) did a series of drawings and engravings for William Cullen Bryant's monumental two volume picture book of 1872, *Picturesque America.* These books consisted of descriptive essays with copious illustrations. There is considerable emphasis given to the Hudson River region and also to the Atlantic Highlands and adjacent Neversink and Shrewsbury Rivers. Other artists contributing illustrative material on this region included David Johnson (1827-1908), Granville Perkins, and A. C. Warren.

During the second two-thirds of the nineteenth century the scenery of the Hudson Valley was popularized by the lithographs of the firm of Currier & Ives. In 1835 Nathaniel Currier (1813-1888) founded his firm in New York City. He took his brother-in-law, James Merritt Ives (1824-1895), an artist, into partnership in 1850. They used the services of many other artists, including Fanny Palmer, Eastman Johnson, James E. Butterworth, Charles Parsons, George H. Durrie, Louis Maurer, and Arthur Fitzwilliam Tait. However, their works always bore the legend Currier & Ives and were usually unsigned and undated. The Hudson River was a popular subject and background and lithographs of the steamboats sold well. Among the most famous of these steamboat prints were *The Steamboats Drew and St. John of the*

William H. Bartlett
(1809–1854)

People's Evening Line, by C. R. Parsons (1878); a view of the *Saloon of the S. S. Drew,* un-signed (1878); and the *S. S. St. John* by Fanny F. Palmer, showing that noble vessel passing through the Highlands. However, the most famous of all these steamboat lithographs was entitled *A Night on the Hudson: Through At Daylight.* This picture shows the night boat *Isaac Newton* and the day boat *Francis Skiddy* of the Hudson River Day Line (which was also suitable for overnight operation), passing between Anthony's Nose and Bear Mountain. This is a very dramatic view and must have inspired wanderlust in many a heart.

Other specifically identified Hudson River views included *Castle Garden* at the Battery; the *United States Military Academy at West Point;* and *Ice Boat Race on the Hudson,* show-ing a train on the Hudson River Railroad in the background. Other views are not specifically identified but are obviously of views in the area. Among the more interesting are the three series entitled *American Homestead, American Country Life,* and *The Four Seasons of Life.* In the *Country Life* series the *May Morning* view shows a typical Italian Villa country house on Staten Island; *October Afternoon* shows Haverstraw Bay and the Ramapo Mountains in the background; and the *Pleasures of Winter* depicts a typical aristocratic house of the Albany area. In the *American Homestead* series *Spring* shows a typical Rockland County Dutch cottage; *Summer* is another typical Dutch Colonial homestead; and *Autumn* depicts a setting typical of the Haverstraw Bay area. *Middle Age: The Season of Strength,* in the *Four Seasons of Life* series depicts a father returning home to his villa on the shores of the Hudson.

Considering the wide circulation obtained by these popular prints, it is easy to understand how Hudson River scenery became part of the popular culture. Other important lithographers who did work descriptive of the Hudson were F. Berthaux of Dijon, France, who reproduced C. B. J. Fevret de Saint-Memin's drawing of *Fulton's Clermont Passing West Point,* and Fritz Meyer, who specialized in Catskill scenes.

In a more painterly tradition, Thomas Chambers (c1808-c1866) did a number of interesting early views. He was born in England and came to America in 1834. His paintings were based upon Bartlett's drawings. Of particular interest are: *Staten Island and the Narrows; Villa on the Hudson near Weehawken;* and *View from West Point.* They are somewhat naive and primitive in execution.

The first important native American painter from the Hudson Valley was John Vanderlyn (1775-1852), who was born and grew up in Kingston. He became a student of Gilbert Stuart and studied in Paris between 1796 and 1815 as a protege of Aaron Burr. He worked in the Classical Style of David and Ingres, and his masterpiece, *Marius Among the Ruins of Carthage,* attracted the interest of Napoleon. However, upon his return home to the United States, he found that there was little market for this style of painting. Retiring to Kingston, he lived a life of penury. Late in life he received a commission for the gigantic *Landing of Columbus* which hangs in the rotunda of the Capitol at Washington, and was popularized by use on the 2ᶜ stamp of the Columbian Issue of 1893. By time of receiving the commission his health was so undermined by poor living that he had to hire assistants to help him and thus saw little profit from the project. This one job did not help him much, and he was eventually found dead of starvation in his apartment in Kingston. It cannot be said that Vanderlyn was influenced by his native environment as he always worked in the monumental style, producing such works as *The Death of Hercules.* Today his works can be seen in the Metropolitan Museum of Art and in the Senate House Museum in Kingston.

Another early painter in the region was Thomas Doughty (1793-1856), who was born in Philadelphia and worked as a leather currier until the age of twenty-seven. He was entirely self-taught in painting. Later in life he lived and worked in New York City, Newburgh, and Western New York. Representative works include: *View of Highlands from Newburgh; Autumn on the Hudson;* and *Scene in the Catskills.*

Probably the most important event in the art history of the Hudson Valley was the first visit, in 1825, of the English-born artist Thomas Cole (1801-1848) to Catskill. Cole is universally recognized as the principal founder of the Hudson River School of painting. He was born in the Midlands of industrialized England, where the sky was obscured by a pall of factory smoke, and came to America as a youth, settling first in Philadelphia and later in western Pennsylvania and Ohio. He was impressed by the paintings in the Philadelphia Museum, and, on one occasion, walked from Pittsburgh to Philadelphia to study them. He first worked as an itinerant portrait artist in Ohio.

After his first visit to Catskill in 1825 Cole was so enthralled by the scenery that he often returned and eventually settled there. His home and studio have recently been established as a museum. He became a frequent visitor to the Catskills, taking long hikes and making sketches, which he would turn into paintings upon his return to New York City. These landscape paintings soon gained critical acclaim. In 1825 one of his works was purchased by Philip Hone, then Mayor of New York. John Trumbull (1756-1843), then considered America's greatest painter, was impressed by the young man's work and advanced his cause. Before long Cole's work was in vogue with fashionable and wealthy New Yorkers. For subject mater Cole was particularly attracted to the areas of Catskill Creek, the Great Wall of Manitou, and North and South Mountains, as well as the Kaaterskill Clove and Falls. Black Tom, fifth tallest peak in the Catskills, with an elevation of 3940 ft., has been renamed in his honor Mt. Thomas Cole. Artist's Rock, atop the Wall of Manitou, near the site of the former Catskill Mountain House, was also named in his honor. Cole was an avid hiker and outdoorsman and explorer of the wilds. He wrote considerable descriptive material and some poetry of high quality of which *The Wild* is an excellent example.

THE WILD[1]

Friends of my heart, lovers of Nature's works,
Let me transport you to those wild blue mountains
That rear their summits near the Hudson's wave
Though not the loftiest that begirt the land,
They yet sublimely rise, and on their heights
Your souls may have a sweet foretaste of heaven,
And traverse wide and boundless.

From this rock,
The nearest to the sky, let us look out
Upon the earth, as the first swell of day
Is bearing back the duskiness of night.
But lo! a sea of mist o'er all beneath;
An ocean, shoreless, motionless and mute,
No rolling swell is there, no sounding surf;
Silent and solemn all; the stormy main
To stillness frozen, while the crested waves
Leaped in the whirlwind, and the loosened foam
Flew o'er the angry deep.

See! Now ascends
The Lord of Day, waking with pearly fire
The dormant depths, See how his glowing breath
The rising surges kindles, lo! they heave
Like golden sands upon Sahara's gales.
Those airy forms disporting from the mass,
Like winged ships, sail o'er the wondrous plain.
Beautiful vision! Now the veil is rent,
And the coy earth her virgin bosom bares,
Slowly unfolding to the enraptured gaze
Her thousand charms.

Cole began to develop a complete aesthetic incorporating mystical elements of a transcendental nature. He viewed the unique beauty of the Hudson River and Catskill scenery as a special manifestation of God's Providence and blessing upon the new nation. This view soon became widely held and was elaborated by the philosophers and preachers of the day. Contemplation of natural scenery was considered a religious experience and the artist capable of representing this natural beauty on canvas was held in high esteem. Cole's own love of this scenery was so great that, upon occasion of a trip to Europe, he wrote home:

"Neither the Alps, nor the Apennines, no, nor Etna itself, have dimmed in my eyes the beauty of our own Catskills. It seems to me that I look on American scenery, if it were possible, with increased pleasure. It has its own peculiar charm—something not found elsewhere."[2]

He painted the view of the Catskills, across Catskill Creek, from Jefferson Heights, near his home, over and over again, in varying moods of atmosphere, and he remained remarkably faithful to the scenery of this area as long as he concentrated upon pure land-

---

[1] *The Wild*, by Thomas Cole. Included in "Picturesque Catskills—Greene County," by R. Lionel De Lisser,
[2] Quoted in "Picturesque Catskills—Greene County," by R. Lionel De Lisser,

scapes. However, later in life, he began to paint large allegorical works in the Romantic manner. These were frequently religiously or philosophically inspired. Among the most famous series of such works are *Course of Empire* and *The Voyage of Life.* They gained critical acclaim but did not sell as well as the pure landscapes. In recent years a new appreciation for Cole's allegorical works has arisen. Among Cole's most famous paintings are *Catskill Mountain House, Sunny Morning on the Hudson,* and *Catskill Creek.*

Another founder of the Hudson River School was Cole's friend, Asher Brown Durand (1796-1886). Although not so well known as Cole, he was perhaps an even greater technician. Born near Newark, New Jersey, he first worked as an engraver, and for the rest of his life his work showed the fine hand and meticulous craftsmanship associated with this trade. Among his engravings was one of Vanderlyn's *Ariadne.* After 1835 he devoted himself to painting and studied in Europe. Upon returning home he devoted himself to local scenery, including the then beautiful Hoboken and Weehawken cliffs, the Hudson Valley, the Catskills, and the White Mountains. His great painting of *Kaaterskill Clove* dates from 1886. In 1849 he had used this same clove as setting for a double portrait of his close friends Thomas Cole and William Cullen Bryant entitled *Kindred Spirits.* It now hangs in the New York Public Library and is universally known and loved. This painting perhaps best summarizes the spirit of the Hudson River school. Durand was one the founders of the National Academy of Design, and served as its President from 1845 to 1861. In later years he made his home in South Orange, New Jersey. Of particular Hudson River interest are his paintings *River, Scene, Hudson River Looking Towards the Catskills,* and *View of Troy.* Good collections of his works are in the Metropolitan Museum of Art, the Montclair New Jersey Museum, and Corcoran Gallery in Washington.

Frederick E. Church (1826-1900) was the scion of a wealthy family resident in Hartford, Connecticut. Evincing great talent at an early age, he studied with Thomas Cole at his studio in Catskill. Church's works tend toward giganticism and are both romantic and realistic in detail. He travelled extensively in North, Central, and South America, producing great canvases of absorbing power and exotic beauty. His most famous production is a mural-like oil of *Niagara Falls* which captures the scope and power of the falls on the one hand, and the individual delicate whitecaps and sprays of foam on the other. It is a work of both delicacy and power, and now hangs in the Corcoran Gallery. He devoted himself less to Catskill and Hudson subjects than did the other important members of the Hudson River School, but he loved the area and built his Victorian Pseudo-Persian mansion *Olana Castle* across the Hudson from Catskill. The house itself is a work of art, and the landscaping, designed by Church and the noted landscape architect Calvert Vaux, is designed as a tremendous "living picture," providing a sweeping panoramic view of the entire Catskill escarpment and the Hudson River south to the Highlands. The entire conception is in harmony with his large paintings. *Olana Castle* has been restored as a museum and is open to the public. Among his paintings of particular interest are, *Winter Landscape from Olana, Autumn View from Olana,* and *View of Catskills from Olana.*

John Frederick Kensett (1818-1872) was born in Cheshire, Connecticut and first worked as an engraver. He began to study oil painting and went abroad to study in England, Dusseldorf, and Rome. In 1849, back in the United States, he became a member of the National Academy of Design. His color palette was cooler than Cole's or Durand's and he made a specialty of rock scenery; concentrating on the Lake George, Hudson Highlands, and Ramapo Mountain areas. His output was prodigious. Of particular interest are: *Lakes and Mountains, View near Cozzens Hotel from West Point,* and *View of Storm King from Fort Putnam.*

Jasper Francis Cropsey (1823-1900) was born on Staten Island and studied in Europe. He was a follower of Cole and later lived in Hastings-on-Hudson. Because of his accuracy, his output is very interesting to students of the Hudson and includes: *Shad Fishing on the Hud-*

Tower of Olana Castle, home of Frederick Edwin Church. (Photo by Arthur G. Adams)

Kindred Spirits, painting of William Cullen Bryant and Thomas Cole in Kaaterskill Clove by Asher B. Durand. (New York Public Library)

son, showing the Palisades in the background; *Hudson River near Hastings; Autumn on the Hudson River; Upper Hudson; View of the Catskills Across Hudson; Sunset-Hudson River;* and *Catskill Mountain House from North Mountain.*

Sanford Robinson Gifford (1828-1880) was born in Kingston, New York and brought up in Hudson in Columbia County. He studied at Brown University and privately with the painter John Rubens Smith in 1845. Later he joined the National Academy of Design and travelled to Europe, where he took up landscape painting and produced such works as *Villa Malta, Tivoli,* and *Valley of Lauterbrunnen.* Returning to the United States, he served in the Civil War. He became a member of the National Academy of Design in 1845, and was strongly influenced by the work of Thomas Cole. His great painting of *Kauterskill Falls* is one of the most impressive items in the American Wing of the Metropolitan Museum of Art, and one of the most successful treatments of this popular but difficult subject. Other pictures of Hudson River interest include: *Sunset Over New York Bay, Sunset on the Hudson,* and *Hook Mountain near Nyack.*

George Inness (1825-1894) was born at Newburgh and raised in Newark, New Jersey. Showing a strong talent for painting and the arts, he was apprenticed to an engraver. In 1845 he opened a studio in New York, and soon the bounty of several patrons made it possible for him to study in Rome and Paris. He was influenced by the Barbizon School, with their interest in atmospheric effects. Returning to the United States, he settled first in Medford, Massachusetts, and later in Montclair, New Jersey. From there he made many trips up the Hudson and Delaware valleys and into the Poconos and Catskills. Among works influenced by local subjects are *Rainbow After a Storm, Autumn Oaks,* and *Vernooy Falls.*

John William Casilear (1811-1893) was a New York City native all his life, and is known for his realistic landscapes. Albertus del Orient Browere (1814-1887) was born at Tarrytown and went to California twice for the Gold Rushes in 1852 and 1856. He made his permanent home in Catskill from 1834. He was the son of John Henri Isaac Browere (1792-1834), who specialized in making life masks of famous Americans. Of greatest interest are his *Catskills* and *Hudson River Landing.*

Regis Francois Gignoux (1816-1882) was born and studied at Lyons, and later in Paris. Settling in New York, he became assimilated to the Hudson River School.

Thomas Prichard Rossiter (1818-1871) was born in Connecticut and later practiced portrait painting in New York. In 1859 he moved to Cold Spring. His painting *A Picnic on the Hudson—Constitution Island* depicts many famous local people, including the poet George Pope Morris, with Crow Nest, and Storm King Mountains in the background.

Frederick A. Chapman (1818-1891) was born in Connecticut and practiced painting in Brooklyn. He did a well known view of *Washington's Headquarters at Newburgh.* A similar view was painted by Edmund C. Coates, who was active between 1837 and 1857. Little is known about his life.

William Hart (1823-1894) was born in Scotland and came to Albany in 1831. He was later active in New York and Brooklyn. Of particular historical interest is his view of *Albany, New York, from Bath.*

Better known is David Johnson (1827-1908) who lived all his life in New York and produced some interesting Hudson River views, including, *West Point from Fort Putnam, Off Consitution Island, Foundry at Cold Spring,* and the plate, *Mouth of the Moodna,* for *Picturesque America.*

James McDougal Hart (1828-1901) was born in Scotland and came to Albany in 1831. In 1851 he returned to Dusseldorf to study before returning to America to specialize in landscapes. Most interesting of his works are: *Picnic on the Hudson,* and *View from Hazelwood—Albany in the Distance.*

Edward Moran (1829-1901) was born in England and came to America in 1844, where he

Ice-Boat Race on the Hudson c1860, by Currier & Ives. Note train of the Hudson River Railroad in background.

specialized in such marine views as: *New York Harbor, Coming Storm in New York Bay,* and *Outward Bound.*

Albert Bierstadt (1830-1902) was born in Dusseldorf, Germany, but grew up in New Bedford, Massachusetts. He later returned to Dusseldorf to study. While following the practice and philosophy of the Hudson River School, he ranged far afield to the Rockies, Sierra Nevada, California, and Alaska to seek spectacular subject matter. He was closely akin to Frederick Church in this way. His large paintings include *The Rocky Mountains, Giant Redwood Trees of California,* and *View on the Hudson.* In later life he built a thirty-five room mansion in Irvington-on-Hudson.

Samuel Colman (1832-1920) specialized in storm and cloud effects and is best remembered for *Looking North from Ossining,* and the very impressive *Storm King on the Hudson.* John Ferguson Weir (1841-1926) was the son of the West Point drawing master. He was a well known landscape painter, best remembered for his *View of the Highlands from West Point.* Other minor Hudson River School painters include Samuel Lancaster Gerry (1813-1891), Frederick Rondel (1826-1892), John George Brown (1831-1913) and Francis A. Silva (1835-1886). This about completes the canon of recognized Hudson River School painters. Let us now consider several artists who followed a more individual bent.

Robert Havell, Jr. (1793-1878) was born in England and came to America in 1839, settling first in Brooklyn and later in Ossining. He transferred Audubon's drawings for *Birds of America* to aquatint. Later he specialized in elaborately accurate landscapes. Most notable are *View of the Hudson from Tarrytown Heights,* and *West Point from Fort Putnam.*

James Bard (1815-1897) worked in New York and specialized in detail ship paintings, including many of Hudson River steamboats.

Although contemporary with the Hudson River School, Homer Dodge Martin (1836-1897) was nearly blind and developed a unique style of great beauty. He was born at Albany. His most famous painting is *Harp of the Winds,* but he did several Hudson River views, including *Lake Sanford,* one of the headwaters of the Hudson in the Adirondacks.

Another anomaly is George Henry Hall (1825-1918) who was a native of New Hampshire but later built a home and studio at La Belle Falls in Kaaterskill Clove. He studied at Dusseldorf and Paris. While maintaining close social ties with the leaders of the Hudson River School, Hall specialized in still lifes and interior scenes.

Although, strictly speaking a New England painter, Winslow Homer (1836-1910) did some interesting drawings of Kaaterskill Falls and watercolors of lumbering on the Upper Hudson.

By the turn of the century there was a great decline of interest in representational and atmospheric landscape painting and the Hudson River School fell into oblivion. Only recently has there been any considerable revival of interest in the work of this school. About 1900 there was an art colony atop the Palisades at Coytesville. Its leading light was George O. "Pop" Hart (1871-1933) who specialized in marine scenes and brooding watercolors. Another member of the Coytesville art colony was Van Dearing ("Dan") Perrine, who styled himself "the painter of the Palisades." His large 1906 painting of dark brooding cliffs and snow-covered talus entitled "The Palisades" hangs in the White House. A few years later there was another art colony at Grantwood, also atop the Palisades. Its leading lights were Manuel Komroff, the muralist, Albert Glaisze, and Marcel Duchamp, who is best known for his sensational *Nude Descending a Staircase.* Glaisze and Duchamp were both Cubists. In the Hudson Valley there were also art colonies at Yonkers, Croton, and Woodstock, but the influence of the River was minimal. The colony at Woodstock still flourishes.

An important marine artist and illustrator of international fame who lived in the Hudson Valley region was Anton Otto Fischer (1882-1962). Fischer was born in Munich, Germany on February 23, 1882. He was orphaned at the age of five and brought up in an orphanage. At the age of 16 he ran away to sea and sailed in square riggers from Hamburg and also in English barks. He decided to become a United States citizen and by 1903 was racing yachts for money on Long Island Sound. He worked for the illustrator A. B. Frost as both a model and handyman and developed the desire to become an artist. Between 1906 and 1908 he studied under Jean Paul Laurens, the famous painter of historical scenes, at the Academy Julian in Paris. He returned to New York City to take up his profession. In 1908 he sold his first illustration to *Harpers Weekly* and from that date his career developed rapidly. In 1912 he married the female illustrator, Mary Ellen Sigsbee, daughter of Admiral Charles D. "Foxy" Sigsbee, Captain of the *U. S. S. Maine* at the time of her sinking in Havana harbor, further reinvigorating his interest in marine subjects. In 1916 Fischer received his final citizenship papers. During this period he was living in New York City and summering at Bushnellsville in the Catskills. With the outbreak of World War I, Fischer became unpopular owing to his German birth. He could not obtain work and gave up his home in New York City and moved into his former summer home at Bushnellsville and took up subsistence farming while continuing to paint. After the War the anti-German mania died down and his career again picked up. He illustrated not only fine editions of Robert Louis Stevenson's *Treasure Island* and Herman Melville's *Moby Dick,* but also many other books by Rudyard Kipling, Joseph Conrad, Rex Beach, Ben Ames Williams, and Albert Payson Terhune--mainly dealing with the sea or outdoors life. He became best known for his illustrations for the *Glencannon, Cappy Ricks,* and *Tugboat Annie* series for the Saturday Evening Post. In 1923 he established a winter home in Kingston, while returning to Bushnellsville for the summers. In 1940 he moved to Woodstock where he spent the remainder of his life. During World War II he was treated quite differently. He was designated Artist Laureate of the United States Coast Guard and served aboard the armed cutter *Campbell* with the honorary rank of Lt. Commander in 1942. When the *Campbell* sank a German submarine Fischer did a series of drawings of the incident for Life Magazine. The original paintings were later exhibited at the Corcoran Gallery in Washington and are now at the U. S. Coast Guard Academy at New London, Connecticut. In 1947 he wrote an autobiographical book entitled *Foc's'le Days* telling of his years aboard the British bark *Gwydyr Castle*. He remained active as an illustrator up until his death but also turned to doing landscapes of the Catskill Mountains. His works are at the Brandywine Museum and New Britain Museum.

A very unique more recent artist who has devoted himself to portraying New York Harbor is Cecil C. Bell (1906-1970). He was born in Seattle and came to New York in 1930, ultimately settling on Staten Island in 1942. His house in Tompkinsville overlooked the Narrows. The ferry boats and harbor craft were among his favorite subjects. His artistic style is akin to the robust manner of Reginald Marsh. Whatever verdict history passes on his art, his paintings will remain a valuable social document, as can be seen from the very titles of his numerous works: *East River Swimmers, White Horse on the Ferry Ramp, Ferry Ride at Night,* and *Coming off the Ferry.* One particularly impressive seascape is entitled *Rough Crossing* and is reminiscent of John Sloan's great painting, *The Wake of the Ferry.* Other Bell paintings with the Staten Island Ferry as topic are: *Bootblack, Sailors' Delight,* showing several sailors ogling a floozy aboard the ferry, and *The Staten Island Ferry Passing a Tug.* He also liked to portray important events in an unlikely manner. Among his documentary pictures are: *The Biggest Cranes in the World,* painted in 1966 and showing the Verrazano Bridge under construction; *The Burning of the Normandie-Hudson River Pier* (1942); *Welcoming the Queen Mary;* (1936); and *Welcoming the Queen,* showing the arrival of the *Q-E 2* in 1966. Perhaps his most novel picture is his 1957 painting entitled *Arrival of the Mayflower.* This is the replica ship sailed across from Plymouth, England by Captain Villiers in 1957 and shows the improbable melange of the *Mayflower II,* a Staten Island Ferryboat, the Day Line Steamer *Alexander Hamilton,* a Moran tug, and a Goodyear Blimp, with the towers of lower Manhattan as background.

At the present time we have a truly great marine artist living and working in the Hudson Valley. William G. Muller of Ossining is perhaps the greatest painter of Hudson River watercrafts of all descriptions of all times. His highly detailed paintings of steamboats, tugs, sloops, ocean liners, and waterfront activity are instinct with life and the true feeling of the river in her various moods. Muller's paintings are truer than the clearest photographs, yet, in a way, more Romantic than the paintings of the earlier Hudson River School. In his youth in the mid-1950's Muller served as Quartermaster pilot of the sidewheel steamer *Alexander Hamilton.* He is a true student of the vessels he paints, often researching original engineering drawings, blueprints, and all other available technical material. With a deep understanding of the life along the Hudson and its economic activity, his paintings are also important social and historical documents. Muller is a founding trustee and academician-member of the American Society of Marine Artists.

The Hudson River and its surrounding landscape and cityscapes continues to provide stimulation to artists and every year brings interesting river views to the galleries and salons. It seems likely that, with a returning general interest in the river, this trend will continue long into the future.

MUSIC OF THE HUDSON

Inasmuch as it has inspired great art, it is generally assumed that the Hudson has also inspired much great music. Unfortunately, this does not seem to be the case. Among the more important works inspired by the Hudson are: Douglas More's short opera *The Legend of Sleepy Hollow,* inspired by Washington Irving's tale and several operas inspired by his *Rip*

Van Winkle, by Reginal De Koven and Robert Planquette. Ferde Grofe's (1892-1972) *Hudson River Suite* was commissioned by Andre Kostelanetz, and is similar in style to his better known *Grand Canyon* and *Mississippi* suites.

Eastwood Lane published a piano suite in 1913 entitled *In Sleepy Hollow.* It is in the impressionist style and has four sections entitled: *In Sleepy Hollow*-A Barcarolle; *On Tappan Zee*-A Boat Song; *A Mid-October Afternoon*-Reverie; and *Katrina's Waltz.* This last referring to Ichabod Crane's sweetheart, Katrina Van Tassel. This is a charming suite in the style of Debussy and Ravel.

The important American Composer, Charles Tomlinson Griffes (1884-1920), who was a student of Englebert Humperdinck, taught and was organist and chapel master at the Hackley School for Boys at Tarrytown. His best known works are *The White Peacock,* and *The Pleasure Dome of Kubla Khan.* These are the musical equivalent of Frederick E. Church's *Olana Castle.*

19 Hudson Valley Resorts

The new interest in landscape scenery, coupled with the new easy travel by steamboat, led to a great spurt of hotel and resort development along the Hudson and in the adjacent mountains. However, resorts were not really anything new in the Hudson Valley. The earliest resorts were health spas built around medicinal springs with water for drinking and bathing of an allegedly curative nature. There are a number of such springs near the Hudson, and many of them ultimately developed into popular resorts.

The earliest known one, near Saratoga, was called "The Medicine Waters of the Great Spirit," by the Mohawk Indians. It is alleged that the French Jesuit Priest, Isaac Jogues, visited the springs in 1643. Better documented is a visit by Sir William Johnson, the British Indian Commissioner, in August 1767. Later on the springs came to be called "High Rock Spring," and later, "Saratoga Springs," from the name of the nearby community on the Hudson. Saratoga is a contraction of the Indian term "Se-rach-to-que," meaning "Hillside Country of a Great River." Saratoga was the scene of an important American victory during the Revolution in 1777.

The fame of the waters spread and by 1802, the year that Gideon Putnam opened the first inn, the springs were attracting numerous visitors. In 1864 a racetrack was opened and Saratoga became the mecca for both high society and the sporting set. It was America's first great popular resort. The greatest hotel was the Grand Union, successor to Gideon Putnam's early tavern. Substantial brick additions were built in 1864 and 1871, making it the world's largest and most lavish hotel. The United States Hotel was almost as large and equally luxurious. The central courtyard and hotel structure covered seven acres. Both hotels featured enormous verandas with tall columns and large dining rooms and ballrooms. Society has deserted Saratoga Springs, but the medicinal baths are still extensively patronized and the August racing season and cultural festival draw great crowds. The Grand Union and the United States hotels are both gone; the Grand Union lasted until 1953. Today the chief hotel is the new Gideon Putnam on the State Spa Grounds. Gambling casinos operated between 1871 and 1907, that of Richard A. Canfield being the best known.

From early times the Hudson River was the principal approach to the springs. Travellers would go by steamboat to Albany or Troy, and change to stage coaches. Later the coaches were replaced by the railroad. In the late nineteenth century Saratoga was a principal stop on a tour that included a steamboat trip up the Hudson, a visit to the Catskill Mountain House, and steamer trips the lengths of Lakes George and Champlain, with Montreal and Quebec

City as the destinations. The tourist could then continue west to Niagara Falls. This route was commonly known as the "Pleasure Highway."

Saratoga was not the only early spa. Ballston Spa, a few miles to the south of Saratoga Springs, was drawing visitors as early as 1771, but never achieved the size or gaiety of its neighbor. Further to the west, Richfield Springs and Sharon Springs, in the hills south of the Mohawk Valley, were drawing visitors from about 1820. Both are still visited for the medicinal value of the waters. Sharon Springs was quite social during the mid-nineteenth century, and was described by Nathaniel Parker Willis. These spas were also reached by the Hudson River and stagecoach connections, later superseded by the railroad.

Nearer to the Hudson itself were the White Sulphur Spring at Berne, in the Helderberg Mountains, and Lebanon Springs, in Columbia County, in the Taconic foothills. Columbia Springs were four miles northeast of the city of Hudson. Further to the south, about three miles east of Ossining, Chappaqua Spring attracted visitors around 1825. Actually the presence of medicinal springs was merely a pretext for the development of a resort. America was becoming richer and people had more leisure to travel and relax. The new steamboats and railroads made travel easy, and were an attraction and pleasure in themselves.

Literary and artistic interest in the Hudson and Catskills served to create a desire on the part of many to visit the region. The nineteenth century was a time when many wealthy people spent summer-long vacations. This was particularly the case with Southerners who wished to escape their own sultry and often unhealthy climate in the cool north. Philadelphia and New York City became unbearably hot, and malaria and other epidemics were common. It must be remembered that there was no air conditioning, and water supplies in the cities were limited and of dubious quality, and sewage systems were often inadequate. The Catskills were the nearest mountains of any size and could be reached easily by steamboat or train. The Adirondacks were still largely unknown and difficult to reach, while the White Moun-

Grand Union Hotel, Saratoga, N.Y. Largest and finest of the old spa hotels. Note Mansard roof and high portico and columns typical of older Saratoga hotel construction. (Adams Collection)

New York State Spa Buildings, Saratoga, N.Y. (Adams Collection)

tains were too distant except for residents of New England. All the ingredients were present to stimulate the growth of a major resort industry in the Hudson Valley and Catskills.

At first the old stagecoach inns began taking in tourists and summer vacationers. Among the early ones was Perez Steele's Windham House, at Windham. It is a gracious old building with Ionic columns and a Garrison Colonial style second floor gallery. Built in 1800, it has been restored and still attracts many guests.

While the old taverns and inns served to a degree, they were usually located in villages and along busy highways, and were not always comfortable nor within easy reach of the great scenic attractions such as Kaaterskill Falls. To meet the need for more attractively located hotels, and the requirements of wealthy and demanding clients, the Mountain House type of hotel was developed. These were the forerunners of today's large resort hotels. Some of the old Mountain Houses, such as Lake Mohonk, remain in operation today.

In 1823, partly at the instigation of stagecoach operator Erastus Beach, a group of Catskill businessmen formed the Catskill Mountain Association to build accommodations at Pine Orchard atop the Wall of Manitou, which was reached by an old wood road from Palenville. On July 4, 1824 a primitive hotel opened its doors. It consisted of ten rooms, including a ballroom and male and female dormitories with bunk beds. A good time was had by all and the view over the Hudson Valley was highly acclaimed.

The fame of this view soon spread and demands for accommodation grew rapidly. Soon control of the enterprise came under Charles L. Beach. He improved the old Turnpike Road from Catskill to Pine Orchard and made additions and betterments to the hotel. The Mountain House was easily reached from the Hudson River steamboats landing at Catskill Point, which was approximately half way between New York City and the popular spa at Saratoga Springs.

By 1845 the Catskill Mountain House had been expanded to fifty rooms, and ultimately, with the addition of two large wings, grew to three hundred. Architecturally it was a

United States Hotel, Saratoga, N.Y. (Adams Collection)

patchwork. Initially it was a simple Federal Style structure. With the addition of a long colonnade with thirteen Corinthian columns fronting the Hudson Valley, it became a really impressive example of Greek Revival architecture. The guest rooms were simple and small, but the quality of the food and drink and the service were good for the day and age. The Catskill

Ballston Springs, N.Y. (William Bartlett)

Catskill Mountain House and the Two Lakes on the Catskills (William Bartlett).

Mountain House eventually acquired a large estate of three thousand acres, over which paths and trails were layed out to such points of interest as Elfin Pass, Fat Man's Delight, Druid Rocks, Puddingstone Hall, Palenville Overlook, Artisits Rock, Bears Den, Glen Mary, Newmans Ledge, and Inspiration Point. There were few formal lawns or gardens and a rustic atmosphere prevailed. The feeling of the forest came right to the doorstep of the hotel and this exactly suited the Romantic temperament of the time.

Entertainment included dances, impromptu concerts, and amateur theatricals. Sunday was a day of quiet with religious observances. The meals were of the old time "ordinary" type with "Family Style" service and no choice of menu—you ate what the host provided. The wine cellar was extensive and of notable quality. A popular activity was to rise early to see the sunrise over the distant Berkshire and Taconic Mountains. Usually the broad Hudson Valley was still clothed in clouds and mist and appeared as a sea of golden waves under the rising sun, as described in Thomas Cole's poem, *The Wild,* quoted in the last chapter. For most of its history the Catskill Mountain House was operated by the Beach family. Its last season was in 1942. After then it fell into ruin and the property was acquired by the State and, in 1963, the hulking ruin was burned down, as it had become a menace to life and limb.[1] Thus "the noblest wonder of the Hudson Valley," ended in a fiery Gotterdamerung.

During the great years of the Catskill Mountain House there were many famous guests: Writers such as Reverend Charles Rockwell, Lucy C. Lilly, Harriet Martineau, Mark Twain, Henry James, and Oscar Wilde; clergymen—Timothy Dwight, Newman Hall; performers—-Jenny Linde and Maude Adams; composer Charles K. Harris (who wrote the popular ballad, *"After the Ball Is Over";* inventor Alexander Graham Bell, who exhibited his telephone when a line was established between the Mountain House and Catskill; artists Thomas Cole,

---

[1]NOTE: The fire was set on a snowy morning, when there would be little danger of the fire spreading, by Edward West of the Department of Environmental Conservation, who has told the writer that this was the saddest duty he ever had to perform for the State.

Catskill Mountain House at Pine Orchard, atop the Wall of Mainitou, overlooking the Hudson Valley near Palenville, N.Y. First built in 1823. Showing final evolution after 1845. Note long portico with Corinthian columns. (From an old advertisement, Author's Collection)

Asher B. Durand, Sanford Gifford, and Jasper F. Cropsey; the poet William Cullen Bryant, and illustrators William H. Bartlett, Harry Fenn, and Winslow Homer; social commentators such as Nathaniel Parker Willis and journalist Thomas Nast. General William Tecumseh Sherman and President Chester A. Arthur visited, as did ex-President Ulysses S. Grant.

To make the hotel easy of access the Beach family operated the famous Otis Elevating funicular railroad, the narrow gauge Catskill Mountain Railroad, and Catskill & Tannersville Railroad, and the Catskill Evening Line of steamers to New York City, not to mention the local steamferry from Catskill to the New York Central Railroad station at Greendale, across the river. At a later time the Ulster & Delaware Railroad operated a direct line in conjunction with the West Shore Railroad, and private cars and through Pullman sleeping and parlor cars came from as far away as Washington, Chicago, and Montreal. This was all in addition to the lines of stage coaches the Beaches operated and extensive livery stables. Proximity to the famous Kaaterskill Falls led to development of an extensive "one-day tripper" trade, and many of the excursionists "took a meal" at the Catskill Mountain House.

Today all vestiges of this activity are gone except for a memorial marker on the site. The Catskill Mountain House summed up the spirit of the Romantic Age in the Catskills and also served as prototype for all the following large resorts.

After the opening of the Catskill Mountain House, need soon arose for auxiliary, and less expensive, accommodations. In 1852 Peter Schutt built the Laurel House at the top of Kaaterskill Falls. It was a simple colonial style building and accommodated fifty guests. It was enlarged in 1881 and again in 1884, when it gained a large Victorian style wing, a cupola and an impressive portico. This almost doubled its size. It was served by private railroad stations on two separate railroads running through its grounds. It remained in operation until 1963, when it was acquired by the State. It then ran rapidly to ruin and was burned down in 1967; also by Mr. West.

Other famous hotels in the Catskills, reached by the Hudson River, were Meads Mountain House (1863) and Overlook Mountain House (1870), both on Overlook Mountain above Woodstock, and both with extensive views over the Hudson Valley. In the Shawangunk Mountains, southwest of Kingston, Lake Mohonk Mountain House opened in 1870, and Lake Minnewaska Mountain Houses, (the Cliff House and the Wildmere), in 1879. Mohonk

House is still in flourishing operation in 1982. Wildmere closed in 1979, but Marriott Corporation plans to build a large new luxury hotel on the site. Meads is now a Buddhist Monastery, and the Overlook House has been out of operation for many years.

The mighty Kaaterskill Hotel, built in 1881, stood atop South Mountain, between the Catskill Mountain House and the Laurel House. This was a giant luxury structure four stories high with two towers six stories high. It was the world's largest mountain hotel and featured rooms for one thousand guests, DeLuxe cuisine, and its own full symphony orchestra. It burned to the ground in 1924 and was never rebuilt.

Further inland, in the Catskills, on the route of the Ulster & Delaware Railroad, which connected with the Hudson River steamers at Kingston Point, were the Mount Tremper House of 1878 at Phoenicia; the Grand Hotel (1881-1966) at Highmount; and Churchill Hall (1883-1944) and the Rexmere at Stamford, at the headwaters of the Delaware River. The Rexmere is still standing, but is now used as a government office building. All-rail routes were used to reach the laterday resorts of the Southern Shawangunks and Catskills of Orange and Sullivan counties, and they cannot properly be considered Hudson Valley resorts.

Other resorts developed right along the banks of the Hudson. Perhaps the largest and finest was the Palisades Mountain House, built atop the Palisades at an elevation of 375 ft. at Englewood Cliffs, New Jersey. It was a large brick and stone structure four stories high with Mansard roofs and towers in the best Victorian style. Porticos on three sides commanded fine views up and down the Hudson. It was built by a syndicate headed by Andrew D. Bogert. The hotel opened on June 7th 1860. The operating lessee was "Dave" Hammond, who also managed the stylish Murray Hill and Plaza Hotels in Manhattan, and through him the hotel drew a high class clientele. To make access easy, the hotel, through a subsidiary company, built a road down the cliffs, today called Palisades Avenue, and a steamboat dock. They also built a well constructed footpath and steps down the cliffs, which are still in use today. The hotel burned down in 1884 and was not rebuilt.

Further north was the Prospect Park Hotel at Catskill which opened about 1860. It had a tremendous piazza, 400 feet long and 16 feet wide, overlooking the river. The roof of the piazza was supported by Corinthian pillars 25 feet high. This large hotel, 250 feet long,

Catskill Mountain House, c1900. (Library of Congress)

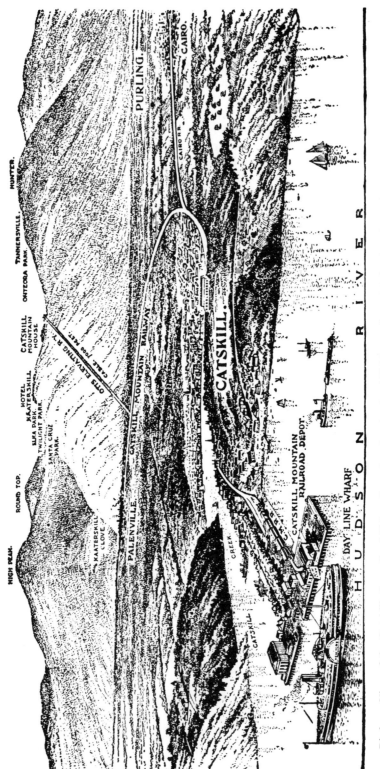

Birdseye View of the Catskills from Catskill Landing, showing the Catskill Mountain and Otis Elevating railways and the Catskill Mountain House and Hotel Kaaterskill.

Laurel House at Kaaterskill Falls. (Library of Congress)

featured many private balconies and scenic views from every room. It was situated in a park adjoining the best residential neighborhood of Catskill and its situation afforded "miles of elegant shady walks and drives near at hand," according to an advertisement which also proclaimed that "the views and scenery from the Prospect are unsurpassed."

Just south of West Point stood the famous Cozzen's or Cranston's Hotel. Cozzens originally operated a resort on the West Point grounds at Trophy Point. In 1849 he built a much larger one south of the military reservation, somewhat north of the present Ladycliff College. About 1860 it burned down and he built a larger one on the high rocky bluff overlooking Buttermilk Falls. Later it was operated under the name Cranston's. The hotel was situated 180 feet above the river and accommodated between 250 and 500 guests. It was visited by the Prince of Wales in 1865. There were cottages attached and extensive pleasure grounds with walks and rustic bridges along and across the Buttermilk Falls. In 1900 it was acquired by a Catholic order for use as an academy and comprises part of the present Ladycliff College complex.

Other riverside hotels included Caldwell's Hotel at Tomkins Cove, and the Octagon House and Fort Lee Park Hotel at Burdett's Ferry, at the foot of the Palisades south of Fort Lee. Further downriver, in the harbor area, were the La Tourette Hotel on the Kill Van Kull in Bayonne, and the Grand View, overlooking the Narrows in Brooklyn. The La Tourette was formerly the private home of Irenee Dupont, one of the founders of the Dupont Chemical Company. He settled in Bayonne in 1800, when he first arrived from France. In later years his home was turned into a resort hotel and greatly enlarged. It was razed in 1926. The eight story Grand View Hotel at Dyker Beach, on the Narrows, was built on piles out over the water in a Swiss Chalet style. There were four levels of balconies running around the building, which sported a Mansard roofed tower.

Hotel Kaaterskill, atop South Mountain, near Palenville, N.Y. Built 1881 and burned 1924. World's largest summer hotel at the time of construction. (Library of Congress)

Of more recent vintage are the Bear Mountain Inn, which opened in 1922, and has recently been enlarged by addition of an annex, and the Hotel Thayer at West Point. The Thayer is located on the Military Academy Grounds and is owned and operated by the United States Government and open to the general public. Built in 1924, it was renovated extensively in 1978. It is named in honor of Sylvanus Thayer, an early West Point Superintendent.

The luxurious and colossal Oriental Hotel, Hotel Brighton, and Manhattan Beach Hotel, which reached their zenith in the 1880s, were located on Coney Island. Rockaway Beach and Long Branch, on the Lower Bay, were high-society resorts in the nineteenth century.

For day excursionists there were many picnic groves along the Hudson and adjoining waters. They were the usual destination of the many excursion steamers. Among the earliest and best known were the Elysian Fields at Hoboken. These pleasure grounds were operative from 1804 until 1839. The Sibyl's Cave, under Castle Point, was a cool rocky cavern with a spring of ice cold water.

On June 19, 1846, the first baseball game of record was played at Elysian Fields between two amateur Manhattan teams—the Knickerbockers and the New Yorkers. The New Yorkers won, twenty-four to one. Further up, along the Palisades, were Alpine Grove and Occidental Grove. Weehawken was also a popular place for picnics.

There were a number of amusement parks along the Hudson. One of the earliest was Eldorado Park at Weehawken, which opened in 1892. It featured Franko's Brass Band and stage spectaculars such as *Egypt Through the Ages* and *King Solomon and the Destruction*

Prospect Park Hotel at Catskill, N.Y. (Author's collection)

Palisades & The Hudson-Eastern Boundary of Bergen County, c1880. Scene is taken from Fort Lee, looking northward from near site of George Washington Bridge. Palisades Mountain House was atop cliffs to right of trees. Note Palisades Avenue climbing up hill. (Author's collection)

Palisades   Mountain House, c1860.
  (Author's collection)

Oriental Hotel, Coney Island, N.Y. c1890. (Author's collection)

Luna Park at night, Coney Island, c1900. (Author's collection)

Coney Island Steamboat, Dreamland. (Author's collection)

Dreamland Park, Coney Island. Note pier for accommodation of excursion steamers. From old broadside poster. (Author's collection)

Burdetts Landing at Fort Lee, showing Octagon House, c1890. (Author's collection)

of Jerusalem, with 1000 performers, camels, horses, and elephants. Palisades Amusement Park, at Cliffside Park, was one of the largest in America. It featured a giant salt-water pool with machinery to simulate ocean waves, three giant roller-coasters (the Scenic Railway, the Sky Rocket, and the Bob-Sled), and a large ferris wheel right at the top of the cliffs. Woodcliff Amusement Park was located just north of Poughkeepsie. Coney Island had three major amusement parks—Luna Park, Dreamland, and Steeple-Chase Park, with its giant Parachute Jump.

Amusements of every kind could be found along the shores of the Hudson, from the most plebian to the most sophisticated. Frequently a trip on the waters was an important part of the experience, whether on an Iron Palace Steamer up the Hudson, or on an Iron Steamboat Company excursion boat to Coney Island. Indeed, the Hudson was a great "Pleasure Highway."

Grand View Hotel at Dyker Beach, N.Y. (Author's collection)

20 Riverside Estates, Country Homes, and Famous Architects

Ever since the early eighteenth century the affluent citizens of New York have been establishing country seats along the Hudson and the waters of the lower bays. Many of these people also owned elegant town houses in Manhattan or Albany, but chose to spend the summers in the pleasant countryside, which could be easily reached by the river. Summers in town could be very unpleasant and rather unhealthy, and consequently the entire shoreline from Atlantic Highlands to above Albany soon became lined with pleasant summer homes and estates. This practice was made even more fashionable when Washington Irving settled at Sunnyside in 1835, and James Kirke Paulding settled at Placentia, just above Hyde Park, in 1837.

In 1705 Peter Fauconier, Private Secretary of Edward Hyde, Viscount Cornbury, Royal Governor of New York, obtained a patent on the east bank and named it Hyde Park, in honor of his patron. In 1772 this estate was layed out by Dr. John Bard, whose wife had inherited part of the patent. His son, Dr. Samuel Bard, improved the property with the importation of fruit trees from France, and England; melons from Italy and vines from Madiera. The property was purchased by Dr. David Hosack in 1827, who put André Parmentier, a professional landscape gardener from Belgium, in charge of developing the estate. After passing through several other hands, the estate was acquired by Frederick William Vanderbilt. Paulding's estate, Placentia, was immediately to the north.

During this same early period, Lt. Governor Cadwallader Colden developed properties on the west bank above Newburgh into the estate of Coldenham. Similar properties were developed on upper Manhattan. In his novel *Satanstoe*, set in 1757, James Fenimore Cooper describes a fictitious estate on the Hudson near present day Dyckman Street in Upper Manhattan, called Lilacsbush:

"A very tolerable road conducted us through some woods, to the heights, and we soon found ourselves on an eminence, that overlooked a long reach of the Hudson, extending from Haverstraw to the north, as far as Staten Island to the south; a distance of near forty miles. On the opposite shore rose the wall-like barrier of the Palisades, lifting the table-land on their summits to an elevation of several hundred feet. The noble river itself, fully three quarters of a mile in width, was unruffled by a breath of air, lying in one single, extended placid sheet, under the rays of a bright sun, resembling molten silver....."

"....he led the party by pretty bridle-paths along the heights for nearly two miles, occasionally opening a gate, without dismounting, until he reached a point that overlooked Lilacsbush, which was soon seen, distant from us less than half a mile."

Nathaniel Parker Willis (1806-1867).

"Here we are, on my own domain," he said, as he pulled up to let us join him, "that last gate separating me from my nearest neighbor south. These hills are of no great use, except as early pastures, though they afford many beautiful views."

"I have heard it predicted," I remarked, "that the time would come, some day, when the banks of the Hudson would contain many such seats as that of the Philipses, at Yonkers, and one or two more like it, that I am told are now standing above the Highlands."

"Quite possibly; it is not easy to foretell what may come to pass in such a country. I dare say, that in time, both towns and seats will be seen on the banks of the Hudson, and a powerful and numerous nobility to occupy the last."[1]

The preceding passage was written in 1845, by which time industrial barons were building in the valley at a rapid rate. By 1853, Nathaniel Parker Willis, in his *Letters From Idlewild, Letter V,* was writing as follows:

FARM LAND AND FANCY LAND

I met one of my neighbors yesterday, seated in his wife's rocking-chair on top of a wagon-load of tools and kitchen utensils, and preceded by his boys, driving a troop of ten or fifteen cows. As he was one I had always chatted with, in passing, and had grown to value for his good sense and

---

[1]James Fenimore Cooper, *Satanstoe,* Complete Works of J. Fenimore Cooper, Leatherstocking Edition in Thirty-two Volumes, Undated, pp. 131, 133, 134.

kindly character, I inquired into his movements with some interest. He was going (to use his own phrase) "twenty miles farther back, where a man could afford to farm, at the price of the land." His cornfields on the banks of the Hudson had risen in value, as probable sites for ornamental residences, and with the difference (between two hundred dollars the fancy acre, and sixty dollars the farming acre) in his pocket, he was transferring his labor and his associations to a new soil and neighborhood. With the market for his produce quite as handy by railroad, he was some four or five thousand dollars richer in capital, and only a loser in scenery and local attachments. A Yankee's pots and kettles will almost walk away on their own legs, with such inducement.

There is another "alluvial deposit," however, besides Taste and Wealth, which helps to drive the farmer from the banks of the river. The steamboat landings occurring every few miles, are nests of bad company, and constant temptations to the idle curiosity of laborers and children. It is a gay sight—at least contrasted with plough and barn-yard—to see the "day boat" sweep up with twice as many inhabitants as the nearest village; crowds of city-dressed people, leaning over the balustrades, and the whole gaily painted and confusedly fascinating spectacle of life and movement. The "evening boat," with her long line of lights, her ringing bells, and the magical glide with which she comes through the darkness, touches the wharf, and is gone; the perpetual succession of freight-boats; the equipages from the surrounding villages; and all the "runners," coachmen, porters, and "loafers," who abound upon the docks, swarming the bar-rooms in the intervals of arrivals, contribute to keep up an excitement, within reach of which a farmer's customary reliances are made vexatiously uncertain. He would scarce need more than this to make him seek a different neighborhood. But for once, the "money down" also pays virtue's expenses, and it is not surprising that the migration of the river farmers to both cheaper lands and a more moral atmosphere, is general and lively. The "opening down the middle" of the Empire State's robe of agriculture, will soon be edged with velvet, and, for its common cloth, we must look to the sides and skirts, broad back and towering shoulders. A "class who can afford to let the trees grow" is getting possession of the Hudson; and it is at least safe to rejoice in this, whatever one may preach as to the displacement of the laboring tiller of the soil by the luxurious idler. With the bare fields fast changing into wooded lawns, the rocky wastes into groves, the angular farm-houses into shaded villas, and the naked uplands into waving forests, our great thoroughfare will soon be seen (as it has not been for many years) in something like its natural beauty. It takes very handsome men and mountains to look well bald.

Yet the mover-back from the banks of the Hudson soon finds, probably, that he has sold more than he meant to sell. The "farm that belonged to his thoughts," has gone with the other farm. He has parted unintentionally with what he was daily in the habit of looking for, measuring time by, thinking about, and finding society in—the rail-trains and steamers, schooners and barges, sloops, yachts and lumber-rafts, of one of the most lively thoroughfares in the world. Stupidly enough, he had included all this in the "scenery"—the mere trees, hills and running water, of which he expected to find plenty where he was going! But a mere landscape—and a landscape alive with moving objects of beauty and interest—are very different places in which even to be yourself a solitary.

It is to this blindness as to the *un-fencible property in a spot,* that Idlewild owes its name. It belonged to a valuable farm; but it was a side of it, which, from being little more than a craggy ravine, the bed of a wayward torrent, had always been left in complete wilderness. When I first fell in love with it, and thought of making a home amid its tangle of hemlocks, my first inquiry as to its price was met with the disparaging remark, that it was of little value—"only an idle wild!, of which nothing could ever be made." And that description of it stuck captivatingly in my memory. "Idle-wild!" "Idle-wild!" But let me describe what belongs to Idlewild, besides its acres of good-for-nothing torrent and unharvest-able crags, and besides the mere scenery around them.

To begin with a trifling convenience, it supplies *a clock* gratis. From the promontory on which stands my cottage, I see five miles of the Hudson River Railroad, and two miles of the Newburgh & Erie—a clock rimmed round with a mountain horizon, the loveliest of landscapes for a face, and half-mile streaks of smoke for the fingers. Once learn the startings of the trains, and every one that passes announces the time of day. The smoke-fingers serve also as a barometer—more or less white and distinct, depressed or elevated, in proportion to the dampness of the atmosphere. It is something of a luxury also to be daily astonished; and I feel no beginning, at present, of getting used to seeing a rail-train slide along the side of a mountain—the swift smoke-tails of the Newburgh & Erie slicing off the top of Skunnemunk several times a day, at an elevation of two hundred feet above the Hudson, and often, when there is a mist below or above it, looking more like a meteor shooting along the face of a cloud, than a mechanical possibility in which a mortal may take passage or send a parcel. To have these swift trains perpetually flying past, one on each side of the river, and meeting at right angles where the ferryboat is seen continually to cross, varies a man's walk, even at the tail of a plough.

But the two railways, though the most wonderful features of the *movement* in my landscape, are the least beautiful. The spread of the river above the pass of the Highlands (upon which I look immediately down), might be a small lake of four or five miles in extent, embosomed in mountains. This would be fine "scenery" to be solitary amidst, though the birds and the tree-tops were the only stirrers. But to be just as picturesquely secluded, as to personal remoteness, and still see the lake beneath my lawn traversed daily by a hundred craft of one sort and another—steamers, tow-boats, sloops, rafts, yachts, schooners, and barges—makes, as I said before, a different thing of solitude. I presume five thousand people, at least, pass daily under my library window; and as one looks out upon the crowded cars and flotillas which bear such multitudes along, it does not require poetry, in these days of animal magnetism, to express how the sense of society is thus satisfied. A man mingles in a crowd, or goes to the play, to satisfy the social craving which is irresistible—but he need not speak or be spoken to, to get rid of his loney feeling altogether. He must have a certain amount of human life and motion within reach of his eye. And, just how near or distant these moving fellow-beings must needs be, to magnetize companionship into the air, would vary, probably, with each man's electric circle. Across the river and over to Skunnemunk is near enough for me.[2]

Sunnyside, home of Washington Irving, c1850. (Currier & Ives)

---

[2]Nathaniel Parker Willis, *Out-Doors at Idlewild, or the Shaping of a Home on the Banks of the Hudson.*

Lyndhurst, at Tarrytown, Front view. Designed by Alexander Jackson Davis in Gothic-Revival Style. Home of the Paulding, Merritt, and Gould families. (Photo: National Trust)

Lyndhurst, River view. (Photo: National Trust)

Such sentiments were not uncommon, and building sites with fine views soon commanded a premium.

In the early days the typical manor house was only an enlarged version of the typical Dutch farmhouse. Settlers of other national backgrounds brought with them a preference for classic revival styles, often called Georgian or Federal in the United States. Structures of this sort were similar to those in other parts of the country. From about 1810 to 1840 the Greek Revival, or Temple Style, of architecture became popular in the Hudson Valley. This style was popularized by two books that circulated widely among carpenters and builders in the region. *The American Builder's Companion* by Asher Benjamin (1773-1845), a Hartford, Connecticut architect; and *The Modern Builder's Guide* by the New York City architect, Minard Lafever (1798-1854). Another influential architect operating from New Haven, Connecticut, and New York City, was Ithiel Town, who later became a partner of the famous Alexander Jackson Davis. All these men originally worked in the Greek Revival style.

Between 1815 and 1840 the, so called, Egyptian Revival style enjoyed a brief vogue. There is very little Egyptian Revival left in the Hudson Valley, although fine Greek Revival structures are fairly common.

The next style to become popular in the region was the Gothic Revival. Initially this was popular for churches and large public buildings; but soon it was being employed for villas and, eventually, for even small cottages. This style was popular from 1840 to about 1900. Among the most famous architects who advocated Gothic Revival was Alexander Jackson Davis (1803-1892), who practiced in New York City and did much work in the Hudson Valley. He is best known for his Custom House (later Sub-Treasury) on Wall Street, Manhattan, in the Greek Revival Style built in 1832. In the Gothic Revival style, he is best known for Lyndhurst at Tarrytown (1838). His Dutch Reformed Church at Newburgh (c1830) is a fine example of his earlier Greek Revival work. While Davis bridged the change

Villa on the Hudson, c1860. House in Italianate style. Note steamboat and sloops on river in distance.
(Currier & Ives)

New York Bay from Greenwood Cemetery, c1870. Note the Gothic-Revival gatehouse designed by Richard Michell Upjohn in 1861 and considered by many critics as the culmination of this style. (Engraving by Harry Fenn)

from Greek Revival to Gothic Revival, his successors worked mainly in the latter style.

Richard Upjohn (1802-1878) was born in England and came to America in 1829. He is best known for Trinity Church in Manhattan (1846), which was the first successful large Gothic Revival church, and was one of the founders of, and first President of, the American Institute of Architects. His St. Philips Episcopal Church at Garrison (1857), in the Highlands, is a good example of his smaller scale work, as is the small church at Locust, in the Atlantic Highlands of New Jersey.

James Renwick (1818–1895) specialized in the Gothic Revival, and is best known for his Grace Church (1846) and St. Patrick's Cathedral (1853–79) in New York City. He also designed the first buildings for Vassar College in Poughkeepsie, and various structures for the Croton Aqueduct project (1842). He designed many private homes, and the first building for the Smithsonian Institution in Washington.

Perhaps the man who had the greatest influence on the architecture and landscaping of the Hudson Valley was Andrew Jackson Downing (1815-1852). He was born, and spent his entire life, in Newburgh, although he did work outside the area and his writings had national significance. He was educated at Montgomery Academy in Orange County and joined with his brother in a nursery and landscaping business in Newburgh. In 1837 his brother left the firm and he assumed full control. Having very definite ideas about architecture and landscaping, he published an important series of books: *A Treatise on the Theory and Practice of Landscape Gardening, Adapted to North America* (1841); *Cottage Residences* (1842); *The Fruits and Fruit Trees of America* (1845); and, most importantly, *The Architecture of Country Houses* (1850). He also published a periodical, *The Horticulturist,* starting in 1846. Shortly after his death, in 1853, a collection of his editorials was published under the title

The Calvin Tomkins House, Tomkins Cove, N.Y. Now the Boulderberg Manor Restaurant. This Tudor Gothic villa had poured concrete walls. (Photo courtesy Boulderberg Manor)

Rural Essays. In his writings and work he championed the picturesque, or natural, style of landscaping rather than the formal classical style, as being better adapted to the American terrain and temperament. In architecture he favored a simple modification of the Gothic Revival and advised against giganticism in residential buildings. He also inveighed against a "gingerbread" style with tortured verge boards and trim—the style sometimes called "Steamboat Gothic." Downing's style might best be called Hudson River Gothic, although he did some work in an Italianate vein. His own home, near Newburgh, *Highland Gardens,* was in the Tudor Gothic style. In 1850 he took a trip abroad and, in England, met Calvert Vaux, a young architect. As his tastes were sympathetic, he invited Vaux to America as a Partner. An earlier attempt at partnership with Alexander Jackson Davis never came to fruition, although the two men sometimes collaborated and shared many ideals.

Downing met a tragic death on July 28, 1852, in a famous steamboat tragedy. The *Henry Clay,* upon which he was travelling with his wife, was engaging in a race with the *Armenia.* The *Clay's* boilers became so hot that their canvas covers ignited, setting fire to the entire ship. She was beached near Mount Saint Vincent, below Yonkers, but only the bow touched the shore and the passengers had to jump into deep water to escape the flames. Downing remained aboard until the end, helping others escape by throwing wooden deck chairs into the water for non-swimmers to use as life rafts. His wife escaped, but his drowned body was found later that afternoon. As Downing was known as a powerful swimmer, it would seem that he had been knocked unconscious and fallen into the water. He was widely mourned. His influence remained powerful.

Clavert Vaux (1824-1895) continued his American career with great success and perpetuated many of Downing's ideas. In 1852 he joined forces with Frederick Law Olmstead to submit plans for the new Central Park in New York City. Their plan was accepted, and many subsequent important commissions came to the firm of Vaux & Olmstead. Among them were Prospect Park, Brooklyn (1857), sections of the Metropolitan Museum of Art, and the American Museum of Natural History, as well as the Downing Memorial Park at Newburgh (1867). This firm also layed out the town of Harrington Park, New Jersey, on the route of the West Shore Railroad. His book, *Villas & Cottages* (1857) was in the tradition of Downing's *Architecture of Country Houses,* and also had considerable influence in the Hudson Valley.

Frederick Law Olmstead (1822-1903) was born in Hartford, Connecticut, but spent most of his active career in New York City while residing on Staten Island. It was his responsibility to execute the designs for Central Park, and, to a degree, he seemed to be the "field man" for the firm of Vaux & Olmstead. His son, also named Frederick Law Olmstead, was born in 1870 and also became a prominent landscape architect.

21 The Upriver Ferries

For most of recorded history in the Hudson River Valley, from the earliest colonial times until relatively recently, the ferries have been the hub of economic and social life along the river. Towns and cities grew up around their landings. Daily crossing of the ferries was woven into the very warp and woof of the lives of millions of residents of the valley, to an extent that can hardly be conceived by younger people and newcomers to the area. For millions of commuters the daily ferry crossings were a part of the daily routine which kept them in close touch with such simple elemental facts of life as the winds and tides and state of the atmosphere. Flood, rain, and fog had direct impact upon their lives. The brief crossing provided time for pleasant relaxation and social contact—a respite from the bustle of daily activity. What is more, it kept people in contact with the river in a very immediate sense. A good case can be made out that rampant biological, chemical, and visual pollution came to the river, and was tolerated, only after the majority of the population lost the immediate contact with the river, made possible by frequent ferry travel. This pollution simply would not have been tolerated if more people had remained in close touch with the river. Abandonment of the ferries for use of tunnels and bridges was among the first signs, and also one of the causes, of people's turning their backs on the river.

In early times, and even into recent years, the ferries have been the scenes of much action of human and historical interest. The Kings Ferry and military ferry at Fishkill were vital to the Revolution. Sneden's Ferry played a part in the espionage of the Revolution, and Major André used the Kings Ferry in his flight with the plans of West Point. Jim Fisk, the rascal master of the Erie Railroad, escaped the hands of justice in New York State by taking a wild and unusual ferry trip. Joyful new immigrants set foot on Manhattan after a brief trip on the Ellis Island Ferry, and for millions, the trip across from Manhattan to the great Jersey City, Hoboken, and Weehawken railroad terminals was the start of the great adventure that was a transcontinental railroad journey. For others, resident in the sweltering slums of lower Manhattan, the ferry provided a short respite from the heat and foul air of the city at minimal expense. It brought millions into touch with the great ice floes of late winter and spring, the balmy waterborne zephyrs of spring, and the bracing winds of autumn. Life on the ferries was a microcosm of life along the Hudson. A study of the various ferry routes tells us as much about the people and the times as about the bare statistics of commerce and technology. There was romance in the ferries—a romance which people are beginning to consciously miss. There was also variety, ranging from bucolic operations using simple home built craft of primitive design and ungainly appearance, to the punctilious operations of large and majestic steamboats on the great lower lines such as the Hoboken Ferry and Staten Island line. In this, and the following two chapters, we take a look at the various ferry routes, giving their different histories from start to finish, in such details as are available and of interest. We begin at the northern end of the river and travel downstream to the lines across the Narrows and Arthur Kill.

The two ferry lines, furthest upstream, of which we have any record, are the Sarles Rope Ferry, six miles below Schuylerville, and the Powers-Briggs Rope Ferry, three miles above Bemis Heights. They seem to have been relatively casual affairs, sometimes changing their exact location of operations. It is unclear when most of them began operations, or just exactly when they ceased, although both lasted into the auto era. As they were in light traffic areas, they were never replaced by steam ferries, and bridges came relatively late. They were similar in operation to the one at Bemis Heights, here described by Benson J. Lossing:

> The river was crossed in several places by means of rope ferries. These, at times, presented quite picturesque scenes, when men and women, teams, live stock, and merchandise, happen to constitute the freight at one time. The vehicle was a large scow or batteau, which was pushed by means of long poles, that reached to the bottom of the river; and it was kept in its course, in defiance of the current, by ropes fore and aft, attached by friction rollers to a stout cable stretched across the stream. There were several of these ferries between Fort Edward and Stillwater, the one most used being that at Bemis Heights.[1]

Troy was originally called Ferry Hook, or Ashley's Ferry, after Captain Stephen Ashley who kept a tavern and ran a ferry here. The name Troy was adopted in 1789. This was an important trading town at the confluence of the Poestenkill and Wynantskill with the Hudson,

Albany North Ferry c1860 (Author's collection).

---

[1]Benson J. Lossing, *The Hudson, From the Wilderness to the Sea,* pp. 95, 96.

Athens Ferry, c1890 (Lionel DeLisser).

and just a short distance below the confluence of the Mohawk River. It was also at the head of free sloop navigation on the Hudson, and the furthest point at which the tides were felt. Greater importance was gained in 1802 when the Troy-Schenectady Toll Road was opened between West Troy (now Watervliet) and Schenectady. The early ferries were row or sail boats, but these were later superseded by small steam boats. On October 6, 1835 the first bridge was opened across the Hudson River between Troy and Green Island. It was built by the Rensselaer & Saratoga Railroad. However, vehicle ferries continued in operation here into the second half of the nineteenth century. While not strictly speaking a ferry line, as late as 1916 a Captain Hitchcock was operating the small steamboat *Victor,* built in 1854, on his Albany & Troy Steam Boat Line. The reason for the existence of this ferry-like short line was that the river offered restricted navigation and light traffic for large steamers above Albany, and this route served as a sort of annex for through traffic to and from downriver.

Considering the present-day constricted breadth of the Hudson, and the fact that it is crossed by such numerous bridges, it might be difficult to conceive that, at one time, as many as three steam ferries operated across the Hudson from Albany. As early as 1637 there is mention of "the ferry at Crawlier (Fort Crailo), over against Albany." The first regularly organized ferry was the *South Ferry* which operated from Ferry Street in Albany to Greenbush. It was started in 1684. On April 1, 1828 it received its first steam double-ender. The line was discontinued in the mid-1880s. The *North Ferry* operated from North Ferry Street in Albany to Ferry Street in Bath. This line began in 1831 and got its first steam double-ender in 1856. It was discontinued during the winter of 1903-1904. The *Albany Railroad Ferry* was not a train transfer type boat, but a regular foot-passenger and vehicle type vessel. It ran from Maiden Lane in Albany to the Boston & Albany Railroad depot at Greenbush. The line started operating with a steam double-ender in 1836 and ceased operations in the mid-1880s, quite some time after the opening of the first railroad bridge at Albany in 1866 by the New York Central Railroad.

Dropping downstream, the remains of the slip of the Coxsackie to Nutten Hook line can still be seen on the eastern shore. This operation began in 1800, and horseboats were being used as late as 1860. By 1894 a steamboat was in use. The line ceased operating in 1938.

Athens, the eastern terminus of the Scoharie Turnpike, was an important ferry place for

Catskill Ferry Landing, c1890. (Lionel DeLisser)

many years. The first ferry was established across to Hudson in 1778. By the late 1800s sidewheel, walking beam, steam double-enders were in use. This line remained in operation until September 7, 1947, long after opening of the Rip Van Winkle Bridge in 1935. This is indicative that a large part of its traffic consisted of foot passengers from the New York Central Railroad mainline at Hudson. However, the opening of the Rip Van Winkle Bridge did do-in the Hudson to Catskill ferry, which catered mainly to automobile traffic, and the Catskill to Greendale ferry, both of which ceased operations shortly thereafter.

The line from Catskill to Greendale, also variously known as Oak Hill Station and Catskill Landing Station, was established in 1851, upon completion of the Hudson River Railroad as far north as Oak Hill Station. It was operated by the Beach family of Catskill who were active in the stagecoach business and also owned and operated the Catskill Mountain House, the Catskill Evening Line of steamers to New York City, and the narrow-gauge Catskill Mountain, Otis Elevating, and Catskill & Tannersville railroads. The western terminus of this ferry was immediately adjacent to the Catskill Point terminal of the narrow gauge line and the Hudson River Day Line landing at the foot of Main Street, upon which ran the village trolley cars. The pride of the fleet was the double-end, walking-beam sidewheeler, *A. F. Beach*.

Further downstream, operations between Saugerties and Tivoli were both unusual and intermittent. The first period of operations was from 1800 to 1842. The longest period of operations was from 1851 to 1924. The first steamboat on the route was in 1857. In 1896 the unusual *single-end* walking-beam sidewheeler *Air Line* was on the route. In construction the *Air Line* was a regular double-ender for purposes of loading and unloading. However, she had a pilot house only at one end and generally only operated in one direction. On July 4, 1926, a regular double-ender was tried on the route. Probably this attempt at restoring ser-

Ferryboat *A. F. Beach* of the Catskill ferry line. Picture taken in 1878. This is a typical upriver sidewheel, walking beam, double ender. (From collection of T. I. Brooks. Courtesy of the Steamship Historical Society Library—University of Baltimore)

vice was unsuccessful, for the next period of continuous operations was from 1931 to 1938.

About 1702 there was a primitive sail and row boat ferry from Kipp Landing near Kipsbergen, in present-day Rhinecliff. Substantial ferry operations in this area began in 1752 when a ferry was chartered to connect the Ulster & Salisbury Pike on the east shore with the Ulster & Delaware Turnpike on the west shore. The Rhinecliff terminal was at the Long Dock. A steam ferry was established in 1815 and in 1842 the *Knickerbocker* was operating on this route, connecting Rhinecliff with Columbus Point, now known as Kingston Point. In 1851 the Hudson River Railroad was completed through Rhinecliff and the new steam ferryboat *Rhine* was put into service. The Kingston terminal was also changed to the Strand in Rondout, about a mile up Rondout Creek. Prior to delivery of the *Rhine* the *Astoria* and the *Wallabout* were chartered to supplement the *Knickerbocker*. At this time Thomas Cornell, of Rondout, was manager of the ferry line. The Rhinecliff dock was also moved to Shatzell's Dock, its present location. The *Rhine* had a wooden hull, because of which she sustained damage in battling winter ice. In 1853 the line was re-incorporated as the Rhinebeck & Kingston Ferry Co. A larger sidewheeler, the *Lark* was put into service in 1860. In 1866 a horsecar line was established from the ferry at Rondout, up the hill to Kingston. This line was electrified in 1894. During this period the Rhinebeck & Connecticut Railroad, which had been chartered as the Connecticut Western, terminated at Rhinecliff. In 1881 the steel hulled 115 foot sidewheel ferryboat *Transport* replaced the *Lark*. She operated on this route until 1938. During these years she was supplemented by the *Steinway* in 1928, *Aquehonga,* a chartered boat, and *Kingston* in 1930. The 1920s and 1930s were the great days of auto traffic on the line. Service was discontinued in 1943, and the *Kingston* was sold. The line was revived in 1946 by the New York State Bridge Authority, using the steel-hulled, diesel-powered propeller, *George Clinton*. She operated until January 6, 1957. The Kingston-Rhinecliff Bridge was opened the next month. Presently there is much agitation to restore at least foot passenger ferry service from Rondout to the Amtrak depot at Rhinecliff, the new bridge proving inconvenient to railroad passengers. The writer remembers an old gentleman who used to sell homemade warm, flat, Birch Beer at the Rhinecliff landing in the summertime. He claimed that this was better than the store variety which was cold and carbonated and "no darn good for your innards." Ferries tended to attract "characters."

Ferryboat *Air Line* of the Saugerties-Tivoli Line. This unique double-ender had a pilot house at only one end, and generally operated only in one direction. (Photo, Lionel DeLisser)

Also at Rondout Creek, the chain ferryboat *Riverside* operated between the Strand in Rondout and Sleightsburg between 1870 and 1922, when the new Route 9W Suspension Bridge across Rondout Creek was opened. This boat was locally called the *Skillypot,* which was a corruption of the Dutch *Skillepot,* or *tortoise,* which she resembled in both appearance and speed. Whereas in rope ferries the cable was strung high above the water, on a cable or chain ferry the cable was dropped across the stream and left sitting on the bottom but securely fastened at each end. This was to enable large boats to pass up and down stream without being obstructed by an overhead cable. Either a steam or gasoline powered winch aboard the ferryboat grips the cable or chain (which is raised up temporarily from the bottom during the passage of the ferry) and pulls the ferry across. The cable keeps the ferry on-route despite cross currents and provides the fulcrum for traction. A similar ferry is still in operation across the south end of Lake Champlain between Fort Ticonderoga and Larrabee's Point, Vermont.

The next ferry line below Rhinecliff was the Poughkeepsie Ferry to Highland, formerly called New Paltz Landing. This ferry was established by Noah Elting in 1793, as a sail and row boat operation. A horse powered flat boat was used in 1819. The Dutchess & Ulster Steam Power Ferry was established in 1830. A sidewheel walking-beam ship, the *Brinkerhoff,* built in Newburgh in 1899, operated on this line for many years, and was very well known on the river, as she later went to serve as a relief-boat on other lines further downriver. The first diesel-electric ferryboat in the east was the *Poughkeepsie* used on this route. The line closed on December 31, 1941, eleven years after opening of the Mid-Hudson Bridge. Terminals close to the West Shore and New York Central Railroad stations probably helped keep the line alive.

A venerable line of the distant past was the Milton Ferry, about four miles below Poughkeepsie. During the Revolution a Patriot blacksmith named Theophilus Anthony lived on the east shore. He forged one of the chains which was stretched across the Hudson in an attempt to block British ships. He also operated a ferry using row and sail boats. In 1860 a horseboat was being operated here by his grandsons, named Gill. However, by 1866 this ferry had ceased to operate. The eastern terminus was at the outlet of Spring Brook.

Another very early operation was the Hampton Ferry which ran between Hampton Point, near Cedarcliff, and New Hamburg. The western terminal was near the important trading post of Daniel Gomez, who was one of the more active of the early day Hudson Valley merchants. There is no record of steamboats ever having been used on this route.

Continuing downstream, a small steamboat belonging to the Sweet Orr Overall Company used to operate out of Wappingers Creek to Newburgh on a daily freight and passenger run until fairly recent times.

The first line we come to of real major stature is the Newburgh to Beacon Ferry. In early times Newburgh was sometimes called Quassaick and Beacon was frequently called Fishkill, and thus this ferry is often referred to by these names in old records. In 1743 King George II granted a ferry charter to Alexander Colden, one of the first English trustees of the Palatine Parish of Quassaick. This ferry was in operation until after the Revolution, during which time it was known as the Continental Ferry. General Washington had his base in Newburgh, and Baron Friedrich von Steuben had his in Fishkill, and the ferry was used frequently by both leaders, as well as the many military personnel based in the area. As the Kings Ferry, south of the Highlands, was prone to British interference, the Newburgh Ferry was the main trans-Hudson link in Patriot communications up and down the Atlantic Seaboard.

Rondout landing of the Rhinebeck-Kingston Ferry, c1896. Note car of Ulster & Delaware RR train in street. (Lionel DeLisser)

Major Patriot cantonments were located at Fishkill and New Windsor, and this ferry was of great strategic importance. The defeated British General, Burgoyne, and his army crossed over the ferry in 1777, after their surrender at Saratoga.

After the Revolution competition developed as the original charter was not an exclusive one. Martin Wiltsie and Daniel Carpenter formed a new company which continued in operation until 1781 or 1782, when Peter Bogardus, John Anderson, and James Denton established a new ferry line. It is believed that this new company acquired the rights to the original Colden ferry. During this period the original charter rights were confirmed. In 1802 the original Colden Charter was sold to Leonard Carpenter for $2500. The two competing ferry systems were combined in 1804, and between then and 1835 the line changed ownership many times. In May of 1835 Thomas Powell purchased the system for $80,000 and remained

Ferryboat *Transport* of the Kingston-Rhinecliff Line. Typical of the mid-river ferries.
(Photo courtesy of the Steamship Historical Society of America Library—University of Baltimore)

sole owner until 1850, when he deeded the property to his daughter, Mrs. Frances E. L. Ramsdell. The Ramsdell family retained ownership for one hundred years until, in 1956, they sold the line to the New York State Bridge Authority. The owners at the time of sale were Homer Ramsdell, and his sister, Mrs. Herbert R. Odell. The line stopped running on November 3, 1963, the day after the opening of the Newburgh-Beacon Bridge. Bells were tolled in mourning when the boats made their last crossings, and 220 years of continuous service were closed out. Well the bells might have tolled, for this was the end of Newburgh's economic vitality as well as the ferry. Despite large and costly urban renewal programs, the new bridge has done more harm than good for both Newburgh and Beacon. People now bypass them on their way to the bridge and business has completely died in the downtown areas. The convenient connection to New York Central (MTA and Amtrak) trains to Manhattan has been broken, and with no more passenger service on the West Shore Railroad, commuters no longer pass through Newburgh, or do their shopping there on their way home; nor do shoppers from Dutchess County go to the stores in Newburgh anymore. This is a classic example of how the ferries served for many years as hubs of economic and social activity. Both Nyack and Edgewater have suffered similarly from loss of ferry services. Ironically, the new bridge is subject to tremendous traffic jams and there is no provision for pedestrians or bicyclists going to the Beacon railroad station. Presently there is considerable agitation for restoration of a passenger ferry.

Sail and row boats were used until 1816, when the horseboat *Moses Rodgers,* named after its inventor, was put into operation. Another horseboat, the *Dutchess,* was later rebuilt as the steam ferry *Jack Downing.* The first paddlewheel boat was the *Caravan.* In 1828 the *Post Boy,* later renamed *Phoenix,* was put in service. Later nineteenth century steamboats were the *Gold Hunter, Fulton, Union,* and *Williamsburg.* Later came the *City of Newburgh* and the *Fishkill-On-Hudson.* In 1910 the *Dutchess* was put in service, and in 1914 the *Orange.* These last two were built at Newburgh. Next came the *Thomas Powell,* and in 1921, the *Beacon.* The last three boats in operation were the *Dutchess, Orange,* and *Beacon.* These last boats burned coal and were hand fired. They generated magnificent clouds of black smoke.

Chain ferryboat *Riverside,* also known as Skillypot c1896. View shows Rondout Landing. Note towboat tied up to right. (Lionel DeLisser)

They were painted green and had gilded lanterns atop their pilot houses.

The Newburgh Ferry was a unique fusion of bucolic charm and bigtime marine operation—in fact it was a miniature copy of the large railroad operated lines to Manhattan. In many ways the line was indeed a part of the local railroad system. The Beacon terminal was across the Plaza from the New York Central Railroad station. New York Central timetables had a symbol next to Beacon indicating: "Newburgh NOTE: Frequent all year ferry service between Beacon (adjacent to railroad station) and Newburgh. Fare 15ᶜ. Railroad tickets not accepted on ferry." A similar notice read: "Rhinecliff NOTE: Ferry service, except during Winter months, between Rhinecliff (adjacent to railroad station) and Kingston. Fare 15ᶜ. Inquire of Agent relative to operation. Railroad tickets not accepted on ferry."

Chain ferryboat *Riverside* and Sleightsburg Landing, 1896. (Lionel DeLisser)

Ticonderoga-Larrabee's Point chain ferry across Lake Champlain, 1957. This is a diesel version of Skillypot. (Photo: Arthur G. Adams)

On the bucolic side, a quaint sign was posted in the pilot houses of the boats. It read:

THE COW BELL MEANS
only one thing
whether engine is working ahead
is stopped or backing
BACK STRONG

The scenery was magnificent, delightful, and picturesque all at once. For many years a trolley line connected the Beacon Terminal with the Mt. Beacon Incline Railway, and this was a popular excursion for both local Newburghers and New Yorkers, who had come up to Newburgh on the Day Line. Winter added a new dimension to the trip. I particularly remember crossing from Beacon to Newburgh on a bright sunny morning after a snowstorm when new skim ice had formed on the river. As the boat cut through the ice it threw up a spray of ice chips which sparkled in the sunlight forming a miniature rainbow, and made a tinkling sound as of tiny crystal bells, which carried clearly through the freezing and exhilarating air.

The Beacon ferryhouse was a copy of the larger terminals downriver. It was of modern steel frame construction with copper sheathing with neo-classic fluting and decorations, in the best Lackawanna Railroad or Jersey Central style, and had two slips. The terminal was incongruous set amidst many weeping willow trees.

The Newburgh Terminal could have come directly from the Rhineland of the 1800s. It was a picturesque Victorian structure with gable ends, towers, turrets, gingerbread vergeboards, and much scrollwork, all painted a light cream color, all surmounted with a red painted Mansard roof and flagpole, from which a large American Flag always flew. The West Shore Railroad depot was only a short way off and the Day Line Landing and the large Schoonmaker's Department Store were immediately to the north. Several bus lines used the ferry to cross the river. The terminal was a bustling place with many cars, trucks and passengers waiting in line. Perhaps the Newburgh Ferry had the most distinct personality of any of the up-river ferries. Details of later-day vessels are given in the Appendix.

Between 1872 and 1902 the sidewheel railroad car ferryboats *Fannie Garner* and *William T. Hart* operated between Newburgh and Denning Point, or Fishkill Hook. It was operated by the Erie Railroad and connected with the New Haven's Fishkill Branch to Hopewell Junction and New England.

Below Newburgh everything, except the scenery, diminished in scale. During the Revolution there was a temporary ferry between Fishkill and New Windsor for use of the Continental Army. Up until World War I several small steamboats plied between Newburgh and Peekskill, stopping at Cornwall, Cold Spring, and West Point, and carrying foot passengers and light freight and hay. These were used more as ferries than for through travel. Between 1850 and 1892 a small single-ended steamer operated a ferry route between Cornwall and the Storm King Depot on the New York Central Railroad, near the base of Breakneck Mountain. From Colonial times, and continuing up until the present, there has been sporadic ferry service between West Point and Cold Spring. In his book *American Scenery* of 1840, Nathaniel Parker Willis, who later lived at Cornwall, makes mention of two ferrymen at Cold Spring, named Lipsey and Andrews, who operated an irregular row and sail ferry. At the present time the U. S. Army operates a ferry-launch service from South Dock, West Point to Constitution Island and Cold Spring for the shopping convenience of base personnel and for tourists.

A Newburgh-Beacon ferryboat as seen from the deck of the steamer *Alexander Hamilton* c1960. Fishkill Range in background. (Photo Arthur G. Adams)

There seems to have been a ferry at West Point since before the Revolution. These were primitive sail and rowboat operations, more like a water taxi service, and it seems that such services survived the coming of the steam ferry, inasmuch as such a service is mentioned as late as 1875. In view of the social life at Cold Spring, and the activities at the West Point Foundry, it seems natural that such a service would have been well patronized. In his *History of American Steam Navigation,* Morrison does not list the West Point ferry as running under steam prior to 1836. It is likely that a steam ferry was inaugurated at the time of the construction of the Hudson River Railroad, in 1851. An anonymous lithograph dated 1858 in the Collection of the New York Historical Society is entitled *West Point from the Ferry Landing at Phillipstown.* It shows the Garrison ferryhouse, which is still standing in 1980, and a double-ended sidewheel steam ferryboat named *West Point.* Later boats were the *Highland* and the *Garrison.* In his 1866 book, *The Hudson,* Benson Lossing gives the following information:

Newburgh ferry terminal, c1963 from steamer *Alexander Hamilton*. (Photo Arthur G. Adams)

The road from the plain to the landing at West Point was cut from the steep rocky bank of the river, at a heavy expense to the government. The wharf is spacious, and there a sentinel was continually posted, with a slate and pencil, to record the names of all persons who arrive and depart. This was for the use of the Superintendent, by which means he is informed daily of the arrival of any persons to whom he might wish to extend personal or professional courtesies.

A steam ferryboat connects West Point with the Garrison Station of the Hudson River Railway, opposite. Near the latter is the old ferry-place of the Revolution, where troops crossed to and from West Point. Here Washington crossed on the morning when General Arnold's treason was discovered, and here he held a most anxious consultation with Colonel Hamilton when that event was suspected.[2]

Landing, as it does, within the limits of the United States Military Academy, the status of the West Point-Garrison Ferry as a common carrier is peculiar. It never seems to have been widely promoted as a popular river crossing. The West Shore Railroad timetable of 1909 notes at West Point "Garrison by Ferry." Regular commercial passenger vehicular ferry service was discontinued in the autumn of 1928. The U. S. Army still operated an irregular service, usually to meet MTA trains at Garrison. The service is sometimes available to the general public and information can be obtained from Military Police at West Point or railroad ticket agents.

Below the Highlands, there was a nineteenth century ferry service between Peekskill and Jones Point, which was then called Caldwell's, and where there was a large and popular resort hotel. On March 19th, 1800 Joshua Colwil and Joseph Travis, for whom Travis Point

[2]Benson J. Lossing, *The Hudson, From the Wilderness to the Sea,* pp. 236, 237.

was named, obtained a charter for a ferry between Caldwell's Point and Peekskill. This first ferry was a row boat, but horseboats were used briefly after 1830. Sometime prior to 1836, the steamboat *Jack Downing,* which had been converted from a horseboat when operating on the Newburgh Ferry, was running on this line. This service was discontinued in the late nineteenth century. On May 4, 1835 an act was passed permitting S. W. Bard of Haverstraw, and Ward Hunter, of Peekskill, to establish ferry communication between those places. In 1852 Captain John Bard ran a small boat named the *John T. Rodman* on this route, but later replaced her with the *Sarah.* There has been no service on this route in recent years.

Of great importance from earliest times was the King's Ferry which ran between Verplanck's Point and Stony Point, near Tomkins Cove. In 1852 Benson Lossing wrote:

> This was the old King's Ferry of the Revolution, where the good Washington so often crossed, and where battalion after battalion of troops, royal, French, and American, at various times spanned the Hudson with their long lines of flat boats, for it was the main crossing place of armies moving between the Eastern and Middle States. It was here, too, that a portion of the forces of Burgoyne crossed the Hudson on their march from Massachusetts to Virginia.'' (N.B. it will be recalled that they used the Newburgh Ferry going from Saratoga to Massachusetts. Author's Note) The landing place on the Stony Point side, in former times, was in the cove at the opening of the marsh, on the north of the promontory. Now the western terminus of the ferry is a little above, at the cottage of Mr. Ten Eyck, the jolly old ferryman, who has plied the oar there, almost without intermission, ever since 1784. He was sitting upon his door stone when his son moored the boat at its rock fastening. As we ascended the bank, the old man held up a bottle of whiskey and proferred a draught as a pledge of welcome to the "millionth" man that had crossed his ferry. Preferring milk to whiskey; I sat down under the rich leaved branches of a maple, and regaled myself with that healthful beverage.[3]

In order to understand the importance of this crossing we must remember that both the Americans and British understood that control of the Hudson between West Point and the Tappan Zee, and particularly the King's Ferry, could determine the entire results of the war. Much of the history of the Revolution revolves around British attempts to gain control of the Hudson and sever New England from the Middle and Southern Colonies. To prevent this the Americans built Forts Montgomery and Clinton in the Highlands. In October of 1777 Sir Henry Clinton, under cover of heavy fog, landed a force of British troops at the western terminus of the King's Ferry, and then proceeded over Dunderberg Mountain and past Doodletown to attack the American forts from the rear. Three hundred Americans were captured, killed, or wounded and the British seized the iron chain across the Hudson at Bear Mountain. Later they sailed up the Hudson and burned Clermont and Kingston. However, in the meantime Burgoyne had surrendered to General Gates at Saratoga and the British grand strategy became abortive and the Americans shortly thereafter regained control of the Highlands. Later in 1779, Sir Henry Clinton's forces captured the promontory at Stony Point along with the small fortification across the river at Verplanck's Point, whereupon they installed a strong garrison. Ultimately Washington sent General Anthony Wayne to recapture Stony Point, which he succeeded in doing in a spectacular manner which did much to raise Patriot morale. They could not hold Stony Point for long, but the British withdrew again of their own accord before the end of the war, and it was in American hands by the time of Benedict Arnold's betrayal in September of 1780.

It will be recalled that, on the night of September 21st, Major André had come ashore from the *Vulture* at Waldberg Landing, near the foot of Long Clove, below Haverstraw. With daylight on the morning of the 22nd, he and Joshua Hett Smith retired to Smith's house, halfway between Haverstraw and Stony Point. Let us follow events as described by Lossing:

---

[3]Benson J. Lossing, *Field Book of the American Revolution,* Vol. I, pp. 751, 752.

Bidding André adieu, Arnold went up the river in his own barge, to headquarters, fully believing that no obstacle now interposed to frustrate his wicked scheme. André passed the remainder of the day alone, and as soon as evening came, he applied to Smith to take him back to the *Vulture.* Smith positively refused to go, and pleaded illness from age as an excuse. If he quaked, it was probably not from age, but from fear wrought by the firing upon the *Vulture*; for he offered to ride half the night with André, on horseback, if he would take a land route. Having no other means of reaching the vessel, André was obliged to yield to the force of circumstances. He consented to cross King's Ferry to Verplanck's Point, and make his way back to New York by land.....A little before sunset, on the evening of the 22nd, accompanied by a negro servant, they crossed King's Ferry. At dusk, they passed through the works at Verplanck's Point, and turned their faces toward White Plains.[4]

It is recorded that, on November 22, 1780, the Marquis de Chastellux crossed from Verplanck's Point to Stony Point on his way to meet Washington at Preakness and Lafayette at Totowa.

The King's Ferry was at the narrowest point of the Hudson, which made it a desirable crossing place for scows, barges, and rowboats, such as were used to transport an Army. However, neither terminus was in a populated area and, once the war was over, other more direct routes of travel along the seaboard became more attractive. The coming of the steam ferry, which made it possible to cross wider parts of the river directly between populated areas, caused the King's Ferry to fall into disuse. It was revived briefly, and unprofitably, between 1922 and 1924, as an automobile crossing. There have been three different landings at the western end. The oldest was at the foot of the eminence of Stony Point. The second one, at which Lossing landed in 1852, was about a quarter of a mile north of the first. The third, and last, was still further north, at the mouth of a small stream which empties into the Hudson there. Near the place of the original landing is Ten Eyck's Beach, named after the Ten Eycks, who were ferrymen there from the earliest times. The remains of an old causeway, covered with grass, leading to the main road, Route 9W, half a mile away, could be discerned until much of it, and the second and third landing places were obliterated by construction of the West Shore Railroad.

In the Haverstraw Bay area, because of its great width, there has only been rather limited ferry operations. On March 25, 1837, Samson Marks of Haverstraw obtained a franchise for a ferry from Call's Dock to Verplanck's Point. Row boats and steam ferries operated sporadically during the nineteenth century between Grassy Point and Crugers. Grassy Point was an important steamboat landing because the channel came in near the western shore here. In 1852 Elisha Pack and Samuel A. Vervalen operated the *Vinton,* a steam ferry, between Haverstraw and the Hudson River Railroad at Crugers. Other early-day boats on this line were the *Three Bells* and the *Ida Pell.* During the early twentieth century a ferry operated between Haverstraw and Ossining.

On May 11, 1835 John Haff of Ossining was given permission to establish a ferry between that city and Slaughter's Landing, now called Rockland Lake Landing, at the foot of Hook Mountain. On April 23, 1844 George E. Stanton, Peter B. Lynch, William H. Pack, Robert Wiltse, Gaylord B. Hubbell, and A. P. Stephens obtained the passage of an act incorporating them into the Sing Sing & Rockland Lake Ferry Company. It is likely that Haff's ferry was a rowboat operation, as it is recorded in Cole's *History of Rockland County,* that during the early days of the Knickerbocker Ice Company business (c1835) at Rockland Lake, a row ferry plied between these points. Possibly the later operators ran a steamboat.

Starting in 1827 Nyack enjoyed steamboat service to New York City. This was provided by the Nyack Steamboat Association, operating the diminutive *Orange,* which measured only

---

[4]Benson J. Lossing, *Field Book of the American Revolution*, Vol. I, pp. 722, 723, 724.

75 ft. x 22 ft. x 7.5 ft. deep, and cost $8,854. In 1830 the Orangetown Point Steamship Company put the *Rockland* into service on the same route, but was driven off in 1831, when the *Orange* was improved and given larger paddle wheels.

Regular ferry service between Nyack and Tarrytown was instituted in 1834 by Isaac S. Blauvelt. The first boat was called the *Dank Ya,* which means "Thank You" in Dutch. The boat was thus christened when Isaac Blauvelt's father refused any remuneration for helping him to build the little ship. The local "Yankees" soon corrupted the name to the *Donkey.* This line operated on a rather loose schedule.

In 1839 George W. B. Gedney began operating the *Charon* on this same route and, on April 1, 1840, was given a formal franchise. This boat ran on a regular schedule and was subject to certain restrictions in its franchise: The ferry must be run from April to December, from 5:00 AM to 9:00 PM, and during the winter months whenever ice conditions permitted. The boat must be equipped with sails and must always be ready to transport passengers, horses, cattle, carriages, and other freight across the river. The boat must also have one or more rowboats with proper and skillful men to row them.

Gedney constructed the first permanent dock and slip, which measured eighty by fifty feet. Fares were fifty cents for foot passengers and seventy-five cents for horse and rider. A one-horse wagon cost one dollar and a two-horse, four-wheel carriage and driver cost one and a half dollars.

In 1853 Abram P. Smith bought a little sidewheel steamer named the *Daniel Drew* and started her as a ferry to Tarrytown. A year later he bought the *J. J. Herrick* for a ferryboat and ran her until he sold the ferry to D. D. and Tunis Smith in 1862. The number of names under which that boat sailed was legion. In the patriotic fervor of the Civil War she was called the *Union,* and at another time the *Nyack,* and the *Tarrytown.* Before she went out of use she reverted to her original name of *Bergen,* by which she is best remembered.

The ferryboat *Tappan Zee* was built in 1874. In the 1800s, the North River Steamboat Company and the North River Ferry Company began a rivalry which continued for many years. On May 21, 1887, the *Tappan Zee* of the North River Steamboat Company caught fire and burned to the waterline. Around 3:00 AM the firemen cut her loose from her dock and let her drift out in the Hudson. The origin of the fire was never discovered. During this period, it was the custom of the ferries to take passengers out to mid-river to board the day boats.

Ferryboat *Orange* and Newburgh terminal c1963. (Photo A. G. Adams)

West Point-Garrison Ferry from Garrison Landing, 1858.
(Anonymous lithograph, New York Historical Society)

Passenger and auto service continued until November 30, 1941. After World War II, Robert N. Lee operated a passenger-only service on the route, but this was discontinued upon completion of the Tappan Zee Bridge in 1956. There is still talk of reviving this line to connect with the commuter trains at Tarrytown.

After construction of the Erie Railroad in 1841, but before the opening of the Hudson River Railroad in 1850, a row ferry operated between the railroad pier at Piermont and Irvington. On March 2, 1849, Benjamin L. James and James L. Shultz obtained a franchise for a ferry from Piermont to the opposite shore, to connect with the new railroad. In 1861 the Erie Railroad started running its through trains from the West to Jersey City, where there was a direct short ferry crossing to Chambers Street, Manhattan, rather than to Piermont, as before. Their own steamer service from Piermont to Manhattan was proving too slow, and they did not like losing patronage to the Irvington Ferry and the competing Hudson River Railroad. Consequently Piermont reverted to branchline status in the Erie System. In 1868 the Erie stopped running its own steamers between Piermont and Duane Street, Manhattan. This sort of left little Piermont very much out of things. Starting in 1859 the new Northern Railroad of New Jersey ran trains from Piermont to Jersey City. However, a ferry connection from Piermont to the Hudson River Railroad at Irvington was still very desirable, particularly for those going to midtown Manhattan, where the Hudson River Railroad had stations. In 1870 the Northern Railroad of New Jersey was extended from Piermont to Nyack. The prosperity of the village of Piermont depended entirely upon the Erie Railroad that had shops there. When the Erie removed these facilities to Pavonia between 1852 and 1861, Piermont lost half its inhabitants. The need for rapid communication across the Hudson diminished, and the ferry to Irvington was soon discontinued.

Service was resumed briefly between 1932 and the Second World War, using two small diesel boats, the *Piermont* and the *Irvington,* which could each carry nine automobiles and thirty-two passengers. They were built at United Drydock Company at Mariners Harbor,

Staten Island, for a cost of only $17,000 each. The *Irvington* was the first ferry built in the United States with an all-welded steel hull. These boats later operated on routes across the Arthur Kill and Kill Van Kull.

Below Piermont we come upon the location of one of the most ancient ferry routes on the Hudson. Dobbs Ferry, or Sneden's Ferry, or Paramus Ferry, operated between 1698 and 1944 between Dobbs Ferry in Westchester County and Sneden's Landing, just north of the New Jersey border, in Rockland County. Originally the land on the eastern shore was called Wecquaskeck, or "Place of the Bark Kettle," by the Indians. This tract was acquired by Frederick Philipse in 1672. One of the first settlers on the Philipse lands was an Englishman named John Dobbs. According to tradition, he and his immediate descendants operated a sail and row ferry across to the "dingle" in Paramus. "Dingle" is an old English word for a deep narrow cleft between hills, or a shady dell, such as the Dutch would call a clove. This clove was at the northern termination of the Palisades and provided easy access to the waterfront. The land on the west shore had been purchased from the Indians on March 17, 1681 by a group of eight white men and three free negroes from Bouwery Village on Manhattan, together with five men from New Jersey. This tract was on the New Jersey-New York border and in dispute between the two states. In New Jersey it was known as the Paramus Patent, and in New York, as the Tappan Patent. Dobbs ran his ferry to a landing at the foot of the dingle, to a location simply called "the ferry," or, at a period before the Revolution, as Rockland. At the time of the Revolution it was called Paramus.

In 1745, or 1752, a person named Robert Sneden purchased property at the landing. Robert's wife was Mary, or Molly, Sneden, who was a most unusual woman. She lived to the advanced age of one hundred years and eighteen days. She supplemented her husband's calling of farmer by serving as ferry mistress, and she may have run the ferry as early as 1745, and the place is shown as Sneden's Landing on maps dating from 1759. This obviously conflicts with the Dobbs operation....

Molly Sneden, and all her children except her son John, were Tories. An interesting Revolutionary order of the Committee of Orange County reads:

> Whereas Dennis Snyden, James Snyden, William Snyden, and Samuel Snyden, all living at or near a place commonly called Snyden's or Dobbs Ferry on the west side of Hudson's River in the County of Orange and State of New York, have refused to sign any or either of the Associations that have been put forth or recommended by our honorable convention; and as the above said persons are greatly suspected of carrying on a treasonable correspondence with our natural enemies, or ships of war belonging to the King of Great Britain, lying in aforesaid river, by the great opportunity afforded them in the privilege they have of keeping the ferry: knowing the aforesaid persons to be inveterate enemies to the common States of America, Therefore Resolved, that the above Dennis Snyden, Jesse (sic) Snyden, William Snyden, and Samuel Snyden are hereby forewarned not to keep ferry, or employ any other person to ferry in their room, or employ a craft on the aforesaid river, upon any pretence whatsoever, and all other persons are hereby forewarned against having any correspondence with the above said Snydens, or any other person or persons whatsoever that are in any degree enemies to the liberties of America. And whereas John Snyder is advertised in the public Gazette as pilot of the ships of war on the above said river, greatly to the damage of the said John Snyder, it is hereby requested that the said Printer shall insert Robert Snyden instead of John Snyder, who has always appeared to be a warm friend to the common cause of America.

PER ORDER OF THE ORANGE COUNTY COMMITTEE, CLARKSTOWN, JULY 29, 1776.

During the Revolution Molly Sneden lived in a white frame house on the road by the river. With her lived her son Dennis, a bachelor. The story goes that a British soldier was pursued down the gully by some patriots; she hid him in her house in a large chest on which she set pans of cream to rise, and when the patriots arrived she misinformed them; they were tired and asked for refreshment, and she offered them all the milk she had, but told them not to disturb the pans of cream which she had just set out; in the evening she is said to have ferried the soldier across the river. Some of her sons settled in Nova Scotia after the war and received grants of land there.

It is possible the Jeremiah Dobbs may have resumed operation of the ferry during the time of the Sneden's proscription. Among the romantic passengers on this ferry during the Revolution was Aaron Burr, then in the Continental Army stationed at White Plains. He was then courting Mrs. Theodosia Prevost, widow of a British Army officer, living at the Hermitage in Hohokus. Both Sneden's Landing and Hohokus were known as Paramus at that time. Hohokus was disputed neutral ground and his nocturnal trips through this area plagued with Skinners and Cowboys, and across the Hudson, patrolled by enemy warships, in a light skiff with his horse, must have been quite an adventure.

After the war the most notable ferryman here was Captain Lawrence J. Sneden (1800-1871), who was also a shipbuilder and served as assemblyman. It is reputed that Martha Washington also crossed this ferry. Inauguration of Erie Railroad steamboat service from Piermont to Manhattan in 1841, and of the Northern Railroad of New Jersey in 1859, precluded any real usefulness for such ferry to such a lightly populated area and the route never thrived in later years. The steam ferryboat *Union* was built and put into operation here in 1832. Sporadic operations continued up until September 14, 1944, when the last boat was wrecked in a hurricane.

Last of the upriver ferries to be considered is the Yonkers Ferry. The earliest record of any ferry at this point is of the "Patroon's ferry sloop *Frederick Closter*," which operated from Yonkers to Closter Dock around 1700. Up until the coming of the steamboat and railroad, the Dobbs Ferry handled what light traffic existed. The foot of the Palisades was lightly populated with wood and stone cutters, and they depended on small sloops and steamboats

Yonkers Ferryboat, *F. R. Pierson* leaving Alpine Landing c1940. (Author's collection)

for communication with New York City. The cliffs posed a great obstacle to east-west traffic and the foot of the Palisades was not an auspicious terminus for a ferry route. However, in 1876 service was started with a steam double ender. This incarnation remained in operation until 1882. Service was restored in 1885, using a conventional single-end steamboat for foot passengers only, until 1892 when a double-ender was put back on the route until 1895, when service was discontinued near the end of the year.

By the 1920s things had greatly changed. The Palisades Interstate Park Commission had taken over the Palisades, largely to preserve them and to also provide recreational facilities. The sparse population had been removed and auto roads were developed to the top of the cliffs. The park was served by several small steamboats from New York City. However, the availability of auto roads up the cliff, coupled with very long waiting lines at the Englewood Cliffs-Dyckman Street and Edgewater-125th Street ferries, created a need for a new east-west ferry crossing between Alpine and Yonkers.

The Yonkers Ferry Company was chartered in 1922. Among the principal incorporators were Jack and Leo Schwarzstein, Frank R. Pierson, and John J. Walsh. Frank R. Pierson was elected President.

On May 15, 1923, service was inaugurated with two old sidewheel beam steamers from the Delaware, Lackawanna & Western Lines—the *Musconetcong,* and the *Paunpeck.* The *Musconetcong* was renamed the *F. R. Pierson.* In 1938 a new vessel, the *John J. Walsh* was purchased. She was a great departure from the earlier boats in that she was designed with a great open deck to handle automobiles and had only one pilot house, from which the pilot could see to operate in either direction. She had a hull designed for ice breaking, was 153 feet long by 48 feet wide and had a 650 hp diesel engine and cost $150,000. She went into service in January and replaced the *Paunpeck*—the *F. R. Pierson* remaining as a relief boat. Initial fares on the line were 5ᶜ for a foot passenger; 15ᶜ for a bicycle and rider; 40ᶜ-50ᶜ for automobiles, depending on the size. The new *Walsh* could accommodate the largest trucks of that time. The crossing took five minutes. In 1937 the line had handled 300,000 vehicles and solicited business by placement of road signs as far away as Pompton Lakes, New Jersey and Middletown, New York, and points in Connecticut. The steamers were painted white with the traditional gold lanterns atop the pilot houses. The *Walsh* was painted metallic silver with black lettering. She was almost oval in shape. In later years the corporation changed its name to The Westchester Ferry Company.

After the discontinuance of the Edgewater-125th Street Ferry in 1950, they acquired the *Weehawk,* another diesel-electric boat, designed for carrying many automobiles. She was painted Army-Olive drab and had considerable upper deck passenger accommodation and the traditional two pilot houses.

After opening of the Tappan Zee Bridge in 1955, traffic began to decline. The *Pierson* had been retired upon acquisition of the *Weehawk,* and now traffic would not support even one boat in operation. The Westchester Ferry Company, which had been so incorporated on March 29th, 1939, decided to call it a day. The last boat crossed on December 26, 1956. The Schwarzsteins still retained ownership and sold the remaining boats to the St. Lawrence Seaway Development Corporation for use between Roosevelttown, New York and Cornwall Island, Ontario. On the human interest side, it is interesting to recall that the Yonkers ferry always attracted itinerant musicians, and accordion players and violinists would serenade the passengers and "pass the cup" for donations, making for a very pleasant crossing. As with other lines, there is constant agitation to restore the line.

22 The Manhattan Ferries

Furthest upriver of the Manhattan ferries was the Dyckman Street to Englewood Cliffs route. This bucolic operation was more typical of the other upriver lines than the great railroad-controlled operations further downtown.

In June of 1860 the large and luxurious Palisade Mountain House was opened atop a bluff of the Palisades in Englewood Cliffs. The owners formed another corporation called the Englewood Dock & Turnpike Company, which built a carriage road down the cliffs and constructed a steamboat dock. During the period of the hotel's operation, from 1860 to 1884, the dock was served by two boats each way daily, connecting it with lower Manhattan. After 1884 the road was taken over by the Palisades Road & Turnpike Company, and provided connection between private residences atop the Palisades and local steamboats. As the area atop the cliffs developed, an alternative to the long trolley trip from Coytesville to the Edgewater or Weehawken ferries became desirable, and agitation began for a direct short-crossing ferry to connect with the subway in upper Manhattan. Better access was also desired for the new Palisades Interstate Park.

On June 17, 1915 ferry service was started from the Englewood Landing at the foot of the cliffs, to Dyckman Street. The Englewood Turnpike had become Palisades Avenue, and was extended on over the Palisades and down the western slope into the village of Englewood, in the Northern Valley. The ferry line operated with three or four sidewheel beam double-enders, including the *Englewood* (1896) and the *Florida* (1896), with extra boats as traffic demanded. The passenger fare was 3ᶜ, but went up to 5ᶜ in later inflationary times. In 1930 the line carried 1,286,177 vehicles and 965,696 pedestrians. Often the traffic line would back up across Route 9W atop the Palisades. In the early days automobiles were pushed on and off the boats, as it was considered dangerous to operate the motors where they might frighten horses. The manager of the line from 1921 to 1931 was George V. Cook, who was a great local celebrity. Famous regular passengers included Thomas Lipton, John D. Rockefeller, Sr., John Ringling, Dwight Morrow, and Billy Sunday. Construction of the George Washington Bridge in 1931 did not seem to hurt business to any substantial extent. The line operated until May 21, 1942, when the only remaining usable float-bridge at Dyckman Street collapsed, pinning the boat in the slip. The Second World War discouraged any thoughts of restoring service immediately. The Hill Bus Company, the forerunner of today's Red & Tan Lines, had been operating from Englewood and Tenafly "over the Hill" to the ferry landing. With cessation of ferry service, they combined operations with the

Rockland Coach Lines, and began operating over the George Washington Bridge to Manhattan. They never resumed bus service to the Englewood ferry landing. Ferry service was resumed in 1948 and continued until 1951. Cessation of service came about more because of dilapidation of equipment than from any lack of traffic. While there would be a good demand for resumption of service even today, siltation of the river would make considerable dredging necessary and new docks would have to be built.

About a mile below the George Washington Bridge, at the foot of the Palisades south of the Fort Lee, and where the present day River Road, Hudson Terrace, and the Henry Hudson Drive come together, there is a location that has been known by various names throughout the years. A trading post and sloop landing was established here in 1658 by Etienne Burdette, a Huguenot merchant. For many years they operated sloops to many points and a row and sail ferry to Carmansville on Manhattan Island, near about 152nd Street. This locality was first called Burdett's Ferry. It is at the foot of a natural clove from the top of the Palisades near Fort Lee, and was a natural location for a colonial period ferry and landing. A stage line ran from here to Hackensack by way of Leonia. In later years the location became known as Tillie Tudlem or Tilly Toodlum, and still later as Pleasant Valley and Fort Lee Park. The large Octagon House Hotel and Fort Lee Park Hotel were located here, and in the nineteenth century this became an important landing for local steamboats. The Fort Lee & New York Steam Boat Company was formed in 1832 and ran to 22nd Street, Spring Street and Canal Street in Manhattan, making way-landings in New Jersey at Edgewater, Bulls Ferry, Guttenberg, and Weehawken. Ships on this line included the *Edwin, Thomas E. Hulse, Fort Lee, Pleasant Valley,* and *Shady Side.* Also, between May 23, 1880 and 1896, a double-ended steam ferry operated from here to 129th Street Manhattan.

In modern times the principal line to upper Manhattan was the Edgewater ferry to 125th

Edgewater-125th Street ferryboat *Tenafly* of 1915 approaching Edgewater slip.
(Courtesy Raymond J. Baxter)

West Shore ferryboat *Albany* c1883. (Author's collection)

Street, sometimes known as the Public Service Ferry. This line was started in 1894. In 1900 it was acquired by the newly organized New Jersey & Hudson River Railway & Ferry Company, that operated an extensive network of electric railways in New Jersey. The line had good connections with the Broadway IRT Subway near its Manhattan terminal. Also, Day Line and Night Line steamers stopped at an immediately adjacent pier, and the Iron Steamboat Company had a pier at 129th Street and operated service down bay and to Coney Island until 1932, making this a popular excursion route. There was also a crosstown trolley car on 125th Street, connecting with the New York Central and New Haven Railroad station. In 1911 the ferry and electric railways were taken over by the Public Service Railways, a division of Public Service Electric & Gas Company. In 1938 the last trolley rolled out of Edgewater Terminal, and up the switch back route up the cliffs, and Public Service put on buses in substitution. Public Service soon lost interest in the ferry line and began running most of their buses directly across the George Washington Bridge, or through the Lincoln and Holland Tunnels to Manhattan. On August 1, 1943 they sold the ferry line, which was now primarily a vehicular traffic route, to the Electric Ferry Company, which operated the line until December 16, 1950. During this period an automobile ferry toll of 25¢ was still an at-

NEW YORK CENTRAL R.R.
WEEHAWKEN FERRY

GOOD FOR ONE PASSAGE IN
EITHER DIRECTION BETWEEN

**WEEHAWKEN, N. J. and
FOOT OF W. 42nd St. N. Y.**

Limited to Thirty (30) Days including date of sale.

Not Transferable. Asst. V.P., Pass. Traffic

Series 7   245247

West Shore ferry ticket c1940. This ticket cost 3ᶜ. (Author's collection)

West Shore Railroad ferryboat *Weehawken*. Painting by William G. Muller from collection of Henry O. Smith III.

Interior cabin of West Shore Railroad ferryboat *Weehawken*. Note elaborate woodwork.
(New York Central photo)

tractive bargain compared to a 50ᶜ bridge or tunnel toll, and long waiting lines were still usual. Only with the gradual loss of value of the dollar, coupled with ever rising labor costs, did the economic margin disappear and the ferries become uneconomic. When rising costs made a 35ᶜ fare necessary, the differential was no longer attractive and traffic fell off tremendously making it unfeasible to continue operations. Shortly after ferry services ended the Port of New York Authority increased bridge and tunnel tolls to 75ᶜ. Since that time Edgewater has become a true "backwater." However, recent major apartment house developments in the area have created persistent calls for resumption of at least foot-passenger ferry service to Manhattan as the George Washington Bridge and the Lincoln Tunnel represent long detours and frequent traffic jams.

The Public Service boats were large two stack steamers named after such local communities along the trolley lines as Tenafly. They had large passenger cabins on either side of the main deck and upper deck passenger accommodations but only two vehicle gangways. They were painted red, with the traditional two pilot houses topped with gilded lanterns. They were exceptionally handsome boats and were always beautifully groomed. The diesel powered boats of the Electric Ferry Company offered a great deal more vehicle space on the main deck. All passenger accommodations were on the upper deck and reached by covered stairways at either end. There were two pilot houses with the traditional gilded lanterns. The boats were painted olive drab with white lettering. One interesting characteristic of this particular line was that the boats often had to make long detours to avoid the nets of the numerous shad fishermen.

In February of 1964 it was announced that Fairwater Excursions would operate boats from the Tri-Terminal area, site of the old Ford Assembly Plant, to the New York World's Fair via the Hudson River, Spuyten Duyvil Creek, and the Harlem and East Rivers to Flushing Bay. Fare was to be $3.50 Round Trip for adults and $1.75 for children. Two new vessels, the *Fairmaid* and the *Teresa* were built for this service and launched at the Blount Shipyard in Warren, Rhode Island on February 22nd of that year. Each measured 60 feet by 30 feet and was capable of carrying 340 passengers. The *Dolly Madison,* of similar design, was also chartered for this service. Backers of the operation were Raymond Wheeler, who was appointed President, Frances Tierney of North Bergen, who was associated with National Export Packaging Company, and Irving Maidman, President of the New York, Susquehanna & Western Railroad, which planned to operate connecting excursion trains to the dock in Edgewater. Maidman was also a principal in the Tri-Terminal corporation. Somehow this well conceived operation turned out a fiasco. The railroad never operated the excursion trains and other traffic did not materialize. The service was discontinued after only a few trips.

A bit further south of the Tri-Terminal area is the neighborhood called Shadyside, but at an earlier time Bulls Ferry or Block House Point. Bulls Ferry took its name from a family named Bull residing in the vicinity in the eighteenth century who operated a sail and row ferry. Originally the name applied to the location of Block House Point, a half mile south of present day Bulls Ferry. This was the location of a British Block House during the Revolution and several skirmishes. In later years the lessees of this ferry were Cornelius Huyler in 1788; Theodore Brower in 1792; Garret Neefie in 1805; Lewis Concklin in 1806; and Abraham Huyler in 1808. This route was used by Bergen County farmers in going to market and was located at the eastern terminus of the old Bergen Turnpike, which ran to English Neighborhood, now Englewood, and the Northern Valley. In later years this came to be called Bulls Ferry Road. With the coming of the railroads and trolley lines, this ferry gave way to other routes. By 1909 the only remaining service was as a landing on the Fort Lee & New York Steam Boat Company line to Spring Street, at which time the landing place was moved from Block House Point north to be convenient to the Shady Side Hotel.

West Shore Railroad ferryboat *Albany* approaching 42nd Street slip. (New York Central photo)

Guttenberg, a bit further south, was also a way landing for the Fort Lee & New York steamboats to Spring Street, from 1832 to about 1909. There was also a direct ferry between here and West 42nd Street, Manhattan operated by the West Shore Division of the New York Central Railroad between 1902 and 1922.

The first informal ferries were operated between Weehawken and Manhattan by Samuel Bayard in 1700. In 1742 he and Francis Kouwenhoven petitioned the Governor and Council of New York "for a ferry to Weehawk." These early boats were sail and row boats. This pioneer route was abandoned in 1834, owing to diversion of patronage to the new Hoboken steam ferry.

On March 25, 1852, the State of New Jersey granted a ferry charter to a group of nine men including Judge Francis Price and Dudley S. Gregory, the first mayor of Jersey City. These same men, on the same day, chartered the Ramapo & Weehawken Plank Road Company, to build a toll road between the said places. Ferry service commenced on New Years Day 1859 between Slough's Meadow in Weehawken and West 42nd Street. It was a miserable rainy day according to early newspaper accounts. The first two vessels were purchased second hand from the Union Ferry Company of Brooklyn. They were named *Abbie* and *Lydia,* and were sidewheel beam double-enders. Federal law precluded changing their names to *Hackensack*

Weehawken ferry terminal, c1958. (Photo Arthur G. Adams)

and *Weehawken* as originally planned. This company never enjoyed any prosperity and was discontinued in 1872 after opening of a new railroad-controlled Weehawken ferry line.

In 1871 laws were passed in both New York and New Jersey providing for the formation of the Weehawken Transportation Company, incorporated by Cornelius. A. Wortendyke, who was also President of the New Jersey Midland Railway, part of the former New York & Oswego Midland System, later to become the New York, Ontario & Western Railway. The New Jersey Midland is today's New York, Susquehanna & Western. The New Jersey Midland purchased the *Roslyn* from the Union Ferry Company of Brooklyn and ordered an entirely new vessel, the *Midland,* from Lawrence & Foulkes. She was launched on May 2, 1872 at Greenpoint, Long Island. On March 9, 1873 the Weehawken Transportation Company changed its name to the Midland Terminal & Ferry Company, and also received authority to acquire waterfront lands, build piers, and lay connecting tracks to the New Jersey Midland. On November 15, 1873 the new company took over the boats and terminals from the railroad. During the Spring of 1875 the Midland Railroad went into receivership.

During the next several years various sections of railroad were shuffled around, and three basic railroads came out of the deal: the New York, West Shore & Buffalo, running from Jersey City to Albany and Buffalo; the New York, Ontario & Western, running between Cornwall-On-Hudson and Oswego, on Lake Ontario, and reaching Jersey City via trackage rights over the West Shore; and the New Jersey Midland Railroad, now the New York, Susquehanna & Western. None of these lines had their own proper terminal on the Hudson River opposite New York, and all operated down the west side of the Palisades to Jersey City, where they gained access to the river and the ferries over the tracks of other railroads—a most unsatisfactory arrangement. Clearly it was necessary to tunnel under the Palisades from North Bergen to Weehawken and establish their own ferry lines. They operated in concert as follows:

Hoboken ferryboat *Fairy Queen,* 1827. (Author's collection)

William H. Truesdale, 6th President of the Delaware, Lackawanna & Western Railroad (1899–1925). (Author's collection)

Samuel Sloan, 5th President of the Delaware, Lackawanna & Western Railroad (1867–1899). (Author's collection)

Union Ferryboat Terminal at 23rd Street Manhattan. (Author's collection)

The Midland Terminal & Ferry Company was reorganized in 1883 as the Open Cut & General Storehouse Company, but was promptly again renamed West Shore & Ontario Terminal Company. Both the West Shore and O & W were co-guarantors of a $10,000,000 mortgage from the Central Trust Company of New York. They made a long term joint agreement covering use of terminals in Weehawken, New York, and Brooklyn. The tunnel was holed through in September of 1883 and a large new passenger terminal was built at its mouth, south of the original Slough's Meadow terminal. The Slough's Meadow to 42nd Street ferry line continued to operate until 1902, when its terminal was moved to West New York. Ferry service from the new Weehawken Terminal to 42nd Street was started on January 1st, 1884. The first scheduled train through the tunnel came through in mid-May of that year. On Sunday, June 21, 1885 a second route was opened downtown to Jay Street. This was known as the West Shore Ferry. This line operated to Jay Street until 1892, and was removed to Franklin Street in 1893. A temporary slip at West 13th Street was used during the summer of 1892. The downtown terminal was changed again in 1909 to Debrosses Street, and finally to Cortlandt Street in 1930.

The West Shore and the O & W had formed the jointly owned North River Construction Company in 1880 to complete the railroad between Weehawken and Cornwall, and to build the new terminal at Weehawken. On December 15, 1883 the two railroads signed a 99 year joint occupancy agreement and issued their first joint timetable. At the beginning, trains operated from the Pennsylvania Railroad Terminal at Exchange Place in Jersey City and ran along the western side of the Palisades from Marion Junction over the former Jersey City & Albany line.

The new Weehawken Terminal had five ferry slips and sixteen passenger tracks. The tunnel beneath the Palisades from North Bergen was 4,225 feet long. A few trains, carrying

Hoboken ferryboat *Ithaca* in drydock. Note horse incline in background.
(Photo courtesy of William H. Ewen, Jr., from the William King Covell Collection)

through cars from the south, continued to operate from the Pennsylvania Exchange Place depot, and thence north along the eastern foot of the Palisades over the New Jersey Junction Railroad to Weehawken, making a stop at Paterson Plank Road in Hoboken.

In 1885, after a disastrous rate war, the New York, West Shore & Buffalo was acquired by the New York Central and was re-incorporated as the West Shore Railroad Company.

Hoboken ferryboat *Binghamton*. (Author's collection)

Hoboken Ferry Tickets. (Author's collection)

From then until the end of operations the ferries have been controlled by the New York Central.

Prior to 1883 the New York, Ontario & Western had ordered for itself four sidewheel double-enders from Ward, Stanton & Company of Newburgh. These were large first class vessels and were named the *Oswego, Newburgh, Kingston,* and *Albany.* Cabin interiors were in Queen Anne style and had stained glass transoms over each window. As they were completed, they were swapped with the New York, West Shore & Buffalo—for ten freight locomotives.

Between 1892 and 1894 the Guttenberg Steam Railroad Division of the North Hudson County Railways contributed traffic to the West Shore ferries. An electric trolley line was

Hoboken ferryboat *Lackawanna,* c1957. (Photo Arthur G. Adams)

completed down along the cliffs parallel to Pershing Avenue in 1894, which superseded the steam railway. In 1897 the large viaduct and elevators of the steam railroad terminal were removed.

This system soon grew into one of the largest ferry operations on the Hudson. The peak year for traffic was 1927, when about 27,000,000 passengers were carried. Traffic declined steadily thereafter, except for a slight increase in 1934. The Holland Tunnel opened in 1930; the George Washington Bridge in 1931; and the Lincoln Tunnel in 1937. In 1957, when seeking to discontinue the ferries, the New York Central Railroad offered the following figures as testimony:

Year	Passengers Carried
1938	12,401,645
1946	3,514,272
1957 (9 months)	783,631

Previously, owing to poor patronage, the Cortlandt Street service had been cut back to rush hours, weekdays only, in April of 1937. Since the Second World War, the two operating routes were from Weehawken Terminal to West 42nd Street and Cortlandt Street.

Despite the great shrinkage in traffic, this remained an impressive large scale operation right up until the very end. The West Shore ferries of the later years were particularly handsome vessels, all designed by the noted marine architect, J. W. Millard. The West Shore was the last railroad ferry line to retain sidewheelers. The first screw propeller ship was the *West Point* of 1900. Originally the boats were painted white, but this later gave way to a light pea green in 1902. There was fine line detailing in red and gold with gold lettering and pilot house lanterns. The stacks were painted black. The boats were beautifully maintained, and the writer can remember as a small boy watching men wash the outside of the cabin windows with brushes on long poles while crossing the river. There was a long cable stretched alongside under the outsides of the window sills and the men walked on the narrow guards.

The last group of boats were all very fast and averaged just slightly under 200 feet in length and 40 feet breadth with 16 feet depth, at an average of 1,350 gross tons. The following boats were built in Newburgh: *West Point* (1900); *Syracuse* (1903); *Rochester* (1905); *Niagara* (1912); *Utica* (1910); and *Catskill* (1914). The *Weehawken* (1914) and *Stony Point* (1917) were built at Wilmington, and the *Albany* (1925) at Mariners Harbor, Staten Island.

I travelled on all these boats innumerable times in all kinds of weather and at all times of year, and writing this list is like recalling the names and personalities of long-departed dear friends. The *Albany* was the only boat designed for possible conversion to upper-deck loading, which was never used on this line, although contemplated at one time. Each of the boats could accommodate 1,600 passengers and 18 automobiles.

After lengthy hearings and a strongly contested legal battle the New York Central was allowed to discontinue the ferries. The last trips were as follows: The *Utica* left West 42nd Street at 12:45 AM on Wednesday, March 25, 1959. The *Stony Point* left Cortlandt Street at 6:00 PM on Tuesday, March 24, 1959. The last eastbound trip was the 1:10 AM departure of the *Weehawken* for West 42nd Street early on the morning of Wednesday, March 25, 1959—closing out 259 years of service. This was the largest single ferry closing on the Hudson up until that time.

The next day patronage on the West Shore trains dropped from 3,500 daily riders to only 549. The end of the ferry also sealed the fate of the West Shore passenger trains, owing to lack of any other good connection to Manhattan from the Weehawken Terminal. The Citizens United Transit Committee had previously interested the Hudson River Day Line in taking over the operation, but they lost interest when the railroad asked for $58,000 annual

Lackawanna Railroad ferryboat *Ithaca* of 1905 approaching slip at Hoboken.
(Courtesy Raymond J. Baxter)

rental for use of a slip at Weehawken. The railroad did not wish this as it would prolong use of the trains which they also wanted to eliminate. The whole procedure was a brutal "axe job," from which the communities served have never fully recovered.

In addition to the ferries, the New York Central also operated a large fleet of lighters, tugs, and carfloats in New York Harbor. The New York Central Marine Shops were located in the north end of Weehawken, near the former Guttenberg-West New York ferry terminal. The Central performed all their own repairs, including drydocking of the large ferries. When the ferries stopped running 85 employees were put out of work. Despite competition from bridge and tunnels, the potential traffic was so substantial and tunnel traffic jams of such frequent and onerous occurrence, that, given proper operation and promotion, this line could have been kept in operation indefinitely. The fact is that the New York Central Railroad was getting into very deep financial troubles and did not wish to spend scarce capital on upgrading and expanding what was, to them, a marginal operation. It was simpler to discourage its use and liquidate the operation entirely. With the construction of many large new apartment houses atop the Palisades, it is again being agitated that the line should be restored, possibly under a public operating authority. However, all the boats are gone, as are all the terminals, and the next incarnation will have to be from scratch. If history provides any key to the future, it is likely that this, and certain other of the more important routes, will again be back in operation within the decade.

Between November 8, 1926 and July 31, 1943, the Electric Ferry Company operated a line from the Undercliff section of Weehawken, at the foot of Baldwin Avenue, to West 23rd Street, Manhattan. These diesel electric boats, which later operated on the 125th Street and Brooklyn to Staten Island routes were designed principally to carry automobiles. This route

Jay Gould, President
of the Erie Railroad.
(Author's collection)

picked up "overflow" traffic from the West Shore and Hoboken ferry lines, and remained in profitable operation for five years after the opening of the Lincoln Tunnel, although their Weehawken Terminal was situated only one block from the entrance to the tunnel! The line was discontinued principally because the Electric Ferry Company found more profitable use for their vessels on the Edgewater-125th Street Line, which they had just acquired from the Public Service Company.

Between 1796 and 1806 Barnet DeKlyn and John Towne operated a ferry to Hoboken from the wharf near the State Prison at Spring Street in Manhattan.

By 1884 various streetcar lines were operating north and west from the north end of Hoboken. The Hoboken Ferry Company established a line from 14th Street, Hoboken to 14th Street, Manhattan on May 30, 1886, with the *James Rumsey* and the *Morristown*. In 1903 the Manhattan terminal was moved to West 23rd Street, and the line was acquired by the Lackawanna Railroad in 1905. Boats on this line included the *Hoboken, Buffalo,* and *Bergen*—all single-deck boats which could accommodate 589 passengers and 24 automobiles. The line closed on April 26, 1942 because the site of the Hoboken landing was required for expansion of a neighboring shipbuilding firm that was building ships for the war effort.

Hoboken is truly the birthplace of the steam ferry. However, long before the practical introduction of the steamboats, the Elysian Fields in Hoboken were a popular pleasure resort for New Yorkers, who came hither in all kinds of small boats for a day's outing. The first charter for a regular ferry operation was granted to Hermanus Talman in 1774. The ferry was then known as the Horsimus Ferry, after a small creek in the south end of Hoboken, which was then virtually an island. This early row and sail operation was given importance by the establishment of a stage line to New Bridge, near Hackensack, by Andrew Van Buskirk in 1775. Van Buskirk was a notorious Loyalist during the Revolution and this line ran through an area more or less under British control. In 1784 John Van Allen purchased the franchise but Sylvanus Lawrence acquired it at auction for thirty-seven pounds, but could not raise the money and defaulted on the franchise.

For the period from 1789 to 1791 Colonel John Stevens purchased the ferry rights. He owned considerable waterfront property in Hoboken and wished to make it more accessible for real estate development purposes. In 1799 the franchise was in the hands of Joseph Smith who operated a periauger. In 1802 the Bergen Turnpike was extended from Bulls Ferry to Hoboken Ferry, and in 1808 the ferry was leased to David Goodwin. However, in 1810 John Stevens again had control and, in 1811, his new steam ferryboat *Juliana* was operated on the route to Vesey Street, and later to Spring Street. Actual operation was farmed out to David Goodwin. Stevens withdrew the *Juliana* in 1813 in order to avoid conflict with the Fulton-Livingston monopoly, and the *Juliana* was sent to Connecticut and dismantled. The Hoboken Ferry was the first regularly scheduled steam ferry line anywhere in the world.

In 1814 the line reverted to the use of periaugers and Moses Rodgers' horseboats. This continued for only a relatively short time, as Fulton and Stevens soon worked out a licensing arrangement which allowed the Hoboken line to return to steam operation.

Erie Railroad ferryboat *Meadville* of 1936 approaching slip at Jersey City about 1950.
(Courtesy Raymond J. Baxter)

Erie Railroad Terminal at Jersey City about 1940. Erie Railroad Photo. (Courtesy Raymond J. Baxter)

In 1817 Colonel Stevens sold his lease to John, Robert, and Samuel Swartwout. The boats operated briefly to Murray Street, but on June 18, 1818 they commenced running to Barclay Street, which was to remain the final steam ferry line operating on the Hudson River in 1967. Talman's line of 1774 had also operated from Barclay Street.

Philip Hone held the lease from 1818 to 1819, and in September of 1819 he was also granted a franchise to operate to Christopher Street. In May of 1821 Colonel John Stevens and Robert L. Stevens repurchased the lease, and on November 3, 1821 formed the Hoboken Steamboat Ferry Company. They put the steam ferryboat *Hoboken (1)* into operation on May 11, 1822. The *Hoboken (1)* was 98 feet long, 200 tons burden, and operated at 9 miles per hour. In July 1823 they opened another line to Spring Street and to Canal Street with the *Pioneer,* in September of the year.

In July of 1836 the Stevens family started a new line to Christopher Street, and the lines to Spring Street and Canal Street were discontinued shortly thereafter. The first night boat was operated in 1856.

Some early boats were the *Fairy Queen,* which replaced the last horseboat on the Canal Street run in 1825; the *Newark* (1828); the *Passaic* (1844); the *John Fitch* (1846); the *James Rumsey* (1846); and the *Paterson* (1854). The *James Rumsey* was destroyed by fire in her Barclay Street slip in 1853, but her engines were salvaged and used in the *Paterson.*

The *James Watt* of 1851 was also destroyed by fire in 1870. The *Chancellor Livingston* of 1853 was chartered by the United States Government for one year in 1861 and used as a transport. The *Hoboken* (2) of 1861 was taken by the government and lost in the Burnside Expedition that same year. The *Hoboken* (3) was built in 1863.

The Stevens started a new line to West 14th Street Manhattan on May 30, 1886. In January of 1896 the Stevens sold their interests to the Hoboken Land & Improvement Company, controlled by Roswell Eldridge and Lewis A. Eldridge, who had previously operated the Astoria and Long Island Rail Road ferries on the East River. In 1903 the Eldridges established a line between the Lackawanna Railroad terminal in Hoboken and West 23rd Street, Manhattan. This line is not to be confused with the line between West 23rd Street Manhattan and 14th Street Hoboken, which, in later years, was also operated by the Lackawanna Railroad.

In December 1904 the Hoboken Land & Improvement Company sold all their ferry lines to the Delaware, Lackawanna & Western Railroad. John M. Emery was appointed Superintendent of the Ferry Department and Benjamin Schoppe was appointed Chief Engineer. William H. Truesdale, President of the Lackawanna, determined to operate the ferries to the highest standards.

In 1905 he commenced building the present massive ferry and railroad terminal, completed in 1907. It is built entirely on piles over twenty feet depth of water and has a total river frontage of 566 feet. It has fourteen railroad tracks, and its six ferry slips have provision for upper deck loading. There are grand concourses leading directly into the palatial railroad waiting room. There was a fine dining room in the ferry terminal, on a level with Delmonico's or Sherry's in Manhattan. This restaurant was popular with high society. The forty foot high ceilings were supported by Ionic columns and pilasters. The building had a steel frame, embedded in concrete to inhibit corrosion, and was sheathed with copper, which turned an attractive green weathering in the salt atmosphere. The entire structure was surmounted by a 203 foot high campanile and clock tower modeled after that of St. Marks in Venice. This stood until the 1940s when it was feared that the supporting pilings were giving way and it was removed. The Union Ferry Terminal at West 23rd Street, Manhattan, used by the Lackawanna, was of similar construction and also had a clock tower of similar design. The Hoboken Terminal still dominates the waterfront and is presently the beneficiary of a $4 million restoration program and has been designated, by its present owner, the State of New Jersey, as an historic building. It is the East Coast's counterpart of the Market Street

Erie Railroad ferryboat *Jamestown* of 1907 entering middle slip at Jersey City about 1945.
(Courtesy Raymond J. Baxter)

Ferry Terminal in San Francisco. Much of the technology used in its construction was developed by E. W. Stern, members of the Stevens family, and Lincoln Bush, Chief Engineer of the Lackawanna Railroad. The architect was Kenneth M. Murchison. The restored building was rededicated on October 3, 1981.

The facility was capable of handling vast amounts of traffic. In 1948, well after bridges, tunnels, and subways had eaten into traffic, the Lackawanna ferries handled 15,000,000 passengers in fifteen boats. In that same year the West Shore ferries handled 11,000,000 passengers in eight boats, according to ICC statistics. This conflicts with the testimony, described above, which the New York Central gave of handling only 3,500,000 in 1946. The lower figure probably represents only passengers using both train and ferry and does not include those reaching the boats by other means than train. In any event, this will give an idea of the volumes handled on the larger ferry lines.

When considering such vast volumes of traffic it is interesting to consider that the Hudson River ferries handled it with extremely little injury or loss of life to passengers. The Hoboken Ferry Company and the Hudson River Day Line probably handled more deck passengers during their combined histories than any other steamboat lines in the world. They handled them in ships of wooden superstructures and operating with only primitive navigational aides and on extremely congested waters in all kinds of weather, including dense fog, and while maintaining fast and demanding schedules. Their ships were registered to carry more passengers than any ocean liners. The *Washington Irving* of the Day Line had the largest certificate ever issued to any ship for over 4000 passengers. Neither line ever labored under the delusion that they operated "unsinkable ships."...and neither line ever suffered a catastrophic loss of lives. Intelligent attendance to duty and safety precautions, and great pride in their operations on the part of everyone from deckhand to corporation president counted for more than the most expensive and elaborate safety devices.

Erie Railroad Ferry Terminal at Chambers Street and West Street, Manhattan. Note small "dinky" trolley car. Erie Railroad photo. (Raymond J. Baxter Collection)

In the early years of operation service was provided by sidewheel double-enders such as the *Musconetcong* (1885), *Paunpeck* (1882), and *Secaucus* (1873). They were all painted white with the usual trimmings. The Hoboken Ferry was a pioneer line to use screw ships, starting with the *Bergen* of 1888. The boats of the later years averaged a little over 200 feet in length by 43 feet breadth by 17 feet deep, and weighed in at an average of 1,400 gross tons. In the final years of operation the most famous of their large fleet were the "four sisters" built in Newport News in 1904 and 1905. They were the *Scranton,* the *Pocono,* the *Elmira,* and the *Binghamton.* They all remained hand fired coal burners up until the end of service. The

Erie Railroad ferryboat *Youngstown* of 1922. (Photo by Raymond J. Baxter)

West Street, Manhattan showing ferry and steamship piers c1900. (Smith's New York Harbor Guide)

Binghamton is now preserved as Binghamton's Restaurant at Edgewater, New Jersey.

The flagship of the fleet was the *Lackawanna,* which was extensively rebuilt and dieselized in 1949, the year the Lackawanna Railroad inaugurated its new streamlined train the *Phoebe Snow* to Buffalo and Chicago. The *Lackawanna* was originally built in 1891 as the steamboat *Hamburg.* She was later renamed *Chatham,* prior to 1949. The *Pocono* had been originally called the *Scandinavia,* when built in 1905. In 1958 there was a consolidation of services with the Erie Railroad and the *Youngstown,* and *Meadville* of the Erie Line were renamed *Chatham* and *Maplewood* when put into service on the Hoboken Ferry. An unusual event in the history of the line took place in 1909 when two boats abandoned their regular route and raced to Newburgh and back.

The first routes to be discontinued were the uptown ones. The Hoboken Terminal to 23rd Street line was discontinued on December 31, 1946. On March 30, 1955 the *Buffalo* closed out service on the Christopher Street run, but the Barclay Street route seemed a permanent institution. Long after all the other Hudson River ferriers were discontinued, the Barclay Street Ferry continued on its appointed rounds. During its last years the line was known as the Erie-Lackawanna Ferry. However, the end came on November 22, 1967. The last two boats in operation were the *Lackawanna* and the *Elmira.* All that afternoon they blew their steam whistles in memorium. While champagne was drunk onboard the ferries, fire boats flung water high in the air in the traditional farewell, and police boats blew sirens. A bugler played taps on board the *Elmira.* At 5:45 PM the 62-year-old steamboat *Elmira* sailed out of Barclay Street for the last time, ending 156 years of steam ferry operation—the first and last steam ferry on the Hudson.

Just below Hoboken, a primitive sail and row ferry operated for a few years starting in 1802 from Budd's Dock in Harsimus Cove to Manhattan. It never used steamboats.

In 1733 King George II of England granted a ferry franchise to Archibald Kennedy to operate a ferry from Pavonia to Manhattan. However, this service was never implemented on a continuing basis until the Pavonia Ferry, Inc. was formed by the New York & Erie

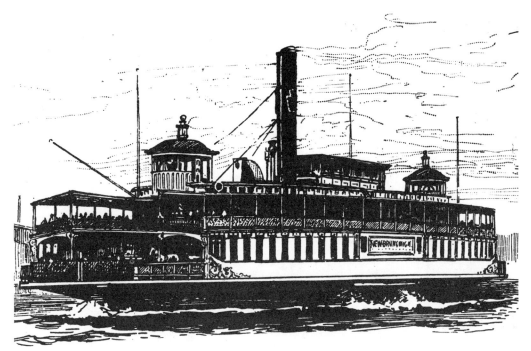

Pennsylvania Railroad ferryboat *New Brunswick*. (Courtesy Raymond J. Baxter)

Cabin of Pennsylvania Railroad ferryboat *New Brunswick*. (Courtesy Raymond J. Baxter)

Railroad elevation across Newark and Railroad Avenues in Jersey City leading to Pennsylvania Exchange Place Depot. (Courtesy Raymond J. Baxter)

Pennsylvania Railroad Ferry Terminal and Bridge Across West Street, Manhattan at corner of Cortlandt Street c1880. (Courtesy Raymond J. Baxter)

Railroad Company in 1849 to take over the ancient charter. At that time the Erie was operating to a terminal at Piermont, with a steamer connection to Duane Street, Manhattan. Completion of the Paterson & Hudson River Railroad and the Paterson & Ramapo Railroad, forming a through line of travel from Suffern, on the Erie's main line, to Jersey City, skimmed off much of the Erie's through traffic. Therefore, the Erie ultimately took over these other lines as part of a new direct all-rail route to Jersey City. Homer Ramsdell, who was to serve as Erie President from 1853 to 1857, was a Director during this period. He began purchasing over two hundred acres of waterfront property in the Pavonia section of the Fourth Ward of Jersey City in his own name, in order to head off speculation.

After signing of leases for the short New Jersey railroads on September 10, 1852, the Erie incorporated the Long Dock Company in New Jersey to build adequate freight and passenger terminals. The charter provided that they must spend $100,000 within five years on these improvements. The plan included a 8000 foot double-track tunnel under Bergen Hill. This was begun on June 1, 1856, but not completed until February 6, 1861. James P. Kirkwood was the principal construction engineer. The project cost fifty-seven lives.

In 1859 the New York & Erie Railroad Company became formal lessees of the Long Dock Company, and the Pavonia Ferry Company. Ferry service began on May 1, 1861, after completion of the tunnel under Bergen Hill. Initially it used three old Brooklyn ferryboats: *Onala, Niagara,* and *Onalaska.* Shortly thereafter the Erie acquired three elegant boats of its own: the *Pavonia* (1861); the *Susquehanna* (1864); and the *Delaware* (1865). The service operated to Chambers Street, and left there "By the hour of St. Paul's Clock," according to an early advertisement.

In 1868 the Erie discontinued its Duane Street to Piermont steamers, but opened a new ferry line from Pavonia to 23rd Street, Manhattan, with the elegant new steam ferries, *Jay Gould, James Fisk, Jr.* and *Erie.* In the 1890s the palatial *Orange* was added to the fleet. It had decorations by Louis Comfort Tiffany.

These were exciting, and rather scandalous days for the Erie. In 1868 the Erie was in the control of Daniel Drew, Jay Gould, and Jim Fisk. The newly completed line represented a distinct threat to Commodore Cornelius Vanderbilt's newly completed New York Central & Hudson River Railroad. Vanderbilt wanted to "buy in" on the Erie in order to defuse this threat. Drew, Gould, and Fisk decided to let the good Commodore buy all the stock he wanted. They purchased a printing press and put it in the cellar of the Duane Street offices, and started printing unauthorized stock certificates, which Vanderbilt just kept buying up. This seriously disrupted the legitimate market for Erie stock. By March 11th, Vanderbilt had spent in excess of $8,000,000 for these "worthless" certificates, and had called in the law, in the form of Judge George G. Barnard, of the New York State Southern District Court. Warrants were issued for a search of the Erie offices, seizure of company records, and funds, and arrest of Drew, Gould, and Fisk. However, the Erie directors had gotten wind of this impending storm of legal action and, during the day, had started moving all the trunks full of money and records across the Chambers Street Ferry to a block of rooms rented at Taylor's Hotel next to the Jersey City Terminal, where they intended to establish new offices outside of Judge Barnard's jurisdictions.

By supper time all the money and records had been removed, but Fisk and Gould felt brave enough to go to dine at Delmonico's Restaurant at Broadway and Chambers Street. During the main course, they were tipped off that the police were about to move in and arrest them. They ducked out a side door and took a cab, *not* to the Chambers Street Ferry dock, where they would be sure to be apprehended, but to the Canal Street dock where Drew's Hudson River Night Boat, the *St. John,* was tied up. They bribed an officer of the ship to let down a lifeboat, manned by two sturdy oarsmen, to row them across to Jersey City. Mr. Fisk directed the men to head up the river, to keep out of the track of the ferry boats, but the fog

Pennsylvania Railroad ferryboat *St. Louis.* (Pennsylvania RR photo) Raymond J. Baxter Collection

was so thick that they lost their reckoning and rowed for some time in a circle. They were at one time nearly run down, only saving themselves by the vigorous use of their lungs. Once they escaped from one ferry boat, only to see another bearing down upon them. Hopelessly lost in mid-river, they hailed another ferry, but could not make themselves heard. They made a clutch at the support struts of the guard, and were drawn so near the paddlewheel as to nearly wash the whole party out of the small boat. However, they saved her from swamping, and climbed on board the ferry boat, arriving shortly thereafter at Jersey City, safe and sound, but thoroughly drenched. Undoubtedly this is one of the most bizzare ferry trips on record.

After much legal warfare, and some actual physical fighting by platoons of hired thugs, the "Erie War" calmed down, and the "Captains of Erie," as they were publicly called, were free to return to Manhattan. It was in that same year, in May, that they opened the second ferry route to West 23rd Street. This route was not chosen at random. At that time 23rd Street was the center of the theatrical life of New York and of many flashy cabarets. Fisk was a true playboy in every sense of the word. He had taken a lease on the elegant Pike's Opera House, on the corner of Eighth Avenue and 23rd Street, and proceeded to produce light opera by such composers as Offenbach, Strauss, and Sullivan. What is more, he moved the offices of the Erie into the opera house itself, and installed his paramour Josie Mansfield in an adjoining Brownstone, having a direct passage to the Erie offices in the opera house. Obviously, he had to have easy access to his private railroad car on a siding at the Jersey City Terminal, in which he and Miss Mansfield took frequent little trips up the Erie to the Orange Hotel at Turner's Station, near present day Harriman for supper and "conversation." The Orange Hotel was a "hot pillow" establishment and was owned by the Erie. It was located across from the station and the Erie had paid $350,000 for it. The building was 400 feet long and built of brick and was three stories in height. The Erie occupied part of the ground floor for general offices, but the hotel complex, which was very lavish with a dining room on the ground floor and a second one for "special" hotel guests on the second, was used largely to entertain politicians and large shippers. Here Fisk and others staged wild parties, coming up from New York on special trains for the weekend. It faded into disuse when Fisk and Gould lost control of the Erie and burned down on December 26, 1873, leaving only gaping external brick walls, which were finally torn down in 1878. I have a letter from Mr. Gerald Best which says that his grandfather, who worked for the Erie in Port Jervis, told him that, in the early 1870s he went down there several times to see the "goings-on," which he said were too racy for small boys to hear about. He said it was impossible to sleep on a Saturday night at the Orange Hotel on account of the noise coming from the various parties in the rooms on his floor. Indeed the Erie was a lively firm in those days.

While the Erie was not paying dividends, Fisk was using company funds to subsidize operatic spectacles and his own personal high living. Factions soon formed to attempt to oust him from control. Stockholders complained that the young company clerks were ogling ballet dancers in the offices on company time. This extravagance was extended to the appointments of the new 176 foot long ferry boats on the 23rd Street run. The *Jay Gould* and the *James Fisk, Jr.* each sported life-size oil portraits of their patrons at either end of the grand saloon. As neither was considered genuinely illustrious by the public, this gave rise to much comment. The railroad offered free omnibus service between the ferry and the Fifth Avenue Hotel, with a stop at the Grand Opera House. All this came to an end when Jim Fisk was shot on January 6, 1872 by Ned Stokes, another of Miss Mansfield's admirers. The Grand Opera House burned down on June 29, 1960. The Erie's 23rd Street Ferry was discontinued on July 5, 1942, and only the Chambers Street line remained.

The Jersey City Terminal was itself a marvel for its time. It boasted every possible facility, including an interpreter who spoke thirteen languages, and public stenographers, barbers, fine restaurants, and much elaborate woodwork. The original terminal opened in May 1861, and the second in 1886. A terrific rush hour traffic poured through this terminal. In 1946, during the evening rush hour between 5:05 PM and 6:05 PM thirty trains departed and two arrived; twenty-eight sets of equipment were backed into the station, and during one forty-

Entrance to Pennsylvania Railroad Ferry at Exchange Place, Jersey City, 1907.
(Raymond J. Baxter Collection)

one minute period twenty-four trains left Jersey City. During this period the traffic was handled with a 99% on-time performance—absolute, to the minute on-time...a skill which modern American railroads seem to have lost. Each day this total traffic was handled by sixty-one trains, six gas-electric cars, fifty-five locomotives, and two hundred and fifty-five coaches of eighty-four seat capacity. Trains ranged in length from two to nine cars, and carried between fifty and eight hundred passengers each.

Pennsylvania R. R. Company's double-ended Drill tug working in Jersey City slip.
(Author's collection)

Another very ancient route was the Paulus Hook, or Powles Hook, ferry. This section of Jersey City, which was originally separated from the mainland by tidal marshes, was named for Michael Paulusen, who established a trading post here in 1633. There was a British fort here during the Revolution. It was connected with the mainland by a wooden bridge at an early date, and soon its strategic location at the end of the Hudson River proper, and above the head of Newark and Upper New York Bay, made it the principal route of overland travel between New York City and Philadelphia. The first sail and row ferry was chartered in 1764, operating to Mesier's Dock at the foot of present day Cortlandt Street. It was operated by Cornelius Van Voorst in 1767. In 1768 Andrew Van Buskirk was operating a line of stages from here to New Bridge, near Hackensack. This line of "Flying Machines" ran twice a week, pulled by four or six horses, and had a two-shilling-sixpence fare.

In 1775 the patriotic Jeredine Elsworth took over this operation from the Tory Van Buskirk and also ran the ferry. In 1794 Colonel John Stevens of Hoboken completed a plank road to Newark which had been authorized in 1765. In 1811 Colonel Stevens also took the lease on the ferry. In March of 1814 the Paulus Hook Ferry Company was organized, but almost immediately changed its name to, York & Jersey Steamboat Ferry Company. This was the line operated by Robert Fulton, with the financial backing of Elisha Boudinot of Newark and Nicholas Roosevelt of Manhattan. The first two boats were the *Jersey* and the *York,* described in chapter twelve.

In 1824 this line was controlled by Francis B. Ogden, Cadwallader D. Colden, and Samuel Swartwout—all affiliates of Fulton and Livingston. The *Washington* was put into service in 1826 and the *Jersey City* in 1827. The line was renamed the Jersey City Ferry in 1836, upon formal incorporation of that municipality. After the breaking of the steamboat monopoly the ferry line came under the control of the New Jersey Railroad & Transportation Company by lease in 1841. They operated the *Essex, Sussex, Washington,* and *New Jersey.* The operation was purchased outright by the railroad in 1853. Up until this time service was operated only to the foot of Cortlandt Street, but on August 1, 1862 another line was opened to

Desbrosses Street. This was known as the Branch Ferry. In 1856 a large new terminal had been built by the railroad in Jersey City. On January 9, 1880 an additional line was opened from there to West 34th Street using the *Mechanic.* In 1881 the *Camden,* formerly of the Camden & Philadelphia Ferryboat Co., was added to the line. On August 8, 1877 General Butterfield opened an independent line operating from this terminal to the foot of Fulton Street, Brooklyn, using steam single-enders. Double enders were put on in March of 1888, and the Brooklyn Annex Ferry, as it was called, operated until November 29, 1910. Around 1935 the Pennsylvania Railroad ran a ferry from here to Atlantic Avenue, Brooklyn. On May 16, 1897 another railroad-owned line opened from Exchange Place Terminal to West 23rd Street Manhattan, using the large double enders *St. Louis* and *Pittsburgh.*

In 1871 the Pennsylvania Railroad acquired the New Jersey Railroad, and also the ferry operations. Exchange Place, as Paulus Hook was then called, now became the busiest terminal on the Jersey shore of the Hudson, and in 1890 the railroad erected a four track elevated structure from near Journal Square to Exchange Place to get the trains off the Jersey City streets. It was three fifths of a mile long and very heavily constructed. This was torn down in the 1960s, at which time it was used only by local freight trains. Typical ferries at the turn of the century were very ornate. The *New Brunswick* had fine friezes and bas-reliefs in rare woods in its passenger cabins. Other boats of this era were the *Washington (2)* and the *St. Louis,* which boasted Corinthian capitals on the pillars supporting the upper deck loading ramps. Ferries of later date were more Spartan.

In 1909 the Pennsylvania Railroad completed its tunnel into Pennsylvania Station in Manhattan. That same year the Hudson & Manhattan Railroad completed its subway tunnel from Exchange Place, Jersey City, to downtown Manhattan. The Pennsylvania Ferries lost most of their traffic overnight. The Brooklyn Annex Ferry was discontinued on November 29, 1910, and the 23rd Street Ferry on November 30, 1910. The Desbrosses Street route

Approaching Central Railroad of New Jersey Liberty Street Terminal. Ferryboat *Bound Brook* is in upper slip waiting to depart for Jersey City. (Raymond J. Baxter Collection)

Central Railroad of New Jersey ferryboat with Baltimore & Ohio train connection limousine bus. Date unknown. (Raymond J. Baxter Collection)

lasted until January 21, 1930. The later c1935 line to Atlantic Avenue, Brooklyn was operated primarily for automobile and truck traffic rather than as a connection for railroad passengers. However, the Cortlandt Street route lingered on, as it served some local electric commuter trains terminating at Exchange Place, as well as the plush club car special train, the *Broker* of the New York & Long Branch Railroad. This operated on an express schedule to the Jersey Shore and carried both club and open observation cars, and was pulled by a steam locomotive which could not operate into Penn Station without a delaying change to an electric locomotive. It provided the fastest service between Wall Street and the plush suburbs of Monmouth County. The Pennsylvania boats were painted the traditional Pennsylvania Railroad Tuscan Red, with gold trim and lanterns. In their later years these boats operated on only one boiler and travelled at a sluggish pace and became rather dowdy. There was provision for upper deck loading. The final trip was made on December 31, 1949, closing out 135 years operation of one of the first steam ferries across the Hudson. The Exchange Place Terminal was demolished in the 1950s.

Furthest downstream of the Hudson River ferries proper was the Communipaw Ferry. In 1609 Michael Pauw had established a trading post in this area at the mouth of the Hudson upon the Upper Bay. In 1661 the New Netherland Council granted authority to William Jansen to operate a periauger ferry from Manhattan to Communipaw for one year. This was under the administration of Peter Stuyvesant. In 1664, under the English, Governor Richard Nicolls authorized Pieter Hetfelsen to operate this ferry. Governor Carteret of New Jersey stipulated that the ferry always operate on Monday, Wednesday and Friday, and established rates for passengers, corn, beer, horses, swine, and sheep—but none for vehicles of any kind. The passenger fare was 12ᶜ which could be paid in coin or wampum. A horse or ox cost $1.60. In later years this line fell into disuse with the establishment of the Paulus Hook Ferry, and was discontinued in 1786.

During the 1860s the Central Railroad of New Jersey extended its line eastward from Elizabethport, crossing Newark Bay on a long bridge to the Bayonne Peninsula near Bergen Point. Thence it ran up the peninsula to Communipaw. They built a mile-long trestle out to a mud flat in Communipaw Bay and thereon built a two-slip ferry terminal. Eventually the land between the terminal and the mainland was filled in and covered with railroad yards. No trace of the trestle now remains. The old ferry steamer route from Elizabethport to Pier 2, North River, via the Kill Van Kull, with stops at Bergen Point and Mariner's Harbor, was also continued until the 1880s, using the steamers *Kill Van Kull* and *Chancellor.*

The new ferry's Manhattan terminal was established at Liberty Street, and remained there up until the end of service. The first trip was on Friday, July 29, 1864 with the new double-ended ferryboat *Central,* commanded by Captain Charles A. Woolsey. President Johnson of the Jersey Central threw an elaborate party aboard the vessel, serving Champagne and claret, and with banquet tables loaded with food running the length of the team gangways. There were many speeches and a good time was had by all.

On November 18, 1876 a passenger train which was not equipped with air brakes shot through the Communipaw terminal and the locomotive plunged into the river via an empty ferry slip. A freakishly similar accident happened in the 1960s when a Jersey Central passenger train shot through the open draw bridge over Newark Bay and into deep water, causing many fatalities.

Another route to Clarkson Street Manhattan was tried between September 1876 and May 10, 1877, but was discontinued because of lack of patronage. Around the turn of the century the Jersey Central came under the control of the Baltimore & Ohio Railroad and began handling their through trains into Jersey City, as well as those of the affiliated Philadelphia & Reading Railroad. About this same time the trains of the Lehigh Valley Railroad and the New York & Newark Railroad needed a better terminal facility. In 1902 a new joint terminal

Central Railroad of New Jersey Liberty Street Terminal icebound with ferryboat *Cranford* of 1905 in upper slip behind CNJ tugboat *Newark*. West Shore Railroad ferryboat *Niagara* is in the adjacent slip. (Raymond J. Baxter Collection)

was established at the foot of Johnston Avenue. The present large terminal complex was opened in April of 1914. The train shed measured 818 feet by 370 feet and had 18 tracks with Bush Train Sheds. The train concourse measured 383 feet by 75 feet, and the upper level 302 feet by 50 feet. The upper level provided for direct communication between the upper deck of ferry boats and trains by ramps and escalators. Four double-decked steel buildings adjoined the ferry slips to accommodate the baggage room, mail room, local ferry waiting room and stationary department. This entire enlarged service was operated with great elegance. The main building of the Jersey City terminal resembles a great French Chateau, with its Mansard roof, cupola, and gilded steeple. It has been completely renovated and refurbished for use as a visitors center to the new Liberty State Park.

A large new ferry terminal was also built at Liberty Street. It was a steel frame building covered with copper with Neo-classic motifs. Stationmaster Ross Appleton presided wearing white gloves, a high starched collar, and a swallow-tailed coat until the 1930s. Two porters passed face towels in the mens room, and, lest the passengers step in the mire, all horse-drawn vehicles were followed by a porter with a broom and shovel. The outside had fluted neo-classic pillasters and columns with ornamental cornices. The great two story high waiting room had rosewood Ionic columns with ornamented cornices and friezes. The brass door handles were polished daily, and the tiffany glass skylight was vacuumed twice a week. The Jersey City terminal had five slips, and the Liberty Street two—all equipped for upper deck loading.

For a number of years, because of inadequate slip space at Liberty Street, a route was operated from Jersey City to the Whitehall Street Terminal of the Staten Island Railway. This facilitated upper deck transfer to the elevated trains in Manhattan without entering the streets. The route was called the Royal Blue Ferry. Service was instituted on July 19, 1897, using the *Easton* and the *Mauch Chunk*. On June 14, 1901, the *Mauch Chunk,* about to enter the east slip at Whitehall street, rammed and sank the Staten Island ferryboat *Northfield,* which was just pulling out with a heavy load of passengers. Only four were killed, but the *Northfield* was virtually demolished. About 1905 the City of New York acquired the Staten Island Ferry, and the Royal Blue Line became an unwelcome tenant at Whitehall Street. The final trip operated on Saturday, June 24, 1905.

To replace this service a single slip terminal was established at the Union Ferry Terminal at West 23rd Street. This was then an important commercial artery with good surface transit connections to other stations, ferries, and hotels. The *Red Bank* made the first trip on this new route on Sunday morning, June 25, 1905. Because of shrinking patronage, the West

Central Railroad of New Jersey ferryboat *Bound Brook* of 1901 heading up river to 23rd Street, off Harborside Terminal, Jersey City, prior to November 1941. (Raymond J. Baxter Collection)

23rd Street route was discontinued on November 14, 1941, leaving only the Liberty Street route.

Until as late as the 1950s such famous trains as the *Queen of the Valley, Blue Comet,* and *Harrisburger* of the Jersey Central, and the *Crusader* and *Wall Street* of the Philadelphia & Reading, and the long distance *Capitol Limited, National Limited, Shenandoah,* and the *Royal Blues* of the Baltimore & Ohio all operated into Jersey City. These trains ran to such distant points as Chicago, St. Louis, and Louisville, with through cars to New Orleans and the west coast. The B & O provided a DeLuxe limousine bus service to various convenient stations in Brooklyn and Manhattan connecting with all through trains. Buses would drive alongside the train and the baggage was transferred directly to the bus, which was then driven aboard the ferry. The passengers boarded the ferry on foot for the short and scenic crossing. Upon reaching New York the passengers boarded the buses to be driven to the various local stations. Many of the through trains were strictly first class, offering parlor, Pullman, and full dining sevices, and operating with observation cars, and Vista Dome cars west of Washington. Many were streamlined with uniformly painted equipment. This was the last of the great New Jersey terminals serving truly DeLuxe long haul trains with a ferry connection. In the 1950s the Jersey Central discontinued its longer routes, and the Baltimore & Ohio cut back service to only west of Baltimore and Washington, eliminating through service to Philadelphia and New York. The Reading's *Crusader* and *Wall Street* continued to run to Jersey City as long as the ferry operated, and then were rerouted to Penn Station in Newark, where they presently terminate, using a PATH subway connection to lower Manhattan.* All ferry service finally ended on Tuesday, April 25, 1967, closing out 306 years of ferry service. At that time the line was carrying only 11,000 daily passengers in four vessels, each of which could accommodate 1470 passangers and 14 vehicles on each trip.

Possibly the service is not finally dead, as there are negotiations with City and State planners to re-establish a passenger only steamboat service in this area in conjunction with the new Liberty State Park. The views are highly interesting and scenic and such service will be a tourist attraction as well as a convenience.**

The ferry crossing took eight minutes. Among the better known of the later day steam ferries on the line were the *Red Bank* (1902), the *Wilkes-Barre* (1904), the *Cranford* (1905), the *Somerville* (1906), and the *Elizabeth* (1901), originally called the *Lakewood.* All these boats were built in Wilmington, Delaware, by the firm of Harlan & Hollingsworth. They had an average gross tonnage of 1197 gt, and were all screw driven. They averaged 191 feet long by 44 feet wide, by 16 feet deep. They all carried radar and could operate in dense fog. Towards the end of operations the steamers were layed up and two Diesel-electric ferries, formerly used on the Staten Island to Brooklyn route were used. They were the *Tides* and the *Narrows,* and have been described elsewhere in this chapter.

Originally all the boats were painted white, and the early boats, such as the *Central* (1863), *Communipaw* (1863), *Elizabeth* (1867), *Plainfield* (1869), and *Fanwood* (1876) were sidewheelers. In 1884 the *Communipaw* was painted cream, but in later years all the boats were painted in two tones of green with white pilot houses and lettering. Stacks were black with the red Statue of Liberty insignia of the Jersey Central Lines. There were the usual golden lanterns atop the pilot houses. The steamers burned coal. The *Cranford* until 1982 was moored at Brielle, New Jersey, on the Manasquan River as a restaurant ship. The *Elizabeth* has again been renamed, *The Second Sun,* and is presently a floating exhibition ship owned by Public Service Electric & Gas, describing the uses of atomic energy, and moored at Salem, New Jersey, on the Delaware River. This line was next to the last to operate on the Hudson River proper. All vestiges of the Liberty Street and Cortlandt Street terminals have been obliterated by new landfill for Battery Park City.

---

*The *Crusader* and *Wallstreet* were discontinued entirely in 1982.
**New York Waterway inaugurated such service in 1995.

23

Ferries of the Lower Waters

Although the most southerly ferry on the Hudson River proper was at Communipaw, there was, and still is, important ferry traffic on the lower waters of the bays and tributary rivers separating areas of dense population. These frequently served islands and military and other government installations.

From the establishment of the United States Immigration Facility on Ellis Island in 1892, until operations were suspended there in 1954, the United States Government operated a ferry on this route for foot passengers only. They used various boats from 1892 until the acquisition of the *Ellis Island,* which was built to special specifications and launched on March 18, 1904 at Wilmington, Delaware. She was built by Harlan & Hollingsworth and similar to the Jersey Central boats. She measured 160 feet by 37 feet, by 9 feet deep and weighed 660 gross tons, and was a screw propelled double-ender. She was put into service in June of 1904. She had two pilot houses, passenger cabins, a sick-bay, a single-funnel, and a wooden superstructure on a steel hull. She was powered by a 450 hp compound steam engine fired by a coal burning Scotch Marine Boiler. In 1932 she was converted to oil. The *Ellis Island* cost $105,000. The Manhattan Terminal was at the Barge Office at the foot of Whitehall Street. The trip was 1½ miles and took fifteen minutes. The ferry operated from 6:00 AM until midnight. Her last trip was on November 29, 1954 commanded by Captain Ives. She had transported 2,000,000 passengers and logged over 1,000,000 miles. After discontinuance of service she was moored at her berth on Ellis Island, and sank there on August 10, 1968, settling into shallow water with a 20° list. Divers discovered a hole in the steel hull. At present she awaits salvage as part of the museum development on the island.

At the present time service to Ellis Island is provided by the Circle Line, operating from the Battery.

There have been sail and row ferries to Governors Island from Manhattan from the earliest times. At the present time the island is occupied primarily by the United States Coast Guard. Six thousand people work there daily and there is a substantial permanent population. There is a free ferry making the 1500 foot run to Whitehall Street in Manhattan. This service is usually available only to those having valid business on the island, although there are occasional open houses. Formerly the small steam ferry, *Major General Wm. H. Hart,* now at the South Street Seaport Museum, was used on this route. Presently it is served by the diesel electric ferries *Nicholas Minue* and *Lt. Samuel S. Coursen.*

Liberty Island, formerly Bedloes Island, site of the Statue of Liberty, is reached by boats of the Circle Line from the Battery. These are small passenger yachts with diesel power. The largest boat regularly assigned to this run is the *Miss Liberty*. Some of the trips continue on to Liberty State Park in Jersey City after calling at Liberty Island.

One of the most important ferry routes on the lower waters was that across the East River between Manhattan and Brooklyn. The first recorded ferry dates from 1642 and was operated by either Cornelius Dirckman, or Cornelius Hooglandt—depending on which authority you choose. They were flat bottomed rowboats. Brooklyn was then known simply as "The Ferry," and as late as 1816 was incorporated as Brooklyn Ferry.

On October 12, 1694 the Corporation of the City of New York purchased from William Morris property in Brooklyn on which to construct a pier, ferry steps, and cattle pens. They later constructed a substantial brick and stone ferry house. The ferry operated to Peck's Slip on Manhattan.

In 1700 the Manhattan landing was moved to Fly Market Slip, at the foot of Maiden Lane, and in 1774 an additional route was established to Coenties Slip, and a landing at Joralemon Street in Brooklyn. In 1789 there were four boats in operation, and in 1805 five scows with sails and six rowboats. This route was known as the "Old Ferry." In 1795 an additional route was inaugurated from Catherine Street, Manhattan, and was known as the "New Ferry." In 1811 it was operated by Rodman Bowne and leased to Cyrus P. Smith and William F. Buckley from 1852 till 1863. In the early days the crossing was dangerous and slow, and the boatmen were often drunk.

The first steam ferry was established in 1814 by Robert Fulton, and his brother-in-law, William Cutting. It operated from Beekman's Slip, at the foot of present day Fulton Street, Manhattan, on land purchased by the Corporation of the City of New York from Peter Schermerhorn. Fulton and Cutting formed the New York & Brooklyn Steamboat Ferry Association, with Capital Stock worth $68,000. While the regular row or sail ferry fare for a foot passenger was 2ᶜ, the new steamboat charged 4ᶜ at first. The first boat was the *Nassau,* the second steam ferry, the *William Cutting,* was put into operation in 1827. Other steam ferryboats were the *Decatur* and *Long Island Star.* All these first steamboats were double-hull catamaran type vessels. Peter Coffee was pilot of the *Nassau.*

By 1833 ownership was in other hands, and in 1836 the single hull steamboats *Olive Branch* and *Relief,* both sidewheelers, were added.

The South Ferry Line, from Whitehall Street to Atlantic Avenue, was opened in 1836, backed by the same parties who were building the new Long Island Rail Road. It was a financial failure, and was absorbed by the Fulton Line in 1839 as the New York & Brooklyn Union Ferry Company. The *Suffolk* was added in 1840, and the *Union* in 1843. In 1844 the line was reincorporated as the Brooklyn Union Ferry Company—Henry E. Pierrepont and Jacob R. Leroy—Directors. In 1846 a route was established from Whitehall Street to Hamilton Avenue.

In 1853 F. C. Havemeyer and S. J. Tilden established a route from Roosevelt Street, Manhattan to Bridge Street in Brooklyn, with three boats. That same year Jacob Sharpe and associates established a two boat line from Wall Street, Manhattan to Montague Street, Brooklyn. Both routes were unsuccessful financially, and in 1854 they, along with another line to Gouverneur Street, were all incorporated into the new Union Ferry Company of Brooklyn, and a 1ᶜ fare was established on all seven routes. This did not work out however, and in 1856 the fare was raised to 2ᶜ. The route to Gouverneur Street was discontinued in 1857, and that to Roosevelt Street in 1859.

In May of 1860 the Union Ferry Company was operating five routes: Fulton Street; South Street; Hamilton Street; Wall Street; and Catherine Street. New cast-iron terminal buildings were erected at Fulton Street, Manhattan in 1863, and at Whitehall Street in 1864. A new terminal was built at Fulton Street, Brooklyn in 1871. That same year the first iron hull boats were put into service. They were the *Fulton* and the *Farragut*. Other boats of this period included the *Ellen,* the *Whitehall,* the *Wyandank,* the *Atlantic,* the *Clinton,* and the *Somerset.*

Construction was started on the Brooklyn Bridge in 1869, and it was opened for traffic on May 24, 1883. This drained considerable traffic from the ferries and all the East River lines were combined in 1896. The Fulton Street Ferry, the pioneer line, was discontinued in 1924. In 1931 there were still lines operating from South Street to 39th Street, Brooklyn, and from Whitehall Street to Hamilton Avenue, Brooklyn, as well as from South Street to Atlantic Avenue, Brooklyn. All vehicular ferries on the East River have now been discontinued. However, it seems that a revival is afoot on the East River. On October 17, 1979 the New York City Department of Ports & Terminals announced the opening of bidding for reestablishment of the Fulton Street Ferry.

Although there were informal sail and row ferries across the Narrows from earliest times, the first organized route wasn't put into operation until July 3, 1912, between St. George, Staten Island, and 69th Street, Brooklyn, by the Brooklyn & Richmond Ferry Company. Service opened with the steam sidewheeler *Garden City,* built at Chester, Pennsylvania in 1872. In 1939 the Electric Ferry Company took over operations and used the Diesel-electric vessels *The Tides, The Narrows, Hamilton, E. G. Diefenbach, Hudson, Gotham,* and *St. George.* These boats were designed principally to carry automobiles; they averaged 560 gross tons and measured 184 feet by 45 feet by 14 feet deep. In 1954 the operation was acquired by the City of New York, who leased the actual operation to private parties. In 1963 they carried 2,700,000 vehicles. Operations ceased after the opening of the Verrazano Narrows Bridge in November 1964.

The Staten Island Ferry from Manhattan is possibly the most famous ferry line in the world, and remains in operation.

The earliest recorded charter for such a ferry dates from 1712, although the New York City Council had chartered quite a few piragues by 1755. Among the early sail operators were young Cornelius Vanderbilt, who in 1810, at the age of sixteen, established a ferry from Whitehall Street, Manhattan, to Clifton, Staten Island. Tradition says he borrowed the money for the boat from his mother, and paid her back by doing farm work. The future "Commodore" was active and progressive, and in 1817 he introduced the steamboat *Nautilus.* The route he served was known as the Richmond Turnpike Ferry until the mid-1840s, when it came to be simply called the Staten Island Ferry. The early boats were rather elegantly furnished single-ender sidewheelers for passengers only. In 1853 Vanderbilt

Manhattan Terminal of Staten Island Ferry c1900. (Author's collection)

consolidated his line with the rival Tompkins & Staples Ferry, founded in 1817 by Daniel Tompkins, and the People's Line, as the Staten Island & New York Steam Ferry Company. Their early single ended boats included the *Hunchback,* the *Sylph,* the *Josephine,* the *Columbus,* and the *Staten Islander.*

The double-enders *Southfield (I), Westfield (I),* and *Clifton (I)* were introduced in the 1850s as vehicle traffic increased. On July 30, 1871 the boiler of the *Westfield* exploded at its slip at Whitehall Street with terrible loss of life. The walking beam double-enders *Westfield (II), Northfield (II),* and *Middletown,* were introduced in 1862, 1863, and 1864 respectively.

The Vanderbilt interests sold out to the Staten Island Railroad Company in 1864, who operated the service as the Staten Island Railway Ferry Company. The Baltimore & Ohio Railroad acquired both rail and ferry operations in July of 1884. They extended the railroad to Tompkinsville in 1884 and to Elm Park in 1886, establishing ferries to Perth Amboy and Elizabeth. These later routes, using small beam sidewheelers such as the *Perth Amboy,* remained in operation until quite recent times. The Baltimore & Ohio also operated some of its Jersey Central ferries from Communipaw to Whitehall Street. On June 14, 1901 the Jersey Central ferryboat *Mauch Chunk* struck the *Northfield* as she was pulling out of her Whitehall Street slip. Fortunately only four people were killed in what might have been a major disaster. The *Northfield* was carrying 995 passengers at the time of the accident, and was damaged beyond repair.

The City of New York took over ownership and operation of the ferries on October 25, 1905. Boats at the time of acquisition included the *Castleton,* the *Robert Garrett,* the *Westfield (II),* the *Southfield (II),* and the *Middletown.* All routes operated to St. George, where the principal railroad terminal was located.

For a brief period, from 1909 until 1913, the City operated a second line from the Battery to Stapleton. It was unsuccessful and discontinued on December 31, 1913. The City purchased the first screw propelled ferries for the Staten Island Line, and they entered operation in 1905. They were known as the "Five Boroughs," and were the largest and fastest ferries of their day. They were the *Manhattan, Brooklyn, Bronx, Queens,* and *Richmond.* All except the *Richmond* were built by the Maryland Steel Company at Sparrow's Point, Maryland. The *Richmond* was built, fittingly, by the Burlee Drydock Company of Staten Island. They measured 250 feet by 66 feet, and carried two funnels, rigged fore and aft. The *Mayor Gaynor* was added in 1914; the *President Roosevelt* in 1922; and the *American Legion* in 1926.

Another handsome series of steamboats was acquired with the *Dongan Hills* in 1929, the *Tompkinsville* in 1930, and the *Knickerbocker* in 1931.

The next group of boats were the *Miss New York, Gold Star Mother,* and *Mary Murray,* all in 1938.

On June 25, 1946 the large terminal at St. George caught fire and burned to the ground. The present new terminal was opened in 1951. The Manhattan Terminal was renovated in 1956 from plans by Roberts & Schaefer. It handles passengers from an upper level and vehicles below.

The last group of steam ferries, measuring 269 feet by 69 feet, by 19 feet deep, were all built by Bethlehem Steel Company on Staten Island. They each weigh 2285 gross tons and are powered with six-cylinder Unaflow engines. They are the *Pvt. Joseph F. Merrell* (1950), the *Cornelius G. Kolff* (1951), and the *Verrazzano* (1951). They are the last large steam ferries in service on Hudson waters.

Three large diesel electric ships, the *Governor Herbert H. Lehman,* the *American Legion (II),* and the *John F. Kennedy,* were delivered by the Levingston Shipbuilding Company of Orange, Texas in 1965. They measure 273 feet by 69 feet by 21 feet deep, and are equipped with four 1600 hp Diesel engines, turning eight 6000 hp electric motors.

On August 6, 1981 a new era began for the Staten Island Ferry when the new 6,000 passenger, $16,500,000 superferryboat *Andrew J. Barberi* was delivered from the Equitable Shipyard in Florida. This new vessel carries passengers on all three decks and does not carry automobiles. After refitting at the Bethlehem Shipyard in Hoboken she entered service on the 6:51 AM sailing from St. George on Monday, October 5, 1981, under the command of Captain Walter Smith. She is to be joined by a new sister ship, the *Samuel I. Newhouse,* in 1982. The *Andrew J. Barberi* is the largest boat to ever operate on the Staten Island run and is licensed to carry 6,000 passengers on voyages in inland waters. This is the largest current certificate granted to any vessel in the world. The previous largest Staten Island ferry was the *Kennedy* class, licensed for 3,533 persons. When both new ships are in service the steamboats of the *Merrell* class will be retired and the *Kennedy Class* boats will be converted to three passenger decks and the Staten Island ferry will cease carrying automobiles or any other motor vehicles. This traffic has fallen off drastically since the opening of the Verrazano Bridge, while rush hour passenger loads have dramatically increased. The new boats are

Ferryboat *Knickerbocker* of the Staten Island Ferry, leaving Manhattan. This is typical of the giant double-stack steamers in use in the 1930s.
(Parslow Collection—Courtesy of the Steamship Historical Society Library—University of Baltimore)

double-enders with single exhaust stack centrally located. They have the traditional rounded pilot houses at either end, but there is only limited open deck space for passengers. There are full snack and refreshment stands inside and the passenger saloons have individual molded plastic seats, some placed in random pattern, in place of the traditional long wooden benches. The boats are propelled by the Voith-Schneider cycloidal propeller system. A variable-pitch makes a rudder unnecessary and allows the ferry to enter the slip and dock without the use of the wooden racks. The boat can revolve 360° on her own axis.

The specifications for the *Barberi* are as follows: Built July 1, 1981; 3335 Gross Tons; 2288 Net Tons; Deadweight 585 Tons; Length 310 feet; Horsepower—7000; and Direct Diesel Propulsion. Passenger traffic on the Staten Island route passed 20 million in 1980. There are, in 1981, 20,000 daily riders. Two and a half million tourists make the 25ᶜ round trip annually to view the Statue of Liberty and other sights of the Upper Bay. The Staten Island-Manhattan Ferry promises to remain the most vital route on Hudson Waters. Success of the new technology on this route, greater operating economies, and increasing congestion of the vehicular crossings, bode well for redevelopment of many other routes.

The population growth of Staten Island, coupled with renovation of the railroad on the Island and the present gasoline situation, augurs well for the future of this line. It is one of New York's greatest tourist attractions and provides unsurpassed views of the harbor, the Statue of Liberty, Robbins Reef Light, and the Verrazano and Brooklyn bridges, besides handling vast numbers of vehicles and commuters.

There were also four important ferry lines across the narrow waters of the Kill Van Kull and Arthur Kill on the north and west side of Staten Island. One of the most important was the line from Port Richmond, Staten Island to Bergen Point, Bayonne. This ferry landed in Port Richmond "opposite the Dutch Church," and was part of the great overland stage route from Jersey City to Philadelphia by way of Staten Island in Revolutionary times. The first ferry here was founded in 1695. In 1750 it was being kept by Jacob Corson. The first steam double-ender came in 1849. Prior to 1937 the line was operated by the Public Service Railways Company. In later years the line was operated by Sunrise Ferries, Inc., using small modern diesel boats of 48 gross tons and measuring 60 feet by 35 feet and only 6 feet deep. They were the: *Altair* (1946), *Deneb* (1946), *Vega* (1946), *Capella* (1948), *Spica* (1949), *Sirius* (1950), and *Orion* (1955). Sometimes the larger *Irvington* (1932) and *Piermont* (1932) of 113 gross tons were used during busy periods. All these small boats were used on all the different routes operated by Sunrise Ferries. Service was discontinued in December, 1961.

A route from near Elm Park to Elizabeth was known as the Howland or Holland Hook Ferry. There were early sail and row operations. In the early days of steamboating, Elizabeth to Manhattan was a popular route, and nearby Mariner's Harbor, on Staten Island, was a regular landing. The first steam double-ender on the Howland Hook Ferry opened service on the short route on September 30, 1850. In later years this route was operated by Sunrise Ferries, using small diesel craft. The final crossing was on January 21, 1961.

Slightly further south on the Arthur Kill, between Linoleumville, Staten Island and Carteret, New Jersey, was the New Blazing Star Ferry. This line had operated from before the American Revolution, starting in 1764, and was discontinued during the Revolution. Service was reinstituted with a steam double-ender on May 5, 1916. Steam operation was discontinued on August 31, 1929. Since that time a "gas" launch was used to carry foot passengers only. This service was discontinued on December 31, 1960.

The most important route across the Arthur Kill was the Tottenville to Perth Amboy Ferry. In 1650 it is recorded that friendly Raritan Indians were operating an informal ferry service here. In 1709 Christopher Billopp established a regular perigua ferry, which remained in the Billopp family until 1781. In 1737 the fare for ferrying was 14 pence in Jersey currency for man and horse, and 5 pence for a single passenger. Isaac Doty (or Dote) operated the ferry under lease from Billopp from about 1757 until his death in 1774. Both sloops and periguas were used. By 1860 the ferry traffic had dwindled to the point where the traffic was served by a rowboat. The ferryman was A. M. Dawson, and the fare was 12½ᶜ each way.

With the construction of the Staten Island Railroad in 1860, things began to pick up. In 1861 the small single-ender *Grace Irving* was on the route, but was withdrawn for inadequate traffic. In December of 1862 the 75 ton steamboat *Enterprise* was put on the route, making connection with all trains. She continued in use until replaced by the forty-four ton sidewheeler *Stillman Witt* in July of 1864.

The Staten Island Railroad Company instituted regular double-ender service on May 12, 1867, with the 148 ton sidewheeler *Maid of Perth*. The first captains were Hunter and White. This boat operated until scrapped in 1905. Other beam sidewheelers used on this route were: *Warren,* 513 tons, built in 1859 and operated on this route from 1898 to 1907; *Perth Amboy,* 618 tons—placed in service new the day *Warren* was retired, and operated until October 14,

S.S. Commander of New Hamburg New York.

1948, when she was scrapped. *Tottenville* was built in 1881 and weighed 831 gross tons. She was originally named *Hoboken*. She was put on this route in 1912 and removed from regular service in 1933, and scrapped during the Second World War. The last steam ferry was the *Charles W. Galloway,* of 587 tons. She was probably the last beam engine sidewheel ferry ever built. She was built new for this route in 1922, and operated here until her final trip on October 16, 1948, under command of Captain James E. Lane. This was the last trip of a double-ended sidewheeler in the northeastern United States. This was also the final trip under railroad auspices. Later that day the *Charles W. Galloway* was towed away for scrapping, and Sunrise Ferries took over with small diesel boats. This service lasted until October 16, 1963. There is presently some talk of restoring passenger service on this line.

As an extreme outpost of Hudson River ferry service, the Rockaway Boat Lines operated a summer only foot passenger ferry between Sheepshead Bay in Brooklyn and Rockaway Point and Breezy Point. They used three dieselized diminutive ancient steamers. The *Commander* (1917), the *Columbia* (1919) and the *C. Washington Colyer* (1913) all weigh no more than 14 gross tons, are no longer than 75 feet, and no deeper than 5 feet. The *Commander* and the *Colyer* were built in Morehead City, North Carolina, and the *Columbia* in Brooklyn. This line was discontinued in 1981 and the boats were sold for cruise service out of West Haverstraw and Hyde Park on the Hudson.

I was aboard the *Commander* on its inaugural trip for Hudson Highlands cruises in May 1982. She has been given a thorough overhauling and drew raves from an invited group of dignitaries because of her charm. Captain Collin Key is the proud skipper.

The *Columbia* was sold to Central Hudson Cruise Lines of Hyde Park. The *Colyer* remains for sale as we go to press.

This chapter completes the survey of ferries which operated across the Hudson River and its principal estuaries. Of all this once great network, only the Staten Island Ferry continues in the Grand Tradition. With developing energy problems, and a renewed interest in both the river and in public transportation, it is likely that where there are suitable circumstances, there will be renewed use of the waterways.

24 Steamboats Come to Maturity

After the breakup of the Fulton-Livingston monopoly, various new steamboat lines were formed. The, so called, "Old Line" consisted of the *James Kent, Hudson, Chief Justice Marshall,* and the *Saratoga.* The Hudson River Line consisted of the *Constitution, Constellation,* and the *Independence.* The *DeWitt Clinton* was operated independently out of Albany, and the Stevens Line operated the *North America, Albany,* and *New Philadelphia* on the Albany route. Competition was keen. In 1832 all these lines were consolidated into the New York, Albany & Troy Line, or Hudson River Steamboat Association—a new monopoly! As with most cartels, attempts were made at apportioning business and fixing freight rates and passenger fares. However, none of these arrangements lasted for very long, and fares fluctuated wildly, reflecting every least change in the competitive situation. So called "opposition" lines sprang up overnight, usually with older and less desirable, or slower, vessels. Eventually these other lines evolved into a sort of second class service in their own right.

By the 1840s steamboat speeds had increased to such an extent that it was possible to make the entire trip between New York and Albany during either a single day or overnight. Up until then most ships had some sleeping accommodations, as most trips took place at least partly at night. With increased speed, separate types of day and night boats were developed. Generally the day boats were somewhat smaller and faster, and frequently did not carry freight. Speed was the great factor, and ships would race each other to be first to pick up passengers at the various way-landings. Often, when racing, they would pass up scheduled landings, or land people "on the fly." While still operating at speed, the ship would shear in towards the shore. The ship's boat would be lowered on a light line, and passengers and baggage to be landed would be tumbled into the boat. A crew member would steer the small boat, still attached to the steamer by a light line, into the beach or wharf. It would stop for a few moments while the steamer continued to pay out line while remaining under way. The passengers would then have to hop nimbly ashore as their baggage was tossed out to them, while embarking passengers jumped into the boat, and their baggage was tossed in on top of them. Quite often the passengers missed the dock or boat and got soaked or, not infrequently, drowned or were hit on the head by their own baggage. Once the embarking passengers and their baggage were in the small boat, the steamer began to pull in the line to bring the small boat back to the ship. This was done by wrapping the line around the paddle shaft, using it as a winch. When the boat came abreast of the steamer, the passengers were taken aboard. This was a very dangerous practice and was later outlawed.

Lighthouse near Caldwell's Landing. (Actually Stony Point). Note early steamboat, lumber raft, and sloops. From engraving by William Bartlett.

Another time saving expedient was for a ferry, or other small boat, to meet the steamer out in the river, and for passengers to jump from one to the other while both were under way, which was very dangerous. However, it was fairly safe if both ships stopped during the transfer, and this practice was continued for many years by the Hudson River Day Line and the Nyack-Tarrytown Ferry.

Steamers would often race, leading to boiler explosions; breakdowns of heavy machinery, often sinking the ship; and running aground in misty weather, snowstorms, or at night. During clear weather two competing ships would often collide in attempting to get to a landing first. On the down-river trip, this often happened at Catskill Point. Sometimes they would attempt to ram and damage each other, or force the competing ship aground in a narrow channel. Runners and ticket agents would grossly slander competing boats and "puff" their own. The boiler explosions became such a fear that the Swiftsure Line inaugurated "Safety Barges" in the 1820s. These were elegantly fitted up and pulled by powerful steam towboats. The first safety barges were the *Lady Clinton* and the *Lady Van Rensselaer*. They did not remain popular for very long, as the desire for speed became overpowering, and the safety barges did not make as good time as the new fast steamers.

Aside from the through Day Line and Night Line, and their lower-priced through opposition lines, other lines, making more way landings, soon sprang up to serve intermediate points. Many of them operated "express" part of the way, and then made many local landings in some particular portion of the river. Often these lines operated very fine ships, such as the *Mary Powell* to Rondout, the *Homer Ramsdell* to Newburgh, and the *Kaaterskill* and *Clermont* to Catskill. Other smaller boats handled local freight, hay, and farm produce, often operating only between mid-river terminals. On the lower river, commuting boat lines developed and operated from Peekskill, Ossining, Nyack, Haverstraw, and Fort Lee, to New York. Every landing along the river soon had some form of through or connecting steamboat service to New York or Albany. From an early date excursion boats were popular, taking people on a day's outing from the larger towns and cities. There were also lines operating down the bay from New York to seashore resorts and points in New Jersey, as well as lines operating into Long Island Sound. Often the same vessels would operate, sometimes on the Hudson, and sometimes on one of the other routes out of New York. In those days there was little difference between Hudson River steamboats and short-distance coastal steamboats. Let us now examine the workings and design of typical day and night boats.

First, in view of the central importance of this technology to the development of commerce and social life along the Hudson River, and in consideration of the fact that few present-day readers have had firsthand experience of them, let us describe the workings of a steam engine as used on board a steamboat.

The prime moving force in a steam engine was the terrifically powerful expansive force of steam, which takes up roughly 1,600 times the space of the water required to generate it. The force is measured in terms of the pressure this steam exerts in a closed vessel, expressed in pounds per square inch on the surface of the vessel. The steam was generated in boilers fired, at first by wood, and later by coal and oil. If the fire was hot, steam was formed quickly and the piston moved rapidly. If the fire was low, steam was formed slowly and the piston moved less rapidly. There were two basic types of boilers. In firetube boilers hot gases from the firebox exhaust passed through tubes inside a large vessel containing water before passing up the stack. The steam was generated inside the boiler shell before being drawn off to the manifold and cylinders. This type of boiler was subject to terrific internal pressures, and often led to terrible boiler explosions in the early days. In the watertube boiler, more commonly in use in later years, the hot exhaust gases passed through the boiler shell on their way to the stack. Water circulating through tubes inside the boiler shell was heated by the passing hot gases. As the water inside the tubes turned to steam it was drawn off to the manifold and cylinders. The reason why wood was abandoned as a fuel in favor of coal was that coal has a higher caloric value per pound and does not pass sparks through the flues. Consequently, less weight of fuel had to be carried. The early coal burners were fired by hand shovels and were known as "Hand Bombers." It is interesting to note that the last coal burning steamboats on the Hudson, the ferryboats *Binghamton* and *Elmira,* were both "Hand Bombers" which used anthracite coal. This innovation was first made by Robert Stevens, one of the founders of the Hoboken Ferry. It was a cleaner burning fuel than soft coal, or certain "dirty burning" oils. Eventually, automatic coal stokers were developed, and by the 1920s oil generally superseded coal as the favored fuel on the river.

The name "reciprocating" steam engine came from the fact that, in this type of engine, a piston moved back and forth inside a cylinder. This was accomplished by admitting live steam into the cylinder through a valve to push the piston. The inlet of steam was stopped about half-way through the piston's stroke so as to take full advantage of the expansive force of the steam. At the end of the stroke, another inlet valve was opened on the other side of the piston, which pushed it back in the opposite direction. Spent steam was exhausted through outlet valves which were mechanically activated in synchronization with the steam inlet valves. This mechanism was known as the valve gear. On more modern engines it was very complex, and differed in design on vertical and inclined piston engines. The critical factors in describing ships' steam engines are the diameter of the cylinder bore and the length of stroke of the piston. In later years it was found that much of the exhaust steam had much expansive force left, and engines were designed with second, third, and fourth cylinders, of increasing diameter, into which the exhaust steam from the next smaller cylinder was utilized as inlet steam. These were known as compound engines. The later large Day Boats, such as the *Hendrick Hudson* and *Alexander Hamilton* had compound and triple expansion engines, respectively. The *De Witt Clinton* had two triple expansion engines.

The next problem of steamboat design was to change the reciprocating, or back and forth, movement of the pistons into rotating movement to turn either a paddle wheel or a propeller. In the early steamboats the cylinder was mounted vertically, so that the piston worked up and down out of the top of the cylinder. Usually there was only one very large diameter cylinder on the early day boats. This piston was connected by a flexible joint to a connecting rod which ran up to the top of the boat, where it was fastened to one end of a balanced beam, similar to a see-saw, and known as a walking beam. As the piston rod and connecting rod pushed one end of this walking-beam up, the other end would go down, and vice versa.

Steamer *Alexander Hamilton,* of the Hudson River Day Line. Last of the large sidewheelers to be built or to remain in service.

At a relatively early date, a beam per se was replaced by a diamond shaped metal frame, known as a skeleton beam. This was both stronger and lighter and less subject to breaking from sudden jars to the machinery. The end of the walking beam, opposite to that connected with the piston, was connected to another connecting rod which ran down through the body of the ship to a crank cam on the paddle wheel shaft, which ran through the hull or, on some boats such as the *Robert Fulton,* was supported on bearings slightly above the waterline. On Hudson River steamboats there was usually only a single monolithic paddle shaft and both paddle wheels always turned in the same direction. On Western Rivers and in Europe, it was not unusual to have two smaller engines, two paddle shafts, and paddle wheels which could operate independently in opposite directions. This aided in maneuverability, but was used only rarely, generally on towboats, on the Hudson.

The second connecting bar, which joined the walking beam and the paddle shaft, was also connected to a "rocker bar" which automatically activated the valve gear. On older vertical beam boats the steam was let into the cylinder by manual valving, using a "starter bar." Once a certain velocity was attained, linking hooks would be attached from the connecting rod and rocker bar to activated the valve gear automatically. This was known to steamboaters as "dropping the hooks," and is the action from which the popular cant phrase "hook her up," is derived.

In later steamboats the cylinders were frequently mounted horizontally, or on a slight slant, and a single connecting rod, or set of rods in the case of a compound engine, connected the pistons with crank shafts on the paddle shaft. This was known as an inclined piston engine. The *Alexander Hamilton* was a well known example. Passengers could easily view the workings of this magnificent machine with the ponderous revolutions of the great crank shafts, which also acted much as does a flywheel.

In sidewheel ships the paddle shaft passed through the lubricated bearings, supported by springs, on either side of the vessel. In early sidewheelers, large paddles radiated out from the hub and slapped the water. This created much wasteful turbulence, and when a paddle blade first hit the water, it exerted a downward force against the water which would tend to raise the ship up in the water. Near the nadir of its revolution it exerted the maximum forward thrust. In the ascending phase of its revolution, the paddle lifted water from the level of the river and thus wasted energy. Efficiency was attained for each blade only when near the nadir in its revolution. This early type of wheel was known as a radial wheel.

John Ericsson is credited with an improvement in paddle wheel design, although there is some good evidence that the Stevenses preceded him in this matter. He perfected what is known as the "feathering" or Ericsson wheel. (In Europe called the Morgan Wheel). In this type wheel the blades, or buckets, as they are sometimes called, are mounted on a type of circular cage similar to the frame of a ferris wheel with swinging cars. They are hinged on one end, and the other end is connected to a radius arm fastened to an eccentric crank on the hub of the paddle shaft. The paddle blades are thus kept in a plane always near perpendicular to that of the surface of the water. Entering the water, they cut right into it, exerting no downward thrust, nor tending to lift the vessel from the water, so that no energy is wasted in this way. Upon coming up from the water, it lifts no heavy splash. As the paddle blade is perpendicular to the surface of the water from first entry, it is so placed as to exert maximum horizontal thrust throughout its entire submerged evolution. It thus conserves power, increases speed, and minimizes splash. The first large Day Boats to be fitted with feathering wheels were the *Albany* and *New York* of the Hudson River Day Line. They were used on most of the later sips.

To protect the wheels from damage, often of a deliberate and malicious nature, and to contain the splashing water, the early radial wheels were enclosed in semi-circular paddle housings, which were often highly decorated and ornate. Just as with the size of locomotive drive wheels, large diameter side wheels were designed for speed, and smaller ones for power. Often the wheel on such early steamboats as the *St. John, City of Troy,* and *Kaaterskill,* would extend to the third and fourth decks. The wheel of the *St. John* had a diameter of forty-eight feet. The paddle housings were often called paddle boxes.

On vertical piston ships, the walking beam was supported on a heavy wooden or steel framework called the "gallows frame," from its obvious resemblance to the structure of that same name.

On screw propelled steamships the cylinders were usually mounted vertically over the propeller shaft or shafts if on a twin screw vessel. The pistons came through the bottom of the cylinders and were connected to connecting rods by a flexible crosshead. The connecting rods were attached to cranks on the propeller shafts. The valve gear was actuated by another set of rods motivated by the propeller shafts. Some ships had as many as four engines, driving two shafts. These could be simple or double, triple or quadruple expansion machines.

Steamer *Kaaterskill* of Catskill Evening Line.

In the earliest steamboats the boilers were mounted on the deck. Later they were mounted down in the hull. However, after some disastrous boiler explosions, people became afraid of injury, and it became common practice to mount the boilers outboard "on the guards," so that there would be less injury to passengers and the ship in case of explosion. The *Mary Powell* was the last important Hudson River passenger steamboat with boilers on the guards. This arrangement also made it easier to store the fuel and made for cooler working conditions for the firemen who had to manually feed the large fires.

On ships with boilers on the guards the stacks were usually on the sides, above the boilers. On some larger ships, with four separate boilers (one forward and one aft of the paddle on either side), there were four separate stacks. Later, with the boilers in the hull, it became common practice to use a third boiler and mount the three stacks athwartship, as in the *Chauncey Vibbard, Albany, New York,* and *Robert Fulton.* Later practice was to place the stacks amidship, one in front of the other. The newer Hudson River steamboats never exceeded the need for two stacks. The *Washington Irving* had a third stack, but the forward stack was a "dummy" used to give an aesthetic design.

Paddle wheels remained in use on the Hudson longer than most other places for a variety of reasons. They were well suited to shallow draft vessels and caused a minimum of turbulence in shallow water. They were easily maneuverable in frequent docking and could reverse directions fast and with good power. They also created less vibration, which is important in a large, shallow hulled, passenger carrying ship with a light wooden superstructure. They were also very fast when equipped with feathering wheels. The *Alexander Hamilton,* built by Bethlehem Steel Company in 1924, was the last sidewheeler built for the Hudson.

The sidewheelers offered another important advantage for a river boat. A rather narrow hull in relation to overall breadth can be attained by fairing the decks out over the guards to the outsides of the paddle boxes. This provides additional deck or cabin space. The ship thus had a great virtual breadth in proportion to waterline breadth, thus maintaining a beneficial metacentric ratio. This is important to provide stability in a passenger ship on which large numbers of persons frequently go to one side either for sightseeing or to unload, or to seek or avoid the sun. To help keep these ships in trim and prevent capsizing or excessive tipping over or list, many were equipped with saddle shaped trimming tanks, with high speed centrifugal pumps, so that fast adjustments could be made. In the later designs of the noted naval architects Frank Kirby, J. W. Millard, and George Sharp, the superstructure was closely bound to the strength hull to minimize vibration and strengthen the superstructure. Earlier ships had to be strengthened by truss frames, known as hog frames, which are prominent in pictures of the older steamboats. There was much use of guy wire bracing, which had to be constantly adjusted by use of turnbuckles to prevent the ship from either sagging in the middle, or "hogging," or digging her nose into the water.

Athough there was considerable variation in details of design, certain features were fairly standard in steamboat design. Passengers usually boarded from a gangway aft of the paddle wheel. The Purser's Office and the main dining room were usually on the main deck aft. The Saloon and third decks were usually given over to either passenger lounge space or, on night boats, cabins. The larger day boats had private staterooms, known as parlors, with private toilet facilities and sometimes private outside decks. These were usually on the Saloon deck. Often crews quarters for the deck officers were located on the Hurricane deck abaft the pilot houses. Other crew quarters were usually below deck in the forecastle, and the crews mess below deck abaft the boilers and machinery. Steering was originally done from a large hand wheel in the pilot house. As the ships grew larger, these were superseded by steam power steering, done from a second smaller wheel, the large hand wheel being retained for emergencies. It frequently took a number of men to steer by hand. On one occasion when the power steering failed on the *Alexander Hamilton,* it took several deckhands to man the wheel.

Captain Lozier in the Wheelhouse of West Shore ferryboat *Albany*. (New York Central photo)

Electricity was generated by small steam engines. Steam pumps kept pressure in the fire fighting water lines and for sanitary systems.

Some of the larger boats of later years carried crews of up to one hundred men and officers. Fourteen men in the engine room alone was not uncommon. There was usually the Captain or Master and a First and Second Pilot, who were also usually licensed to serve as

Master in an emergency. There were also the First and Second Mates, Chief and Assistant Chief Engineer, Purser, and Chief Steward, in addition to numerous deckhands, ablebodied seamen, waiters, porters, chefs, cooks, kitchen help, and bartenders and stewards. Passenger loads frequently ran over four thousand passengers on a busy trip. It was much like a miniature ocean liner. Up until 1949 the better boats were all carpeted on the upper decks and nicely furnished and decorated with objects de art, oil paintings, and murals. There was much carved fine wood and fancy metalwork and chandeliers. Bands would play at sailing time and for dancing and string orchestras would give concerts and play in the dining room at luncheon and dinner. Besides the main dining room, similar to those in the finest hotels, there was usually a separate, lower priced, cafeteria. The Day Boats offered the height of luxury until after the Second World War. Naturally, the small excursion boats did not offer the same luxury as the through liners, although some of them, such as the *Great Republic,* were impressively magnificent in their appointments. On the through Day Line a gentleman would not be admitted aboard without a white shirt, collar, and jacket. It is unfortunate that many people today, who remember only the last sad years of decline with greatly lowered standards of ship operation and passenger behavior, have misconceptions about the nature of this operation throughout most of its years.

Some of the large night boats had staterooms arranged around a grand gallery abaft the stack housings, and there was usually a "Grand Staircase," often built of expensive woods and decorative metalwork. The gallery was often two or three decks in height, with the cabins opening off circular balconies on each deck level, much like the new Hyatt House Hotel in Atlanta, or the Brown Palace in Denver. The gallery of the Night Boat *Berkshire* was particularly impressive, with large fluted Corinthian columns, carved corbels, and decorative friezes. These were painted white with gilding for trim. For many years the great Hudson River day and night boats were called "Iron Palace Steamers," and they set high standards which were famous and emulated throughout the world. No trip to America was complete without a voyage up the Hudson on one of these great liners. It is truly unfortunate that some modern version of this great tradition has not been able to survive.

25 The Hudson River Steamboat Lines

The first night services were operated by the Fulton-Livingston monopoly. After the breaking of the monopoly many competitors entered the field, and shortly thereafter the more successful ones formed the Hudson River Steamboat Association. In 1835 A. P. St. John and Daniel Drew formed the People's Line, in opposition, for the night trade, although the company had originally been projected as a day line. Competition was keen and, in 1840, Drew formed a People's Line Association, which was later incorporated as the New Jersey Steamboat Company in 1854. Its principal ships were the *Hendrick Hudson, Isaac Newton,* and *New World,* which were monsters for their time. Between 1864 and 1866 these were replaced with the even larger *Dean Richmond* (348 feet), *Drew* (366 feet), and *St. John* (393 feet). They all had boilers on the guards, stacks abreast, and beam engines, and were very elaborately decorated inside. In 1896 the *Adirondack* (388 feet) replaced the *St. John,* which had burned in winter quarters in 1885. At this time the company was also running the *Dean Richmond.*

The Citizens Line operated somewhat smaller ships to Troy, including the *Thomas Powell, Sunnyside, City of Troy,* and *Saratoga.*

In 1902 C. W. Morse, an operator of steamboats on Long Island Sound, acquired the Peoples Line and the Citizens Line. He immediately ordered a mammoth new steamboat, the *C. W. Morse* (411 feet), which entered service in 1903. The name of this ship was changed to *Fort Orange* in 1921, after Morse lost control of the line. The *C. W. Morse,* and the *Berkshire* (422 feet) of 1913 were the two largest night boats ever in regular service on the Hudson. Other ships of the combined People's-Citizens Line were the *Greenport,* the *Rensselaer* (317 feet), and the *Trojan* (317 feet)—this last one built in 1909.

The company went bankrupt in 1921 and C. W. Morse lost control. It was reorganized as the Hudson Navigation Company, and the names of People's Line and Citizens Line were dropped in favor of Hudson River Night Line, by which name it was known for the remainder of its life. This final reorganization came in 1926. Owing to increasing direct highway competition, the line again went bankrupt in 1932. Operations were taken over by D. F. McAllister and the Hudson River Day Line, who operated the line jointly under the trade name, Hudson River Steamboat Company. McAllister withdrew in 1935 and, in that same year, the entire operation was sold to Samuel R. Rosoff, a contractor sometimes known as "Subway Sam." He struggled to keep the line running until September 9, 1939, when all overnight service ceased. Towards the end of operations the *Trojan* had been renamed the *New Yorker.*

Nightboat *St. John*

Nightboat *City of Troy*

Nightboat *Berkshire* of the Hudson Navigation Company. Largest to ever operate on the Hudson.

Nightboat *Adirondack* of the Hudson Navigation Company.

Nightboat *C. W. Morse* of Hudson Navigation Company.

Early day boats on the Hudson included the *Armenia,* the *Alida,* the *Rip Van Winkle,* the *Rochester,* the *Manhattan,* the *Eureka,* the *Confidence,* and the *Cataline.* In the 1840s and 1850s the *Columbia,* the *Reindeer,* the *Joseph Belknap,* the *Baltic,* and the *Henry Clay* were known as fast day boats. The *Henry Clay* caught on fire and burned with great loss of life on July 28, 1852, while racing with the *Armenia.* This disaster led to stricter enforcement of safety laws. In 1852 Cornelius Vanderbilt built the *Francis Skiddy,* which was a notably fast boat.

In 1856 Commodore Alfred Van Santvoord commenced operation of the famous Hudson River Day Line. He started operations with the *Alida* and the *Armenia.* In 1863 Van Santvoord purchased the *Daniel Drew.* Other fine boats were added regularly: *Chauncey Vibbard* (267 feet-1864); *Albany* (1880 - Originally 284 feet. Lengthened to 314 feet in 1892); *New York* (1887 - Originally 301 feet. Lengthened to 335 feet in 1898); and the great *Hendrick Hudson* (1906 - 379 feet).

The *Robert Fulton* (377 feet), last of the walking beam engine Day Liners, was built in 1909 for the Hudson-Fulton Celebration. She was followed by the largest Day Liner of all, the *Washington Irving* (400 feet) of 1913. She was the only ship the Day Line ever lost in service, when she sank in 1926, but except for the loss of two lives, with virtually no injury to

Hudson River Day Line steamer *New York*.

Hudson River Day Line steamer *New York* at Kingston Point, c1896. (Lionel DeLisser)

Hudson River Day Line steamer *Robert Fulton*.

Hudson River Day Line steamer *Peter Stuyvesant* c1959. (Photo by Arthur G. Adams)

any passengers. These were all sidewheel ships. In 1913 the Day Line purchased the *DeWitt Clinton* (320 feet), a screw propelled ship. She was of ocean going design and later served as a transatlantic troop ship. Other screw propelled Day Liners were the yacht-like *Chauncey M. Depew* (194 feet) of 1913 and the larger *Peter Stuyvesant* (269 feet) of 1927. The last sidewheeler to be purchased was the *Alexander Hamilton* (349 feet), of 1924. She was the last sidewheeler built for the Hudson, and operated until September 6, 1971—the last sidewheeler on the river.

Motor Vessel *Dayliner* of the Hudson River Day Line. (Photo courtesy of Frank Wilson)

William Henry Vanderbilt, who purchased the West Shore Railroad for his New York Central System.

Chauncey M. Depew. Statesman and railroad executive. Under his direction New York Central passenger service reached high levels of luxury.

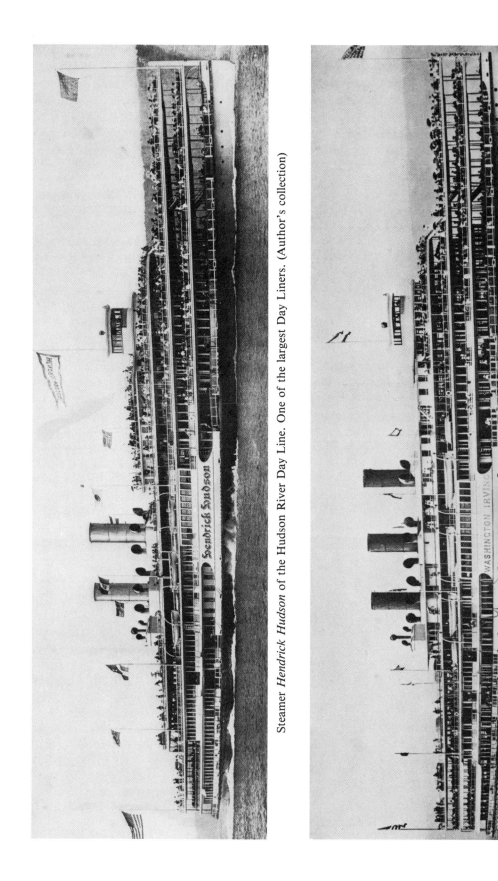

Steamer *Hendrick Hudson* of the Hudson River Day Line. One of the largest Day Liners. (Author's collection)

Steamer *Washington Irving*, the largest liner of the Hudson River Day Line.

For many years the Hudson River Day Line remained in control of the Van Santvoord family and their descendants, the Olcotts. In 1948 they sold the line to George Sanders, operator of the Sutton Line. The last through sailing from Albany on a regular basis was under Olcott control, when the *Robert Fulton* departed on September 13, 1948. The next season Sanders cut operations back to Poughkeepsie, the present regular terminus. In 1962 Sanders sold the line to the Circle Line, headed by Francis J. Barry, which operates tour boats around Manhattan and to the Statue of Liberty and Ellis Island. Mr. Barry reincorporated the Day Line and continued operations from Pier 81 as in the past. He made many material improvements in the terminals and kept the sidewheel steamer *Alexander Hamilton* in service after retirement of the *Peter Stuyvesant*. However, under this management the quality of operations were reduced to the most Spartan excursion boat standards with minimal on-board amenities and very limited food and beverage services. All inter-line arrangements with railroads and bus lines were eliminated and the Day Line was virtually out of the through transportation business, except for traffic to Bear Mountain State Park and West Point. The landings at Newburgh and Poughkeepsie were eliminated and the ship only cruised to Poughkeepsie without landing. He did not even run an occasional special excursion to Albany as Sanders had for many years. These changes in operations were reflected in a drastic change in the clientele which lacked the typical refinement of earlier years. However, the beauty and reputation of the Hudson still drew numerous tourists to a day on the river. By 1971 the *Alexander Hamilton* was getting into poor condition and having difficulty passing the regular Coast Guard inspections. Consequently it was decided to order a new ship—this time a diesel. This broke a tradition of 164 years and 2 days of sidewheel steamboat service starting with Fulton's *North River Steamboat* of Clermont.

On June 10, 1972 the Day Line commissioned the new *M. W. Dayliner,* a 308 foot, twin screw, diesel-electric vessel of 3600 horse power and 3800 gross tons. She was built by the Bellinger Marine Works, of Jacksonville, Florida, and continues the Day Line tradition of operating with modern equipment. However, while she may be modern, she is extremely Spartan as presently fitted out, and does not draw the same crowds as were attracted by the *Alexander Hamilton*.

In 1979 Mr. Alfred V. S. Olcott and I studied the possibility of putting a new small first class sidewheel steamboat on a through route between New York and Albany. This concept received encouragement from people in state government and the project looked promising, especially in view of the energy shortages of the time, which were expected to limit automobile travel and severely tax the railroad's carrying capacity.

Let us consider some other important steamboat lines which served the various way-landings on the Hudson. The New York & Catskill Steamboat Company, and the Catskill Evening Line and Central-Hudson Steamboat Company all specialized in providing service to Coxsackie, Stuyvesant, Hudson, Athens, and Catskill. The Catskill Evening Line was owned by the Beach family who also operated the Catskill Mountain House and a network of narrow gauge railroads operating from Catskill Landing to the mountains. Their more famous boats included the *Thomas Powell,* the *New Champion,* the *Frank,* the *Andrew Harder,* the *Walter Brett,* the *Charlotte Vanderbilt,* the *Escourt,* the *City of Catskill,* the *Kaaterskill,* the *William C. Redfield,* the *Thomas McManus,* the *Onteora,* and the *Clermont,* all passenger steamers, and the small freight propeller *Catskill*. Passenger service ended in 1918. Other small freighters serving these landings were the *Storm King* and *Reserve.* They specialized in transporting fruit until 1932; mostly from small way-landings.

The Saugerties Line served landings between Hyde Park and Saugerties. Their boats included the *Ansonia,* the *Saugerties,* which also was called *Robert A. Snyder,* and *Ulster* at various times, and the *Ida.*

Steamer *City of Kingston*. (Courtesy John F. Matthews)

Steamer *William F. Romer* at Rondout Landing.

Steamer *James W. Baldwin* at Rondout Landing.

Famous Hudson River speed queen *Mary Powell*.

Rondout and Kingston were served by the Romer & Tremper Line, Cornell Steamboat Company, and the Mary Powell Steamboat Company, and more lately, by the Central Hudson Line. Rondout was the outlet of the Delaware & Hudson Canal, and many towboats operated from there. Rondout Creek had many boatyards at Rondout, Wilbur, Connelly, and Ponkhockie. Adjacent Sleightsburg was home to many steamboat men. It is in tribute to this tradition that the Hudson River Maritime Center is establishing its base and collections at Rondout.

Among the more famous boats operating from Rondout were the *James W. Baldwin, Thomas Cornell, City of Kingston, Henry E. Bishop,* and the famous speed queen, *Mary Powell.*

Poughkeepsie and Newburgh were served by the Central-Hudson Steamboat Company and the Homer Ramsdell Transportation Company. Principal ships serving these ports were the *Isaac Smith, John L. Hasbrouck, Daniel S. Miller, William Young, Thomas Powell, Highlander,* and *James Madison.* The *John L. Hasbrouck* was later renamed *Marlborough,* and the *Daniel S. Miller* renamed *Poughkeepsie.* Later large passenger vessels included the *Newburgh, Homer Ramsdell,* and *Benjamin B. Odell.* There was always a close community of interest between the Central-Hudson Lines and the Erie Railroad. Homer B. Ramsdell was President of the Erie Railroad from 1853 to 1857. Benjamin B. Odell was Governor of New York from 1901 to 1905. During the steamboat era Newburgh was an important center of economic and political influence and its native sons had far-reaching interests. Regular passenger line service to Poughkeepsie and Newburgh by the Central-Hudson Line ceased in 1931, and the ships were disposed of to other lines. This was a typical pattern in the 1930s. The former *Clermont* of the Catskill Evening Line was operated by the Sutton Line on behalf of the Palisades Interstate Park Commission, under the name *Bear Mountain.* The *Onteora* was operated in the same service, but kept her original name.

The Lower Hudson Steamboat Company, serving Peekskill, Ossining, Nyack, and Tarrytown, as well as Grassy Point and Haverstraw, were formed in 1865. Ships serving these

Popular lower river steamboat *Chrystenah.*

ports through the years include the following: *Sunnyside, Sleepy Hollow, General Sedgwick* (later known as *Bay Queen*), *Thomas Colyer, Orange, Rockland, Arrow, Broadway, Isaac P. Smith, Peter G. Coffin, John Faron, Adelphi, Chrystenah, Raleigh,* and *Riverdale.* Between 1854 and 1941 Ossining was served by the *Ora, Eureka,* and *Sarah A. Jenks,* later renamed *Ossining.* These small, unglamorous, sturdy little steamboats served thousands of people daily and provided the lifeblood of local commerce. It is fitting that their names not be forgotten.

Between 1841 and 1868 the Erie Railroad operated a line of steamboats between its Duane Street, Manhattan terminal and the railhead at Piermont, where the Erie built a long pier out into the river to contain its terminals. The railroad was completed from Piermont to Dunkirk, on Lake Erie, in 1851. Steamers operating on this route were the *Arrow,* the *Santa Claus,* the *Robert L. Stevens,* the *Eureka,* the *St. Nicholas,* the *Thomas Powell,* the *New Haven,* and the *Francis Skiddy.* The flagship was the large *Erie,* formerly called the *Iron Witch.* On May 14, 1951 the Day Line ship *Peter Stuyvesant* carried a party from Duane Street to Piermont in commemoration of the Centennial of the completion of the Erie Railroad from Piermont to Dunkirk.

The Fort Lee & New York Steam Boat Company was formed in 1832 and served Fort Lee, Edgewater, Shadyside, Bulls Ferry, Guttenberg, and Weehawken, with terminals at 22nd Street, Spring Street, and Canal Street in Manhattan. Its ships included the *Edwin,* the *Thomas E. Hulse,* the *Fort Lee,* the *Pleasant Valley,* and *Shady Side.*

26 Down Bay Steamboats

"The Mandalay goes down the bay"—Old New York City
Children's Chant

Not all steamboats operated upstream from Manhattan. There was considerable steamboat activity on the lower Hudson, or North River, and the Upper and Lower New York Bays which are part of the Hudson, as well as the Kill Van Kull and Arthur Kill and Harlem and East Rivers, which are actually secondary channels of the Hudson proper, not to mention such tributaries as the Passaic, Hackensack, Raritan, Neversink, and Shrewsbury Rivers. Vast numbers of people in the Metropolitan Area used the steamboats to go to the seashore, or as transportation short-cuts around Raritan Bay, or as connections to the early day railroads terminating on the Raritan River or the Arthur Kill.

Between 1885 and 1932, among the most popular lines was the Iron Steamboat Company which operated from 129th Street, Manhattan, down the Hudson and Bay to Coney Island. The line advertised: "They cannot burn—they will not sink." This was most impressive in the days before compartmentalization was common and when most excursion boats were built entirely of wood—hull and all, and disastrous sinkings and fires were common. Furthermore, this was before the tragic lesson of the *Titanic*. Their fleet consisted of the small, classically named sidewheelers: *Cygnus, Sirius, Cepheus, Cetus, Pegasus, Perseus,* and *Taurus.*

The Iron Steamboat Company was not alone in operating downriver. The Mandalay Line operated the *Bear Mountain* to Coney Island, and of course, the *Mandalay* went down the bay. Coney Island was a very popular excursion destination, with the various steamboats landing either at the Steeplechase Open Pier or at the head of Gravesend Bay.

Coney Island seemed to be a particularly popular destination for people from Newark, New Jersey, on the Passaic River. The boats would sail down the Passaic River and Newark Bay, and then either through the Kill Van Kull, Upper New York Bay, and Narrows; or down the Arthur Kill and across Raritan Bay and Lower New York Bay. Many excursions operated one way going and returned by the other route to offer a circle excursion. All the old time Hudson River skippers used to work in this trade at one time or another. Popular boats in this trade included the: *Suffolk,* the *Santa Claus,* the *Taminend,* the *Thomas P. Way,* the *Magenta,* the *Jesse Hoyt,* the *Martha's Vineyard,* the *J. S. Warden,* the *Majestic,* the *William Penn,* the *Fairview,* the *Elizabeth Monroe Smith,* and the *Manhattan.* Most of these were walking-beam radial sidewheelers.

For a tributary of its size, the Passaic River supported a surprising number of steamship companies. These included the Stephens & Condit Line, the T. V. Johnson Company, the Belleville Steamboat Company, Lister Brothers Line, the Passaic Steamboat Company, the Central Railroad of New Jersey Steamship Division, the Knickerbocker Steamboat Company, and the New York & Keansburg Steamboat Company. Clearly Newark and Passaic were a lucrative market for the excursion trade, with its great number of German and Slavic immigrants. A great number of these excursions headed up the Hudson River after sailing down Newark Bay and through the Kill Van Kull. The various groves along the Palisades were the most popular destinations in early years, and Bear Mountain at a later date. The largest and best known boats operating from the Passaic River were the: *United States,* the *Newark,* the *Fanny,* the *Passaic,* the *Fore-Runner,* the *Olive Branch,* the *Jonas C. Heartt,* the *Edward Payson,* the *Josephine,* the *Americus,* the *Novelty,* the *Cinderella,* the *Passaic Queen,* the *Henriette,* the *Susquehanna,* the *Cherokee,* the *Mayfair,* and the *Chrystenah,* not to mention the present-day boat, *Passaic Queen (II).*

The Hackensack River had far less population along its banks, and consequently far less steamboat activity. It was served by the *Thomas Swan, Hackensack,* and *Wesley Stoney,* plying between Hackensack and Manhattan via Newark Bay and the Kills.

Boats to Kill Van Kull and Arthur Kill operated from Whitehall Street and Dey Street in Manhattan. North Shore ports of call were New Brighton, Snug Harbor, West Brighton, Port Richmond, and Elm Park on Staten Island, and Bergen Point in Bayonne. This route was served by the North Shore Ferry Company with single-end sidewheel steamboats. Both Cornelius Vanderbilt and John H. Starin operated boats on this route. The Tompkinsville & Stapleton Ferry Co. also served these points at various times, while the Central Railroad of New Jersey Steamboats operated to Elizabethport through the Kill Van Kull with landings at Mariner's Harbor, Staten Island, and Bergen Point. Best known ships on this route were: The *Huguenot,* the *Pomona,* the *Thomas Hunt,* the *Flora,* the *Castleton,* the *Citizen,* the *Westfield,* the *Southfield, Middletown,* and *Northfield.* Also the *Red Jacket,* the *Kill von Kull,* the *Water-Witch,* the *Thomas Collyer,* the *Black Bird,* the *D. R. Martin,* and the *Sunshine.*

Service to the Amboys and New Brunswick was first established by the Fulton-Livingston interests with the *Raritan* in 1809, and the *Olive Branch* in 1818. Thomas Gibbons and Cornelius Vanderbilt also served this route with the *Atalanta,* the *Bellona,* the *Thistle,* and the *Swan.* Shortly afterwards the Stevens interests and the Camden & Amboy Railroad became the major factors on the Raritan River route. Ships operated by these interests included: *Phoenix, Independence, New Philadelphia, Napoleon, Antelope, Reindeer, Trenton, John Potter, John Neilson, Richard Stockton, William Cook, Joseph Belknap, Transport, Amboy, Princeton, Bordentown, Weehawken, G. T. Olyphant, Wyoming,* and *New Brunswick.*

Many of these names are familiar from upriver lines, which demonstrates the homogeneity of lower bay and upriver steamboat operations. With completion of railroad lines across New Jersey all the way to the shores of the Hudson at Jersey City, the Raritan River lines quickly lost importance, but they were immensely important in the days of the first railroads, which terminated on the Raritan.

The first steamboat to serve Keyport, at the mouth of Matawan Creek on Raritan Bay, was the *Monmouth* in 1836. The operating company was the Steamboat Company of Middletown Point, as Keyport was then known. In its later years its vessels were the *Hope,* the *Rockland,* the *Joseph E. Coffee,* the *John Hart,* the *Ocean Wave,* the *Golden Gate,* and the *Chingarora,* named for a local creek. The Keyport & Middletown Steamboat Company was organized in 1853 and operated the *Keyport,* the *Eagle,* the *John Hart,* the *Armenia,* the *D. R. Martin,* the *T. V. Arrowsmith,* and the *Matteawan.* It is interesting to see how a once Blue

Steamer *City of Keansburg* of the Keansburg Steamboat Company. (Steamship Historical Society Library—University of Baltimore)

Ribbon Day Liner eventually wound up in a secondary service, in the case of the *Armenia*. While these small operations frequently had small new vessels built for themselves, invariably their larger boats came off more important routes.

Early service to Keansburg, then known as Waquake, was provided by the *William V. Wilson* and the *Accomak*. In 1910 the Keansburg Steamboat Company was formed by William A. Gehlhaus, who operated brickworks in the vicinity and was interested in selling real estate. This line operated many old boats and was affectionately known as the "Gehlhaus Navy." Ships operated on this line included the *Nantasket,* later renamed *Keansburg, Chrystenah, Marthas Vineyard,* renamed *Keyport,* the *Nantucket,* renamed *Point Comfort,* the *Majestic,* the *Mobjack,* the *Pocohontas,* the *Smithfield,* and the *City of New York*. This mongrel collection demonstrates that many old ships from New England and Chesapeake Bay waters found their way to the Hudson. The flagship of the Gehlhaus fleet was the *City of Keansburg,* a 270 foot, double stacker, built for them new by the Marvel Shipyard in Newburgh, in 1928. It was the last steamboat ever built on the Hudson and is presently being refitted for use as a floating restaurant and museum ship. She operated until 1971.

The New York & Keansburg Steamboat Company operated briefly around 1916, using the *Chrystenah,* the *Forest Queen,* the *Clermont,* and the *Patchogue*. Service to Keansburg ended in 1962 when a hurricane destroyed the dock. The Keansburg Steamboat Company removed operations to Atlantic Highlands until 1965, when that pier burned down, and then operated cruises from Manhattan until 1968, and sporadic charters thereafter. For many years they provided a pleasant direct route from Manhattan to the Raritan Bay and Sandy Hook Bay shore area.

In 1860 the Raritan & Delaware Bay Railroad began building south from Port Monmouth on Raritan Bay, and they inaugurated connecting steamboat service to New York using the *Eagle,* the *Argus,* the *Alice Price,* the *Taminend,* the *Naushon,* the *Aurora,* the *Thomas Col-*

Atlantic Highlands—Beacon Hill, Twin Lights and entrance to the Shrewsbury River.

lyer, the *Twilight,* and the *Wyoming.* Other ships in this service included the *J. D. Beers,* formerly the *Jesse Hoyt,* the *Magenta,* the *Neversink,* the *Nelly White,* and the *Josephine.* By now certain of these names should be familiar, and this teaches how operations were in constant flux during the great days of steamboat activity. Furthermore, these simple ships were so well built that they never seemed to wear out. They remained economical to operate for an incredible number of years—something that our over-complex society might take a lesson from. They were so simple that there was little to break down or wear out.

The Raritan & Delaware Bay Railroad was reorganized in 1869 as the New Jersey Southern Railroad Company, and also acquired the Long Branch & Sea Shore Railroad from the Edwin A. Stevens estate at this time. This later line was extended from Long Branch and Spermaceti Cove on Sandy Hook to a deep water terminal at Horse Shoe Cove, further out on the Hook. For some time prior to this, the Long Branch & Sea Shore Railroad had been operating the *William Cook, Richard Stockton,* and *River Queen* between New York City and Spermaceti Cove. Upon completion of the Horse Shoe Cove terminal in 1870 the New Jersey Southern contracted with James Fisk and Jay Gould to operate the larger steamers *Plymouth Rock, Metropolis,* and *Empire State,* formerly of the Fall River Line, on the new route. These boats were supplemented by the *Jesse Hoyt* and the *Long Branch,* formerly the *Sleepy Hollow.* This arrangement ended in 1874, and after this period the ships operated were the *Jesse Hoyt,* the *River Belle,* the *Jane Moseley,* the *Day Star,* the *Crystal Wave,* and the *Empire State.*

In 1879 the New Jersey Southern was acquired by the Central Railroad of New Jersey. They put the large *Kill von Kull* on the route, along with the *Cape Charles* and the *City of Richmond.* In addition, the *Jesse Hoyt* was recommissioned, and the *St. John* chartered. In 1888 they built the large *Monmouth,* and in 1889 the *Sandy Hook.* The *Asbury Park* was built in 1903, but proving too slow for the route, was sold to California interests in 1918. The *Monmouth* and the *Sandy Hook* were each 260 feet long and very fast twin screw vessels. The *Monmouth* was requisitioned for military use in 1941, and the *Sandy Hook* in 1943. They were both returned to the railroad in 1946, but were never put back in service and were sold as scrap. This line, in conjunction with the New York & Long Branch Railroad, offered a fast and pleasant route to the North Jersey Shore, and was used by many summer commuters.

Various lines served the piers at Atlantic Highlands. The first pier was built in 1879. The Central Railroad of New Jersey built a 2400 ft. pier in 1892, which was destroyed by fire on May 6, 1966. This had been served at various times by ships of the Keansburg Steamboat Company, Hudson River Day Line, and Central Railroad of New Jersey. In recent years there was a bus connection from there to the Monmouth Raceway.

In the nineteenth century Long Branch was a very popular society resort. The center of social life was Leland's Ocean Hotel. At various times attempts were made to operate steamboats to an "ocean pier" at Long Branch. None of these services, using large ocean-going or Sound type steamers, ever lasted for very long, as the piers themselves did not stand up to the rough water, which often made docking very difficult or impossible. The Bath House Pier lasted from 1828 until 1854. The East End Excursion Pier lasted for only the season of 1872. Ocean Pier lasted from 1879 till 1881, and was replaced by the Iron Pier in that year. This lasted until 1908. The last pier was built in 1911 and lasted until shortly after 1966, but it was not suitable for docking ships.

Steamers that docked at the Ocean Piers in Long Branch included the *New Era,* the *Plymouth Rock,* the *City of Richmond,* the *Columbia,* the *Cygnus,* the *Taurus,* and the *Adelaide.* The *Cygnus* and *Taurus* belonged to the Iron Steamboat Company.

Steamboat service ran from New York City to the Navesink, or Neversink River points of Rumson, Locust Point, Brown's Dock, Fair Haven, and Red Bank, from 1834 until 1932.

Locust Point Landing on the Navesink River, c1870. (Granville Perkins)

For many years this service was operated by the Highlands, Long Branch & Red Bank Steamboat Company. This was a very shallow river, with shifting shoals. All the boats on this route were small, shallow-draft, sidewheelers. In early years the boats used were the: *Frank, Osirrus, Orus, Edwin Lewis, Confidence, Thomas Hunt, Thomas G. Haight, James Christopher* (later renamed *Long Branch*), *Ocean Wave, Golden Gate, Alice G. Price,* and *Highland Light.* In later years service was provided by the *Meta,* the *Helen,* the *Sea Bird,* the *Nelly White,* and the *Albertina.*

The Shrewsbury, or South River, was even shallower than the Neversink. Principal ports were Branchport and Pleasure Bay, at Long Branch, Oceanport, Sea Bright, Ocean House Landing, and Swift House Dock at Highlands. The first service between New York and Long Branch by the "inside route" was offered by the *Franklin* in 1819. Principal operators on this route were the Merchants Steamboat Company and the New York & Long Branch Steamboat Company, known as the Patten Line, after its founder, Thomas Patten. This line operated until 1942. Principal ships on the route were the *Edwin Lewis,* the *J. G. Christopher,* the sternwheeler *Wilber A. Heisley,* later renamed *City of Long Branch,* the *Shrewsbury,* the *Pleasure Bay,* the *Elberon,* the *Mary Patten,* the *Citizen,* the *Gilpin,* the *Helen,* the *Herald,* the *Tourist,* the *Union,* the *Little Silver,* and the *Thomas Patten.* Most of these were diminutive, walking-beam, sidewheelers. If we only had one of these left in operating condition on Hudson waters!

This and the preceding chapter should provide a good overall view of the variety and great amount of steamboat activity on Hudson River waters. People today tend to have no conception of the unused potential of these beautiful waterways. It is my hope that this long catalog of routes will stimulate the imagination of planners and other government officials as to the great possibilities available to them. We are working to clean up the waters. Now let us use them again.

27 The Coming of the Railroads

The nineteenth century was the age of railroad building in America and the Hudson Valley came in for its goodly share of this activity. This development was complex, and traffic and corporate alignments still remain in a constant state of flux in 1980, as freight tonnages reach all time highs. As a major port and metropolis, New York was a natural center for railroad growth. However, inasmuch as it was located on an island, and there were mountains of considerable size to the immediate northwest, many of the early railroads ran to tidewater at such places as South Amboy, Catskill, Albany, and Troy, and relied upon steamboat and barge connections to New York. The great width and depth of the Hudson River prevented rails from entering Manhattan from the west until 1908, when the Hudson & Manhattan Tunnel was opened. Most railroads relied upon ferry boats, lighters, barges, and car-floats to service New York City, with the actual railheads on the west bank of the Hudson. North of Manhattan the two natural, low-level, routes to the west were along the Mohawk River, west from Albany, and through the Sparkill Gap and Ramapo Clove in Rockland and Orange Counties. The first alternative was used by the New York Central System, and the second by the Erie Railroad. Availability of easy shipping on the Hudson River, and opposition of waterside estate owners, delayed construction of the Hudson River Railroad, along the east bank from Manhattan to Albany, until around 1850.

The first railroad to impinge upon Hudson waters was the Camden & Amboy, which was chartered by the State of New Jersey in 1815. It was for a line across the narrow middle part of New Jersey connecting South Amboy, on the Raritan Bay, with Camden, on the Delaware River, across from Philadelphia. This was a very busy stagecoach route and there was considerable ocean coastal shipping between Philadelphia and New York, sailing around Cape May. This valuable charter was granted to the noted engineer and real estate developer, Colonel John Stevens, who was among the earliest developers of steamboats and railroad locomotives. The line he built ran from South Amboy to Bordentown, on the Delaware, at the head of tidewater navigation just below Trenton. At first, before tracks were extended to Jersey City, and to Camden, and before ferries were established at these points, the railroad depended on steamboat connections at either end. Colonel Stevens's son, Robert L. Stevens, also a notable mechanical and civil engineer, was made Chief Engineer of the Camden & Amboy and imported the famous steam locomotive, the *John Bull* from England. The Camden & Amboy was the original nucleus of the great Pennsylvania Railroad system, which later abandoned the Camden & Amboy as its chief line upon acquisition of the parallel New

Jersey Railroad, the present Northeast Corridor-Amtrak Mainline. At present the Camden & Amboy is operated as a secondary freight line by Conrail. It is electrified and serves a considerable industrial area.

The next railroad development connecting with Hudson waters was at Catskill, at the mouth of Catskill Creek. In 1828 the Catskill & Ithaca was chartered to cut across the northern Catskills to the Finger Lake region. There was delay in raising capital and the line was built under the name of Canajoharie & Catskill in 1840. Even this more modest project was never completed, as the line never got further west than Cooksburg. Completion of the Albany & Schenectady in 1831 lessened the incentive to complete the line, and in 1842, after a serious accident, the Canajoharie & Catskill was abandoned. Years later, parts of its grade were used by the narrow gauge Catskill Mountain Railroad.

The Erie Canal was completed in 1825, reaching Albany from Schenectady by a circuitous route by way of Cohoes. To circumvent this detour and save time, the Albany & Schenectady Railroad was completed in 1831. It was later reincorporated as the Mohawk & Hudson. The first through train was powered by the steam locomotive *DeWitt Clinton,* and the passenger cars were modified Concord coaches. This line was the first segment of the later-day New York Central System, and by 1840, there was a chain of short connecting railroads all the way from Albany to Buffalo. While the first segments were built to supplement the Erie Canal, eventually the railroad came to completely supplant the canal for the passenger and fast freight trade. For a few years passengers transferred to steamboats at Albany in order to reach New York. These were golden years for Albany and hotels, taverns, warehouses, and transfer agents flourished and great fortunes were made. However, Albany was soon to lose importance upon completion of through rail lines all the way to New York City.

In October 1851 the Hudson River Railroad was completed from New York City, up along the east bank of the Hudson River, to Greenbush, across the river from Albany. It was then necessary to take a ferry in order to reach Albany. The original southern terminal of the

Albany Union Station, built 1899.

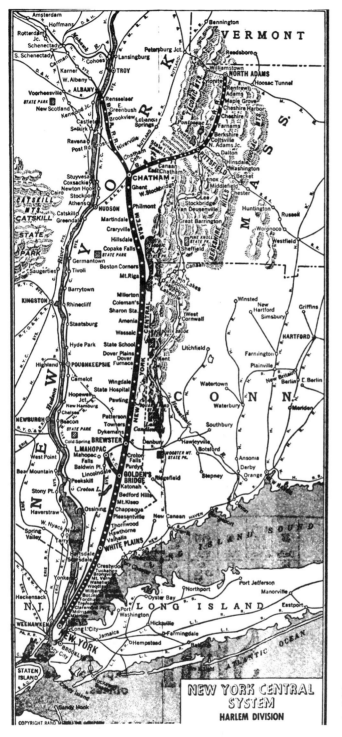

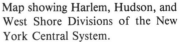

Map showing Harlem, Hudson, and West Shore Divisions of the New York Central System.

Hudson River Railroad was at St. John's Park on Manhattan's West Side. The line ran north in the middle of Eleventh Avenue, which soon came to be called Death Avenue, because of the many accidents harming pedestrians and horse drawn vehicles. After proceeding north past Manhattanville, Audubon Park, and Carmansville, the line crossed Spuyten Duyvil

Creek to Berian's Neck in the Bronx. It continued north to Yonkers, Peekskill, Poughkeepsie, Hudson, and Greenbush. As mentioned before, property owners along the Hudson did not like the new railroad, which was noisy and dirty and cut them off from the riverbank. Washington Irving, who lived below Tarrytown, was particularly annoyed. However, it is recorded that he soon became a frequent traveller on the railroad. Many people thought it foolish to spend a great deal of money building a railroad when the river navigation was free to all. Much rock blasting and tunneling was required along the line, and Spuyten Duyvil and other creeks had to be bridged at their mouths. The large 1,500 foot long Cortlandt Bridge was built across the mouth of Annsville Creek at Peekskill. Other major bridges were built across the Croton River and Wappinger's Creek. However, despite this expense, it was seen as a good investment by a prominent steamboat operator, William C. Redfield, who was the principal backer and promoter of the new railroad. He well realized the great advantage of year around operation during the annual freeze-up of the Hudson, and the fact that the fast trains paralleling the Erie Canal had siphoned off the most lucrative portion of the canal's traffic—the high rated express freight and the passengers. Furthermore, another shrewd steamboat operator, Cornelius Vanderbilt, was attempting to cut himself in on the New York and Albany traffic. It was clear that the new railroads were where the action was, and that it was attracting the "smart money."

We might note that upon construction of Grand Central Terminal at 42nd Street and Park

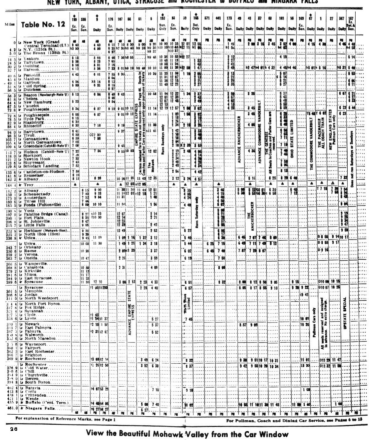

Timetable of the New York Central's Hudson Division in 1940. This is one of four similar pages for this portion of line.

WEEK DAY TRAINS—NEW YORK TO PEEKSKILL

♦ 195	Mile	EASTERN TIME	♦ 277	♦ 235	♦ 279	♦ 711	♦ 191	♦ 241	♦ 281	♦ 111	153	2
PM	0	Grand Central Term......	PM	PM	PM	PM	PM	PM	PM	PM	PM	P
5 06		Upper Level	.....	.....	.....	.....	‡5 24	5‡32	.....	.....	‡5 43	..
.....		Lower Level...........	5‡11	5‡17	5‡19	5k20	.....	.....	‡5 35	5‡38	.....	5
h5 16	4	Lv 125th Street.............	h5‡21	h5‡27	5‡29	h5k30	‡5h34	h5‡42	‡5h45	w	‡5h53	h6
.....	5	Lv The Bronx (138th St)....	.....	.....	5‡31	h5k32		.....	.....	w	.....	..
.....	7	Ar High Bridge (W.169th St.)	.....	.....	5‡36	5k37		.....	‡5 51	w	.....	..
.....	8	Ar Morris Hgts (W. 177th St.)	.....	.....	5‡38	5k39		.....	.....	w	.....	..
.....	9	Ar Uni'sity Hts (W.207th St.)	.....	.....	5‡41	5k41		.....	‡5 55	w	.....	..
.....	10	Ar Marble Hill (W.225th St.)	.....	5‡38	5‡43	5k42		.....	‡5 58	w	.....	..
.....	11	Ar Spuyten Duyvil.........	.....	.....	5‡47	5k46		.....	‡6 00	w	.....	..
	12	Ar Riverdale...............	5‡34	.....	5‡50	5k49		.....	‡6 04	w		..
	13	Ar Mt. St. Vincent.......(b)	.....	.....	5‡52	5k50		.....	.....	w		..
	14	Ar Ludlow...................	5‡38	5‡46	5‡55	5k52		.....	‡6 08	w		6
	15	Ar Yonkers.................	5‡41	5‡50	5‡58	5k55		.....	‡6 12	w		6
	16	Ar Glenwood............(b)	5‡44	5‡52	6‡01	5k58		.....	‡6 15	w		6
	17	Ar Greystone..............	—	5‡56		6k00		.....	—	w		6
	19	Ar Hastings-on-Hudson......	.....	6‡00	.....	6k03		.....	.....	6‡10		6
	20	Ar Dobbs Ferry............	.....	6‡04	.....	6k06		.....	.....	6‡13		6
	21	Ar Ardsley-on-Hudson......	.....	6‡07		6k09		.....	.....	6‡16		6
	22	Ar Irvington..............	.....	6‡10		6k12		.....	.....	6‡18		6
	....	Ar Sunnyside Restoration...	.....	.....		.....		.....	.....	..		..
.....	25	Ar Tarrytown...........(g)	.....	6‡15		6k16		6‡11	.....	6‡23	.....	6
.....	26	Ar Philipse Manor.......(b)	.....	6‡18		6k19		6‡15	.....	6‡26	.....	6
.....	29	Ar Scarborough............	.....	6‡24		6k23	.....	6‡20	.....	6‡31	.....	6
5 53	30	Ar Ossining................	.....	6‡29	.....	6k27	‡6 i09	6‡24	.....	6‡34	‡6 i28	6
5 57	33	Ar Harmon................	.....	6‡34	.....	6k31	‡6 13	6‡32	.....	6‡39	‡6 33	7
6 07	34	Ar Croton-on-Hudson.......	.....	6‡40	.....	6k36	.....	.....	.....	c 6‡49	.....	7
.....	36	Ar Oscawana...............	.....	—	.....	—	.....	.....	.....	c 6‡52	.....	—
.....	37	Ar Crugers..................	.....	.....	.....	.....	.....	.....	.....	c 6‡55	.....	..
.....	38	Ar Montrose................	.....	.....	.....	.....	.....	.....	.....	c 7‡00	‡6 49	..
6 17 PM	41	Ar Peekskill..............	PM	PM	PM	PM	‡6 31 PM	PM	PM	c‡7 06 PM	‡6 54 PM	P
Notes: Will not run Holidays. See Note "✠"			See Note "✠" Will not run Holidays. Does not run Saturdays.	See Note "✠" Will not run Holidays. Does not run Saturdays.	See Note "✠" Will not run Holidays. Does not run Saturdays	Runs Saturdays only.	See Note "✠" Does not run Saturdays. Will not run Holidays.	See Note "✠" Will not run Holidays. Does not run Saturdays.	See Note "✠" Will not run Holidays. Does not run Saturdays.	Does not run Saturdays	Does not run Saturdays	See Note "✠" Will not run Holidays. Does not run Saturdays.

Timetable of New York Central Hudson Division showing a few of the local trains operating between New York and Peekskill in 1950.

Avenue in Manhattan, a new line was built from Berian's Neck, along the north side of Spuyten Duyvil Creek, and down along the Harlem River in the Bronx and thence across to Manhattan on the East Side, to link the new terminal with the Hudson River Railroad. The original line to St. John's Park reverted to branchline status, although even today the Hudson Division of Conrail, who now owns all the lines involved, still runs from St. John's Park to Albany. Between the years 1930 and 1941 a great construction project was undertaken to build depressed rights or way, tunnels, and viaducts to get the tracks off the Manhattan streets. In recent times there has been no passenger service on the West Side Manhattan Line. This line, first built in 1847, is now primarily a freight terminal route, but even this use is in decline with changing operations in the Port of New York. There is some talk of Amtrak building a connecting track between this line and Penn Station, but in view of the extremely high construction costs and the rather limited benefits to be gained, it is likely that this will never transpire and that they will continue all operations into Grand Central. The new New York Convention & Visitors Center is being built over the main freight yards at 34th Street.

Cornelius Vanderbilt, who had been active in Hudson River steamboating, was becoming anxious to control a railroad between New York and Albany. The eleven separate railroads between Albany and Buffalo had been amalgamated into the single New York Central Railroad in 1853. If Vanderbilt could control this line, he would have a stranglehold on traffic west from Albany and could cause Redfield to sell out of the Hudson River Railroad. In order to get a line from New York to Greenbush, Vanderbilt first sought control of the New York & Harlem Railroad. This line was founded in 1831 as a horse-car line running north from City Hall in New York City to the village of Harlem on Manhattan Island, near the present 125th Street. It followed roughly the line of The Bowery and Park Avenue. Eventually the New York & Harlem had been extended north through White Plains, Brewster, Dover

Plains, and Copake Falls to a connection with the Albany & Stockbridge Railroad at Chatham. Vanderbilt undertook some secret stockmarket manipulations and drove New York & Harlem stock down to $9.00 per share, and then bought controlling interest. By 1862 Vanderbilt was President of the line. Next he purchased control of the New York & Hudson, a short line that connected the New York & Harlem with Greenbush, across the Hudson River from Albany. Then he sought to gain control of the New York Central. In 1866 a railroad bridge had been built at Albany, and the New York Central and the New York & Hudson were exchanging through cars. Because of the competition offered by the New York & Harlem, Vanderbilt had been able to acquire the Hudson River Railroad by 1864. Thus, by 1867 Vanderbilt controlled all the lines between Albany and New York. Vanderbilt's technique to acquire the New York Central was to drive its stock down by embargoing interchange traffic during the winter months when the Hudson was frozen and there were no steamboats available as a relief route . . . . and this he did on January 14, 1867. The New York Central stock fell, and fell, and fell, and Vanderbilt bought, and bought, and bought. On December 11, 1867 Cornelius Vanderbilt became President of the New York Central. In 1869 he merged his holdings into the New York Central & Hudson River Railroad. The New York & Harlem was not included in the merger, but was leased to the larger road. It retains its separate corporate identity in 1980. In 1871 Vanderbilt built a major new terminal at East 42nd Street and Park Avenue, known as Grand Central Terminal, to serve as principle depot for trains of his new system. He continued to operate a connecting horsecar line as far south as 26th Street. A second, larger, Grand Central Terminal was built in 1884, expanded in 1898 and 1900, and finally replaced by the present structure in 1913. Eventually Vanderbilt, and his son William H. Vanderbilt, expanded their holdings into the Great New York Central System through acquisition of the Lake Shore & Michigan Southern, Michigan Central, New York, West Shore & Buffalo, Cleveland, Cincinnati, Chicago & St. Louis, Rome, Watertown & Ogdensburg, and Boston & Albany railroads, not

The original Grand Central Terminal, 1871. (New York Central photo)

The second Grand Central Terminal, 1884. (New York Central photo)

to mention numerous shorter lines. Ultimately the Central's tracks reached such distant points as Boston, Montreal, Chicago, St. Louis, and Cincinnati. It controlled lines running along both shores of the Hudson, and advertised itself as the Waterlevel Route.

The Vanderbilt family retained control of the system from 1869 until the 1950s. During that decade the New York Central began to get into serious financial difficulties and was losing traffic to trucks on the new Federally subsidized highways, and passengers to the airlines and private automobiles. This led to decreased dividends and stockholder disenchantment with the Vanderbilt designated management headed by William White. A dissident group, headed by Robert R. Young and Allen Kirby, waged a great proxy fight and succeeded in gaining control. They installed Alfred E. Perlman as President. In attempts to immediately increase and maintain dividends, Perlman cut maintenance to the point of causing frequent breakdowns and impairing the railroads' ability to offer acceptable service. This led to diversion of traffic to competing lines and loss of revenue. The line was in such bad physical and financial shape by the mid-1960s that it sought merger with its arch-rival, the Pennsylvania Railroad, which was experiencing similar difficulties. On February 1, 1968 the two roads were merged to form the Penn-Central Railroad. Shortly thereafter the Penn Central sought to diversify greatly into many other fields, and changed the name of the company to simply Penn-Central Corporation, in an attempt to play down their image as a railroad. Much revenue that should have been put into refurbishing the railroad plant to properly service increasing freight tonnage was spent on acquisition of many speculative properties of dubious value, and all the while substantial dividends were paid and executive salaries increased. The

The present Grand Central Terminal, 1913. (New York Central photo)

plant and service deteriorated still further and more traffic was diverted to competing systems. Management, under President Stuart A. Saunders, kept up a brave front, although at this time they had begun borrowing substantially from European Banks to meet railroad operating expenses, and misrepresented the value of the collateral to these banks. The great Penn-Central seemed unsinkable. Then, in June 1970, the inevitable happened and bankruptcy was declared—the biggest one in United States history! The great system built up by the Vanderbilts, whose prime interests were in the transportation field, was brought to ruin by financial speculators and mismanagement. Only the Federal Government had sufficient funds to help this debacle and keep the line operating. On April 1, 1976, it was incorporated, along with other bankrupt railroads in the northeast, into the Conrail Corporation. Since May 1, 1971 all long distance passenger trains had been operated by the National Railroad Passenger Corporation, better known as Amtrak. Various commuter and local passenger operations are maintained by Conrail on account of various local and state transportation authorities, such as the Metropolitan Transportation Authority, MTA, in New York.

Many former New York Central branch lines, once independent short lines, were not included in Conrail and were put up for sale. Several, such as the Adirondack Railway and the Ulster & Delaware are back in independent operation as short lines. The fate of other lines, such as the Wallkill Valley and parts of the New York & Harlem, are still undecided. Conrail operates freight service over most of the former New York Central and West Shore mainlines. Amtrak provides both coach and sleeping car services between Boston and New York in the east and Chicago in the west via Albany and Buffalo and a connecting service to Montreal over the Delaware & Hudson north of Albany.

In 1863 the Saratoga & Hudson River Railroad was completed from Athens to Schenectady. At Athens it connected with steamers to New York operated by Daniel Drew. This line never paid and was known for many years as the "White Elephant Line." For many years it remained as the Athens Branch of the West Shore, and a short section was incorporated into the West Shore mainline. The Athens Branch has long been abandoned.

The West Shore Railroad was built as a "nuisance road" by interests that may have been backed by the competing Pennsylvania Railroad. This is a matter still in dispute among rail historians. The idea was to directly parallel the highly profitable New York Central from Albany to Buffalo, and to also serve some new markets on the west bank of the Hudson between Jersey City and Albany. The west bank had previously been completely dependent on steamboats and ferry connections to the Hudson River Railroad on the east bank. Naturally this left them completely cut off during the freeze up of the river, and there was considerable agitation for a railroad on the west side.

In the 1870s the New York, West Shore & Chicago was surveying a route to Buffalo, but the enterprise was abandoned in 1877 during a financial panic. This route was to include the Ridgefield Park Railroad, built in 1866 from Jersey City to Ridgefield Park, New Jersey. It ran west of the Palisades, and along the Hackensack River. In 1873 the new Jersey City & Albany Railroad incorporated the Ridgefield Park Railroad into its projected line, which was in turn to be part of the New York, West Shore & Chicago. The Jersey City & Albany got as far as South Haverstraw, now called Congers, before funds ran out in 1880. North of Congers an expensive tunnel was required to get the line from the Hackensack to the Hudson Valley.

During this same period, the Wallkill Valley Railroad, which connected the Erie Railroad, at Montgomery, with Kingston began building a Northern Extension from Kingston to Athens. Also, the New York, Ontario & Western, which ran from Middletown to Oswego through the Southern Catskills, was looking for a good entry to New York City. It had been originally built as the New York & Oswego Midland, and it depended on a connection to Jersey City over the New Jersey Midland Railroad, which was then coming under the domination of the competing New York & Erie. This was most unsatisfactory. It decided to build its own line east from Middletown to Cornwall-On-Hudson, and thence south along the Hudson to a connection with the Jersey City & Albany at Congers. A new corporation, the New York, West Shore & Buffalo, was formed to take over the Jersey City & Albany and complete the line north from Congers to just south of Albany, and thence westward to Buffalo along the route previously surveyed by the New York, West Shore & Chicago. This new line was to pass through Haverstraw, West Point, Cornwall (where a junction would be made with the New York, Ontario & Western), Newburgh, Kingston, and Athens. This new line was to incorporate the Wallkill Valley's Northern Extension and the Saratoga & Hudson River. Totally new construction would be required from Congers to Kingston and from Rotterdam Junction to Buffalo. A branch was to be built from Ravena, near Coxsackie, to Albany. To eliminate dependence upon use of the New York, Lake Erie & Western and the Pennsylvania Railroad's Jersey City terminals, a new tunnel was to be drilled through the Palisades from North Bergen, on the Jersey City & Albany line, to Slough's Meadow in

TWENTIETH CENTURY LIMITED

DINNER SPECIALS

CHICKEN OKRA SOUP *with Rice*.....................in Cup 25; Tureen 35
COLD TOMATO BOUILLON....................................in Cup 25
CONSOMME *Hot or Cold*....................................in Cup 25

FRIED FILLET OF FLOUNDER *with Tartar Sauce* 70
 BROILED FRESH MACKEREL, *Boiled Potato*.......................... 75
  BROILED SCROD *with Bacon*................................. 75
MIXED FRUIT OMELETTE... 65
FRESH VEGETABLE DINNER.. 70
ROAST BEEF HASH, *Browned in Pan*................................ 65
LAMB CHOP *en Casserole with Vegetables*.......................... 90
FRICASSEE OF CHICKEN *with Rice Curry* 90
ROAST PRIME RIBS OF BEEF, *with Mashed or Boiled Potato* 90
COLD BAKED HAM $\big)$
COLD ROAST BEEF $\big\}$ *with Potato Salad*......................... 85
COLD ROAST PORK $\big)$
SALMON OR SHRIMP SALAD *with Mayonnaise*......................... 60
LETTUCE WITH TOMATOES OR CUCUMBERS......................... 40
PINEAPPLE SALAD *with Cream Cheese*................................... 50

FRESH SPINACH... 25
 NEW CABBAGE 20
  BAKED WHITE ONIONS.................................... 25
   MASHED OR BOILED POTATO 20
    NEW POTATO *in Cream* 25

BANANA CREAM CUSTARD............................ 25
 COFFEE JELL, *Whipped Cream* 25
  ICED WATERMELON................................... 25
   CANTALOUPE *a la mode*............................ 50
    FRESH BLUEBERRY PIE................................. 25
     ORIENTAL FRUIT CAKE.............................. 20
      VANILLA ICE CREAM OR FROZEN PUDDING 30
       BLUEBERRIES WITH BOWL OF CRACKERS AND MILK ... 55

Special Combination No. 1 — $1.25

FRIED FILLET OF FLOUNDER *with Tartar Sauce or*
 BROILED FRESH MACKEREL, *Maitre d'Hotel*
FRESH SPINACH POTATO *in Cream*
 ASSORTED BREAD *or* ROLLS
COFFEE JELL, *Whipped Cream* BANANA CREAM CUSTARD
 TEA, COFFEE, MILK

Special Combination No. 2 — $1.50

CHOICE OF COLD MEATS *with Potato Salad or*
FRICASSEE of CHICKEN *with Rice Curry or*
ROAST PRIME RIBS OF BEEF *au Jus*
BAKED WHITE ONIONS MASHED POTATO
 ASSORTED BREAD *or* ROLLS
PIE BANANA CREAM CUSTARD ICE CREAM
 TEA COFFEE MILK

Dining car menu from the 1920s. This was then the nation's most expensive railroad dining car.

Weehawken, opposite 42nd Street, Manhattan. A large terminal was to be built at Weehawken and ferries established to West 42nd Street and Jay Street. The New York, Ontario & Western was to have trackage rights from Cornwall to Weehawken, and use of the new terminal and ferry services. This great amalgamation took place in 1881, and by January 1, 1884, trains were operating from Weehawken to Buffalo.

Among the principal backers of the New York, West Shore & Buffalo were General Horace Porter and George Mortimer Pullman. Pullman was mad at the Vanderbilts for using the sleeping cars of the competing Wagner Palace Car Company rather than his own, and thought he saw a good opportunity to make a profit while getting some delightful revenge.

General Porter was a personal friend of the late President Ulysses S. Grant, and an active railroad builder and promoter. Actually, both may have been simply front men for the Pennsylvania Railroad, as President Grant himself, much to his subsequent grief, invested heavily in what seemed a "sure thing."

The new railroad was built to the highest engineering standards and even had lower grades than the New York Central & Hudson River Railroad. For this reason Conrail is using it today as their principal route for heavy tonnage. However, the new railroad was undercapitalized and it was soon engaged in a vicious rate war with the parallel New York Central. This rate war was so sharp that, at one time, the passenger fare from New York to Chicago dropped to only $8.00. By 1885 the New York, West Shore & Buffalo was bankrupt. A secret deal was worked out aboard J. P. Morgan's yacht, the *Corsair,* whereby William Vanderbilt would stop construction of the South Pennsylvania Railroad and acquire the West Shore line for a nominal amount. The South Pennsylvania Railroad was another nuisance line financed by the Vanderbilts, parallel to the main line of the Pennsylvania Railroad, from Harrisburg

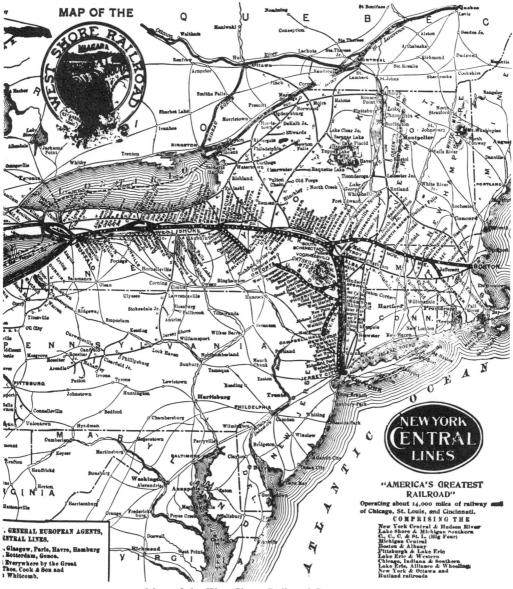

Map of the West Shore Railroad System.

to Pittsburgh. Its old alignment is now used by the Pennsylvania Turnpike. In this deal only the other stockholders in the two nuisance roads—the South Pennsylvania and the West Shore—really lost anything, and it was rumored that J. P. Morgan earned a commission of $3,000,000 for arranging the compromise. The New York Central took over a 475 year lease on the New York, West Shore & Buffalo, with an option to renew for a like period. A new corporation, the West Shore Railroad Company, was created to operate the line under New York Central control, and to complete further terminal improvements, including construction of a large grain elevator at Weehawken.

The West Shore operated DeLuxe through passenger service to Chicago until the First World War. Its top train was the *Continental Limited,* which operated between Buffalo and Chicago over the tracks of the Grand Trunk Railroad. The Grand Trunk was affiliated with the Grand Trunk Western, which ultimately built to Prince Rupert, British Columbia, on the Pacific Coast. Ultimately a through *Continental Limited* route was extended to Prince Rupert and Vancouver. The Grand Trunk and the Grand Trunk Western later became part of the Canadian National System, and the name *Continental Limited* survives in today's *Super Continental,* which is now operated betwen Montreal and Vancouver by VIA, Canada's counterpart to Amtrak. The West Shore advertised itself as "The Niagara Falls Route," and its monogram showed a picture of the Horseshoe Falls.

However, the West Shore's greatest importance in the early years was to provide service to the plush resorts of the Catskill Mountains and Saratoga. Other important trains were the

Typical New York Central dining car of the early 1950s. A long way from Amtrak's Spartan Amdinettes. (New York Central photo)

Saratoga & Mohawk Valley Express and *Rip Van Winkle Flyer,* which was operated in conjunction with the Ulster & Delaware Railroad. They offered through parlor car and drawing room service from points as distant as Washington and Philadelphia by connections over the Pennsylvania Railroad. Cars to Saratoga and Lake Champlain continued from Albany over the Delaware & Hudson. The *Mountaineer* and the *Ontario Express* of the New York, Ontario & Western also operated over the West Shore as far as Cornwall. Through passenger service between Weehawken and Albany was continued until 1958. After that date only commuter service was operated as far north as West Haverstraw.

After a very nasty and prolonged legal battle the New York Central was allowed to discontinue this once extensive service on December 10, 1959, on which date I was the last passenger ever to board a regularly scheduled West Shore passenger train. The New York, Ontario & Western had been totally abandoned on March 29, 1957.

Under Perlman management, the West Shore was cut down from four to two tracks between Weehawken and Dumont, New Jersey; and from two tracks to one, between Dumont and Rotterdam Junction. Most of the line from there to Buffalo was completely abandoned, only short sections being retained as industrial spurs. Under Penn-Central austerity the line deteriorated greatly under very heavy use, and from lack of the barest maintenance, until it reached the point where there were many derailments and slow orders were imposed over long stretches. As this was the Penn-Central's main freight line, this deterioration of service hurt Penn-Central by driving away traffic. On April 1, 1976 Conrail took over the West Shore, and immediately began reconstruction of the line and installing welded rail. However, it was a "cheap and dirty" job without proper attention to rebuilding the track substructure and, under even heavier tonnage use, the track and the expensive new rails, are in worse shape than ever and the derailment-delay syndrome is back in effect, again driving away business.

There have been various plans and proposals for restoration of commuter passenger service to New Jersey and Rockland County points under state auspices. Until Conrail improves the track, this does not seem feasible, although recent population growth and the present gasoline situation make this inevitable eventually. Any such service would operate to Hoboken Terminal, which has just undergone major renovation.

The Ulster & Delaware Railroad was completed from Kingston Point, where connections were made with Day Line steamers, to Oneonta, on the Susquehanna River, in 1900. At Oneonta the Ulster & Delaware connected with the Delaware & Hudson Railroad, and there were trains to Cooperstown on Lake Otsego. The Ulster & Delaware also had direct standard gauge branches to Hunter and Kaaterskill Station, near the Catskill Mountain House and Kaaterskill Falls. The *Rip Van Winkle Flyer* operated through from Weehawken to Kaaterskill Station offering first class service.

In 1932 the Ulster & Delaware was acquired by the New York Central. Passenger service was operated until 1954. The Hunter and Kaaterskill branches were abandoned in 1940. In 1965 twenty-one miles of track between Bloomville and Oneonta were abandoned, leaving only a connection with the West Shore at Kingston. When Penn-Central declared bankruptcy the Ulster & Delaware was not included in the Conrail System. In April of 1979 the County of Ulster purchased the portion of the Ulster & Delaware in Ulster County from the Executors of the Penn-Central Estate for $1,500,000. Delaware County has done the same for that section within its borders. It is planned to resume operation as independent, short lines, offering freight services, and steam powered passenger train excursions through the most scenic portions of the Catskill Mountains.

The Wallkill Valley Railroad, opened in 1872 from Montgomery to Kingston, was acquired by the New York Central in 1932, and passenger service was discontinued in the 1940s. This line was included in Conrail. In February 1980 it was announced that Conrail would operate

Steamlined steam power by Henry Dreyfus. (New York Central photo)

the portion between Montgomery and New Paltz, but that the section between there and Kingston was up for abandonment. However, under the complicated provisions of the reorganization courts, first refusal would be offered to anyone interested in acquiring and operating the line, which opened up several promising opportunities. However, the line was abandoned and tracks torn up in 1984.

The narrow gauge Catskill Mountain Railroad ran from Catskill Point to Palenville and Cairo, using, in part, alignments of the earlier Canajoharie & Catskill. There were steamer connections with both the Hudson River Day Line, and the Catskill Evening Line to New York, which was controlled by the same interests, dominated by the Beach family, who also owned the Catskill Mountain House and controlled several other connecting narrow gauge lines. These lines were the Otis Elevating Railway, a funicular line from Otis Junction to Mountain House Station, and the Catskill & Tannersville, a narrow gauge line from Mountain House Station to Tannersville, by way of Kaaterskill Falls and Haines Falls. Together they formed a through route for passengers to the mountaintop hotels and boarding houses and, from 1882 until 1918, when they were all abandoned, they handled vast numbers of tourists and vacationers.

In 1841 the New York & Erie Railroad was completed from a large mole, or pier, at Piermont as far as Goshen, in Orange County. Piermont was located at the south end of the Tappan Zee at a gap between Tallman Mountain and Mount Nebo, through which the Spar Kill flowed into the Hudson River at near sea level. Many geologists think this gap was the original course of the Hudson River. It is the only break in the long line of hills west of the

GOING WEST.

Miles from Weehawken

STATIONS.

Where Time is Omitted Trains Do Not Stop.

- Lv. N.Y., ft. Desbrosses St., N.R.
- Lv. N.Y., ft. W. 42d St.
- Lv. BROOKLYN, by Annex
- Lv. JERSEY CITY, P. R. R. Sta.
- Lv. HOBOKEN, W. S. Sta.
- Lv. WEEHAWKEN W.S. Sta.
- New Durham
- Little Ferry
- Bogota (Hackensack)
- Teaneck
- West Englewood
- Bergenfield
- Dumont
- Harrington Park
- West Norwood
- Tappan
- Orangeburgh
- Blauvelt
- West Nyack
- Valley Cottage
- Congers, Rockland Lake
- Haverstraw
- WEST HAVERSTRAW
- Stony Point
- Tomkin's Cove
- Jones' Point
- Iona Island
- Fort Montgomery
- W. Point (Garrison by ferry)
- CORNWALL
- NEWB'H (Fishkill by ferry)
- Roseton
- Cedarhill
- Marlborough
- Milton
- Highland, (P'k'psie by ferry)
- West Park
- Esopus
- Ulster Park
- Port Ewen
- Ar. KINGSTON (Restaurant)
- Lv. KINGSTON
- Lake Katrine
- Mt. Marion
- Saugerties, Tivoli by ferry
- Malden
- West Camp
- Alsen
- Catskill, Greendale by ferry
- W. Albany, Hudson by f'ry
- Coxsackie, N'ton H'k by f'ry
- New Baltimore
- Ar. Ravena
- Ar. Selkirk
- Wemple
- Glenmont
- Kenwood Junction
- Ar. ALBANY (Union Sta.)

Selected train-column notes visible in the table:
- Leaving New York Saturday night will run through to Newburgh.
- Does not carry baggage except for Buffalo and points beyond.
- On Sunday, train 47 will run between Weehawken and West Haverstraw only.
- DOES NOT CARRY BAGGAGE
- No. 71 runs daily except Saturday and Sunday.
- Does not carry baggage.
- Albany Special. Does not carry baggage.

West Shore Railroad timetable of early 20th Century. Note through trains such as *West Shore Limited; Hudson River & Mohawk Express; Continental Limited; Chicago & St. Louis Limited;* and *Buffalonian.*

Hudson from Jersey City to Cornwall, and thus was a valuable and likely place to bring a railroad to tidewater from the west. The New York & Erie Railroad was built westward from this location because of this gap, and because the charter from the State of New York demanded that the line remain within that State, and only permitted a few short dips into Pennsylvania, along the Delaware River, to avoid having to do a great deal of blasting on the Hawks Nest Cliffs. The State of New York did not cotton up to the idea of its great Southern Tier railroad having its terminus in New Jersey. Consequently the railroad built its terminal on a long, manmade, mole and established a steamboat connection to Duane Street in Manhattan. The little village took its name from the new pier and the surrounding mountains. It was the goal of the builders of the New York & Erie to connect the Hudson River with Lake Erie and provide service through the Southern Tier of New York State, to appease the many citizens in that area who were envious of the prosperity brought about by the Erie Canal. The State provided some financial backing, but mostly it was a private undertaking. The man who originally conceived this line was the industrialist Eleazor Lord, who lived near Piermont and appreciated the value of the Sparkill Gap. He later became the first President of the new railroad. The new line was to run westward, through the gap, and to Suffern's at the foothills of the Ramapo Mountains. Thence it would follow the Ramapo River through the mountains to Turner's, and then run westward to Goshen, the Orange County seat. From there it would cross over the Shawangunk Mountains to Port Jervis, at the junction of the Delaware and Neversink rivers. It would then head up along the Delaware to Deposit, before striking westward over the Randolph Hills through Glen Summit to the valley of the Susquehanna, near its confluence with Starucca Creek. It would follow the Susquehanna to Binghamton, and the Chemung River to Elmira. Proceeding westward it would pass through Horseheads and Painted Post to Corning, Wellsville, and Salamanca, and then turn northward to strike Lake Erie at Dunkirk, where port facilities would be built. On May 14, 1851 the line was completed from Piermont to Dunkirk, and great celebrations were held

Storm King Mountain with West Shore train c1900.
(Hudson River Day Line photo, courtesy A. V. S. Olcott, Jr.)

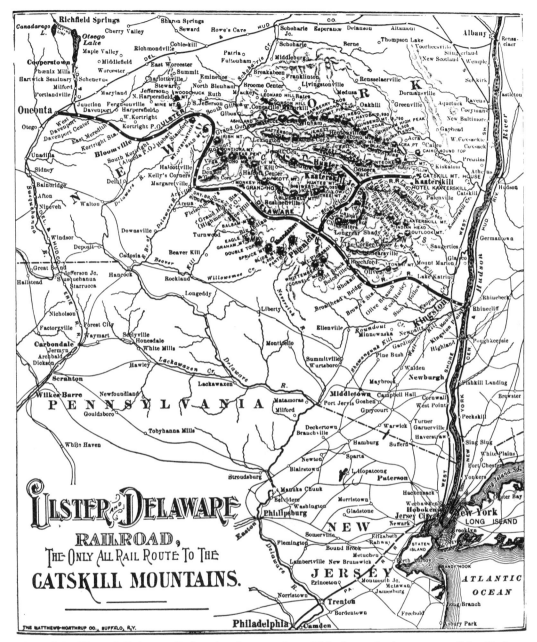

Map of the Ulster & Delaware Railroad and connections. This shows the importance of the Hudson River as an access route to the Catskill Mountains.

all along the route. A special train carrying such notables as Daniel Webster and United States President Millard Fillmore made a joyous excursion the length of the new line.

However, by 1861 the long steamboat trip between Manhattan and Piermont was proving a detriment, and a new all-rail route was established to a large new terminal at Pavonia, in Jersey City. This new route went through New Jersey and incorporated the lines of the Paterson & Hudson River Railroad, the Paterson & Ramapo Railroad, and the .25 mile long Union Railroad, which had been siphoning off Erie traffic at Suffern. A ferry was established to Chambers Street in Manhattan. A second ferry from Jersey City to West 23rd Street was

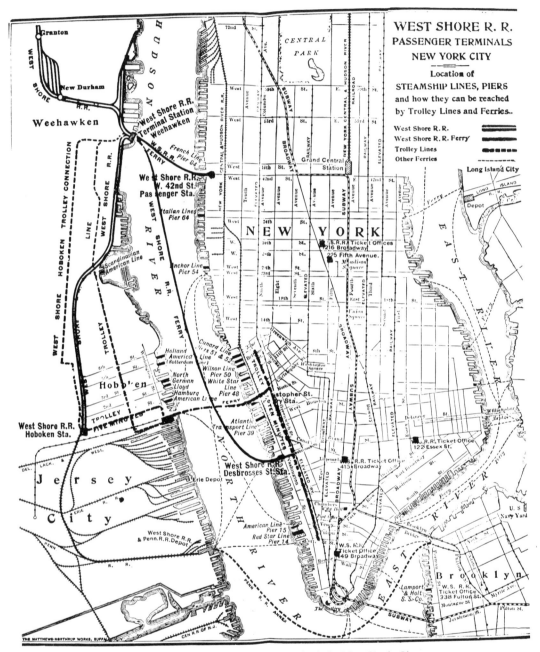

West Shore Railroad Passenger Terminals in New York City.

opened in 1868, and the steamboat from Piermont to Duane Street was discontinued. The line from Suffern to Piermont became a local branch.

During this period another local, New Jersey based, railroad came into the picture. The Northern Railroad of New Jersey, backed by real estate developers John Van Brunt and Thomas W. Demarest, was chartered in 1854 to build a line northward from Jersey City, up along the foot of the western slopes of the Palisades, to the New York State Line. It was to follow the valleys of the Hackensack River, Overpeck Creek, and the Tenakill Brook. The principle idea was to help sell suburban real estate on these gentle western slopes of the

Palisades by providing businessmen with convenient train service to the metropolis. This area was heavily wooded and very picturesque, and a perfect setting for the type of villas and cottages recommended by Andrew Jackson Downing in his various books. Eventually the valley through which this line passed came to be known as the Northern Valley, which name remains in current usage in 1980. The route passed through North Bergen, Ridgefield, Leonia, Englewood, Tenafly, Cresskill, Demarest, and Closter, and terminated at Norwood, which it reached in 1854. In 1859 it built an extension into New York State to connect with the Erie at Sparkill, and continuing through the Sparkill Gap to Piermont on the Hudson. After 1870 it was extended northward along the Hudson, on a ledge one third the way up the side of Clausland Mountain, through Grand View to a terminal at Nyack. This line afforded fine views out over the Tappan Zee, and the towns along the line became a popular location for summer homes and villas—many in the Steamboat Gothic and early Victorian styles. The track from Sparkill to Nyack was ripped up in the 1960s, and today the Northern, which later became part of the Erie and now belongs to Conrail, offers only freight service from Jersey City to Piermont. There is a spur from Sparkill to Orangeburg, which was part of the old Erie Main Line. The portion from Orangeburg to Nanuet has also been abandoned, thus severing the original Erie Main Line.

On January 8, 1850 the Erie Railroad completed a branch line from Greycourt on its main line near Goshen to Newburgh. The line was originally projected in 1845, at which time Newburgh merchants had subscribed $100,000 towards the project. The idea was to establish

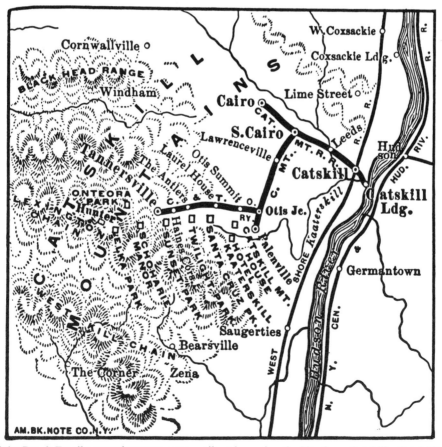

Map of the Beach Family owned narrow gauge railroads serving the Northern Catskills: Catskill Mountain Railroad; Otis Elevating Railway; Catskill & Tannersville Railroad.

a railroad carfloat ferry from Newburgh to Fishkill across the Hudson. There were to be rail connections eastward into New England, and the New York & Erie Railroad could thus tap the lucrative Southern New England market for traffic to the west. The Boston, Hartford & Erie Railroad had completed a line between Boston and Hartford in 1867, and sought Erie financial backing for its completion to Fishkill. Ultimately the western extension came into being as the Newburgh, Dutchess & Connecticut, which was ultimately absorbed into the New York, New Haven & Hartford as its Fishkill Branch. This railroad car ferry operated between 1872 and 1901 using the sidewheel ferryboats *Fannie Garner* and *William T. Hart*. Completion of the great Poughkeepsie Railroad Bridge in 1888 rendered this ferry concept superfluous.

In 1871 a charter was granted to build a railroad bridge across the Hudson River at Poughkeepsie. This began a seventeen year struggle to complete the structure. From the outset political and economic difficulties hampered progress. In spite of a great controversy about bridge piers being built in the river, an amendment to the charter was granted permitting construction of four piers.

In 1873 the Pennsylvania Railroad, through its representatives J. Edgar Thompson and A. D. Dennis, bought $1,000,000 worth of stock in the company, which was about half the projected cost at that time. Control passed into their hands, and the immediate building of the bridge seemed assured. However, because of the 1873 financial panic and the death of Thompson, the scheme collapsed and the project remained inactive until 1876 when a contract was entered into with the American Bridge Company of Chicago, and work on two of the piers began. Because of construction and financial difficulties, work was suspended in 1878. The charter was kept alive by time extensions, and in 1886 the Manhattan Bridge Building Company was organized to finance construction, with the Union Bridge Company under subcontract to build the structure.

Dawson, Symmes & Usher for the concrete, masonry and timber work; the Atlantic Dredging Company; the United Lumber Company for the false work; and John F. O'Rourke, P. P. Dickinson, Arthur P. Paine and John Flack Winslow were the structural engineers. Winslow, who was also the President of the Poughkeepsie & Eastern Railway, was a specialist in steel construction. He had been active in manufacturing steel and introduced Bessemer Process steel to the United States, which he supplied for the famous Civil War battleship *Monitor* built in 1862. The new Bessemer Steel was used extensively in construction of the bridge.

Operations resumed in September, 1886 but, once again, opposition to the four river piers was organized by boatmen. Finally their lobbying efforts were defeated and work was resumed. In addition to overcoming these political and economic obstacles, the engineers had to devise solutions to such physical obstacles as a deep, wide tidal river, great depth to bearing rock, height of the palisades, and the great length (6,767 feet) of the structure. The bridge's length was a record for a steel structure as was its 546 foot channel span. The track is 212 feet above the water and the length of structure over water is 2,260 feet, the rest being over part of the City of Poughkeepsie and the western palisades. Construction was finished on August 29, 1888, and approaches were completed later that year. The first train crossed December 29, 1888. Final cost of the bridge was about $10,000,000.

For several years after its opening the Poughkeepsie Bridge was operated under the control of the Philadelphia, Reading & New England Railroad, a subsidiary of the Philadelphia & Reading Railway. By 1906 the entire network of lines on the east side of the Hudson had passed to the control of the New York, New Haven & Hartford, except for the Poughkeepsie & New England, which ran east to Boston Corners near the Connecticut and Massachusetts state lines. The New Haven controlled these various lines through its subsidiary, the Central New England Railroad. Its main line ran from Hartford, Connecticut to Campbell Hall,

WESTBOUND—WEEKDAYS

Miles	NEW YORK TO NYACK	k 1183 N.B.	c 1101 N.B.	k 1185 N.B.	c② 1103 N.B.	c① 1105 N.B.
		PM	PM	PM	PM	PM
0.0	Lv. **NEW YORK** Port Authority Bus Term. 41st St. & 8th Ave. (1 block from Times Square)	1.17	.....	.....	5.30	......
0.0	Chambers St. Ferry.....	1.12	5.00	5.10 ②	5.23 ①	6.20
....	Jersey City.........(Lv.	1.27	5.15	5.23	5.40	6.35
....	Susquehanna Transfer...	1.37	.....	.....	5.49	......
10.2	Ridgefield.............	1.43	5.30	5.39	5.56	6.51
11.5	Palisades Park.........	1.46	5.34	5.42	6.00	6.54
12.5	Leonia................	1.48	5.37	5.44	6.03	6.56
15.0	Englewood.............	1.54	5.41	5.50	6 08	7.00
16.0	Hudson Ave., Englewood	1.58	5.44	5.55	6.11	7.02
17.0	Tenafly...............	2.02	5.47	5.58	6.14	7.05
18.2	Cresskill.............	2.05	5.51	6.01	6.17	7.07
19.2	Demarest.............	2.08	5.54	6.05	6.20	7.10
20.2	Closter...............	2.11	5.57	6.08	6.23	7.12
21.9	Norwood..............	2.14	6.00	6.10	6.26	7.15
22.7	Northvale.............	2.16	6.03	6.13	6.29	7.18
24.7	Sparkill..............	2.20	6.07	6.16	6.34	7.22
25.8	Piermont.............	2.24	6.12	6.23	6.38	7.31
27.1	Grand View...........	f 2.28	6.16	6.26	6.42	....
28.5	South Nyack..........	2.31	6.20	6.30	6.46	7.37
29.0	Nyack............. (Ar	2.34	6.22	6.33	6.48	7.39
		PM	PM	PM	PM	PM

Vertical notes in columns: k Saturdays only — Will not run Saturdays and Holidays — c — k Saturdays only — Will not run Saturdays and Holidays — c — Will not run Saturdays and Holidays — c

NO SUNDAY SERVICE

1952 Timetable of the Northern Railroad of New Jersey.

New York. Here it had strategic connections with the Erie Railroad, the New York, Ontario & Western, the Lehigh & Hudson River, and the Lehigh & New England railroads. Under later direct New York, New Haven & Hartford control the terminals were changed to Devon, Connecticut and Maybrook, New York. This route served as a high-speed freight bypass around the carfloats used on the lower Hudson and across New York Bay. At one time the New Haven seriously considered acquisition of the New York, Ontario & Western as a western extension which would turn it into a trunk line carrier. It is interesting to speculate what would have been the ultimate fate of the New Haven if it had pursued this course instead of continuing to divide the traffic at Maybrook among four different connecting lines and ultimately being absorbed by Penn-Central and Conrail.

The Poughkeepsie Bridge Route served briefly as a through passenger route for a Boston to Washington train known as the *Federal Express,* and the route was frequently called the Federal Express Route. At that time most through Boston to Washington passenger trains were put upon a car-float in the Bronx and floated around Manhattan Island to Jersey City. Completion of the Hell Gate Bridge across the East River, and of tunnels under the East River and Hudson River, along with the construction of Pennsylvania Station in Manhattan, obviated the need for this inconvenience, and the Poughkeepsie Bridge lost its value as a passenger train bypass. However, it remained a very important freight line. A famous scheduled fast freight called the *Central States Dispatch* operated through between Cumberland, Maryland and Providence, Rhode Island by the Poughkeepsie Bridge, over the lines of the Western Maryland, Reading, Central Railroad of New Jersey, Lehigh & Hudson River, and New Haven railroads. The Poughkeepsie Bridge was also utilized by an Interurban electric railway operating between Poughkeepsie and New Paltz, entering the streets of both terminal cities over the local trolley tracks. After the amalgamation of the New York Central, Pennsylvania, and the New Haven into the Penn-Central, the Poughkeepsie Bridge Route fell into disfavor. It tended to divert traffic from Southern New England to the competing Lehigh & Hudson River and Erie-Lackawanna railroads, instead of keeping it on Penn-Central tracks for the entire journey south or west. Consequently, after a minor fire damaged the eastern approach trestle on May 8, 1974 no efforts were made to repair the bridge. All traffic was rerouted over other lines and crossed the Hudson on the Penn-Central

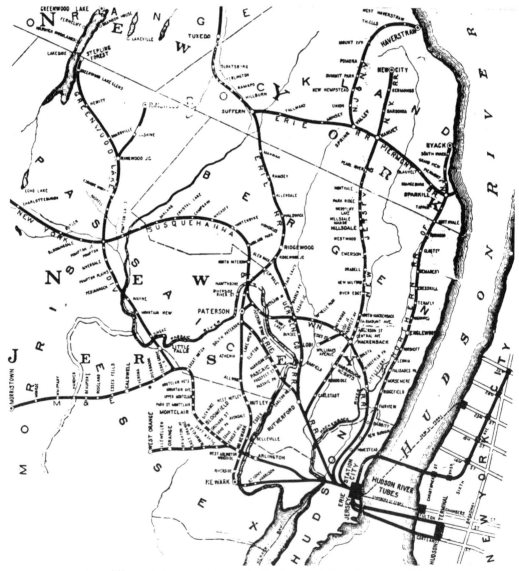

Local lines of the Erie Railroad in the lower Hudson Valley, c1912.

Poughkeepsie Railroad Bridge and Hudson River Day Line screw propelled steamer *De Witt Clinton*. (Hudson River Day Line photo, courtesy A. V. S. Olcott, Jr.)

Castleton Bridge below Albany. The Lehigh & Hudson River and the Erie-Lackawanna entered legal complaints about loss of valuable interchange traffic and this loss helped drive both of them into bankruptcy shortly thereafter. When Penn-Central went bankrupt, all the various lines were lumped together into the new unified Consolidated Rail Corporation, better known as Conrail. As a monopolistic carrier Conrail has shown no interest in reopening the Poughkeepsie Bridge Route and prefers to pass on the additional cost of operating via the Castleton Detour to New England shippers and receivers in the form of large surcharges. In 1982 it remains out of service. Shippers in New England and mine owners in Pennsylvania have exerted political pressure to get it reopened and Congress passed legislation in 1978 mandating its repair, modernization, and reopening and authorizing $9,000,000 to do so. Conrail countered with new wildly inflated repair estimates and false references to "iron construction" and "rotting wooden pilings," when in fact engineering studies confirm the basically good condition of its Bessemer Steel structure and all-masonry piers. Agitation to reopen the bridge continues and Conrail seems more stubbornly set against it than ever before. Possibly this is because they fear such a reopened bridge will fall into the hands of a competitor and break their monopolistic strangle-hold. Several plans for competing independent railroads to take it over from Conrail under a Federally administered "controlled transfer" process have been proposed and are under study. Among those interested were Timothy Mellon's Guilford Transportation Company; the Lehigh, Erie & Wallkill Transportation Company; and Niel St. John Raymond, the Boston financier. Presently the bridge is proposed for formal abandonment under ICC Docket AB-167, Sub. 168 N filed on November 13, 1981, and will take effect 90 days from then. It carried on Conrail's books at a negative value of $5,000,000 and can be purchased for only $35,000, the value of the easily removable running rails. Otherwise the bridge would cost more to remove than its value as scrap. Several consulting engineering firms estimate that it can be put effectively back in service for under $3,000,000. The reason nobody has made a bid for the bridge is that Conrail is refusing to sell other track on either side needed to reach the bridge. Buyers cannot be assured of being able to reach it and are therefore hanging back. Meanwhile, if no buyers appear after a second 90 day period, they would be free to begin dismantling. The whole matter has become a political cause celebre and the results seem problematical at this writing.*

The writer was President of the Lehigh, Erie & Wallkill, one of the firms studying possible purchase. Destruction of this vital defense link would be seriously harmful to the economy

---

*The bridge was ultimately sold for $1.00 to Mr. Gordon S. Miller, agent for Railway Management Associates of St. Davids, PA. They have since done nothing with the bridge, which is becoming dilapidated.

NEW YORK DIVISION BRANCHES.

NEW YORK TO NEWBURGH.

Miles.	Eastern Time. Dec. 16, 1906.	Excpt 148 Sun.& Hols.	Excpt 150 Sun.	Sat. Only.	Excpt 154 Sun.& Hols.	ExSat 156 Sun.& Hols.	Daily 160	Hols. 788 Only.	Sun. 782 Only.	Sun. 784 Only.	Sun.& Sp'l Hols. Note.	
	Leave	A.M.	A.M.	P.M.	P.M.	P.M.	P.M.	P.M.	A.M.	P.M.	A.M.	
. .	N. Y., 23d St..	3.55	9.10	12.40	3.53	4.38	7.25	12.55	9.10	1.40	9.25	
0	N. Y., Chamb St.	4.15	9.15	12.50	4.00	4.45	7.30	1.00	9.15	1.45	9.30	
48	Turner . . . Leave	7.28	10.55	. . .	. . .	. . .	9.00	3.05	10.55	. . .	. . .	
49	Central Valley .	7.43	11.06	2.32	5.25	6.26	9.13	3.18	11.13	3.52	10.54	
50	Highland Mills	7.52	11.09	2.35	5.31	6.29	9.16	3.21	11.19	3.55		
52	Woodbury	8.01	11.12	2.39	5.34	6.33	9.20	3.25	11.26	3.59		
54	Houghton Farm	f8.05	f11.15	f2.43	. . .	f6.36	9.23	3.28	f11.29	f4.03		
55	Mountainville	8.10	11.18	2.46	5.40	6.39	9.26	3.31	11.33	4.06		
57	Cornwall . . .	8.14	11.22	2.51	5.44	6.43	9.30	3.35	11.37	4.10		
59	Vail's Gate Junc.	8.21	11.26	2.56	5.49	6.48	9.34	3.39	11.44	4.14		
61	New Windsor . .	8.25	11.31	3.00	5.53	6.52	9.38	3.43	11.48	4.18		
62	West Newburgh	f8.29	f11.34	3.05	f5.57	f6.56	9.41	f3.46	11.51	4.22		
64	Newburgh	8.33	11.38	3.09	6.01	7.00	9.45	3.50	11.55	4.28		
	Arrive	A.M.	A.M.	P.M.	P.M.	P.M.	P.M.	P.M.	A.M.	P.M.	A.M.	

NOTE.—See notes on page 80 in reference to holidays.
NOTE.—See Note for Special on page 12.

NEWBURGH TO NEW YORK.

Miles.	Eastern Time. Dec. 16, 1906.	Excpt 149 Sun.& Hols.	Hols 781 Only	Excpt 151 Sun.& Hols.		Excpt 153 Sun.& Hols.	Hols. 785 Only.	Excpt 155 Sun.& Hols.	Daily 157 Note.	Sun. 788 Only.	Sun. 789 Only.	Sun.& Sp'l Hols. Note.	
	Leave	A.M.	A.M.	A.M.		A.M.	P.M.	P.M.	P.M.	A.M.	P.M.	P.M.	
0	Newburgh	5.48	6.35	7.10		8.10	12.25	3.45	6.32	7.19		5.16	
2	West Newburgh	5.53	f6.39	Note.		f8.15	f12.29	f3.50	6.37	f7.24	f5.20		
4	New Windsor . . .	5.57	6.43	f7.17		f8.19	12.33	3.54	6.42	7.28	5.24		
6	Vail's Gate Junc.	6.02	6.48	7.25		8.26	12.38	3.59	6.48	7.33	5.30		
7	Cornwall	6.06	6.51	7.29		8.29	12.41	4.03	6.53	7.37	5.34		
10	Mountainville	6.11	6.56	7.34		8.35	12.46	4.08	7.00	7.41	5.39		
10	Houghton Farm	f6.14	f6.58			f8.37	f12.48	f4.10		f7.44	f5.41		
13	Woodbury	6.21	7.02	f7.43		8.44	12.52	4.16	7.12	7.49	5.46		
15	Highland Mills	6.27	7.06	7.51		8.49	12.56	4.21	7.19	7.53	5.50		
15	Central Valley	6.30	7.09	7.55		8.53	12.59	4.24	7.21	7.56	5.52	5.15	
19	Turner . . . Arrive		7.20			9.03	1.10	4.35	7.46	8.07	6.05		
64	N. Y., Chamb. St.	8.14	9.14	9.22		10.37	3.07	6.42	10.12	10.07	8.07	6.27	
	N. Y., 23d St. . .	8.30	9.30	9.30		10.45	3.15	7.00	10.20	10.15	8.15	6.45	
	Arrive	A.M.	A.M.	A.M.		A.M.	P.M.	P.M.	A.M.	A.M.	P.M.	P.M.	

NOTE.—See notes on page 80 in reference to holidays.
NOTE.—See Note for Special on Page 12.

NEWBURGH BRANCH VIA GREYCOURT.

Sun. 786 Only.	Sun. 788 Only.	Excpt 168 Sun.	Excpt 166 Sun.	Excpt 164 Sun.	Excpt 162 Sun.& Hols.		Miles.	Eastern Time. Sept. 16, 1906.	Excpt 161 Sun.& Hols.	Daily 165 Note.	Excpt 165 Sun.	Excpt 167 Sun.	Sun. 787 Only.	
P.M.	A.M.	P.M.	P.M.	P.M.	A.M.			Leave Arrive	A.M.	P.M.	P.M.	P.M.	P.M.	
12.25	9.10	4.25	2.55	9.10	3.55			. . . . N.Y., 23d St . . .	9.30	1.15	7.00	10.20	8.15	
12.30	9.15	4.30	3.00	9.15	4.15			N. Y., Chamb. St.	9.22	1.02	6.42	10.12	8.07	
6.08	11.05	6.30	4.44	11.25	7.40		0	Lv. Greycourt Ar.	7.22	9.50	4.12	6.05	5.34	
6.13	11.09	6.34	4.47	11.28	7.44		3	Craigville	7.17	9.45	f4.06	6.00	5.29	
6.18	11.17	6.37	f4.55	11.32	7.52		5	Blooming Grove	f7.11	f9.40	f4.01	5.58	5.22	
6.28	11.21	6.43	5.10	11.38	7.57		7	Washingtonville	7.07	9.36	3.57	5.45	5.14	
6.34	11.25	6.49	5.16	11.43	8.03	10	Salisbury Mills	7.03	9.31	3.52	5.39	5.08	
6.41	11.32	6.56	5.23	11.50	8.10	13	Vail's Gate	6.56	9.25	3.45	5.32	5.00	
6.46	11.34	6.58	5.25	11.52	8.13	14	Vail's Gate Junc.	6.54	9.23	3.43	5.29	4.57	
6.50	11.38	7.02	5.29	11.56	8.17	16	New Windsor	6.49	f9.18	f3.39	5.24	4.53	
6.54	f11.41	7.06	f5.34	f12.00	8.21	17	West Newburgh	f6.45	f9.15	f3.35	f5.20	f4.49	
6.58	11.45	7.10	5.39	12.04	8.25	19	Newburgh	6.40	9.10	3.30	5.15	4.45	
P.M.	A.M.	P.M.	P.M.	P.M.	A.M.			Arrive Leave	A.M.	A.M.	P.M.	P.M.	P.M.	

NOTE.—See notes on page 80 in reference to holidays.

MONTGOMERY BRANCH.

Excpt 129 Sun.	Daily 115	Excpt 105 Sun. C. N. E	Excpt 117 Sun.	Miles.	Eastern Time. Sept. 16, 1906.	Excpt 142 Sun.& Hols.	Hols. 790 Only.	Excpt 102 Sun.	Excpt 110 Sun. C. N. E.	Sun. 792 Only.	Excpt 126 Sun.	
P.M.	A.M.	A.M.	A.M.		Leave Arrive	A.M.	P.M.	P.M.	P.M.	P.M.	P.M.	
2.55	9.10	7.10	2.55	. . .	. . . N.Y., 23d St . . .	10.45	1.15	7.15	7.15	7.15	10.20	
3.00	9.15	7.15	3.00		N. Y., Chamb. St.	10.37	1.02	7.07	7.07	7.07	10.12	
4.54	11.22	11.12	7.27	0	Lv . . . Goshen . . . Ar	8.26	10.05	4.35	4.12	5.00	5.52	
f4.59	11.30	.	f7.32	3	Kipps	f8.22	f9.57	4.27		4.50	5.47	
5.04	11.40	.	7.37	6	Campbell Hall	8.17	9.51	4.16		4.38	5.41	
5.06	11.42	11.24	7.39	6	Campbell Hall June.	8.15	9.49	4.11	4.00	4.34	5.38	
f5.11	11.48	.	f7.43	8	Seely Town . . .	f8.12	f9.46	4.06		4.29	5.35	
f5.14	f11.51	.	f7.48	9	Beaver Dam .	.		f3.57		f4.17	.	
5.19	11.56	.	7.52	11	Montgomery . . .	8.06	9.40	3.54		4.14	5.29	
P.M.	A.M.	A.M.	A.M.		Arrive Leave	A.M.	A.M.	P.M.		P.M.	P.M.	

Erie Railroad New York Division Branches. The Erie once provided frequent service between New York and Newburgh.

of the region and would further stifle regional economic revitalization which would be a real crime.

In the late nineteenth and early twentieth century another short line operated on the east side of the Hudson. The Rhinebeck & Connecticut Railroad, which had been chartered as the

TABLE 1

MAIN LINE
ALBANY AND TROY TO MONTREAL

Miles	NYC61 D&H9 Daily	NYC163 D&H1 Ex. Sun.	NYC55 D&H3 Daily	NYC95 D&H37 Daily	17 Sun only	NYC49 D&H5 Ex. Sun.	NYC167 D&H41 Ex. Sun.	NYC21 D&H7 Daily			
	PM	PM	AM	AM	PM	PM	PM	PM			
NEW YORK (N.Y.C. RR.).Lv.				See Note							
Grand Central Term...... "	10 50	11 25	7 10	8 15	......	1 00	3 15	8 00	......		
125th Street........... "	......	......	r7 20	r8 25	......	......	......	......			
	AM	AM	AM	PM	PM	PM	PM	PM			
0 **ALBANY, D & H**......Lv.	......	6 15	11 00	12 05	......	4 20	6 30	11 50			
3.3 Menands (✛)........... "	......	f6 22	......		......	4 27	......				
3.9 Cemetery (✛)......... "											
4.7 Colonie (✛)........... "	......	6 26	......		......	4 31	......				
6.0 Watervliet............. "	......	6 30	11 13		......	4 37	6 43	12 03			
7.8 **TROY**.............. "	1 53	......	......		......						
8.8 Cohoes............... "	......	6 37	11 21		......	4 45	6 50	12 11			
10.7 West Waterford........ "	......	6 44	j11 25		......	4 51	6 55				
18.9 Mechanicville........ "	......	7 02	11 39		......	5 03	7 07	12 30			
25.4 Round Lake.......... "	......	7 12	j11 48		......	5 13	7 16	f12 39			
31.6 Ballston Spa......... "	......	7 28	12 02		......	5 25	7 28	12 53			
38.3 Saratoga Springs......Ar.	......	7 40	12 12	12 59	......	5 35	7 38	1 03			
38.3 Saratoga Springs......Lv.	......	7 47	12 18	1 02	......	5 40	......	1 11			
55.4 Fort Edward..........Ar.	......	8 10	12 42	1 25	......	6 04	......	1 36			
55.4 Fort Edward..........Lv.	......	8 22	12 53	1 28	......	6 08	......	1 48			
62.9 Smith's Basin (✛)...... "	......	8 34			......						
66.8 Fort Ann............. "	......	8 41	f1 07		......	f6 22					
70.8 Comstock............ "	......	8 48	f1 12		......	f6 27		f2 08			
77.4 Whitehall............Ar.	......	9 02	1 25	1 55	......	6 40		2 20			
77.4 **Whitehall**..........Lv.	......	9 12	......	2 03	3 00	x6 50		2 30			
87.2 Dresden............. "	......	9 30	......		f3 17	x7 f06		f2 46			
92.2 Putnam (✛).......... "	......	9 40	......		f3 25	x7 f13					
99.5 Fort Ticonderoga........... "	......	9 57	......	2 35	3 37	x7 26		3 07			
(Ticonderoga)											
108.9 Crown Point......... "		10 14			f3 52	x7 f41		f3 21			
116.6 Port Henry........... "		10 29		2 58	4 03	x7 53		3 35			
127.6 Westport............ "		10 52		3 17	4 24	x8 14		3 57			
137.1 Essex.............. "		11 09			f4 44	x8 f30		f4 12			
141.8 Willsboro............ — "		11 20		f3 38	f4 53	x8 f39		f4 21			
149.8 Douglass (✛)........ "		f11 39				x8 f55	g4 37				
154.3 Port Kent........... "		11 54			f5 17	x9 f04		f4 46			
167.4 **Plattsburg**.................Ar.		12 24		4 26	5 45	x9 25		5 12			
167.4 **Plattsburg**.................Lv.		12 45		4 32	5 55			5 26			
176.7 West Chazy.......... "		1 02			f6 15			f5 39			
183.0 Chazy.............. "		1 12			f6 24			5 47			
190.7 **Rouses Point (D. & H.)**.....Ar.	6 35	1 25		5 03	6 40			6 00			
Rouses Point (D. & H.).....Lv.	6 40			5 08				6 10			
Montreal West (N. J. Ry.).. "	7 45			6 15				7 20			
Westmount.... " .. "	7 52			6 22				7 27			
MONTREAL.. " ..Ar.	8 00			6 30				7 35			
(Windsor Station)	AM	PM	PM	PM	PM	PM	PM	AM			

Vertical notes within columns: "Montreal Limited Air Conditioned" (NYC61 D&H9); "The Laurentian" (NYC95 D&H37); "No baggage carried" (NYC167 D&H41).

NOTE: Commencing June 16th this train will operate via Troy leaving New York at 9:00 A. M., Troy at 12:20 P. M., due Montreal at 7:00 P. M.

Timetable of the main route between New York and Montreal via the Hudson River Valley and Lake Champlain over the New York Central and Delaware & Hudson railroads. 1951.

Connecticut Western, ran from Rhinecliff to Silvernails, New York. It was controlled by the Reading Company in its later years.

Returning to the consideration of the New York & Erie Railroad, it is found that shortly after completion to Dunkirk, on Lake Erie, it attracted the interest and attention of Daniel Drew, the steamboat man who had founded the People's Line in 1839. He was a fierce rival of Cornelius Vanderbilt and sought to counterbalance Vanderbilt's increasing control of the New York Central, New York & Harlem, and Hudson River Railroad routes by obtaining control of the New York & Erie. By 1854 Drew was on the Erie's board of directors. Soon he joined forces with James Fisk and Jay Gould in obtaining complete control of the Erie. The financial antics of this clique are not examined here, as they have been described in great detail by many others. Suffice it to say that there was gross mismanagement of the Erie Railroad and its properties were allowed to decay, much like those of the Penn-Central in this century. Only Gould seemed to have any real interest in proper development of the railroad itself, and this was mainly owing to its potential value as part of a contemplated Transcontinental System. This regime brought the Erie to its knees financially by 1872 and it took subsequent administrations until 1942 to rebuild its plant and financial structure and declare a genuine earned dividend. During the intervening years the Erie had extended its lines to Buffalo, Chicago and Cincinnati through acquisition of connecting lines, the principal one being the Atlantic & Great Western.

Another railroad which came into the Erie fold was the New Jersey & New York, which is now known as the Pascack Branch of Conrail. Its main line ran from Jersey City to Spring Valley, on the Old Main Line of the Erie, following the valleys of the Hackensack River and the Pascack Brook through Carlstadt, Hackensack, Oradell, and Montvale, New Jersey, and Pearl River and Nanuet, New York. There was a northern extension from Spring Valley to West Haverstraw, on the Hudson, where connection was made with the West Shore Railroad. In later years this line was cut back to Theils, and ultimately abandoned. There was also a branch from Nanuet to New City, also abandoned. It retains passenger service between Hoboken and Spring Valley, operated by Conrail under the auspices of the New Jersey Department of Transportation and the Metropolitan Transportation Authority, who also operated the new Erie Main Line passenger services between Hoboken and Port Jervis.

On October 17, 1960 the Erie Railroad merged with the Delaware, Lackawanna & Western to form the Erie-Lackawanna Railway, which, in turn, was incorporated into Conrail in 1976 after experiencing very great flood damage during a major hurricane while still seriously feeling the loss of the Poughkeepsie Bridge traffic. At present Conrail still operates most of the former Erie Railroad lines, but the status of many segments is still clouded. The State of New York has spent many millions of subsidy dollars to upgrade the main line, but Conrail favors downgrading it and concentrating traffic on other routes. A number of competing railroads including the Pittsburgh & Lake Erie, Delaware & Hudson, Delaware-Otsego Corporation, and Lehigh, Erie & Wallkill would like to acquire the line, but Conrail prefers downgrading and abandonment to selling.

One of the most powerful and successful railroads from the earliest times, contrasting with its present financial misery competing with an unfriendly Conrail as its major connection, was the Delaware & Hudson. It was chartered in 1823 to build a canal from the Northeastern Pennsylvania coalfields to the Hudson River at Kingston. The canal ran from Honesdale, Pennsylvania to Rondout, New York, following the valleys of Lackawaxen Creek, the Delaware River, the Neversink River, and Rondout Creek. The canal was completed in 1828 and operated from Honesdale until 1899 and for a short segment of its Eastern end until 1904. Its history has been described in detail in Chapter 17. As early as 1829 the Delaware & Hudson Canal Company built a short gravity railroad from the coalmines near Carbondale to Honesdale and experimented with the early steam locomotive *Stourbridge Lion*. Gradually railroads proved superior to canals for year-round movement of commodities and in 1899 the company divested itself of canal operations and expanded its railroad activities, changing its corporate name to Delaware & Hudson Railroad in 1904.

Its first major railroad acquisition was the Albany & Susquehanna, which had been completed by other owners in 1869. It ran between Binghamton on the Susquehanna River and on the main line of the Erie Railroad to Albany by way of Oneonta. This line enters the Hudson Valley at Kenwood, just below Albany through the Normanskill Ravine. There it joins the Albany Branch of the West Shore, with which it shares tracks into downtown Albany.

Map of the Delaware & Hudson Railroad System. 1951.

Eventually the Delaware & Hudson built a more direct line to the Pennsylvania coalfields, dropping south from the Albany & Susquehanna at Nineveh Junction to Carbondale, Scranton, and Wilkes-Barre. For many years the anthracite traffic on these lines was the financial backbone of the Delaware & Hudson, and these lines still remain vital segments in todays greatly expanded trunk line operations.

In 1871 the expanding Delaware & Hudson acquired a small empire of shortlines in the Upper Hudson Valley. After the successful completion of the Mohawk & Hudson Railroad between Albany and Schenectady, another railroad called the Saratoga & Schenectady was

TABLE 3   BRANCH LINE
FORT EDWARD TO LAKE GEORGE

(Also connections from New York and Albany)

Miles	N.Y.C. RR.	163 Daily				
		PM				
0.0	Lv. New York (G.C.T.)	11 25	......	......	......	......
4.2	" 125th St........	......	......	......	......	......
14.5	" Yonkers........	r11 49	......	......	......	......
32.7	" Harmon........	12 21	......	......	......	......
142.2	Ar. Albany........	3 20	......	......	......	......
148.4	Ar. Troy..........	......	......	......	......	......
		AM				
	D. & H. RR.	1 Ex. Sun.				
		AM				
0.0	Lv. Albany........	6 15	......	......	......	......
	Lv. Troy..........		......	......	......	......
55.4	Ar. Fort Edward....	8 10	......	......	......	......
		AM				
	D. & H. RR.	161 Ex. Sun.				
		AM				
0.0	Lv. Fort Edward....	8 30	......	......	......	......
2.4	" Hudson Falls (✛)	f8 38	......	......	......	......
5.5	" Glens Falls......	8 50	......	......	......	......
14.5	Ar. Lake George.....	9 15	......	......	......	......
		AM				

built in 1832 to link Schenectady with the popular resorts of Ballston Spa and Saratoga Springs. In 1835 businessmen in Troy built a line from Troy to Ballston Spa by way of Cohoes, and Waterford. In 1853 this line was incorporated as the Rensselaer & Saratoga Railroad. In the same year it acquired the Saratoga & Schenectady. This line built the first railroad bridge across the Hudson. It was between Troy and Green Island. The bridge was opened on October 6, 1835. On May 10, 1862 this first wooden bridge caught fire from the sparks of a locomotive and, owing to a high wind from the north, resulting in a great fire which devasted Troy, burning over five hundred major buildings and killing many people. After crossing to Green Island the railroad ran northward on the various islands at the confluence of the Mohawk and Hudson rivers, crossing the various sprouts of the Mohawk, on smaller bridges. The main bridge into Troy was rebuilt in 1884, and again in 1925. In 1963 rail operations over this route were discontinued and the bridge was turned over to Albany and Rensselaer Counties for highway use. For many years the *Montreal Limited* operated over this line.

While not now part of the Delaware & Hudson system, it is of interest to note the construction of the Troy & Schenectady in 1842, and the Troy & Greenbush in 1845. Both these lines were ultimately acquired by the New York Central, and are now part of the Conrail system.

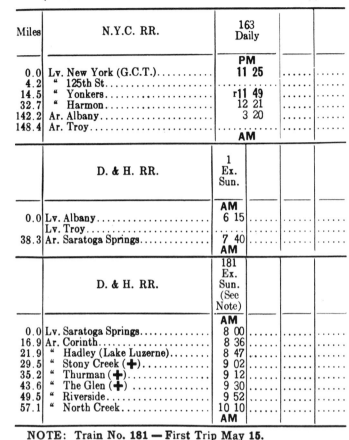

TABLE 2 **BRANCH LINE**
SARATOGA SPRINGS TO NORTH CREEK
(Also connections from New York and Albany)

Miles	N.Y.C. RR.	163 Daily		
		PM		
0.0	Lv. New York (G.C.T.)............	11 25	......	.....
4.2	" 125th St.......................	....	......	.....
14.5	" Yonkers.....................	r11 49	......	.....
32.7	" Harmon.....................	12 21	......	.....
142.2	Ar. Albany......................	3 20	......	.....
148.4	Ar. Troy.......................	....	......	.....
		AM		
	D. & H. RR.	1 Ex. Sun.		
		AM		
0.0	Lv. Albany......................	6 15	......	.....
	Lv. Troy.......................	....	......	.....
38.3	Ar. Saratoga Springs.............	7 40	......	.....
		AM		
	D. & H. RR.	181 Ex. Sun. (See Note)		
		AM		
0.0	Lv. Saratoga Springs.............	8 00	......	.....
16.9	Ar. Corinth.....................	8 36	......	.....
21.9	" Hadley (Lake Luzerne).......	8 47	......	.....
29.5	" Stony Creek (✚).............	9 02	......	.....
35.2	" Thurman (✚)................	9 12	......	.....
43.6	" The Glen (✚)	9 30	......	.....
49.5	" Riverside....................	9 52	......	.....
57.1	" North Creek.................	10 10	......	.....
		AM		

Timetable of North Creek Branch of Delaware & Hudson RR. 1951.

NOTE: Train No. 181 — First Trip May 15.

In 1854 the Troy Union Railroad was incorporated to operate a Union Depot and terminal tracks within Troy for the various lines serving that city.

In 1848 the Saratoga & Washington Railroad was built north from Saratoga Springs to Whitehall, at the south end of Lake Champlain. Here it connected with lines east into Vermont and steamboats on the lake. This line crossed the Hudson River at Fort Edward. Later, from 1855 until its inclusion in the Delaware & Hudson, it was known as the Saratoga & Whitehall. The Glens Falls Railroad, between that place and Fort Edward, was opened in 1869. It once extended to Lake George where connection was made with steamboats serving lakeside resorts. It was also possible to sail the length of the lake to Baldwin, and after a short overland trip to Ticonderoga, continue north up Lake Champlain by steamboat. These lines, in conjunction with a steamboat trip from New York to Albany or Troy, formed a popular through tourist route for many years. The track between Glens Falls and Lake George has been abandoned, and the rest is now operated as the freight-only Glens Falls Branch of the Delaware & Hudson.

The Albany Northern Railroad was completed in 1853, running north from Albany, along the west bank of the Hudson, to Cohoes, and then across the Mohawk River to Waterford Junction, and thence across the Hudson River and east to Eagle Bridge, New York, where connections were made with lines into Vermont. In 1859 this line was acquired by the Rensselaer & Saratoga interests, and was subsequently called the Albany & Vermont. The line from Waterford Junction to Eagle Bridge was abandoned in 1859. The portion between Albany and Waterford is now part of the Delaware & Hudson main line.

While not in the Hudson Valley, it is interesting to note the completion of the New York & Canada Railroad along the western shore on Lake Champlain, with connections to Montreal in 1875. This completed what is today's Delaware & Hudson through route between Albany and Montreal, and was the route utilized for many years by the famous *Laurentian* and *Montreal Limited.* Today this route is followed by Amtrak's *Adirondack,* between Grand Central Station, New York, and Montreal.

In 1849 a charter was granted for construction of the Troy & Rutland Railroad to run northeast out of Troy to the Vermont border. This line was incorporated in the Troy, Salem & Rutland Rail Road in 1865 and, in the same year, was consolidated with the Rensselaer & Saratoga. Today it is part of the Delaware & Hudson. In recent years the Delaware & Hudson has come under the control of the Norfolk & Western through a holding corporation, the Dereco Corporation. However, it has remained an independent entity and is not part of the Conrail system. Since 1976 the Delaware & Hudson has vastly expanded in size by acquiring portions of the former Lehigh Valley Railroad, and extensive trackage rights over former portions of the Penn-Central, and Erie-Lackawanna, giving it access to Port Newark, New Jersey; Philadelphia; Harrisburg; and Buffalo. Consequently it has become the nucleus of an independent system competitive with Conrail. It remains a vigorous railroad in the third quarter of its second century.

In 1853 the Troy & Boston Railroad was built from Troy to Williamstown, Massachusetts. This line was later acquired by the Boston, Hoosac Tunnel & Western and the Boston & Maine in 1879. The line into Troy has been abandoned and traffic on the Boston & Maine now moves across a bridge over the Hudson River to Mechanicsville, where there is a major freight interchange with the Delaware & Hudson. The Boston & Maine line is freight only, and passenger service to Albany from New England is operated by Amtrak over the former Boston & Albany Railroad, now part of Conrail. For many years the Boston & Albany was controlled by the New York Central and Penn-Central. Passenger trains operate into the Rensselaer-Albany station, and freight goes over the Castleton Bridge to the large Alfred E. Perlman Classification Yard at Selkirk, where it is turned over to Conrail's West Shore Line to be sent further south or west. This bridge was built during the New York Central years.

Prior to completion of the Pennsylvania Railroad's twin tunnels under the Hudson River to Penn Station, Manhattan, on November 18, 1909, all steam railroad trains from the south and west terminated on the New Jersey side of the Hudson, where ferry connections were made. Overseas freight was transferred to lighters for movement to Manhattan and Brooklyn piers, or for direct transfer to oceangoing ships. Railroad cars destined for Manhattan were rolled aboard car floats. The various railroads maintained extensive fleets of passenger ferry boats, tugboats, barges, and lighters to handle this vast traffic. Around the turn of the century, the railroads owned almost the entire New Jersey shoreline from Jersey City to Edgewater. With the coming of Conrail, and rationalization of through freight routes, most through traffic has been re-routed by way of the Castleton Bridge. Most shipping has moved from Manhattan piers to Elizabethport and Port Newark, where there are more modern loading facilities and less labor trouble, and where the railroad tracks extend directly to shipside. A great portion of the merchandise and produce freight destined for New York City now is shipped either in containers or by piggy-back. The containers and truck trailers are now delivered over the road through the vehicular tunnels and George Washington Bridge, and most of the freight yards in the Bronx and Manhattan have fallen into disuse.

All passenger service now operates either into Penn Station, or to the former Lackawanna

Delaware, Lackawanna & Western RR streamliner *Phoebe Snow.*

Terminal at Hoboken, which has been refurbished and modernized at great expense by the State of New Jersey. The railroad owned passenger ferries have all been discontinued, as described in Chapter 22. The various former passenger terminal and ferry operations are tabulated in the Appendix. Passengers now reach Manhattan by the Port Authority Trans Hudson system, known as PATH. This is an electric rapid transit line serving Newark, Jersey City, Hoboken, and Manhattan. This system was originally built as the Hudson & Manhattan Railway. Its first tunnel, between Hoboken and Morton Street, Manhattan, was completed on March 11, 1904, and opened for traffic on February 25, 1908—the first tunnel under the Hudson River. The builder was William Gibbs McAdoo, who later became the United States Railroad Administrator during World War I, and Secretary of the Treasury. His chief engineer was Charles M. Jacobs. Later this line was extended uptown, beneath Sixth Avenue, to 33rd Street. A second tunnel was built from Exchange Place, Jersey City, to Cortlandt Street in downtown Manhattan. This was opened on July 17, 1909. Large twin office buildings, which were known as the Hudson Terminal Buildings were built on Church Street. They were torn down to make way for the present World Trade Center, which is simply a much larger version of the earlier complex. Eventually the Hudson & Manhattan, which was essentially an interurban type electric line, was extended to Journal Square in up-town Jersey City, and across the Hackensack Meadows to Newark. It provided connections with the Erie, Pennsylvania, and the Lackawanna railroads, supplementing the ferry services.

With completion of vehicular tunnels and bridges, much of the lucrative vehicle traffic was drawn away from the railroad operated ferries, and they began to lose money. Eventual-ly, by the early 1960s, they were all discontinued, and the entire passenger load fell upon the Hudson & Manhattan "tubes," as they were then known. However, by this time the Hudson & Manhattan was in serious financial difficulties itself, with deteriorating equipment and an obsolescent plant. The Hudson & Manhattan was bankrupt and could not handle the addi-tional traffic thrown upon it by discontinuance of the ferries. An arrangement was made whereby the Port of New York Authority, very reluctantly, took over the deficit producing operation and agreed to modernize and operate it, in return for permission to construct the profitable new World Trade Center upon the site of the old Hudson Terminal Buildings. The

Port Authority has lived up to its bargain and now operates a fast, clean, and attractive modern service and has reconstructed most of the line and built new stations. However, with the recent return of commuters to the New Jersey railroads, even the modernized PATH is reaching saturation point during rush hours, and there is again talk of reviving passenger ferries to supplement PATH.

A number of freight terminal lines were built on the New Jersey side of the Hudson. The Hoboken Shore Railway operated industrial track in the north end of Hoboken. The New York, Susquehanna & Western Railway has a spur from Edgewater to Weehawken along the waterfront and a tunnel under the Palisades to its main line in the Hackensack Meadows at Little Ferry Junction. This line was formerly the Hudson River Railroad & Terminal Company. It is now in horrible condition. In past years it served several large plants, including the former Ford Motor Company assembly plant at Edgewater, and various coastal container ship lines, and coal dumping piers. Conrail now controls the former waterfront trackage of the West Shore Railroad at Slough's Meadow in Weehawken, as well as the New Jersey Junction Railroad, which runs from Jersey City to Weehawken. At the present time its principal function is to connect the former Pennsylvania Main Line at Journal Square with the West Shore at Weehawken, and is used by through freights between Philadelphia and Selkirk. In past years both the Erie and Central Railroad of New Jersey had trackage rights over the Jersey Junction. There is an unused track permitting access to Lackawanna Terminal in Hoboken, and this can be used by revived West Shore passenger trains.

The Delaware, Lackawanna & Western Railroad was an amalgam of many smaller short lines. By 1883 it had assembled a through direct route from Hoboken to Buffalo. The oldest unit of the Lackawanna system was the Morris & Essex chartered on January 29, 1835 to build from Newark to Morristown, New Jersey. On October 1, 1860 authorization was granted to the Hoboken Land & Improvement Company, controlled by Edwin A. Stevens, to build a railroad from Hoboken to a connection with the Morris & Essex at Newark. Morris & Essex trains started running to Hoboken in 1863 where they connnected with Stevens' Hoboken Ferry Company boats to New York. The main line of the Lackawanna was as follows: Hoboken, Newark, Scranton, Binghamton, Elmira, Corning, Bath, and Buffalo, with many short branches and secondary main lines in New Jersey. Its principle freight business was carrying anthracite from the Pennsylvania coalfields both eastward and westward. Branches extended northward to Utica and Oswego on Lake Ontario and southward to Northampton, Pennsylvania. There were several short branches in New Jersey concentrating on commuter traffic, which was very substantial. Several of these commuter lines were electrified in 1930. On October 17, 1960 the Delaware, Lackawanna & Western merged with the Erie Railroad to form the Erie-Lackawanna Railway, which became part of Conrail in 1976. Much of the trackage in New Jersey is now owned by the State and operated under contract.*

The former Lackawanna mainline passes from Hoboken Terminal, located on the waterfront, through two separate two-track tunnels under the Palisades to the Hackensack Meadows, where the different lines fan out. The former Erie Railroad line from the Pavonia Street Terminal on the Jersey City waterfront ran up a gently inclined trestle, known as the Penhorn Trestle, to a shallow four-track open cut through the Palisades with numerous short tunnels beneath roadways known as the Bergen Archways. Construction was started on the Archways in 1907 and completed in 1910. It was the first major open cut through this ridge and largely superseded an earlier tunnel completed in 1861 by the great Scottish civil engineer, James P. Kirkwood. This is an 8000 foot, two-track bore through solid rock for more than half its length. It took seven hundred men more than five years to complete and cost fifty-seven lives to build. Today it is used by Conrail freights going to Croxton Yard and

---

*The Blairstown Cutoff Line of the former Lackawanna was abandoned by Conrail in July 1984, thus breaking the through line of the former DL&W.

Jersey City Terminal and Yards of Central Railroad of New Jersey in 1957.

to connect with the West Shore Railroad. To facilitate its construction, eight shafts had to be drilled from the top of the hill.

The Pennsylvania Railroad had its own shorter open cut through the Palisades south of the Erie's Bergen Archways. There was a station at Journal Square in Jersey City, deep in the cut, and reached by escalators. The Hudson & Manhattan also operated its electric rapid transit trains over this line, which is now used by PATH, which has built a large new intermodal transportation center and parking garage at Journal Square with modern shops, restaurants, offices, and bus loading ramps. Almost all of the New Jersey railroads originally ran over this line to get to the Paulus Hook Ferry prior to building their own various terminals on the riverfront. East of the cut the Pennsylvania had two lines to the Hudson River waterfront, both operating over long low elevated trestles above the streets. The more southerly one went to the Exchange Place Passenger Terminal, the more northerly one went to the freight yards and car float bridges at Harsimus Cove. This one is still used by Conrail. There is also a connection track to the Jersey Junction Line still operated by Conrail and an abandoned line connecting with the Lehigh Valley and Central Railroad of New Jersey at Communipaw. Hudson & Manhattan (PATH) trains enter a subway tunnel immediately east of the open cut. They operate over the old Pennsylvania Main Line between Journal Square and Newark.

Formerly the Central Railroad of New Jersey, the Lehigh Valley, and the Baltimore & Ohio had extensive freight and passenger yards all along the waterfront in the Claremont, Communipaw, Black Tom, and Greenville sections of Jersey City and in Bayonne. The New York & Newark branched off from the Jersey Central main line at Claremont and ran west through a deep narrow open cut through the Bergen Ridge and then across the Hackensack and Passaic Rivers to Newark by way of Kearny. This line is now abandoned.

Both the Lehigh Valley and the Pennsylvania Railroad had modern lift bridges across the upper end of Newark Bay from Greenville, near the Jersey City-Bayonne City Line to Oak Island Yard, near Port Newark. These are still operated by Conrail and serve the heavy industry on Constable Hook in Bayonne and the Navy Ocean Terminal. A major new export coal terminal is planned by the Port Authority for construction at Greenville. In past years, before they were rerouted to Penn Station over the Pennsylvania Railroad, Lehigh Valley passenger trains operated over this route to the Jersey Central ferry at Communipaw. The main line of the Jersey Central ran south from Communipaw, past Claremont and Greenville and down the Bayonne Penninsula to near Bergen Point, where it turned west and crossed a great long lift bridge across the mouth of Newark Bay to Elizabethport. This route was also used by Baltimore & Ohio and Reading Company trains. This bridge was demolished in 1981 by the Port Authority of New York & New Jersey as they considered it a menace to navigation to and from Port Newark and Port Elizabeth. Removal was by a planned explosion as cutting it apart piecemeal was deemed too costly. From Elizabethport the main line continued directly west to Elizabeth and Plainfield, and branches ran north to Newark and south to Perth Amboy. The main line was used by through passenger trains of the Baltimore & Ohio such as the *Royal Blues, National Limited,* and *Capitol Limited* and of the Reading Company, which operated *The Crusader* and the *Wall Street.* Named Jersey Central trains included the *Queen of the Valley* and the *Harrisburger* and the famous *Blue Comet* to Atlantic City. Baltimore & Ohio passenger trains ceased running east of Baltimore before 1971. The remaining Reading Company trains were operated by Conrail and are currently terminated at West Trenton, where they now only connect with electric trains to Philadelphia. They have been rerouted to Penn Station, Newark where connection is made with PATH.

Staten Island is served by the lines of the Staten Island Rapid Transit Railway Company. The first railroad on the island was the Staten Island Railroad Company organized in 1850 and completed on April 23, 1860. It extended thirteen miles from Tottenville, at the southern tip of the island, to Vanderbilt Landing where there was a steamboat connection to Manhat-

DAYLIGHT SAVING TIME **MONDAYS TO FRIDAYS Inclusive Excep**

TRAIN NO. / SOUTHBOUND STATIONS	Miles from New York	3303	1201	4001	7301	AC 3306	AC 3307	1205	1207	4019
		AM	AM	AM	AM	AM	Noon	PM	PM	PM
New York Liberty-Cortlandt St.. Leave	......	3.00	5.45	6.55	‡6.55	8.33	12.00	2.30	‡3.00	3.30
Jersey City Terminal...Lv.	1.0	3.32	5.58	7.07	‡7.07	8.45	12.13	2.42	‡3.12	3.42
Bayonne, W. 8th St.......Lv.	7.6	......	6.17	7.25	‡7.25	8.55	12.24	2.57	‡3.22	4.04
Newark Broad St........Lv.	......	......	......	‡7.13	7.13	‡8.42	‡12.10	.....	‡3.10	‡3.50
Newark Ferry St.........Lv.	......	......	......	‡7.15	7.15	‡8.44	‡12.12	.....	‡3.12	‡3.52
Newark East Ferry St....Lv.	......	......	......	‡7.17	7.17	‡8.46	‡12.14	.....	‡3.14	‡3.54
Kearny.................Lv.	......	......	......	......	.....	......	......	.....	......	‡3.56
Elizabeth...............Lv.	......	......	‡6.10	‡7.26	‡7.26	‡8.55	‡11.55	‡2.55	......	......
Elizabethport............Lv.	10.6	3.53	6.23	7.32	7.35	9.02	12.30	3.03	3.34	4.11
Elizabeth Ave............Ar.	11.5	......	6.26	7.36	7.38	......	......	3.05	3.37	4.14
Bayway....................	12.4	......	6.30	......	7.42	......	......	3.08	3.40	......
Tremley....................	14.5	......	......	......	.....	......	......	......	......	......
Port Reading...............	17.9	b4.05	......	7.47	.....	......	......	......	......	4.21
Sewaren....................	19.0	......	......	7.51	.....	......	......	......	......	4.23
Barber.....................	20.2	......	......	7.57	.....	......	......	......	......	4.27
Perth Amboy.............	22.1	4.20	......	8.07	.....	9.17	12.45	......	......	4.35
South Amboy............ (N.Y.&L.B.R.R.)	24.1	4.41	......	8.16	.....	9.21	......	......	......	4.40
Morgan (Laurence Harbor).	25.8	......	......	......	.....	......	......	......	......	4.43
Cliffwood................	28.1	......	......	8.23	.....	......	......	......	......	4.46
Matawan................	29.3	5.03	......	8.27	.....	9.31	12.56	......	......	4.50
TRAIN NO.						4001	5007			
Matawan............Lv. (C. R. R. of N. J.)	29.3	↓	......	......	.....	9.34	1.00	......	......	↓
Keyport...............Ar.	30.9	↓	......	......	.....	a9.39	a1.04	......	......	↓
Union Beach Railroad Station....	32.6	↓	......	......	.....	a9.43	a1.08	......	......	↓
Union Beach Union Av. & Highway #36.	......	↓	......	......	.....	......	......	......	......	↓
Keansburg...............	34.7	↓	......	......	.....	a9.48	a1.12	......	......	↓
Port Monmouth...........	36.6	↓	......	......	.....	a9.52	a1.16	......	......	↓
Belford..................	37.4	↓	......	......	.....	a9.55	a1.18	......	......	↓
Leonardo.................	39.1	↓	......	......	.....	a9.59	a1.22	......	......	↓
Atlantic Highlands........	40.2	↓	......	......	.....	a10.05	a1.26	......	......	↓
Hiltons..................	41.6	↓	......	......	.....	......	......	......	......	↓
Water Witch..............	42.8	↓	......	......	.....	a10.12	a1.33	......	......	↓
Highlands............Ar.	43.7	↓	......	......	.....	a10.17	a1.36	......	......	↓
Hazlet.................. (N. Y. & L. B. R. R.)	31.1	5.07	......	......	.....	......	......	......	......	......
Middletown..............	35.3	5.14	......	......	.....	......	......	......	......	......
Red Bank...............	39.1	5.39	......	......	.....	9.43	1.08	......	......	......
Little Silver—Oceanport....	41.5	5.44	......	......	.....	......	......	......	......	......
Monmouth Park..........	43.0	......	......	......	.....	......	①1.13	......	......	......
Long Branch Long Branch.....	45.1	6.07	......	......	.....	9.54	1.18	......	......	......
Long Branch Elberon-Oakhurst.	47.3	6.11	......	......	.....	9.58	1.22	......	......	......
Allenhurst (Interlaken).....	49.3	6.17	......	......	.....	10.02	1.26	......	......	......
N. Asbury Park-Wanamassa	50.1	......	......	......	.....	......	......	......	......	......
Asbury Park-Ocean Grove	50.8	6.27	......	......	.....	10.09	1.31	......	......	......
Bradley Beach (Neptune)...	51.7	6.40	......	......	.....	10.12	1.34	......	......	......
Avon (Neptune City)......	52.6	......	......	......	.....	10.14	1.36	......	......	......
Belmar..................	53.4	6.50	......	......	.....	10.18	1.39	......	......	......
Spring Lake—Spring Lake Hgts.	55 5	6.57	......	......	.....	10.22	1.43	......	......	......
Sea Girt.................	56.9	6.59	......	......	.....	......	1.45	......	......	......
Manasquan...............	57.6	7.04	......	......	.....	10.26	1.48	......	......	......
Point Pleasant..........	59.6	7.21	......	......	.....	10.30	1.52	......	......	......
Bay Head Junction......	60.7	7.39	......	......	.....	10.33	1.55	......	......	......
Arrive		AM	AM	AM	AM	AM	PM	PM	PM	PM

Through Service to Bay Head

EXPLANATION OF REFERENCE MARKS

a—Stops on notice to take passengers.
b—Stops on notice to conductor to leave passengers.
f—Stops on notice to take or leave passengers.
B—Leaving time of connecting Motor Coach, change Matawan
R—Connecting Motor Coach, change at Red Bank.
AC—Air-Conditioned equipment regularly assigned to this train, but right is reserved to

Jersey Central Railroad timetable showing route along southern shore of Raritan Bay.

tan. In 1872 it was reorganized in bankruptcy as the Staten Island Railway. On July 31, 1884 control was acquired by the Baltimore & Ohio Railroad and the line was extended north to St. George, Richmond, Mariners Harbor and Arlington, and south to Arrochar and South Beach. A large railroad and ferry terminal was built at St. George and is still in use although rebuilt after a great fire. Another line was built along the north shore to Elm Park in 1886. In 1891, under the name Baltimore & New York Railroad, it was extended to Port Ivory and across a bridge over the Arthur Kill to the Bayway section of Linden, New Jersey. Thence it continued west to a connection with the main line of the Central Railroad of New Jersey at Aldene Junction, east of Cranford.

The new Baltimore & Ohio controlled company was known as the Staten Island Rapid

Transit Railroad Company. The passenger lines on Staten Island were electrified in 1925.

On February 2, 1864, the predecessor Staten Island Railway had acquired control of the east shore ferries and operated them under the name of a subsidiary company, the Staten Island Railway Ferry Company. Upon completion of the new St. George Terminal in 1886, all ferry services from both east and north shore were combined on March 8th for operation by the new corporation. For a while some long distance Baltimore & Ohio passenger trains terminated at St. George. This situation continued until October 25, 1905, when the City of New York acquired the ferry operation and the St. George Terminal. However, the railroad continued operation of a small ferry line across the Arthur Kill between Tottenville and Perth Amboy until 1948.

Today a modern lift bridge spans the Arthur Kill, and the Staten Island Rapid Transit Railway Company operates a freight service from Aldene Junction to Tottenville. Electric, multiple-unit, rapid transit type passenger trains are operated from the St. George Ferry Terminal to Tottenville by the Staten Island Rapid Transit Operating Authority, a governmental agency. Formerly this service had been operated by the Baltimore & Ohio Railroad under a subsidy agreement.

Back on the New Jersey shore of the Arthur Kill, a line of the former Jersey Central, now operated by Conrail, ran south from Elizabethport to Perth Amboy, serving heavy petrochemical industry. Formerly Jersey Central trains to Atlantic City and the North Jersey Shore utilized this line. There are short spurs to Carteret and Chrome. At Perth Amboy this line is joined by a connecting line of the former Pennsylvania Railroad coming from the Pennsylvania Main Line at Rahway and passing through Avenel and Woodbridge. It is used by all North Jersey Coast passenger trains originating at Penn Station, Manhattan or Newark. It is now operated by Conrail.

Below Perth Amboy the combined railroad crosses the mouth of the Raritan River on a low-level swing drawbridge to South Amboy, where the former Camden & Amboy continues south; the Raritan Valley Railway heads west to New Brunswick; and the New York & Long Branch continues east along the south shore of Raritan Bay to Red Bank. This is the principal route for North Jersey Shore passenger trains operated by Conrail. Electrification extends east to Matawan, and the Camden & Amboy line to the south is also electrified. Both the Camden & Amboy and Raritan Valley have long offered only freight service. The Raritan Valley is an independent short line, not part of Conrail.

The New York & Long Branch runs southeast from South Amboy to Middletown, Red Bank, Long Branch, Asbury Park, Point Pleasant, and Bay Head. It is operated by Conrail and remains the principal rail passenger route to the Jersey Shore. There is heavy commuter patronage, and the State of New Jersey has plans to electrify its entire length.* Formerly this line operated no passenger trains on its own account, and only provided trackage rights to the Pennsylvania Railroad, which operated trains to Penn Station, New York, and Exchange Place, in Jersey City, and to the Central Railroad of New Jersey, which operated its trains to Communipaw Terminal in Jersey City, or to Broad Street in Newark. Today all operations are combined to Penn Station, Newark, with some trains continuing into Penn Station, Manhattan. Downtown Manhattan is reached by a connection between Newark and the World Trade Center operated by PATH. In past years a line of the Pennsylvania Railroad continued down the Atlantic Coast from Bay Head to Seaside Heights, where it turned westward and crossed Barnegat Bay on a long low wooden trestle. This line then continued through Toms River Junction to Camden and Philadelphia, but it has been abandoned since the 1940s.

There was a branch of the Jersey Central which left the New York & Long Branch at Matawan and ran along the south shore of Sandy Hook Bay to Keyport, Atlantic Highlands, and Water Witch, to Highlands, on the banks of the Shrewsbury River, which it crossed on a

*June 1989 electrification completed as far as Long Branch.

Pennsylvania Railroad K-4 type Pacific locomotive number 5409 such as was used in express passenger service on the New York & Long Branch trains to the North Jersey Shore from Exchange Place, Jersey City. (Raymond J. Baxter collection)

drawbridge. Here one line ran out onto Sandy Hook, while another line ran south along the beach to Long Branch and another junction with the New York & Long Branch. The history of these lines is given in Chapter 26, as these lines were largely dependent on steamboat connections.

The Southern Division of the Jersey Central left the New York & Long Branch at Red Bank and ran south the length of New Jersey to Bayville on the Delaware. This was the route to Atlantic City used in past years by the Jersey Central's crack *Blue Comet*. At present the line is operated by Conrail only for freight. However, it is a likely candidate for future express service between New York and Atlantic City to serve the new casinos and hotels.

In Brooklyn the various present subway routes all evolved from short railroads running from the Manhattan ferries to Coney Island. The Long Island Rail Road has a terminal at Flatbush Avenue in Brooklyn. From there its main line runs east to Jamaica, where it connects with the nation's busiest passenger railroad and is wholly owned by the State government and not part of either Conrail or Amtrak. The Bush Terminal Railroad, the Eastern District Terminal, and the Brooklyn Dock Railway are all independent industrial switching lines serving factories and piers in Brooklyn. Some segments have no connection with other rail lines except by car floats. A line of the former New York Connecting Railroad ran from 69th Street and the Upper Bay to Sunnyside, Queens, where it connected with the Long Island Rail Road and Hell Gate Bridge to the Bronx. For many years this line was owned by the New York, New Haven, & Hartford, who also owned the Hell Gate Bridge. It is now a Conrail freight line. An important car float operation connected the 69th Street Bay Ridge terminal with the Pennsylvania and Lehigh Valley railroads at Greenville, Jersey City. Since inception of Conrail, most of this traffic has been re-routed via the Castleton Bridge.

This concludes our survey of railroads in the Hudson Valley. It has been a complex history of constant change to meet changing requirements. The entire system is presently in a state of flux and rejuvenation and, with the present energy problems, railroads promise to play an increasingly important role in the immediate future.

28 Mid-Nineteenth Century Developments

In 1817 New York State passed a law abolishing slavery, although it did not take full effect until 1827, which was called the Year of Emancipation. Slavery had been an established institution along the Hudson from earliest settlement times. Many of the slaves did not favor emancipation. This viewpoint is stated in great detail in James Fenimore Cooper's novels *Stanstoe* and *Afloat and Ashore*. In the latter novel he describes a common situation of a Hudson Valley farm family:

> "I had a dozen slaves, also; negroes who, as a race, had been in the family almost as long as Clawbonny. About half of these blacks were singularly laborious and useful, namely four males and three of the females; but several of the remainder were enjoying otium, and not altogether without dignitate, as heir-looms to be fed, clothed, and lodged, for the good or evil they had done."[1]

The great immediate problem of emancipation was what to do with the old slaves who had no possessions or savings and could not take care of themselves. This was the economic side of the question. There was also a strong amount of emotional attachment. The Hudson Valley slave was never simply a fieldhand or "element of production," as on the great southern plantations. He was virtually a member of the family. In later years the freed slaves drifted to such cities as Newburgh, Poughkeepsie, and Albany, creating a labor pool for the new industrialism, while a considerable number remained with their masters.

During this period freedom was on the move. In 1840 New York Governor William Seward refused to give up any more fugitive slaves. Less conducive to freedom was a new system of prison discipline introduced in the New York City and Auburn state prisons in 1823. Under this new system the workhouse feature was introduced. The prisoners were made to work diligently all day, and were incarcerated in separate cells at night. This new system required more room than previously and in 1826 construction was started on a large new prison at Sing Sing, which was also known as Mount Pleasant. This new structure was completed in 1829 and is still, with many additions, in use today. Goods manufactured in the prison were all imprinted Made in Sing Sing. As this was also the name of the neighboring village, local industrialists, afraid that their merchandise would be thought to be prison-made goods, voted to change the name of their village to Ossining in 1901.

---

[1] James Fenimore Cooper, *Afloat and Ashore; Leatherstocking Edition*, p. 11.

The year 1837 saw completion of America's first great dam, the Croton Dam containing the waters of the Croton River as a reservoir for New York City. This original dam was swept away by a flood in 1841, but immediately rebuilt to a higher level. Also in 1837 construction was begun on a great aqueduct to New York City. The principal engineer was John Bloomfield Jervis, who had built the Delaware & Hudson canal. The new aqueduct was 38 miles long and opened in 1842. The system was enlarged in 1884 and again in 1890 to the capacity of 100,000,000 gallons per day. Today the old aqueduct is out of use, but the reservoirs continue to contribute their waters to the Catskill and Delaware Aqueduct systems.

The importance of this engineering achievement can be gathered from the following lines from *The Croton Ode,* written in 1842 by Colonel George Pope Morris at the request of the Corporation of the City of New York to celebrate the opening of the first Croton Aqueduct. It was sung by members of the New York Sacred Music Society near the Park Fountain upon completion of the Aqueduct on October 14, 1842:

> *"Water leaps as if delighted,*
> *While her conquered foes retire!*
> *Pale contagion flies affrighted*
> *With the baffled demon fire!*
> *Safety dwells in her domains,*
> *Health and Beauty with her move,*
> *And entwine their circling pinions*
> *In a sisterhood of love."*

> *"Round the aqueducts of story,*
> *As the mists of Lethé throng,*
> *Croton's waves in all their glory*
> *Troop in melody along.*
> *Ever sparkling, bright and single,*
> *Will this rock-ribbed stream appear,*
> *When posterity shall mingle*
> *Like the gathered waters here."*[2]

On July 4, 1845 the long-festering anti-rent discontents broke out again when a group of farmers met in the old red brick Lutheran Church in Berne, in the Helderberg Mountains. They met to draft a new Declaration of Independence. They vowed to stop paying rents to the Van Rensselaers and other large landowners for lands which they and their ancestors had cleared and improved themselves. The movement soon spread into Rensselaer, Columbia, Greene, Delaware, Schoharie, and Ulster counties. Farmers dressed up as Indians with masks, calico costumes, and other paraphernalia to evade recognition by the law. They resisted rent collectors and law officers and gave warning of their approach by blowing on loud tin horns. Much hard feeling ensued. Resistance was made at Lake Hill and Cooper Lake and at Bearsville in the Catskills. Sheriff Schoonmaker of Ulster County had to send a force of 100 men to Bearsville to break up the resistance and the ring-leaders were indicted by a Grand Jury in Kingston.

These activities, now also becoming prevalent in Columbia and Dutchess counties, across the river, came to a head when Dr. Smith Boughton, alias "Big Thunder," was brought to trial and convicted at Hudson. In September of 1845 he was given a life sentence. This was

---

[2]George Pope Morris, *Croton Ode,* p. 25.

during the Governorship of Silas Wright (1845-1847), a Democrat who was friendly to the landowner class.

In 1846 there was a bloody incident at Lake Delaware in the western Catskills and popular sentiment began to show itself in the political arena. In 1846 John Young, a Whig, was elected as Governor for the term (1847-1849). His first move was to pardon Dr. Boughton. Soon legislation took place which abolished the old landlord-tenant system by a Constitutional Act in 1846. This old system of land tenure had inhibited settlement and agricultural development since earliest times, fostering early settlement of Western New York State rather than intensive development in the Hudson Valley.

The years 1846 to 1848 witnessed the Mexican War—a gigantic United States land grab with little moral justification. This was a period of "Manifest Destiny" and the continued settlement of English speaking people in Texas, New Mexico, and California led to discontent with Mexican rule. The immediate cause of the war was the annexation of Texas in 1845, but this was little more than a pretext. The war was short and nasty with an efficient U.S. Army fighting the forces of a disunited nation that had changed presidents twelve times during the war. The most popular Mexican leader was Santa Anna who fought bravely at Buena Vista. A number of popular heroes came out of the war on the American side. Generals Zachary Taylor, Winfield Scott, John C. Fremont, and Stephen W. Kearny all made names for themselves. Principal battles were fought at Palo Alto, Resaca De La Palma, Cerro Gordo, and Chapultepec. In the final result the United States gained California, New Mexico, and Texas, representing two fifths of all Mexican territory. The United States paid an indemnity of $15,000,000 and assumption of all claims by U.S. citizens. While engendering shame in the consciousness of many, it also served to weld a national purpose and demonstrate the capability of American arms under the leadership developed by the United States Military Academy at West Point, although the commanders in chief, named above, were veterans of earlier times and not themselves West Pointers. While giving the United States its "Natural" boundaries, one less fortunate result was to strengthen a bellicose spirit which helped strengthen Southern resolve to secede from the Union.

In 1808 a temperance group was formed in Saratoga, New York, and in 1857 they succeeded in passing a stringent Temperance Law in New York State providing for local option, which for many years provided a good political issue between "drys" and "wets" in local elections.

In 1837 and 1857 there were severe financial panics which temporarily slowed the growth of Hudson Valley industry.

The years 1860 through 1865 saw the great tragedy of the Civil War, with its great draft riots of 1863 in Troy and New York City. Otherwise, there was relatively little direct effect upon the Hudson Valley. The tanning industry boomed because of the increased demand for leather and many Hudson River steamboats were purchased by the Federal Government for conversion to shallow draft gunboats for use along the coast. The war also gave impetus to local industry at a time when there was a serious manpower shortage. Great fortunes were made overnight in military supplies. After the war President Lincoln's Funeral Train traversed the line of the Hudson River Railroad and the various communities erected memorial arches over the tracks and whole towns turned out to pay their last respects.

The War was followed by a great boom, which gave rise to the many new resorts in the Catskills and along the Hudson. This was followed by a financial panic in 1873.

During this period there were several important changes in the nature of agriculture in the Hudson Valley. The old tenant farms gave way to family farms in which the owners had more incentive to improve the land. With the opening of large new wheat and grain growing areas in the Genesee Valley of Western New York the Hudson lost its previous importance as a "bread basket." Farmers turned their attention to specialty farming and truck farming for the New York City market. Among the most important specialties were wine grapes, small fruits, and orchard crops. At an early date it was found that the western bank of the Hudson has a combination of sunlight, moisture, chalky soil, and good drainage conducive to growing good wine grapes, and especially those used in making Champagne. At Tellers Point Dr. R. T. Underhill and his brother operated a vineyard and a winery. There were 80 acres devoted to the growing of Isabella and Catawba grapes. By the turn of the century about 10,000 gallons were bottled annually. Dr. C. W. Grant had extensive vineyards on Iona Island that covered over 20 acres. Today these early attempts have been superseded by commercial vineyards and wineries concentrated in the stretch between Newburgh and Highland. There are also wineries at Washingtonville and High Tor.

Orchard culture began its first major development during this period, and remains the dominant crop in the region today. The early settlers had planted apple and pear trees, but this was only as a part of mixed farming and little scientific attention was given to the matter. Under the influence of Andrew Jackson Downing and André Parmentier serious attention was given to the study of varieties and yields. Dr. C. W. Grant had over 3,000 bearing pear trees planted on his estate at Iona Island during the mid-nineteenth century. He had eleven propagation houses, and produced more grape and other fruit plants than all other establishments in the United States combined. In later years the orchard industry tended to move upriver, on both banks, in Orange, Ulster, Dutchess, and Columbia counties. Today the emphasis is on apples for cider, vinegar, and eating. Principal centers are Marlboro, Modena, New Paltz, Plattekill, Rhinebeck, Red Hook, and Barrytown. Many varieties are grown, but the MacIntosh is presently the dominant one.

The estate of Robert L. Pell at Cliffwood had a 1,200 acre model orchard and fruit farm. He had over 25,000 trees in his orchards and was one of the largest fruit shippers in the world. He shipped apples to Queen Victoria, as well as large quantities of table grapes, currants, and other small fruits.

Actually small fruits were no small business in the Hudson Valley. In the nineteenth century Milton shipped large quantities of strawberries, raspberries, currants, and grapes. It is claimed that the fragrance from the "Raspberry Boat" could be enjoyed for miles down the river as it passed. Marlboro dispatched a steamboat load of raspberries daily during the season until the 1930s. Dr. Grant at Iona Island also produced large quantities for market. The clergyman and novelist, Edward Payson Roe, was deeply interested in the growing of small fruits and carried an extensive experimentation at his home in Cornwall. He wrote a number of books on the subject, including *Play and Profit in my Garden, A Manual on the Culture of Small Fruits, Success With Small Fruits, Nature's Serial Story,* and *The Home Acre.* This gentleman-scholar interest in small fruit growing seemed endemic to the Newburgh area. In the eighteenth century Cadwallader Colden had experimented in this direction at his estate *Coldenham,* and had carried on a correspondence on the subject with the early Philadelphia botanist John Bartram, and his son William Bartram. At a later time Andrew Jackson Downing published the journal, *The Horticulturist,* and in 1845 wrote *The Fruits and Fruit Trees of America.* The writers N. P. Willis and Washington Irving also took great interest in their fruit plants and orchards. At a later date, the naturalist-philosopher John Burroughs devoted himself to pomology and horticulture at his estate *Riverby* near West Park.

Dairy farming came to the fore with the development of the railroads and fast transportation to the New York and Albany markets. Washington, Saratoga, Columbia, and Orange counties were particularly well suited for providing pasturage, and this remains an important industry today.

It was soon found that the "black dirt" of the Wallkill and Schoharie valleys were particularly well suited to vegetable growing. The Wallkill Valley area around Pine Island is noted for its onions, potatoes, celery, and asparagus. The Schoharie valley produces particularly fine carrots. Formerly it had been a great center for hops growing, but this was destroyed by a great blight in the late nineteenth century, but not before giving impetus to a substantial brewing industry in Utica and Albany.

In the early nineteenth century interest turned to the exploitive industries of mining, quarrying, ice harvesting, and brick and cement making.

Although the early explorers were somewhat disappointed in their quest for precious metals, they did locate some substantial deposits of commercially valuable metals and stones. The Dutch discovered and worked copper mines at Pahaquarry on the Delaware River in New Jersey, and brought it to tidewater at Rondout over the Old Mine Road, which some historians consider to be the oldest highway in America. In the nineteenth century copper mines were worked at Kingsland on the Hackensack River, and right on the banks of the Hudson at Ossining for a short time after 1820.

Traces of silver were found throughout the Ramapo Mountains, but not in commercial quantities. However, some silver was commercially mined in the late eighteenth and early nineteenth centuries at Ossining.

The development of the iron and steel industry has been described in Chapter 14. Marble was quarried at Sing Sing during the early and mid-nineteenth century. The stone was mainly dolomitic marble which was an excellent building material, and much was shipped from there. Also, a great deal was burned to make builders lime.

Another quarrying industry that reached major proportions was the bluestone industry. This stone, sometimes called flagstone, or slate, was "lifted" from deposits of sedimentary rocks in the Catskills. It was an attractive blue-gray color, and had the additional advantage of not becoming slippery when wet. This made it an excellent sidewalk paving material. During the second half of the nineteenth century immense amounts of this stone were quarried for America's growing cities, and much of this moved through the Port of Rondout. Principal cutting centers were near Palenville, Hurley, and Phoenicia. Much was also used locally for walls and as a building material. It was quarried mainly by Irish immigrants, as the marble at Sing Sing was mined by Italians.

Rockland Lake, atop Hook Mountain with an elevation of 300 feet above the Hudson, is an ellipse, half a mile in length and three quarters of a mile at its greatest width and covers about 500 acres. It is the headwater of the East Branch of the Hackensack River. It is supplied by springs in its own bosom and clear mountain brooks. The water is of singular purity. In 1835 John F. Felter, John G. Perry, and Edward Felter cut a sloop load of ice from the lake and sold it at an almost clear profit in New York. In 1836 they formed the firm of Barmore, Felter & Company, with a capital of $2,000. They purchased Slaughter's Landing and soon built a gravity railroad to lower the ice to boats in the river. Business grew rapidly and the firm soon evolved into the great Knickerbocker Ice Company, which was still active in New York City in 1978. During the heyday of natural ice this was the largest of many such firms doing business along the river. Other principal ice cutting facilities of the Knickerbocker Company were at Verplanck's Point, where Lake Meahagh, or Knickerbocker Pond, had been formed by damming Meahagh Creek, and at Bear Mountain.

Hessian Lake, at an elevation of 155 feet above the Hudson, is on the eastern slope of Bear Mountain. It was originally called Lake Sinnipink, but was called Hessian Lake or Bloody Pond after the Battle of Fort Clinton. The bodies of Hessian troops were thrown into the lake and incarnadined the waters. In the nineteenth century the Knickerbocker Ice Company cut 30,000 tons of ice here annually. The name Bloody Pond would certainly never do for use by a natural ice company, and it was then called Highland Lake. The company built a slide down to Doodletown Bight where they had great storage sheds and docks.

Further upriver, and particularly in the Coxsackie area, ice was cut directly from the Hudson and stored in great sheds along the waterfront for summertime shipment to New York. Melting was prevented by insulating the ice with sawdust. Development of mechanical ice making equipment and refrigeration took the profit out of the natural ice business and all these operations were discontinued. For years the great sheds sat empty, but in the 1920s it was discovered that they were excellent for growing mushrooms, and a few survive being used for this purpose. Possibly, with developing energy shortages, this industry may have a comeback.

The limestone and cement industry date from the earliest times in the Hudson Valley. In the eighteenth century limestone ridges below Poughkeepsie were exploited. Kilns were built and the calcined lime was shipped up and down the Hudson. The flames flaring out of the many kilns in the area gave rise to the name of Barnegat, or "firehole."

Another principal center of the limestone quarrying industry was at Tomkins Cove. As early as 1789 John Crom built a small lime kiln here, but nothing much else developed during the next half century. In 1838 Daniel Tomkins discovered the limestone in this area only by searching carefully from Hoboken to the present Tomkins Cove. The limestone beds which he discovered occupies a superficial area of nearly six hundred acres, extending in the rear of Stony and Grassy Points, where it disappears beneath the red sandstone formation. It is traversed by white veins of carbonate of lime. Some of it is black and variegated, and made pleasing ornamental marbles, and most of it was blue.

In 1838 Daniel Tomkins purchased twenty acres for $100 an acre. He organized the firm of Tomkins, Hadden & Company, which was later changed to Calvin Tomkins & Company. After 1859 operations were carried on under the name Tomkins Cove Lime Company. Besides the manufacture of lime, the company added to its business by crushing limestone for macadamizing purposes.

The principal cliff workings were nearly 200 feet high and stretched along the river for one half mile. Several wharves were erected for the easy transfer to sloops and barges. The lime

Bluestone workers at Wilbur on Rondout Creek c1896. West Shore Railroad Wilbur Viaduct in background. (DeLisser)

was slaked previous to shipment to prevent combustion. By 1865 the works were producing 1,000,000 bushels per year and employed one hundred men. Thousands of tons of stone were shipped annually to kilns in New Jersey. Each year between twenty and twenty-five thousand tons of "gravel" were shipped to New York City, where they were used to macadamize roads in Central Park and private driveways.

Another area that was exploited for limestone was the Kalkberg, or chalk rocks, below Catskill. It is a long limestone ridge of abut 250 feet elevation, parallel to the Hudson, running from Cementon, on its south end, to Quarry Hill, west of Catskill. Many large cement plants are still operating in the area.

In 1828 it was discovered that the local limestone near Rosendale on Rondout Creek made an excellent hydraulic cement. An active industry soon developed and much was shipped down to Rondout on the Hudson by the Delaware & Hudson Canal. Eventually Rosendale Cement was superseded by Portland Cement. Some Rosendale Cement is still produced for underwater work. Rosendale Cement was used for the Brooklyn Bridge foundations and towers, and its fame spread rapidly thereafter.

Brickmaking was another industry whose development was made possible by the cheap transportation afforded by the river. The early Dutch settlers were used to building in brick. While they built their early homes of local stone—limestone in the upper valley and sandstone in the lower section—some brick came into the colony from Europe as ballast in ships. This was used for building material at Manhattan and Albany by the more affluent settlers. Brick homes became a status symbol and soon clay deposits were developed along the Hudson. Major brickmaking centers were located along the river between Newburgh and Poughkeepsie, and also at Verplanck Point and near Haverstraw.

Haverstraw was the greatest center of the brickmaking industry. In the 1820s red sandstone was quarried here in great quantities. Ten to twelve vessels a day would leave the docks beneath Hook Mountain. In the early 1800s James Wood discovered the modern method of burning brick. As there was abundant good clay and straw, the two principal ingredients, brickmaking soon became an important industry. At first the bricks were mass produced in molds compressed by a device known as Hall's improved machine. However, in the 1850s a local man, Richard A. Ver Valen, developed a better machine, which was soon adopted and which gave great impetus to the industry. Coal dust and sand were mixed with the clay to impart durability to the bricks. This gave the industry a great advantage in the neighborhood, as there was also suitable sand in good quantity. In 1883 there were 42 brick yards in operation between Long Clove and Jones Point, employing 2,400 men and with a production of 302,647,000 bricks. At the height of production there were 40 brickyards in Haverstraw alone, producing 326,000,000 bricks per annum. While bricks were being produced at other points upriver, Haverstraw was the capital of the industry. With the advent of poured concrete construction and the playing out of the clay beds, the industry gradually faded away to nothing. Old clay pits, usually filled with water, can be seen in the grassy meadows between Haverstraw and Grassy Point, along the Minisceongo Creek. There were major strikes in 1853 and 1877, when it was necessary to call in the militia. Both were caused by the manufacturers cutting of wages.

By the end of the mid-nineteenth century, the Nation had weathered some rather severe crises and the economic base of the Hudson Valley was in a flourishing state.

29 The Late Nineteenth Century

The late nineteenth century was a golden age in the Hudson Valley. It was a period of consolidation of earlier developments, and of taking stock. It was a period when a sense of tradition and history began to manifest itself. The country had come through the difficult years of the Civil War with a new sense of purpose. The industrial north was now the dominant power in the United States, and New York State was unquestionably the dominant state in the Nation. Floods of immigrants were providing the labor force for industrial expansion, and foreign investors were eager to purchase shares in American corporations, especially in the rapidly building new railroads.

It was a "spacious" age. People built on a grand scale. Houses were built with large porches, verandahs, and windows, and with towers, cupolas, bay windows, and lots of decoration. Immigrant labor was cheap and people kept large lawns and flower beds on their grounds, and staffed the large homes with Irish and Italian servants. Food was cheap and nobody had heard of calories and cholesterol. People ate hugely, and became huge themselves. President Taft, a product of that era, tipped the scale at three hundred pounds, and was considered "a fine figure of a man." Taste was sometimes vulgar, but always opulent. Owners of small and medium sized businesses built "Rhine Castles" along the Hudson, as well as the great Barons of Industry. Cities and towns such as Rhinecliff, Poughkeepsie, Newburgh, Nyack, and Yonkers blossomed forth with blocks of large late Victorian and Edwardian mansions—owned by the local shoe store proprietor or blacksmith.

It was an age of optimism and contentment. Picture an early August evening in 1881, and take an imaginary trip along the valley.

Down in the lower bay the swanlike sidewheelers of the Patten Line are bringing the wage-earners of the family home to their summer cottages and villas along the Navesink and Shrewsbury Rivers in the Atlantic Highlands.

People are boarding open trolley cars to head home from the clean sands of Midland Beach on Staten Island, as the endless procession of transatlantic and coastal ships passes through the Narrows. In the Upper Bay tired commuters on the great sidewheel Staten Island ferry boats *Northfield* and *Westfield* contemplate the passing scene and the Robbins Reef lighthouse.

Up in the North River the late railroad ferries scurry across to Communipaw, Paulus Hook, Pavonia and Hoboken, while the lights of Manhattan blink on in the gathering dusk. Abreast of Edgewater, Undercliff, and Piermont the fishermen are hauling in their nets.

In the yards of Irvington and South Nyack the children run through the flag and iris beds surrounding the villas, chasing fireflies, as the adults rock on the porches, the women shelling peas and the men puffing on their cigars while weighing the relative merits of Rutherford B. Hayes and James A. Garfield.

At West Point the Corps bugler is blowing retreat as the colors are lowered and the cadets retire to their tents on the green, worn out from a strenuous day of summer maneuvers.

Up in Newburgh Bay the *Mary Powell* is hurrying home to Rondout with a passenger load of tired shoppers who had spent the day visiting the great emporiums of Manhattan. The lights in the windows of the trains passing on the Hudson River Railroad look like gleaming necklaces.

As night settles down the great resort hotels atop the Wall of Manitou in the Catskills come to life. The great Hotel Kaaterskill is particularly astir with the gaiety of the noveau riche. The symphony orchestra is striking up a waltz by Johann Strauss in the ballroom, as young couples wander down the grassy paths towards Druid Rocks and Elfin Pass, while others walk to the cliff edge at Belleview to see the sunset over Kaaterskill Clove and Haines Falls. At the more sedate Catskill Mountain House the guests are selecting canoes on South Lake for an evening regatta with Japanese Lanterns.

Down in the village of Catskill, children run around playing tag and hide and seek in the narrow alleys of the old town, while shopkeepers sit outside their doors and on their stoops, as in earlier Dutch colonial times. A crowd of loafers are fishing on the end of the pier, awaiting the momentary activity of the arrival and departure of the down Night Boat from Albany. The lighthouse tenders at Hudson Light and Fourmile Point lights are trimming their wicks and polishing their reflector mirrors. Couples are strolling on The Parade at Hudson watching the sun go down behind the distant Catskills.

Somnolence is settling down upon the busy commercial centers of Albany and Troy. The guards are closing up the gates of the new State Capitol Building as the last of the clerks depart. The dockmaster is about to go home after seeing the New York nightboats off on their journey. In the Erie Canal Basin the boats are all moored for the night and the captains and their wives are sitting out on deck in windsor chairs enjoying the fine weather.

Above Waterford the farmers have driven their cows back to the barn and about completed the evening milking. The millhands at Cohoes and Glens Fall have gone to their small homes and completed their simple meals and are enjoying a few moments relaxation, while at Saratoga Springs the great Grand Union and United States Hotels are coming alive with the parade of fashion and dancing to waltzes and quadrilles in the great ballrooms. "Bet A Million Gates" and his friends contemplate visiting Canfield's Casino. God's in his heaven and all is well with the world—especially the Hudson Valley.

Truly, this was a period of relative security and optimism. Even the litany of the names of the United States Presidents from the Civil War to the turn of the century exudes an aura of solidity and security: Ulysses S. Grant; Rutherford B. Hayes; James A. Garfield; Chester A. Arthur; Grover Cleveland; Benjamin Harrison; and William McKinley. Most of these men had intimate contacts with the Hudson Valley and loved it enough to vacation there. In his later life Grant resided in Manhattan and visited the Catskill Mountain House. During his painful terminal illness, he retired to a cottage at Mt. McGregor, near Saratoga Springs, where he died. Rutherford B. Hayes, and his wife "Lemonade" Lucy, vacationed at Lake Mohonk Mountain House among other teetotalers. However, Hayes was a great trencherman, and his portrait still adorns the corridor leading to the dining room at the Mountain House. Their "dry" habits were in perfect tune with those of the proprietor and the other guests.

James A. Garfield had a brief and tragic connection with Hudson Valley resorts. He was shot in 1881 by Charles J. Guiteau, a disappointed office seeker, in the Washington railroad

Brooklyn Bridge (Courtesy New York Convention & Visitors Bureau)

station. The wounded President was put aboard a train to the seaside resort of Long Branch, New Jersey, to recuperate. He died shortly after arrival at the resort. Chester A. Arthur was a New York City "machine" politician who turned honest and competent upon attaining the White House. He also took a vacation in the Catskills and, for a brief time, turned the Hotel Kaaterskill into the Summer White House. Grover Cleveland had been Governor of New York from 1883 to 1885, prior to his first term as President. Benjamin Harrison also vacationed at Lake Mohonk.

William McKinley's connection with the Hudson was more tenuous and also tragic, although this tragedy took place in 1901. McKinley was shot by Leon Gzolgosz, an anarchist, while attending the Pan American Exposition in Buffalo on September 5, 1901. He died a week later on September 14th.

His Vice President, Theodore Roosevelt, was a true Hudson valley man. A native of New York City, Roosevelt had been Governor of New York from 1899 to 1901. Roosevelt, a great trout fisherman, had frequently vacationed in the Catskills at Peekamoose Lodge, on the headwaters of Rondout Creek, and at Stamford, at the headwaters of the Delaware, as well as at Katskill Bay on Lake George. At the time of McKinley's Assasination Roosevelt was camping near the Tahawas Club near the headwaters of the Hudson in the Adirondacks. Upon receiving word of the tragedy he hastened to the Delaware & Hudson Railroad depot at North Creek, on the upper Hudson. Upon arrival there he was advised by telegraph that McKinley had died. The oath of office was administered in the depot before Roosevelt boarded train to attend to his new duties as President. This was the second U.S. Presidential inauguration on the banks of the Hudson; the first having been Washington's in Manhattan.

Let us now consider some significant events in the region chronologically. After the Civil War there was a great boom in business, followed by the great panic of 1873. However, the setback was only temporary.

In 1873 the New York & Oswego Midland Railroad was completed from Jersey City to Oswego on Lake Ontario, passing through central New York State. It promptly went into receivership and was reorganized as the New York, Ontario & Western in 1880. It was of prime importance in opening up the Southern Catskills to development. In 1875 the Ulster & Delaware Railroad was completed from Kingston Point to Bloomville, on the upper Delaware, opening up the Central Catskills, particularly for the new and booming resort trade. Down in Manhattan 1878 saw the opening of the first elevated railroad, controlled by capitalist Jay Gould of the Erie Railroad and *Lyndhurst* on the Hudson at Tarrytown.

Between the years 1867 and 1898 a large new Capitol Building was erected at Albany. It was a gigantic French Chateau designed by a series of notable architects, including Thomas W. Fuller, Leopold Eidlitz, Henry Hobson Richardson, and Isaac G. Perry. The $25,000,000 building was subject to much ridicule and criticism at the time of construction, but has weathered the years well and is now considered a fine example of Victorian Eclectic architecture.

A major engineering feat was accomplished during this same period. The Brooklyn Bridge, considered by many the most beautiful suspension bridge in the United States, was built between 1869 and 1883 by John A. Roebling and his son, Washington Augustus Roebling. Early in the bridge's construction Roebling suffered a serious injury on a ferry boat while supervising the work, and died a few days later. His son supervised completion of the bridge; but he also was a victim of his work. He was stricken with caisson disease in 1872 as a result of continuous underground work. Although an invalid, he supervised from his bed in Brooklyn Heights, until the bridge was opened to traffic on May 24, 1883. A few days later, on May 30th, a great panic took place when someone among the crowd of strollers screamed that the bridge was giving way. People fought to get off and became jammed together in the stairways. Forty people were injured and twelve were crushed to death.

Statue of Liberty, photo c1900. (Smith's New York Harbor Guide)

The bridge, the engineering wonder of its time, as originally built carried two dual width vehicle roadways, two horse-car tracks, and a wide boardwalk in the center. During later years it carried electric streetcars and rapid transit railway trains. Various authorities give the initial cost of construction as between $13,000,000 and $15,000,000. However, within the first twenty-six years in service, increasing loads—most particularly electric trains—made it necessary to spend an additional $15,000,000 on partial reconstruction and strengthening. Twenty workmen lost their lives in the construction of the bridge.

The year 1884 saw the completion of the New York, West Shore & Buffalo Railroad from Weehawken to Buffalo. Completion of this line brought about economic revitalization of the west bank of the Hudson and stimulated suburban development of Bergen County in New Jersey and of Rockland County in New York. It also made the west shore cities less dependent on steamboats and ferry connections to the Hudson River Railroad on the eastern shore.

In 1889 the great railroad cantilever bridge at Poughkeepsie was completed. Work was begun in 1873, but stopped for several years. It was resumed in 1886 and finished in less than three years time by the Union Bridge Company. The river is 3,094 feet wide at this point; the bridge cost $10,000,000; and was the first rail crossing of the Hudson to be built below Albany.

Another structure of engineering interest was somewhat less functional. In 1875 the historian Edward de Laboulaye conceived the idea of a monument commemorating the alliance of France and the United States in achieving American Independence, and symbolizing the friendship of the two nations. This monument was to be a gift from the people of France. He organized the Franco-American Union and raised about $250,000 by 1882.

The promoters turned to Frederic Auguste Bartholdi, an Alsatian sculptor, who specialized in such colossal monuments as *Switzerland Succoring Strasbourg, Vercingetorix,* at Clermont-Ferrand, and the gigantic *Lion of Belfort,* at the Citadel in Belfort, which commemorated the heroic defense of that fortress in 1870-1871 during the Franco-Prussian War.

Bartholdi conceived the idea for the statue as he sailed into New York Harbor. The statue was to be called *Liberty Enlightening The World.* It was to be the figure of a woman uplifting a lighted torch in her right hand. The statue was to be 152 feet tall and made of copper sheets, which would soon oxidize to a green patina in the salt air. It was to be supported by a wrought-iron armature.

First Bartholdi made a model nine feet high. Today this model stands near the Pont Grenelle across the Seine in Paris. Workmen then hand-hammered copper sheets 3/32'' thick on wooden forms.

The supporting armature was designed by Alexandre Gustave Eiffel, who was to build the famous Eiffel Tower in 1889. A circular stairway with 168 steps led to an observation platform in the diadem, with a straight ladder branching off near the top and ascending through the uplifted right arm and hand, and through the base of the torch, to a circular platform around the flame of the torch. The entire statue weighed 225 tons and was shipped from France in 214 cases in 1885.

Joseph Pulitzer, editor of the *New York World,* organized an American subscription to build a suitable base. He raised $225,000 and engaged the American architect Richard Morris Hunt to design the base. Hunt had been the first American to study architecture at the Ecole des Beaux-Arts in Paris, and was later one of the organizers of the American Institute of Architects. He designed a pedestal 154 feet high in Neo-Grec Style built of concrete faced with granite. This sat atop the eleven pointed rampart of Fort Wood, dating from 1811.

The statue was formally presented to the United States in 1884, shipped in 1885, and assembled in less than eighteen months. It was dedicated by President Grover Cleveland on October 28, 1886.

Another important Hudson River landmark erected only a few years later was Grant's Tomb. This houses the sarcophagi of President Ulysses S. Grant and his wife, Julia Dent Grant. It was built between 1892 and 1897. There was a competition for the best design, which was won by John H. Duncan. The design was in the classic eclectic style. The square base was in the Doric mode, and was surmounted by a circular peristyle in the Ionic mode, with a stepped conical dome. It was built of white granite and cost $600,000.

Possibly the most significant national event of this period was the Spanish-American War which lasted only from April 21st to August 12th of 1898. This was in support of Cuban Independence from Spanish Rule. A short and sharp campaign, staffed entirely by American volunteers, backed by the regular U.S. Navy, succeeded in bringing the Spanish to their knees. Principal actions were at Siboney, El Caney, and San Juan Hill in Cuba. It was there that Theodore Roosevelt and his "Rough Riders" gained fame and popularity. Admiral George Dewey also captured Manila in the Philippines on May 19th, and there was some light action at Puerto Rico. As a result of the war Cuba gained independence under U.S. protection, and the United States gained the Philippines and Guam as indemnity. This began an era of American involvement in Latin America and the Far East. The only event of specific Hudson Valley involvement was the detainment of returning Yellow Fever and Malaria victims at the Quarantine Station at Rosebank, Staten Island, and on Hoffman and Swinburne Islands below the Narrows. More American soldiers fell victim to these two diseases than to Spanish sword or bullet. The war also immensely enhanced the popularity of Teddy Roosevelt.

In 1898 New York City took one of the most significant steps in its history and adopted a new charter, which transposed it into a metropolis of five Boroughs, with a hugely increased population. The modern history of New York City can be dated from this event.

During this period there was a great interest in Centennial Expositions. The great National one was held in Philadelphia in 1876. However, this only whet the public appetite for such spectacles. In 1883 the Hudson Valley held its own unique event. This was held at Newburgh, to celebrate the centennial of the disbanding of Washington's Army at the end of the American Revolution. Washington had kept his base here and at neighboring New Windsor in 1783, pending completion of the formal peace treaties. It was at Newburgh that he bade farewell to his troops and disbanded the army. To celebrate these events a great festival was held on October 17, 1883. It was quite a celebration:

At sunrise the celebration was ushered in by ringing of bells on all public buildings and the booming of cannons from Washington's Headquarters, and from the seven ships composing the fleet of Rear-Admiral Cooper, which were drawn up in line in front of the city. At the same time there was an exhibit of Japanese day fire works.

At 9:00 AM the yards of the ships were manned, and at 10:00 AM a simultaneous landing was effected from every ship of the line. At 11:00 AM three guns, at intervals of twenty seconds, were fired from the flag-ship as a signal for the moving of the procession, which consisted of: A squad of mounted police; a platoon of New York City police; the Grand Marshalls and their Aides; buglers, color-bearers, and orderlies; the Seventh Regiment of the National Guard of the State of New York, with Cappa's Seventh Regiment Band of 55 pieces with a 30 piece drum and bugle corps; Officers of the Day with distinguished guests in 50 carriages; these included Wallace Bruce as poet-orator, and Governor Grover Cleveland. Then came the Fifth Battalion of United States Artillery, stationed at Governor's Island, accompanied by a band; an 800 man Naval Brigade from the North Atlantic Squadron, with a 20 piece Marine Band; numerous National Guard regiments from Newburgh, Albany, Brooklyn, Elizabeth, New Jersey, Peekskill, Yonkers, Poughkeepsie, Mount Vernon, and Hudson. These were followed by the veterans of the Grand Army of the Republic. Then followed brigades from the Knights Templar, Knights of Pythias, Odd Fellows, German Mannerchor of Newburgh, Juvenile Temperance Association and fire companies from throughout New York and New Jersey. The parade took until 2:00 PM and wound its way throughout downtown Newburgh, ending at the Hasbrouck House, which was Washington's Headquarters.

A monument to Washington was dedicated before the afternoon ceremonies. At 2:00 PM broadsides were fired from the entire fleet. Cappa's 7th Regiment Band played the *William Tell Overture*. This was followed by a call to order by Mayor Peter Ward, and a prayer by the Rev. Irenaeus Prime, D. D. The prayer was followed by a Te Deum, "We praise Thee, O God," by Dudley Buck, sung by a Grand Chorus of 500 voices and band. Then United States Senator Thomas F. Bayard was introduced as President of the afternoon. This was followed by a singing of "Hail Columbia" by chorus and band and a reading of the poem, *The Long Drama* by poet Wallace Bruce. There were then various military tatoos and inspections, followed by the chorus, "No King but God," and an oration by Hon. William M. Evarts. The final chorus with band was the "Hallelujah Chorus" by Handel. Final Benediction was by the Rev. J. Forsyth, D. D., and a concluding March was played by Cappa's Band.

In the evening there was an enormous display of fireworks from barges anchored in the Hudson, and also at Temple Hill in New Windsor and at Fishkill.

The following Navy ships were in attendance: *Tallapoosa,* flagship bearing Secretary of the Navy and Commodore J. H. Upshur; *Tennessee, Vandalia, Alliance, Saratoga,* and *Portsmouth.* There were also innumerable excursion boats from points up and down the river. This great spectacle set the pattern for all subsequent river festivals.

On a commercial level, the great limestone, cement, ice, brick, and iron industries described in previous chapters were flourishing mightily during this period. They were now joined by two additional industries.

About this period the basalt and diabase rocks of the southern Hudson Valley began to be quarried extensively for trap rock. Many riverside quarries went into operation, benefitting from the cheap barge transportation. The most extensive ones were along the Palisades, at High Tor Mountain, in the Highlands, and near Danskammer Point. The largest quarries in the Highlands were at Crow Nest Mountain, Breakneck Mountain, and Bull Hill. A typical operation was at Rockland Lake. In 1872 John Mansfield established a stone-crusher which he later sold to M. M. Miranda. Around 1884 an average of from seventy five to ninety vessels loaded with crushed stone were shipped annually, and employment was given to from twenty five to sixty five men, according to the demand.

Eventually such damage was done to the landscape that limitations were imposed upon the industry. Conveyors carried the rock from inland quarries to fleets of barges on the river, which carried the rock to the city. New York Trap Rock Company division of Lone Star Industries remains in operation today with principal operations near Van Keurens and Milton. Operations also continue on the backside of High Tor Mountain, out of view of the river.

Another interesting exploitive industry was the making of shale bricks. Shale was common in the Catskill foothills, and commencing in 1894 shale bricks were manufactured at Catskill, utilizing deposits of red Chemung shale located near Cairo. This produced a particularly durable brick.

By this period the lumbering industry had moved largely up into the Adirondack Mountains. By 1900 cutting was reaching such proportions there that serious erosion of the Adirondack soil was taking place. This had its effects in the lower Hudson, along the Palisades and New Jersey shoreline, where extensive silt deposits came to rest upon reaching salt water, and seriously hampered navigation. The situation was so serious that laws were passed to limit cutting and to create the Adirondack Park. However, much cutting still goes on today. Much of the timber is used as pulpwood for the paper industry at Ticonderoga and Glens Falls.

On a recreational level, this period saw the laying out of some of the nations first golf courses in the Hudson Valley. The first American golf game was played at Yonkers on the St. Andrews Golf Course on November 1, 1888. The second course in the United States was the Dinsmore Golf Course near Staatsburg. Another very early course was that of the Powelton Country Club near Newburgh.

By the turn of the century the stage was well set for the important and spectacular events of the twentieth century. Much had been accomplished on a material level, and people's attention was now turning to cultural and historical matters. A new appreciation of the scenery was developing, and people were both using and enjoying the Hudson. It was an age which faced the river.

30 The Interurban and Trolley Era

The late nineteenth and early twentieth centuries were the age of the electric trolley and interurban railroad. Long before the extensive use of the private automobile, the trolley and interurban helped in the orderly growth of cities and began suburbanization. They made access to private homes on plots large enough to allow for lawns and gardens accessible to low and medium wage city workers. Their linear route structures brought about orderly development and sensible, non-wasteful, land use patterns and, while allowing suburbanization, discouraged urban sprawl. Development was effectively held to within "walking distance" of the car tracks—usually three blocks on either side. Many lines were built and developed by real estate promoters and developers. If the lots sold well, the streetcar line proved an extra benefit to the developer. If lots did not sell, he was usually stuck with a bankrupt electric railway system, unless the line served two existent terminals providing through traffic.

Trolleys and interurbans took many forms, ranging from dinky little "Toonerville Trolleys," with only four wheels operating on tracks running down the street, to great, multiple car, electric railway trains operating on private rights of way at high speeds, similar to today's Metroliners and the Japanese Bullet Trains. Many intermediate forms existed. The electric streetcar was fast, quiet, and pollution free. It was also very versatile. It could operate on tracks running down village, city, or suburban streets; it could operate on regular railroad tracks; it could make sharp turns easily and climb stiff grades; because it was relatively light weight; trestles and viaducts could be built inexpensively to light standards; it was easy to operate and maintain; and the cars were durable and "lasted forever."

Unlike many present day railway electrifications, built to unnecessarily high standards and with over-sophisticated technology, the early systems, utilizing wooden poles and a simple trolley wire, were inexpensive to build and operate—an art which Americans seem to have lost. As a result of these factors, streetcar lines and electric railways developed very rapidly, and the Hudson Valley was extensively served by such lines.

As early as 1835, Thomas Davenport, a Vermont blacksmith, had built a miniature electric railway. In 1838 a Scotchman, Robert Davidson, built a battery carry that carried passengers at four miles per hour on the Edinburgh-Glasgow Railroad. Back in America, in 1847 Professor Moses Farmer built a small electric line in Dover, New Hampshire. A locomotive taking current from a third rail was exhibited at the Berlin Exposition of 1879 by Ernst W. von Siemens, founder of a firm which still leads the electric equipment industry in Europe. That same year a similar electric car was built by Stephen D. Field of Massachusetts. Following up on this, Thomas Edison built a similar engine in 1880. However, none of these pioneer attempts solved the problems of power distribution or motor design adequately. It remained for an American engineer, Frank J. Sprague, an Annapolis graduate, to develop a serviceable traction motor and solve other problems of electric distribution. In 1886 Sprague built a small trolley system in St. Joseph, Missouri, and another in Richmond, Virginia in 1888. The system was so popular and successful that there were over two hundred systems operational in the United States and Canada by 1890—in only two years! Boston alone motorized 2,300 horse cars. City streets became cleaner and more attractive and electric streetcars became de rigueur in the best residential neighborhoods.

This pattern of development is well demonstrated in the Hudson Valley. By far the largest electric traction system operating in the area was the 130 mile long system of the Hudson Valley Railway Company, which had lines between Waterford and Warrensburg via two separate routes. The Main Line was as follows: Waterford, Mechanicsville, Stillwater, Schuylerville, Thomson, Fort Miller, Fort Edward, Sandy Hill, Glens Falls, French Mountain, Caldwell (Lake George Village), and Warrensburg. There was a branch from Thomson to Greenwich. The alternate route left the Main Line at Mechanicsville and ran through Round Lake, Ballston Spa, Saratoga Springs, Wilton, South Glens Falls, and rejoined the Main Line at Glens Falls. There was a branch from Saratoga Springs to Kaydeross Park at the north end of Saratoga Lake. This system was acquired by the Delaware & Hudson Railroad's United Traction Company in 1906. All rail operations were discontinued in the 1930s. The Hudson Valley Railway served as an important route between the Capital Area and the closer Adirondack resorts and integrated its services with those of the connecting railroad and steamboat lines.

The United Traction Company, which was controlled by the Delaware & Hudson, had its own lines connecting Albany and Troy. There were two routes between Troy and Waterford. One ran up the east side of the Hudson by way of Lansingburgh. The other operated by way of Green Island, Watervliet, and Cohoes. These interurbans offered stiff competition to the Albany & Troy Belt Line Railroad, a New York Central subsidiary, along the east shore and offering frequent service. The United Traction cars ran along the west shore to a bridge just south of Troy. Until relatively recent years, Boston & Maine and New York Central timetables still carried the notation: Frequent service offered by United Traction Company between Troy and Albany. This continued even after the interurbans were replaced by buses. United Traction also operated local streetcar systems in Albany, Troy, Lansingburgh, and Glens Falls.

The Troy & New England Railway had a line from Troy to Averill Park, southeast of the city. As late as 1923 the Albany Southern Railroad Company, which had absorbed the line of the Albany & Hudson, operated lines from the Plaza in downtown Albany, across the bridge to Greenbush, and then fanning out to Electric Park and North Chatham, and to Nassau, East Greenbush, and Hudson. This last line was operated by third rail rather than overhead trolley wires and was noted for high speed running. The company also provided commercial and residential electric service to the communities along its lines.

The Schenectady Railway, which was controlled by the New York Central Railroad, had lines from Schenectady to Troy, Albany, and to Ballston Spa, with connections to Saratoga Springs. It also operated some local streetcar routes in Schenectady and Albany as late as 1923. The little Eastern New York Railroad, and its affiliate, the Ballston Terminal Railroad, operated from Ballston Spa to Middlegrove, while the larger Albany & Schoharie Valley Railway ran forty-four miles from Albany to Schoharie.

Moving downriver, we find that Catskill Railways had twenty-three miles of line from Catskill Point Landing to Leeds, Cairo, and Oak Hill. The five mile long Rhinebeck & Rhinecliff Railway connected those two points, and the Kingston Consolidated Railways offered local service in Rondout and Kingston.

The Poughkeepsie City & Wappingers Falls Railway offered local service in Poughkeepsie, with an interurban line to Wappingers Falls. The New Paltz, Highland & Poughkeepsie Traction Company had a most interesting and unusual route. It started as a local village trolley line in New Paltz and then ran over its own private right of way as an interurban line to Highland. From Highland to Poughkeepsie it operated across the Poughkeepsie Railroad Bridge on the tracks of the Central New England Railroad. Once in Poughkeepsie, it operated on the tracks of the local streetcar system to reach downtown. The electric cars were pulled across the bridge by steam locomotives.

The Orange County Traction Company operated local lines in Newburgh, and an interurban line to Orange Lake and Walden. Across the river, the Citizens Railroad, Light & Power Company operated cars between Fishkill-on-Hudson and Fishkill, and the Beacon Mountain Railway operated four and one half miles of line from the ferry landing at Fishkill-on-Hudson to the foot of the Mt. Beacon Incline Railway. This was a very popular picnic excursion line, and offered excursion tickets in conjunction with the Hudson River Day Line.

South of the Highlands of the Hudson, the Peekskill Lighting & Railroad Company offered local streetcar service and had interurban lines to Mohegan Lake and Verplanck Point. This line operated until 1926.

Between 1893 and 1924 the Westchester Traction Company operated local lines in Ossining and a line to White Plains. Across the river, the Rockland Traction Company operated lines in and around Nyack. A much larger system was that of the Bronx, Yonkers & White Plains Railroad, which operated to all those points until the late 1940s and was one of the giants of the traction industry. The streetcar lines of the Bronx, Queens, Manhattan, and Brooklyn were too numerous to cover in this book. They provided one of the world's densest networks of service and, developing from early horse-car and cable-car lines, operated until the 1940s, and in Brooklyn, until the 1950s, when they were changed over to buses. The main instigator of this massive change was Mayor Fiorello LaGuardia. The lines were privately owned for many years, and the largest operator was the Third Avenue Railroad Company. Later they were city owned and operated. After converting to buses most of the routes were operated by the Manhattan and Bronx Surface Transit Operating Authority (MABSTOA).

As in many other cities, the buses have not lived up to expectations. They are noisy, expensive to maintain, short lived, and emit noxious black fumes in great clouds, nearly asphyxiating pedestrians. At the present time New York City is, like many other cities, giving serious consideration of restoring electric streetcars on the busiest routes. Current plans are to begin with the 42nd Street Crosstown route as part of an area upgrading program. Buses will probably remain in use on the more lightly used routes for many years, but the gasoline shortages may give impetus for expediting the reconversion.

On Staten Island, the Richmond Light & Railroad Company ran lines between South Beach and Richmond, along with several branches.

The situation in New Jersey was very interesting, and as it has not been well documented elsewhere, and as it was intimately tied in with ferry operations on the Hudson, we shall consider it in some detail. In later years several independent lines had consolidated to form the giant Public Service Railway, predecessor of today's large Public Service Electric & Gas Company. Among the more important of these early electric railways was the North Hudson Railway. It was the brainchild of real estate developer John Hillaric Bonn. He was attempting to sell building lots atop the Palisades, and found it necessary to provide transportation from the ferries at the foot of the cliffs. He founded the railway company in 1860 and commenced operations with a horse-car line from Hoboken to Jersey City. As the hill provided difficulties to the horses, he installed a steam operated inclined plane from Hoboken to Ferry Street in Jersey City in 1874. Next he built an elevated railroad, one and a half miles long, from the incline to Lackawanna Terminal in Hoboken in 1884. Originally this line was

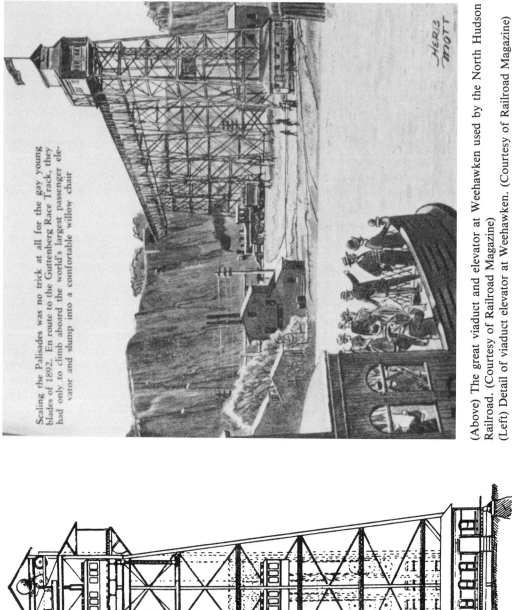

Scaling the Palisades was no trick at all for the gay young blades of 1892. En route to the Guttenberg Race Track, they had only to climb aboard the world's largest passenger elevator and slump into a comfortable willow chair

(Above) The great viaduct and elevator at Weehawken used by the North Hudson Railroad. (Courtesy of Railroad Magazine)
(Left) Detail of viaduct elevator at Weehawken. (Courtesy of Railroad Magazine)

operated by cables, but was converted to electric traction operation in 1892. This line, known as the "E1" ran above Observer Highway, connecting with local streetcar lines in Jersey City until August, 1949. When the "E1" was built the incline was converted to a wagon elevator which operated until 1928.

Bonn's next major undertaking was in 1892. On April 20th of that year Bonn opened the Guttenberg Steam Railroad division of the North Hudson County Railway. Its terminal was located atop a spectacular 148 foot high and 900 foot long viaduct running out at right angles from near the top of the Palisades to the shores of the Hudson at Weehawken, at the West Shore Railroad terminal. From here there were ferries to Manhattan. Passengers were lifted from the ferries to a complete station atop the two track viaduct by three of the largest passenger elevators ever built. The cars measured 21'6" x 12'6" x 10' high. The height of the lift was 148 feet and the trip took forty-five seconds. Each car carried 130 passengers at a time and offered seating in comfortable deep willow chairs. The elevators could transport 9000 passengers an hour. The elevators were designed by the same man who designed those for the Eiffel Tower in Paris. The station atop the elevators was a four-story structure surmounted by a high flagpole. The elevators and waiting rooms were finished in polished mahogany. Besides the two tracks, two wide walkways ran straight to the top of the cliffs—or almost. Actually the cliffs are 200 feet high at this point, and the viaduct was only 148 feet high. The railroad entered a short tunnel beneath the present Boulevard East, and then came out in a shallow cut between Liberty Place and Clifton Place. Here were located the picnic ground, casino, and amphitheater of *Eldorado Park,* which was owned by the Palisades Amusement & Exhibition Company, John H. Bonn-President. The park offered such spectacles as Franko's Brass Band and such stage shows as *"Egypt Through the Ages," King Solomon, and The Destruction of Jerusalem,* with one thousand performers, camels, horses, and elephants. Strudel, pretzels, beer, and Rhine Wine abounded.

Beyond *Eldorado Park* the railroad turned sharply north on a double track line with stone ballast and Georgia yellow pine ties, passing quarry pits, swimming holes, goat pastures, and *Monitor Park,* a gypsy encampment. At 65th Street and Dewey Avenue, where was located the *White House Tavern,* the line again turned sharply right and then again left, to run along Broadway, making a stop at Herman Avenue Station. It then turned left again to end at Bergenline Avenue near *Pat Sullivan's Hotel* and *Nungesser's Guttenberg Racetrack.* This was near the present North Hudson Park, and atop the then famous Dan Kelly's Hill, a turnpike road up the steep western slope of the Palisades from the neighborhood of Ridgefield and bridges across Wolf Creek, Overpeck Creek, and the Hackensack River. It was an important farm to market road. The area around the racetrack is now called Fairview. Later the North Hudson Railway line was continued northward atop the Palisades to Cliffside Park, Grantwood, Fort Lee, and Coytesville. Trains were pulled over the virtually gradeless route by an H. K. Porter "end tank steam motor" locomotive with Eames vacuum brakes, and an 18-ton Baldwin 0-4-0 "dummy" engine. This engine had been used previously to pull night runs on the Hoboken Elevated when the cables were closed down, and prior to electrification of the "E1." The cars were built by the Gilbert Company of Troy and Green Island, and similar to those used on the Manhattan Elevated Lines. The trains were four cars long.

In 1893 New Jersey banned racing, and the *Guttenberg Racetrack* closed down. This was the railroad's principal source of traffic. In 1894 the Guttenberg Steam Line was electrified and a trolley line put down along Pershing Avenue to the Weehawken Ferry Terminal. This line was used until the 1950s. This sealed the doom of the great viaduct and elevators, which were demolished in 1897.

In 1893 the North Hudson Railway built its Hillside line from ferries in Hoboken, up the cliff to Park Avenue, Weehawken. This line was electric from the start and connected with the now electrified Guttenberg Steam division atop the cliff. The Hillside line had a horseshoe curve and several spirals, overcoming 160 feet of ascent in 700 feet of horizontal line. It operated until 1928. An independent company built the, so called, *White Line* from Hoboken to the Paterson Plank Road in West Hoboken, atop the cliffs, in 1884. This was later absorbed by the North Hudson Railway, and operated until 1936. The company also operated another horse elevator incline from Hackensack Plank Road to Union City, which operated until 1928. By the 1920s the entire system was absorbed by Public Service Railways.

Another major network operated from the 125th Street-Edgewater Ferry. In 1893 the Palisades Railroad trolley re-incarnation of the North Hudson Railway's Guttenberg Steam division was completed north to Fort Lee and Coytesville. In 1894 the Bergen County Traction Company built a line from the Edgewater Ferry Terminal, up the Palisades and around a horseshoe curve, to a junction with the Palisades Railroad at Palisades, or Fort Lee, Junction, and thence down the western slopes of the Palisades to Palisades Park, Leonia, and Englewood. A few years later the line was extended to Tenafly. The Bergen County Traction Company completed a line from Fort Lee to Bogota in 1899. In 1900 the company was merged with the Ridgefield & Teaneck Railway Company to become the New Jersey & Hudson River Railway & Ferry Company. That same year it reached Hackensack. It reached Maywood in 1901 and the Passaic River Junction in East Paterson (present Elmwood Park) in 1903.

In 1894 the Union Traction Company was formed, and by 1899 was operating a line between Arlington and Carlstadt. This line failed, but was completed as the Newark & Hackensack. In 1899 the Jersey City, Hoboken & Paterson Street Railway Company was formed out of nine smaller companies. It acquired the old Bergen Turnpike, of which Colonel John Stevens was once President, which ran between Hoboken and Hackensack. It completed a line along the old turnpike in 1903. In 1902 the Hudson River Traction Company was incorporated, and in 1903 purchased the Newark & Hackensack Traction Company. In 1904, it in turn, was leased by the New Jersey & Hudson River Railway & Ferry Company. A principal source of traffic was *Palisades Amusement Park,* atop the Palisades in Grantwood. The New Jersey & Hudson River Railway & Ferry Company was taken over by Public Service Railways in 1911, at which time it operated fifty five cars over forty eight miles of line.

In 1909 the North Jersey Rapid Transit Company built a fifteen mile line north from a connection with the New Jersey & Hudson River Railway & Ferry Company line at Passaic River Junction. This junction was also called Broadway Station and was located near where the present Route 4 Crosses the Passaic River in Elmwood Park. This line ran north to Suffern, New York, by way of Fairlawn, Glen Rock, Ridgewood, Ho-Ho-Kus, Waldwick, Allendale, Ramsey, Cragmere, and Mahwah. In conjunction with the Hudson River Line it provided a through route from Suffern to the 125th Street Ferry at Edgewater. It was planned to build branches to Spring Valley and Greenwood Lake, and also along the Saddle River Valley. None of these were ever constructed. A direct connection with the Hudson & Manhattan Tubes was also contemplated. In 1928 the North Jersey Rapid Transit was taken over by the Public Service Company, because it could not meet its electric bill. It was merged with the Public Service Railways, who by now also owned the Hudson River Line. They operated it until 1929, and then abandoned it in favor of buses. Possibly the direct competition of the parallel Erie Railroad did not leave enough traffic to support two railroads.

The Public Service Railway was a giant. It was an affiliate of the Public Service Electric & Gas Company and, by purchase or merger, had acquired a system that covered the State of New Jersey from Coytesville, atop the Palisades in Bergen County, to Camden and Atlantic City. Its big yellow cars remained on some lines as late as the 1950s. It also still operates the Newark City Subway system on behalf of the government. The last surface route ran along Bloomfield Avenue from Newark to Caldwell.

In the area bordering the Hudson River, in addition to the lines of the New Jersey & Hudson River Railway & Ferry Company, and the North Jersey Rapid Transit Company, it took over the former lines of the North Hudson County Railway, extending from Coytesville on the north to Weehawken, Hoboken, and Jersey City on the south. It operated the Edgewater to 125th Street Manhattan ferry, and operated streetcar lines in Bayonne, Elizabeth, and Perth Amboy. It also operated the Hoboken Elevated until August 1949. It abandoned the Hillside-Park Avenue Line in 1928 and the White Line in Hoboken in 1936. In 1937 the Tenafly Branch was abandoned, and on August 5, 1938 the great Edgewater to Paterson "Hudson River Line" was changed to buses. In the 1940s Public Service abandoned most of its other electric railway and streetcar lines in favor of buses. The Pershing Avenue streetcar to the Weehawken Terminal, once part of the North Hudson Railways, was one of the last survivors in the 1950s. Many of the new bus lines still continued to run to the various ferry terminals, but gradually Public Service buses began running directly into Manhattan via the George Washington Bridge and the tunnels. By doing so it deprived the remaining ferries of traffic and did them great injury. After the Second World War Public Service sold its Edgewater-125th Street Ferry to the Electric Ferry Company.

We remember the railroads because they, or their unused tracks, are still with us providing freight service, and there is always the hope of restoration and modernization of passenger service. However, most vestiges of the interurban and streetcar lines have been obliterated by time and can be located only by interested historians armed with good maps. Consequently, many residents of the Hudson Valley are not aware that they even existed in the area. Nevertheless, electric traction may offer an excellent transportation alternative in a time of urban sprawl, widely spread suburbs, and gasoline shortages. The streetcar is completely non-polluting and flexible. It can operate either on streets or on railway tracks and is more attractive and comfortable than buses. It offers the best features of both trains and buses. The only reason they were abandoned in the first place was that the operating companies found it cheaper to operate buses on the public highway than to maintain tracks and wires. Often the trolley companies were subjected to unfair requirements with respect to maintaining road surfaces along their routes, for the benefit of the new increasingly frequent automobiles which were helping to take their traffic away, and they were subject to unreasonable assessments and franchise taxes. They could not be blamed for making the changeover to buses under these burdens. Economics, rather than social or environmental considerations, took precedence. Today, in many cities, there is a trend towards modernization and expansion of remaining streetcar systems, and Buffalo, Detroit, and Denver are beginning to build completely new systems after many years without any. This can be a good option in areas of North Jersey and the Hudson Valley. The past is parent to the future.

31 The Turn of the Century

In Chapter 29 it is noted that Theodore Roosevelt, a Hudson Valley man, was Vice President of the United States in 1901. He had served as Governor of New York for the term 1899-1901. After the assassination of McKinley at the Pan American Exposition in 1901 Roosevelt became President of the United States. During the period 1901-1905 Benjamin B. Odell, Jr., a steamboatman from Newburgh, was Governor. Consequently both the White House and Governor's Mansion were vitally aware of the Hudson Valley during these crucial years, and we are indeed fortunate that this was the case. Roosevelt's outdoor interests were also of great value to the Hudson.

During the late nineteenth century extensive quarrying was developing along the Hudson. Both the Palisades and the Highlands were subject to disfiguring excavations and the scenic beauty of the region was in serious jeopardy. A mechanism was sought to check this devastation. The New Jersey Federation of Women's Clubs sought legislation to protect the Palisades in New Jersey. In New York, Andrew H. Green worked diligently for similar legislation. Green was the founder of the Historic Preservation Society and had the strong support of Governor Theodore Roosevelt, an avid outdoorsman and nature lover. As a result of these efforts the Palisades Interstate Park Commission was formed in 1900, jointly by the states of New Jersey and New York. During these first days of the Commission, most funds came from the Commissioners and other interested individuals. Great thanks must be given particularly to George W. Perkins, Sr. who was the organizing genius and served as the Commission's first President. He served until his death in 1920, and the park took its present form under his direction. During these formative days J. Pierpont Morgan, who had an estate at Highland Falls, was also most generous.

In 1908 the State of New York acquired the site of Fort Clinton, near Bear Mountain, as a new site for Sing Sing Prison, and prisoners were actually moved there and work started on clearing the land. There was a great public outcry against this misuse of the area, and shortly thereafter Mrs. Mary A. Harriman gave a gift of 10,000 acres in the vicinity, with the stipulation that the prison project be abandoned. Her generous offer was accepted and served as the nucleus of the present Bear Mountain and Harriman State Parks. Complete recreational facilities were built, and the Bear Mountain Inn was opened in 1922.

In 1933 John D. Rockefeller, Jr. donated large acreage atop the Palisades for construction of a Parkway from the George Washington Bridge to Bear Mountain. This beautiful highway, after many delays in construction, was completed in 1958. Other property was donated by the Twombley family and the estate of W. O. Allison, who had developed a private park near Coytesville.

In the 1930s the New York Trap Rock Corporation started quarrying out the back of High Tor. The Hudson River Conservation Society, headed by Alfred Van Santvoord Olcott, President of the Hudson River Day Line, raised $12,000 and purchased the mountain from the heirs of Elmer Van Orden. In 1943 the property was conveyed to the Palisades Interstate Park Commission. Other important parcels were acquired at Tallman Mountain, Hook Mountain, Rockland Lake, Crow Nest Mountain, Storm King Mountain, and at Lake Minnewaska in the Shawangunk Mountains of Ulster County. Since 1937 the New Jersey and New York portions of the parks have been jointly administered in the interest of the citizens of both states.

While the Palisades Interstate Park system represents the essence of scenic beauty, its very antithesis, the New York Subway System, also had its beginnings in the same year of 1900, when the first line was opened in lower Manhattan.

The year 1902 saw a much more glamorous railroad development in the institution of the *Twentieth Century Limited,* which was accurately advertised as "The greatest train in the world." This train was the brainchild of George Henry Daniels, the General Passenger Agent of the New York Central Railroad, one of the greatest railroad marketing men of all time. For many years previously the Central's best train had been the *Lake Shore Limited.* Daniels had previously dreamed up the record breaking speed run of the *Empire State Express,* and the fast twenty hour schedule of the *Exposition Flyer* between New York and Chicago for the great Chicago Exposition in 1893. The new *Twentieth Century Limited* was to make the fast twenty hour schedule of a first class Pullman train a regular permanent service. By dint of providing superb service and equipment, and astute public relations, riding the *Century* soon became a recognized status symbol, and the train was generally accepted as the finest in the nation for all the years of its operation into the 1960s. Thus the Hudson Valley enjoyed the cachet of possessing the finest train in the nation, as well as the finest steamboats.

The period before the First World War saw the construction of the first tunnels beneath the Hudson. The first tunnel was that of the uptown line of the Hudson & Manhattan electric railroad. It was completed on March 11, 1904, and opened for traffic on February 25, 1908. The twin single track tunnels of the Pennsylvania Railroad were completed in October of 1906 and, along with Pennsylvania Station in Manhattan, were opened for traffic in 1909. That same year, on July 17th the downtown tunnels of the Hudson & Manhattan Railroad were completed.

Another monster river festival was held in 1909. The Hudson-Fulton Celebration marked the tercentenary of Henry Hudson's voyage up the Hudson River, and the centennial of Fulton's successful sailing of the *Clermont* . . . albeit actually the 102nd anniversary. The major feature was a great naval parade up the river from New York on Saturday, September 25th. Almost 750 vessels actively participated. There were over 100 steamboats and ferryboats and about 270 yachts and motorboats, and more than 300 lighters and tugs. The procession was headed by the *U.S.S. Gloucester* under the command of Captain J. W. Miller, The first squadron, comprised of twelve divisions of steamboats, was under the command of the Hudson River Day Line's assistant general manager, Captain George A. White. The first division included the *Hendrick Hudson, Robert Fulton, Albany, Providence, City of Lowell, Puritan,* and *Rensselaer,* as well as the venerable sidewheel towboat, *Norwich,* which was then the oldest active steamboat in the world. There were also authentic operating replicas of the *Half Moon* and the *Clermont.* This great flotilla went from New York to the head of navigation at Troy, with many ceremonies enroute. The celebration was the brainchild of President Eben E. Olcott of the Hudson River Day Line.

Observation car of the *Twentieth Century Limited.* Symbol of railroad luxury in the Hudson Valley.
(New York Central photo)

This certainly was the high-noon of Hudson River steamboating. The resorts and little connecting railroads were all in full operation and the automobile still had not effectively appeared on the scene. There was a great deal of traffic and the times were prosperous. Many of the largest of the steamboats were put into service during this period. The *Hendrick Hudson, C. W. Morse, Trojan, Rensselaer,* and *Berkshire* were all products of this era.

The turn of the century was also a period of flood-tide immigration. In 1892 the United States Immigration Service established its major immigration depot on Ellis Island. The monumental buildings date from 1898. The island served in the capacity of receiving station until 1943. Over 15,000,000 new Americans entered the "Golden Door" passing through Ellis Island. New York is still the largest immigration port of entry, welcoming over 100,000 new citizens each year. However, most enter by way of airports and the new liner piers.

32 The Early Twentieth Century

As described in the previous chapter, the United States, and more particularly the Hudson Valley, entered the twentieth century enjoying great prosperity and an expanding economy. Conditions remained much the same until 1917.

The principal event of the period under consideration was the First World War (1914-1918). While the underlying political and economic causes went back into the nineteenth century, the precipitating cause incident was the assassination of Archduke Francis Ferdinand, heir to the Emperial Throne of Austria-Hungary, on June 28, 1914 by a Serbian Nationalist. Before the year was out all of Europe was embroiled in a great war, largely as a result of interlocking alliances. American interests were first perceived to be in danger when the Germans sank the Cunard passenger liner *Lusitania* in 1915 and a great number of United States citizens were lost. In 1916 Germany announced unrestricted submarine warfare against anyone trading with the enemy. The United States found this unacceptable and declared war on Germany on April 6, 1917. American involvement was vast and total. A draft was implemented and the American Expeditionary Force greatly enlarged. During the war the American railroads were taken over by the United States Railroad Administration (USRA), under the direction of William Gibbs McAdoo, who had just completed the new Hudson & Manhattan Railroad tubes under the Hudson. Government administration of the railroads was not very efficient and tremendous bottlenecks of freight cars developed in the port of New York area. A large embarkation and demobilization camp was established in New Jersey at Camp Merritt, near Cresskill.

This camp was named after Major General Wesley Merritt. The camp accommodated between 40,000 and 51,000 men and included 2,000 buildings and 14 miles of concrete roads. A total of 578,566 men debarked from the base between November 1917 and November 1918. Later approximately 500,000 returned to Camp Merritt to be mustered out. A great influenza epidemic ravaged the country in the fall and winter of 1918, and took a heavy toll at Camp Merritt. Over 10,000 cases were reported there and the mortality was high, as men who had escaped the dangers of battle perished on home ground.*

The war touched the Hudson Valley in other important ways. In August of 1916 German saboteurs demolished an American munition plant at Black Tom in Jersey City, six months after the had destroyed the Kingsland, New Jersey Arsenal. They caused spectacular explosions and did approximately $50,000,000 worth of damage.

The war ended in 1918 and the country returned to peace. However, President Woodrow

---

*Since this was written, new evidence has proven conclusively that the allegations of German sabotage were false propaganda to cover the maladroit handling of an unfortunate accident of American workers. The strong anti-German sentiment of the time allowed this story to pass as true.

Hamburg-American Line steamship terminal at Hoboken with New York skyline in distance c1900.

Wilson was not supported in his efforts to get the United States to join the League of Nations to support the peace. After his death in 1921, Warren G. Harding became President and the country returned to "Normalcy." During the war the Port of New York had served as America's principal port of debarkation and of shipment of military supplies....a function which its magnificent facilities enabled it to perform admirably.

During the 1920s the nation embarked upon a great economic expansion, and a formerly rural population gradually drifted to the cities. This was a period marked by great consolidations of corporate power and by financial speculation. This had reached fever pitch by 1929 when the stock market crashed in October, putting the nation into a prolonged depression lasting through the 1930s.

The first third of the century saw some very important local developments in the Hudson Valley.

In 1904 a drought left New York City with only five days supply of water. At this time the City depended largely upon the Croton Reservoir and Aqueduct System on the east side of the Hudson in Westchester County. This situation had been developing for some time, and shrewd speculators had acquired water rights to most of the watersheds near New York City in the Ramapo Mountains and Highlands of the Hudson. Consequently the City decided to go further afield to the Catskills—one hundred miles away. There were a number of legal battles before the City's rights of condemnation were recognized, but by 1909 construction began on the Ashokan Reservoir on Esopus Creek. This was the largest component of the Catskill Reservoir System with an area of 10,000 acres, and measuring twelve miles long. It has a capacity of 132 billion gallons. The system of dams and dikes is four miles long, and the main dam at Olive Bridge is 1000 feet long and 240 feet high. Here water is inducted into the 92 mile long first segment of the Catskill Aqueduct for delivery to a distribution reservoir at Kensico in Westchester County. The Ashokan Reservoir was completed in 1919.

To deliver the water to New York City a new Catskill Aqueduct was built. It is a surface level, gravity-flow, aqueduct at its northern end. It passed beneath the Hudson River at Cornwall-on-Hudson, to Breakneck Mountain on the east shore, through a pressure siphon 1,400 feet beneath high water level in the river. It then continues to Kensico Reservoir, where the waters are chlorinated and sent seventeen miles further to Hillview Reservoir in Yonkers. From there it is distributed through Manhattan and Brooklyn by a deep level, eighteen mile long, tunnel blasted through solid rock. From Brooklyn a bell and spigot pipeline continues under the Narrows to Silver Lake on Staten Island—120 miles from Ashokan Reservoir.

Additional capacity was added in 1924 by construction of the Schoharie Reservoir and the Shandaken Tunnel, which conducts its waters for eighteen miles to the Esopus Creek, above the Ashokan Reservoir.

In 1918 the redevelopment of the old Erie Canal into the New York State Barge Canal System, first authorized in 1903, was completed. The new system was 525 miles long and cost $175,000,000. Construction was started in 1905.

Aiding in continued growth of the Port of New York, the Port of New York Authority was created in 1921 by treaty between the states of New York and New Jersey, 'to plan, develop, and operate terminal, transportation, and other facilities of commerce, and to improve and protect the commerce of the bi-state Port.'' Six Commissioners are appointed by the Governors of each state, and serve without pay for overlapping terms of six years. In 1972 its name was changed to the Port Authority of New York & New Jersey. It has continued as the dominant force in development of the port and related facilities and serves as an example of a well and efficiently conducted public authority. Its major weakness has been a continuing reluctance to help solve the railroad and rail commuter problems in the area under its jurisdiction, continually pleading the danger of impairing its bond ratings by getting so involved. Its facilities, until recently, were well run, well maintained, and kept modern, and the authority has remained free of any taint of scandal for over half a century.

In 1923 the Hudson River Day Line opened its Indian Point Park, below Peekskill. This park offered facilities for picnicking, dining in a cafeteria, swimming, strolling through the woods, and simply relaxing. It covered 320 acres and included a farm for raising of vegetables for use on the steamers. There were two piers. The park remained in operation as a popular destination for excursionists until 1956, when it was sold to Consolidated Edison Company for construction of an atomic power plant.

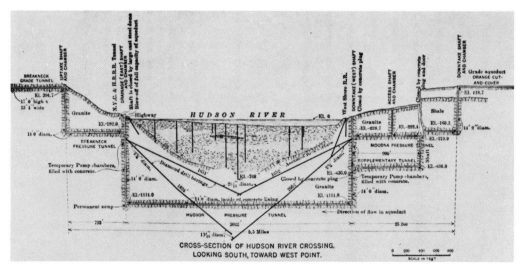

Cross-section of Hudson River crossing of Catskill Aqueduct.
(American Society of Civil Engineers, Vol. 86, pp. 1–92, 1923; courtesy of A. V. S. Olcott, Jr.)

The year 1924 saw construction of the Bear Mountain Bridge, then the world's longest suspension span. As early as 1889 a railroad bridge was projected for this "natural bridge-point." The present highway bridge was privately built at a cost of $5,000,000. It was designed by Howard Baird. The central span is 1,632 feet long and 185 feet above the water. It was acquired by the State of New York in 1940.

The last sidewheel steamboat for Hudson River use, the *Alexander Hamilton,* of the Hudson River Day Line, was built at Sparrow's Point, Maryland, by Bethlehem Steel Company in 1924. Subsequent ships have all had screw propulsion. The *Alexander Hamilton* operated through the 1971 season, the last sidewheeler on the river, and ending an era.

The last steamboat to be built on the upper Hudson was the *City of Keansburg,* launched at the Marvell Shipyard at Newburgh in 1928. She operated until 1971 on the bays and lower Hudson.

The Hudson Valley was now entering a great age of bridge building. On June 29th, 1928 the new Port Authority opened two great vehicular bridges across the Arthur Kill, between Staten Island and New Jersey. The *Outerbridge Crossing,* connecting Tottenville with Perth Amboy, was named for Eugenius H. Outerbridge, first Chairman of the Port of New York Authority. It is a cantilever truss structure with a total length of almost two miles and 135 feet above the water. The companion *Goethals Bridge* was a memorial to Major General George W. Goethals, builder of the Panama Canal, and first consulting engineer of the Port of New York Authority. It connects Port Ivory and Elizabethport. It is over 7000 feet long and also 135 feet above the water.

The Port Authority completed a third important bridge in 1931. The *Bayonne Bridge,* across the Kill Van Kull, is the longest steel arch bridge in the world, with a mid-span clearance of 150 feet, permitting the largest ocean going vessels to reach Port Newark and Elizabethport. Total length is just short of 7,000 feet.

The Port Authority also turned its attention to tunnel building. On November 13, 1927 it

Pennsylvania Railroad carfloat bridges at Harsimus Cove. (Author's collection)

Erie Railroad carfloat slip north of Jersey City passenger terminal at Pavonia Avenue. These floats were designed to carry refrigerated boxcars of perishables to the produce markets along West Street in Manhattan. Note Erie tugboat *Binghamton* and stacks and pilot houses of ferryboats beyond the pier in the background, c1950. (Raymond J. Baxter Collection)

opened the first vehicular tunnel beneath the Hudson—the *Holland Tunnel.* It connects Canal Street, Manhattan with Jersey City. The $70-million tunnel was named for its chief construction engineer, Clifford M. Holland, who died of exhaustion in 1924, just two days before sandhogs, digging from each side, met in one of the tunnel's two tubes. This was the first major tunnel to pose a ventilation problem, as previous ones had served electric railways rather than motor vehicles. It was solved by construction of four ventilation buildings, two on each side of the river, housing immense fans which can provide a change of air every 90 seconds. This was the first tunnel with forced ventilation. The tunnels are approximately 8,500 feet long.

Chelsea Transatlantic Piers at 23rd Street, c1900. (Smith's New York Harbor Guide)

Erie Railroad tugboat *Oradell* and carfloat. The *Oradell* was built in 1891 and sold in June 1936. Photo from Erie Railroad Magazine Centennial Issue, May 1951. (Raymond J. Baxter Collection)

Further upriver, the enlarged Port of Albany was opened to ocean going ships with a channel depth of 27 feet in 1932. Depths have since been increased to 32 feet in 1954 and 34 feet in the 1960s.

During this period the Port of New York was at its zenith, with many lines operating from finger piers along the North River in Manhattan. In 1934 operations were being conducted by the following lines: Railroads: Lehigh Valley Railroad; Central Railroad of New Jersey; Pennsylvania Railroad; West Shore Railroad; Delaware, Lackawanna & Western Railroad; Erie Railroad; Baltimore & Ohio Railroad; New York, Ontario & Western Railway; New York Central Railroad; Southern Pacific Railroad (Morgan Line); all providing passenger ferry and freight lighterage service, and the Southern Pacific operating a coastal steamship line to New Orleans and Texas ports.

River, Bay, and Sound Steamship Lines: Iron Steamboat Company; New England Navigation Company (Fall River Line); Eastern Steamship Company; Metropolitan Steamship Company; Hudson River Steamship Company (Night Line to Albany); Morgan Line; Hudson River Navigation Company; and Hudson River Day Line.

Ocean Steamship Companies: United Fruit Company; North German Lloyd Line; Clyde Line; Clyde Mallory Lines; Royal Mail Steam Packet Company; Italian Line; Savannah Line; Cunard Line; French Line; Atlantic Transportation Company; White Star Line; American Leyland Line; American & Cuban Steamship Company; Anchor Line; Panama Steamship Company; Furness Prince Lines; United American Line; Furness Withy Lines; and Italian-American Line.

Most of these companies operated three or more piers and the activity in the river and along the waterfront is unimaginable to those who are only acquainted with today's desolate waterfront. This was truly the economic lifeblood of Manhattan. Passengers did not simply fly into Kennedy Airport from inland cities and transfer to overseas flights—or fly directly overseas from inland airports. They came by train to New York City by the millions, stayed overnight at Manhattan hotels, attended the theater and ate in the restaurants, and then departed overseas in whole armadas of ocean liners—all paying toll to the City of New York, and providing innumerable jobs. The jet airplane has done untold economic damage to New

York City in loss of this lucrative traffic. This is a major factor behind its present problems which is often overlooked.

The freight movement was even more vast. Whole trainloads of merchandise were loaded onto lighters on the New Jersey shore and pushed across the Hudson by tugboats. They were tied up alongside freighters moored at the Manhattan piers, and the freight was lifted aboard the freighters by cranes and booms. Other whole trains of cars were put aboard railroad carfloats and pushed across the Hudson by tugs, to be moored alongside railroad owned piers in Manhattan. They would be unloaded directly onto the piers and the merchandise was distributed locally by truck. Fruits and vegetables were unloaded onto the piers and directly auctioned off to wholesalers on the spot before being trucked away. The Erie Railroad for many years thus conducted the largest produce market in the City. All the railroads also operated lines of passenger ferries to slips every few blocks apart along the Hudson. The round the clock activity on the waterfront and on the water was inconceivable. Ferry boats had to weave their way between lighters, tugs, carfloats, tows of canal and river barges, coastal liners, excursion boats, freighters, and oceanliners.

This activity continued up until after the Second World War. Then the rot set in. To begin with, the operations were fundamentally uneconomic, and necessitated extra handling of merchandise. At the new terminals on the New Jersey side railroad cars and trucks could be brought right up alongside the ships. Furthermore, there was far less pilferage and theft in the more easy to secure New Jersey terminals. The Unions were less demanding, and there was less gangsterism and corruption. Other ports such as Baltimore and Philadelphia constructed more modern facilities. The railroads, never happy with having to conduct extensive marine operations in New York Harbor, and tired of excessive taxation in New Jersey, began to favor other ports in their rates and marketing policies. The passenger shipping of the great liners was lost largely to the jets. Coastal passenger services were never restored after the war. The ships had been requisitioned by the government for wartime use and were worn out and obsolete when returned to their owners. They would cost too much to replace and the services were discontinued.

Many older excursion boats became unsafe or uneconomical to operate, and gradually went out of business. As described in earlier chapters, the railroads gradually went out of the ferry business. The City of New York built a large new produce market at Hunters Point

Erie Railroad tugboat *Scranton* and covered lighter 416. From Erie Railroad Magazine, Centennial Issue, May 1951. (Raymond J. Baxter Collection)

An Erie Railroad carfloat and tug *Olean* c1957.

which was served directly by rail. More merchandise freight moved into and out of the city by truck, and even the railroads shifted to using piggyback and containers, which were unloaded at New Jersey railyards and brought into Manhattan by truck via the tunnels and George Washington Bridge. Eventually all that was left in Manhattan were a few cruise ships, the Hudson River Day Line and a few local sightseeing boats. *THEN,* the City took action and built a new Passenger Liner Pier. It is a beautiful and efficient new structure, but gets only sporadic use, mainly in the summer. Most cruise operators have shifted to Florida ports, and only a few still operate to New York. Only the Hudson River Day Line, operating with only one ship, is left as a regular liner operation, and this is only for a short season. Conditions have returned to those at the time of Robert Fulton's *Clermont.* Most of the old piers have been removed. Possibly changing times and technology and a renewed interest in both the Hudson River and water transportation in general will bring a revival.

33 The Mid-Twentieth Century

The dominating fact of the beginning of this period was the Great Depression which ensued after the Stock Market Crash of 1929. Credit had been overextended and the country suffered from an excess of productive capacity. Recovery was slow and painful and many local firms failed. People did not have money to spend at resorts, or on cruises, or one-day excursions. Many of the smaller steamboat lines went out of business as farmers took their own produce to market in the family truck. The private passenger car and new highways cut into the business of the excursion and day liners. There was much unemployment in the river towns such as Troy, Poughkeepsie, and Newburgh. The bloom was definitely off the rose.

In these difficult times a Hudson River man came to the fore on the national scene. Franklin Delano Roosevelt was a native of Hyde Park, near Poughkeepsie. He came of an old and distinguished local family and had deep roots in the Hudson Valley, which he loved very dearly. He was an avid antiquarian and active in The Holland Society of New York. While an antiquarian by advocation, he was also a disciple of the most advanced Keynesian economic and social theory and a liberal politician. He was also a humane man and promised to try various economic and social experiments in an attempt to alleviate the misery caused by the depression. Roosevelt served as Governor of New York from 1929 to 1933, when he was elected President of the United States, in which capacity he served until his death in 1945. Roosevelt loved Hyde Park and his estate called Crum Elbow, and the life of the Hudson Valley. He always thought and felt as a Hudson Valley man, and after his death he was buried at Hyde Park. Roosevelt saw the nation through hard years of depression, painfully as both Saint and Devil, and as both traitor to his country and as its saviour. It is not the place of this book to pass judgment, but it is proper to note that he generated strong feelings among people of diverse background. Let us simply say that he was a great citizen of the Hudson Valley who exerted a profound influence upon his times.

With the popularization of the private automobile, suburbanization spread up the Hudson Valley into portions of Rockland and Westchester counties not particularly well served by the railroads. People began taking evening and Sunday drives on the new parkways along the Hudson, such as the Henry Hudson Parkway in New York, and the Henry Hudson Drive along the Palisades in New Jersey. The Bear Mountain Parkway, leading to the Bear Mountain Bridge and Bear Mountain State Park provided a very popular Sunday drive.

New bridges connected the growing highway network. The *Mid-Hudson Bridge* at

George Washington Bridge. (Courtesy Port of New York Authority)

Poughkeepsie was opened on August 25, 1930. It is a beautiful suspension span 3,000 feet long, designed by Ralph Modjeski, who had also designed the great *Huey P. Long Bridge* at New Orleans, across the Mississippi, and the *Ben Franklin Bridge* across the Delaware at Philadelphia. Modjeski, born in Cracow, Poland, and the son of the famous Shakespearean actress, Helena Modjeska, was one of the world's most renowned bridge builders at the time of the construction of the *Mid-Hudson Bridge,* which bridge connoisseurs consider his most beautiful and perfect design. In later life he resided at Saugerties.

The cantilever *Rip Van Winkle Bridge* above Catskill was opened to traffic in 1935, and the steel-arch *Henry Hudson Bridge,* across the Spuyten Duyvil Creek, was opened in 1936.

However, the crowning glory of all the Hudson River bridges was the *George Washington Bridge.* It was designed by Othmar H. Ammann. Ground was broken in October 1927, and it was opened for traffic on October 25, 1931.

The *George Washington Bridge* spans the Hudson River between West 178th Street, Manhattan and Fort Lee, New Jersey, passing directly over Jeffery's Hook Lighthouse. Upon its completion it was the longest suspension bridge in the world with a main span of 3,500 feet, and overall length of 4,760 feet between anchorages. The great supporting towers are 604 feet high, and the roadway is 212 feet above the water. Completion of this bridge had a profound effect upon the development of Northern New Jersey. It led to dense suburbanization and increased use of automobiles and buses in place of railroads, trolleys, and ferries. Hailed as a great advance at the time of its opening, a half-century later its role is being questioned. It shifted the emphasis away from moving people to moving vehicles. Because it was owned by the Port of New York Authority, which depended upon bridge toll revenues to pay back the construction bonds, that authority artificially promoted automobile and bus use, much to the detriment of the railroads and ferries, and abetting traffic strangulation of Manhattan. Similar policies arose from their ownership of tunnels and major bus stations. The *George Washington Bridge* also had the ultimate effect of removing the Hudson River from the consciousness of the population. It made the river so easy to cross that people no longer noticed the Hudson. While being a magnificent structure in itself and a great engineering accomplishment, and while it allowed speculators and real estate developers to reap great profit from sprawling suburbanization in New Jersey, it has proven to be somewhat of a villain so far as the Hudson River per se is concerned.

December of 1937 saw the opening of the center tube of the *Lincoln Tunnel* from West 40th Street, Manhattan to Weehawken. This is similar in design and construction to the

Transatlantic Liner Piers c1950. Steamships: *Independence; America;* and *United States* in foreground. *Queen Elizabeth* docking.

George Washington Bridge. (Courtesy Port of New York Authority)

Holland Tunnel. It is 8,216 feet long. Additional tubes to north and south were opened in 1945 and 1957 respectively, making it the world's only three tube vehicular tunnel.

Its completion has served to compound the problems started by the *George Washington Bridge.* Despite institution of rush hour, "bus only" lanes, it daily develops the world's greatest traffic jams at rush hours and dumps many thousands of vehicles on the overcrowded streets of Manhattan. It is beginning to become apparent that "engineering marvels" are not always the best economic or social solution to transportation problems.

An engineering marvel of undoubted social value is the new Delaware Aqueduct System completed in the 1950s. By 1930 the Catskill and Croton Systems were becoming inadequate and New York City determined to tap the waters of Rondout Creek, the Neversink River, and the Delaware. Construction started in the 1930s. It is a deep driven pressure tunnel through solid rock from the Merriman Dam at Lackawack on Rondout Creek to Hillview Reservoir in Yonkers—a total distance of 85 miles. It passes beneath the Hudson at Chelsea. The Rondout Reservoir was completed in 1955. The Neversink Reservoir and tunnel and the Pepacton Reservoir and tunnel were also both completed in 1955. The Pepacton Reservoir is on the East Branch of the Delaware. In 1965 the Cannonsville Reservoir and tunnel were completed from the West Branch of the Delaware. The tunnels connecting Rondout Reservoir to the Pepacton and Cannonsville Reservoirs are great engineering accomplishments in themselves, running beneath the southern Catskill Mountains. The Pepacton tunnel is 26.5 miles long and the Cannonsville tunnel 42 miles long.

The New York World's Fair was held in 1939 and 1940. It drew large crowds from around the world and purported to demonstrate the new technology which would bring about the world of the future. Its symbol and centerpiece was a gigantic Perisphere and Trylon. Among the most notable and influential exhibits was General Motor's "World of Tomorrow" exhibit.

The last year of Hudson River Night Line operations was 1939. The Night Line had been experiencing difficult times under various ownerships. It was hoped that the World's Fair would stimulate traffic. It did—but not enough. The last sailing was on September 9th when the *New Yorker,* formerly called the *Trojan,* left Albany.

In the late 1930s the war clouds were again gathering over Europe. In 1939 King George VI and Queen Elizabeth of England visited President Roosevelt at his home in Hyde Park. At this time preliminary agreements were reached for providing England with economic help in the anticipated crisis. On September 3, 1939 England and France declared war on Germany after Hitler's troops invaded Poland. Russia entered the war on the side of the allies on September 17th. Early in 1941 Congress approved the Lend-Lease program of economic aid to England. In August of 1941 President Roosevelt and Prime Minister Winston Churchill met at sea and drew up the Atlantic Charter, which served as the memorandum of agreement throughout the Second World War.

On December 7, 1941 the Japanese attacked and destroyed the United States Naval Base at Pearl Harbor, Hawaii. On December 8th Congress declared war against Japan, and a few days later Germany declared war on the United States. The Second World War was now in full swing.

The events of the war were too important and numerous to treat even in summary fashion in this book. In the Hudson Valley area the main activities again centered about the Port of New York, which once again served as a prime staging area for sending men, materials, and economic aid overseas. A large army camp, similar to Camp Merritt, was established at Orangeburg, in Rockland County, on the lines of the West Shore and Erie Railroads. This was called Camp Shanks. A similar large camp was established in Edison Township, New Jersey, near New Brunswick, called Camp Kilmer. They served the same functions as had Camp Merritt in the First World War. In early 1944, before the Allied invasion of Norman-

Tappan Zee Bridge from steamer *Alexander Hamilton,* 1960. Note double wake from sidewheels.
(Photo: Arthur G. Adams)

dy, the West Shore Railroad, between Orangeburg and Weehawken was the scene of the intensest railroad traffic that the world had ever seen, with constant troop movements and ammunition trains, in addition to the extensive regular through passenger, freight, and commuter operations. Most of the troops were debarked at Weehawken, and the old Erie pier at Piermont, for transfer to such ships as the *Queen Mary,* for runs across the sub-infested North Atlantic. There were great military supply terminals at Bay Ridge, Brooklyn and at Bayonne. The Keyser Shipyard on Newark Bay was turning out Liberty Ships, as were the Bethlehem and Todd shipyards in Weehawken and Hoboken, and the large Brooklyn Navy Yard. New York City played momentary host to millions of servicemen on leave and the entire port area was a scene of ceaseless activity. This time the railroads were left under private control and handled the tremendous additional traffic smoothly and efficiently. Many old Hudson River boats were requisitioned for use either as floating barracks or for use in the Invasion of Normandy. Few ever returned. The Hudson River Day Line was granted an Army-Navy E For Excellence in helping carry troops and passengers during these years of severe gasoline shortages and rationing. Altogether these were frightening and exciting years along the Hudson.

On April 25, 1945 the United States and Russian armies met and Germany collapsed. Germany signed an unconditional surrender at Rheims on May 7th, thus ending the European phase of the war.

On August 6, 1945 President Harry S. Truman, who had become President upon the death of Franklin D. Roosevelt on April 12th, authorized the dropping of an atomic bomb on Hiroshima. Another was dropped on Nagasaki on August 9th. This quickly brought Japan to her knees, and an unconditional surrender was signed on August 14, 1945, thus ending the war.

The United States did not repeat the mistake of standing aloof from a new world organization and became a member of the new United Nations. The headquarters was moved from San Francisco to Lake Success, Long Island, in 1945, and ultimately to Manhattan, upon completion of its headquarters buildings on East 42nd Street. By a stretch of the imagination, it might be said that New York City was now the Capital of the World, on the banks of the Hudson River.

The end of the war saw a great boom. Consumer demand that had been pent up during the depression and the war now had an outlet. Many people had earned good wages in war industry and there had been no unemployment. War industries quickly converted to manufacturing consumer goods and the boom was on. Suburbanization galloped ahead throughout New Jersey, Long Island, and around Albany and Troy in the Hudson Valley. New industries such as IBM had brought a measure of prosperity to the mid-Hudson region. Automobiles became common and gasoline cheap and plentiful. Happy times were here—but not on the river.

With expanding population more raw sewage was dumped into the Hudson. The new industries dumped such unusual wastes as PCBs and cadmium. New atomic power plants were built. People with money in their pockets took trips to Europe and up the Rhine and Danube, rather than up the Hudson. They hurried over the river on bridges, and under it through tunnels. They no longer took the time to savor it from the decks of ferry boats, and note what was happening. Patronage fell off the day boats.

On September 13, 1948 the last regularly scheduled Day Liner, the *Robert Fulton,* left Albany for New York. There have only been sporadic excursion trips to Albany since then. Regular steamboat service was cut back to Poughkeepsie. Respect was lost for the steamers. The many new motor boats and water skiers would now frequently race the steamers and attempt to "cut their bow" at risk of life and limb. The motor boats and cabin cruisers seemed to represent the only public interest in the Hudson, as the river was becoming too polluted for fishing and swimming. Even this use was to dwindle as the river became dirtier, gas more costly, and docking fees prohibitive.

The Korean War, between 1950 and 1953, had little direct effect on the Hudson or the Port of New York. The action was primarily on the west coast.

Development was now concentrated on the highways. In the early 1950s the New York State Thruway, then called the Governor Thomas E. Dewey Thruway, was under construction from Yonkers to the State Line near Westport on Lake Erie. On December 15, 1955 the *Tappan Zee Bridge* was completed from Tarrytown to South Nyack. This monstrous bridge is three miles long and crosses one of the widest sections of the Tappan Zee. While it is an engineering marvel, it destroys the scenic beauty of one of the most beautiful portions of the river. Utilitarianism now reigned supreme on the river of Thomas Cole, Asher Durand, and Frederick E. Church.

The main structure of the bridge is a cantilever through-truss span of 1,212 feet, with anchor spans of 602 feet. The remainder of the west end consists of conventional steel stringer design, and the east end of deck truss. The bridge's roadway comprises six lanes, separated by a ten foot center mall. The height of the two main towers is 293 feet above the water and there is a minimum clearance of 138 feet above the channel. The designers were Madigan-Hyland Consulting Engineers. One of the unique features of the bridge is the use of eight concrete caissons, supported on steel piles driven to rock, which serve as buoyant underwater foundations to support approximately 70% of the structure's dead weight. The largest of these caissons is half the size of a city block and weighs 15,000 tons. The bridge is a marvel of sheer brutal size—and it brutalizes the river.

Another ugly behemoth is the *Kingston-Rhinecliff Bridge,* opened in 1957. This monster is of continuous deck design with an overall length of 7,793 feet, and a main span of 5,200 feet with vessel clearance of 152 feet. There are two vehicle lanes. It was designed by D. B. Steinman, and is operated by the New York State Bridge Authority.

The *Castleton-On-Hudson Bridge* of the Berkshire Extension of the New York State Thruway was completed in 1959. It is slightly over a mile long and of cantilever truss design providing 144 feet clearance above the river. This beauty was also designed by Madigan-Hyland Consulting Engineers. However, as it is close to and parallel with an equally ugly railroad bridge, it does not represent any new blot on the landscape.

The opening of these bridges all resulted in loss of ferry services and consequent public contact with the Hudson as people went lickety-split above the waters.

The year 1957 saw completion of the South tube of the *Lincoln Tunnel* and total abandonment for both freight and passenger service of the New York, Ontario & Western Railway from Cornwall-On-Hudson to Oswego. It was the largest railroad abandonment in the United States to date, and the first one of an entire Class I railroad. Ironically the O & W had been the first Class I railroad completely dieselized. People now drove or took the bus to the Catskills.

On December 10, 1959 the last West Shore passenger train ran. This was a melancholy affair and I was the last passenger to board a regularly scheduled West Shore train, as I was the last holder of a regular commutation ticket. There were now more buses crowding the *George Washington Bridge* and *Lincoln Tunnel.*

In 1959, over Labor Day Weekend, a much scaled down celebration was held in honor of the 350th Anniversary of Hudson's voyage of discovery. The steamer *Alexander Hamilton* made a special cruise to Albany, and this, in a minor way, commemorated the 150th anniversary of steamboating. It was a pathetic far cry from the great Hudson-Fulton Celebration fifty years earlier.

The year 1961 saw the United States' entry into the unfortunate fourteen year long Viet Nam War. This insidious conflict had little apparent direct effect upon the Hudson Valley other than a few ugly "demonstrations" on the part of hard-hat workers in Manhattan.

In 1962 the *Alexander Hamilton* made its last special trip to Albany over Labor Day Weekend—the last sidewheel steamboat to ever depart from Albany....and final closing of an era.

In 1963 the Indian Point Atomic Power Plant of Consolidated Edison Company went into operation. This plant, sitting atop the Ramapo fault line, cost $90,000,000. In 1978 plans were underway to double the size of this facility. Conservationists voiced concern about the warm water being returned to the river, and, in 1963, there was an incident where large numbers of striped bass fingerlings were drawn into the water intakes and killed. Since the incident at Three Mile Island on the Susquehanna River there has been considerable public concern about the safety of the Indian Point Plant. At the time of writing (April, 1980), the plant is entirely shut down and its reopening seems problematical.

The year 1963 saw the opening of another scenically destructive bridge across Newburgh Bay. The *Newburgh-Beacon Bridge* is a combination deck truss and continuous deck bridge, owned by the New York State Bridge Authority, who previously operated the Newburgh Ferry. It carries Interstate Route 84 across the Hudson. Overall length is 7,855 feet with a main span of 1,000 feet, and a clearance of 135 feet. It has only two vehicle lanes, which soon became inadequate, and a parallel twin span is presently under construction. The writer has no quarrel with the necessity for a bridge in the vicinity, but this one should have been built a mile further north where far less scenic damage would have been done. The point is that in the late 1950s and early 1960s there was relatively little public concern about preserving the beauty of the river.

Fortunately the last large bridge to be built turned out to be both massive and beautiful in its lines and natural in its placement. The *Verrazano Narrows Bridge,* connecting Brooklyn and Staten Island, across The Narrows, was opened in November of 1964. It was designed by the firm of Ammann & Whitney for the Triborough Bridge & Tunnel Authority, an organization which usually pays great attention to the aesthetics of its facilities. Like most large suspension bridges, it was the longest in the world when opened. The center span is

Verrazano Narrows Bridge (New York Convention & Visitors Bureau).

4,260 feet long and 228 feet above mean high water. The two supporting towers are 690 feet high, and total length is 13,700 feet, including approaches. There are two vehicle decks. Opening of this bridge led to an immediate building boom on Staten Island, which continues in 1980.

The first half of the twentieth century witnessed the construction of a number of power plants along the Hudson. Among the earliest ones were those of the Hudson & Manhattan Railroad in Jersey City and of the Interborough Rapid Transit Company at 60th Street, Manhattan, as well as the Glenclyffe Generating Station of the New York Central Railroad at waters edge in the Glenwood Section of Yonkers. The first major plant for public power generation was that of the Niagara Mohawk Power Company at Kenwood, below Albany.

In more recent times Central Hudson Gas & Electric built a major plant at Danskammer Point near Marlborough, and Orange & Rockland Utilities built plants at Bowline Point, above Haverstraw, and the Lovett Plant at Tomkins Cove. Consolidated Edison Company also has a plant at Bowline Point. Little attention was given to either scenic or thermal pollution in locating these facilities.

The mid-twentieth century saw the economic decline of such mid-Hudson cities as Haverstraw, Newburgh, Poughkeepsie, and Kingston. Heavy diversified industry moved and was replaced by sweat shops of the garment industry, utilizing the low skilled labor which has moved into these cities as the former, better educated, and more skilled, residents moved either entirely out of the region or into surrounding towns. The International Business Machine Corporation has become the dominant firm in the region with major plants at Poughkeepsie and Kingston. There is considerable unemployment and a large number of relief recipients at Newburgh. Some students of the situation blame the flight of industry on the tax policies of the river cities, but this seems to be only part of the problem.

34 The Last Third of the Twentieth Century

The last third of the twentieth century in the Hudson Valley might best be described as a period of ultimate collapse, reassessments, and new beginnings. There has been a new look at the Hudson River and what it represents and offers to the future. New respect has been gained for our heritage. Old technologies are being reevaluated and relics of our past are being preserved and studied. People are seeking their personal and racial roots and clarifying their values. There is considerable interest in industrial and urban archeology, social studies of earlier times, and transportation history. Certain urgent problems are finally finding relief.

The year 1967 was a sad one for lovers of the Hudson River ferries and the leisurely life they represented. On April 25th the Central Railroad of New Jersey Communipaw Ferry ceased operations, and on November 22nd the Hoboken Ferry made its last crossing from Barclay Street—the last regularly scheduled ferry across the Hudson River proper.

The following year saw the amalgamation of the New York Central Railroad, the New York, New Haven & Hartford Railroad, and the Pennsylvania Railroad into the Penn-Central Railroad. This ill-assorted behemoth lasted only two years before filing bankruptcy in 1970.

On May 1, 1971 the National Railroad Passenger Corporation, best known by the tradename Amtrak, took over all intercity passenger train operations in the United States. This included those of all lines operating in the Hudson Valley with the exception of those of the Long Island Railroad. They have gradually upgraded facilities and improved services, with the former New York Central route providing exemplary service with newly modernized long distance trains and fast Turboliners operating to Albany, Syracuse, and Buffalo.

On September 6, 1971 the sidewheel steamship *Alexander Hamilton* made its last trip between New York and Poughkeepsie and return, ending an unbroken tradition from the first trip of Robert Fulton's *Clermont*. She was replaced by a new ship on the Hudson River Day Line in 1972. The new diesel powered *M. V. Dayliner* made her first trip on June 10th, 1972 on the Poughkeepsie run, maintaining a traditional route and service to Bear Mountain and West Point. She remains in operation in 1982.*

The long, drawn-out Viet Nam War came to an end in 1975 and a festering public malaise came to an end. Inflation and a stagnant economy were producing a new phenomenon called stag-flation. However, the nation was on the brink of its third century and new ideas were in the air.

---

*Regular upriver runs discontinued at end of 1987 season, and completely ended Labor Day 1989.

In 1976 the Penn-Central, Erie-Lackawanna, Central Railroad of New Jersey, Lehigh & Hudson River, Reading, Lehigh Valley, and Pennsylvania-Reading Seashore Lines were all bankrupt, and were amalgamated into the new, Federally Financed, Consolidated Railroad Corporation, or Conrail. The properties had suffered tremendously from deferred maintenance and derailments were an hourly occurrence and freight service badly deteriorated. Commuter service provided by the various lines also was suffering in many instances, despite large investments by New York, New Jersey, and Pennsylvania in new passenger cars and locomotives. Since 1976 Conrail has been improving both its plant and service and finally shows some promise of becoming an economically viable system. The former Pennsylvania Mainline, which is part of the Northeast Corridor, was sold to Amtrak and is undergoing a thorough upgrading for very high speed service.

Nineteen seventy six will be best remembered as the Bi-Centennial Year. This occasioned many local celebrations and much delving into local history, leading to restoration of historic structures and publication of local histories, and a feeling of renewed interest and pride in our past. It was a very uplifting experience. The population of the United States had reached 215,318,000.

The greatest Bi-Centennial Celebration in the Hudson Valley, and probably in the nation, was Op Sail-'76, and the Parade Up the Hudson, on July 4th. This great spectacle was the conception of Frank O. Braynard, a celebrated marine historian and consultant to the Port of New York Authority. It consisted of a parade of sixteen of the world's remaining twenty tall ships up the Hudson River to the vicinity of the *George Washington Bridge*. This was accompanied by an International Naval Review with fifty-four vessels from around the world participating. Altogether there were 225 sail vessels participating, from large square rigged ships and four-mastered barques to racing yachts, Chinese Junks, Viking Ships, and small brigs and sloops. Thirty thousand private small craft crowded the harbor as six million viewers crowded the shores. The event was televised nationwide. In the evening there was a great fireworks display. At 9:00 PM the show started over Upper New York Bay beginning with a 200-gun salute from the anchored warships. This was indeed a fitting sequel to the great Hudson-Fulton Celebration of 1909. The greatest benefit of this festival was the creation of a mood of calm and brotherhood among the spectators. Those who witnessed this event will never forget it. A bonus of the festival is that it turned people's attention to the water again. There has been continuing strong popular interest in the Hudson River and other neighboring waters ever since.

A cause celebre throughout the 1970s has been the attempt of the Consolidated Edison Company of New York to build a pumped storage facility at Storm King Mountain in the Hudson Highlands. This projected tampering with the most majestic scenery along the Hudson led to a great public outcry. Anti-pumped storage forces were mobilized by the *Clearwater* organization under Pete Seeger, and the Scenic Hudson Preservation Conference. Large publicity and legal campaigns were waged, with the result that a number of landmark scenic protection legal decisions have been gained and Consolidated Edison has backed off, at least for the time being. It seems likely that they will be dropped for good.

In September, 1979 the Hudson River Maritime Center was formed for the purposes of preserving the maritime heritage of the Hudson River. It is based on Rondout Creek in Kingston and plans to undertake an active program of activities to educate people in the history of the river and to collect documents and artifacts illustrative of this history. If funds allow, actual ship preservation projects will be undertaken.

35 Situation in 1983

In looking back over the last four hundred years we have seen how an idyllic region, sparsely populated by "Savage" Indians of relatively high cultural attainments, has developed into a densely populated one with great ecological, economic, and social problems under "civilized" control, after going through a long era of commercial and cultural prosperity. At the present time we stand on the threshold of a new era of positive development which promises to correct the problems of the moment and amalgamate the achievements of the past with new approaches and technology to build a future of uncompared prosperity and attractiveness.

Much of the development thus far has been predicated upon the bounty and advantages offered by the Hudson River and its associated waters. The Hudson has been both an asset and a commanding challenge to the imagination, inventive genius, and enterprise of the dwellers along its shores.

It provided the Indians with plentiful seafood with its great clam and oyster beds and plentiful shad and sturgeon, and with rich bottom lands on which to build their villages and grow their maize. The deeply forested woods abounded with wildlife for their hunters. The climate was equable. The great marshes drew abundant fowls and migratory flocks of such birds as the passenger pigeon. The many cliffs and rocks provided shelter, and it would be difficult to find a more beneficial environment for people having attained the Eastern Woodland culture.

When the first white explorers and settlers arrived they found a land rich in the pelts and furs which brought quick wealth, and this stimulated rapid development. The Hudson, Hackensack, Passaic, and Raritan provided easy access to the interior. Trading posts developed at Fort Orange, Rondout, Ambos Point, and New Bridge, as well as on Manhattan and Staten Islands, and along the New Jersey shore and in Brooklyn. The great Upper Bay provided safe anchorage for the small sailing ships of the times. We have seen the small trading post of Fort Orange grow into the large city of Albany, with a 1976 population of over 115,000, and the small outpost of New Amsterdam grow into one of the world's greatest cities with a population of over 7,895,000. We have seen the Hudson, and associated waters, serve as the birthplace of successful commercial steam navigation, and the Hudson become literally the commercial key to the continent.

The commerce of the Hudson River was the lifeblood of New York State's economy. Cheap water transportation made possible the development of the limestone, cement, brick, iron, bluestone, and trap rock industries, and provided a path to market for agricultural produce. Its scenic beauty drew tourists, writers, and artists and thus fostered a blooming of the arts. The Hudson was more used and appreciated for many years than it was abused. Only when people lost consciousness of the Hudson River and its importance was abuse allowed, unperceived, and unchecked. Just when did people lose consciousness of the river? I think it is quite easy to pinpoint the date for any given area. It was when a bridge or tunnel was built and the natives lost daily contact with the river on the ferries. In some areas this was quite early and in others quite recently. In the twentieth century the Hudson became an open sewer and dumping ground for industrial wastes, and marine life declined, while the remaining fishery harvest was unsafe to eat.

However, by now public opinion is awake to the harm that has been done and the need to correct it. We are particularly indebted to two men for bringing attention to the needs of the Hudson.

Robert H. Boyle, an editor and writer for *Sports Illustrated,* is a naturalist and conservationist, who closely identifies with the problems of the river and the efforts of the Hudson River Fishermen's Association. His book *The Hudson River; A Natural and Unnatural History,* published in 1969, has done much to raise consciousness.

Pete Seeger, folk-singer and conservationist, has done a great deal to bring attention to the Hudson and its plight with his 106 foot long sloop *Clearwater,* which is used in anti-pollution and environmental education programs. Both Mr. Boyle and Mr. Seeger have been outspoken and valuable opponents to the Storm King Pumped Storage Project. The battle is far from over, but today there are many hopeful signs.

Some upriver towns and cities are constructing secondary and tertiary sewage treatment plants, and New York City is presently building a tremendous treatment plant above 125th Street to facilitate ending dumping of raw sewage into the Hudson. The water is measurably and perceptibly cleaner and many varieties of marine life are returning. Many cities and towns are undertaking major waterfront cleanup programs. The U. S. Army Corps of Engineers is helping to remove old hulks from the New Jersey waterfronts. People again consider the river a good place to live. Old Brownstones are being rehabilitated in Hoboken and Jersey City, and in Edgewater the large Alcoa Plant is being converted into the world's largest condominium apartment complex. Smaller cities such as Beacon, Peekskill, Nyack, Newburgh, Poughkeepsie, Hudson, and Kingston either have, or are presently, undertaking waterfront park developments. Much old junk has been removed from the shoreline. In Jersey City the large new Liberty State Park has been created on the site of obsolescent freight yards, and it is hoped to obtain the *Battleship New Jersey* as a tourist attraction. The old Central Railroad of New Jersey passenger train and ferry terminal has been restored as a visitor's center, and the Lackawanna Terminal at Hoboken is undergoing a multi-million dollar renovation for both continued transportation use and as an historic building. Jersey City is undertaking a major redevelopment at Exchange Place, terminus of Robert Fulton's first trans-Hudson ferry. The Hudson River Maritime Center is establishing itself on Rondout Creek in Kingston, and the South Street Seaport Museum and National Maritime Historical Society are giving significant attention to Hudson River topics. In Manhattan a large new Convention & Visitors Center is being built facing the Hudson, as does the already existing World Trade Center. The future of the Westway Project in Manhattan is still undecided, but there is a consensus that the aesthetics of the waterfront must be enhanced and public access must be improved and maintained.

The restaurant ships *Binghamton,* on the Hudson River at Edgewater, and *Chauncey M. Depew* at Secaucus, on the Hackensack River are proving very popular.* People are returning to the riverbanks to fish, crab, participate in small boating, and to simply enjoy being there. Once again the Hudson is being perceived as an attraction.

Depew foundered at dock in 1987.

On a practical level, there is thought being given in various official circles to resumption of certain passenger ferry services, and resumption of first class passenger steamer services all the way to Albany is being considered by private entrepreneurs.

The Storm King Mountain Pumped Storage has been stopped, and the atomic power plant at Indian Point is shut down at the time of this writing. All things considered, things are once again looking up for the Hudson.

NOTE: New problems are arising. PCBs and Dioxens make Hudson River crabs and eels highly dangerous and carcogenic. It is illegal to fish for or possess them. *1982.*

36 Status Report 1996

Since completing the first edition of this history in 1979, a decade and a half of subsequent history has unfolded along the Hudson. While the final chapter of the original edition concludes on a moderately hopeful note, many of the contemplated beneficial developments have either proven completely abortive or of much less permanent benefit than anticipated. Many old enemies have again arisen and old problems have resurfaced. I will try to give a brief description of major developments during this period, with somewhat of an emphasis on transportation topics inasmuch as this has been a major theme in earlier river history. In fact, much of the present economic stagnation comes from the diminishing impact of transportation on the region. Where earlier freight transportation on the river supported thriving riverside industries, as did the early railroads, today, while the river corridor remains of great importance, there is far less beneficial local impact. Today fast express trains operate along the east bank and mile-long high speed freight trains operate non-stop along the length of the west bank. Trucks and cars on the New York Thruway barrel through the area between New York City and Albany, often without even stopping at one of the rest areas. This commerce has little impact on the local riverside economy.

The lower mid-Hudson valley is continuing to develop as a bedroom community, but largely for people working in the metropolitan area or northern New Jersey. For many years the region was dangerously overdependent upon a single firm: I.B.M. When that firm ran into financial difficulties and began downsizing and phasing out facilities, extreme local economic distress ensued. Much unemployment and underemployment remains and, even with a moderate upswing at I.B.M., the mid-Hudson remains a depressed area. With the continuing decline of the middle class which traditionally provided the bulk of vacationers visiting the adjacent Catskill and Adirondack regions, these too are in a state of depression. Naturally, all this has severe impacts on local service industries, tax revenues, and, consequently, local government spending.

Although the Hudson has been greatly cleaned up and is in a more healthy state than when this book was first published, a growing commuter population is putting additional pressures on the recently improved sanitation systems at a time when ideologically-inspired cuts are being made in the funding of necessary treatment plants and toxic cleanups, and there are renewed proposals for pumped storage generating plants.

Many of the riverfront communities have completed their cleanups and have developed waterfront parks, largely with federal, state, and county funds, only to post them "off limits" for nonresidents. Kingsland Point, Bowline Point, Grassy Point, and Cornwall are only a few among many with such restrictive policies. It is much more difficult today to simply drive up, park your car, and take a walk along the shore. It was easier in the time of decaying waterfront industry, and I personally preferred it. The few people you met were friendly lovers of nature and of the Hudson, instead of scowling parking lot attendants and deputy law enforcement officers telling you to "move on." Similarly, with the great resurgence of passenger and freight rail traffic and a push for Very High Speed trains, Conrail, Amtrak, and MetroNorth are instituting tighter controls on access to the waterfront while ever tighter budget limitations cut back on plans for the necessary pedestrian over- and underpasses to the water's edge.

Despite the existence of such major preservation groups as Scenic Hudson and the Sierra Club, the New York State Department of Transportation has gouged out great scars in the faces of Dunderberg, Anthony's Nose, Crows Nest, and Storm King Mountains. While some of this may have been genuinely needed in the name of safety and rock stabilization (especially on the approaches to the Bear Mountain Bridge), much of it appears to be gratuitously excessive, the main interest being the generation of large construction contracts.

In the area of development, possibly the largest single issue concerns the redevelopment of Stewart Field as a major freight and passenger air terminal. Certainly it is advantageously situated to serve much of the mid-Hudson and lower Hudson regions, and has proven very popular with travelers from those areas. However, highway access from those regions is still limited and rail access still nonexistent, although not particularly difficult to build. Truck access for air freight is presently excellent over existing interstate highways, serving somewhat different traffic pattern demands than travelers have. There is no doubt that this airfield will see continuing development one way or another. The problems are with aircraft noise pollution in the mid-Hudson, Taconic, and Shawangunk regions and, more importantly, with the potential for unplanned urban sprawl in the immediately adjacent areas of Orange and Dutchess Counties. With the stagnation of other industry in the area, many interests are pinning excessive hopes on inappropriately overscaled commercial development around Stewart. This is creating a great amount of controversy between "preservationists" and "developers" (both of which perjorative nominations are gross oversimplifications). The trick will be to keep Stewart a genuine asset while holding development within realistic boundaries.

One great dream that boomed-and-busted was the Riverfront Gold Coast along the Hudson in Bergen and Hudson Counties in New Jersey. Redevelopment of unused terminal areas along the waterfront opened opportunities for redevelopment. In the 1980s things moved along merrily: developers put up large office and residential buildings in such areas as Newport City, Port Liberté, and Lincoln Harbor. When overall business slowed, the developers found themselves overbuilt. Only now is much of this empty development filling up, and there are plans for additional buildings—at the moment the old Colgate-Palmolive Complex at Exchange Place in Jersey City is the newest and most active development. National Westminister Bank and Colgate have erected two of the tallest and most beautiful office buildings in New Jersey and there is a new, redesigned PATH station, ferry service to Manhattan, and plans to have it served by the new WatersEdge Light Rail Transit line now under construction. However, in a sluggish economy, much of the area is still awaiting redevelopment. Here, transportation matters seem to be the key. Highways are overflowing and plans for new rail transit are long in coming. The many new ferry services we will discuss soon are having a strong stimulating effect on this redevelopment.

In the mid-1980s New Jersey Transit ripped up two of their four tracks on the Erie Line in Bergen County, while Conrail and MetroNorth single-tracked their former two-track line between Suffern and Harriman and completely eliminated the original Main Line between there and Middletown, leaving service only over the single-track Graham Freight Line via Salisbury Mills and Campbell Hall—a much more sparsely developed area than around

Monroe, Chester, and Goshen on the old Main Line. Since then there has been a great boom in suburban home building along the Graham Line, but also along the old Main – a classic case of facilities being destroyed just before they are needed. Now, MetroNorth, which is still benefiting from a sales tax surcharge in Orange County, is scrambling around trying to figure out how to serve these new commuters and is finding minimum cooperation from New Jersey Transit (which is suffering from its own misguided policies) and contemplating building either a rail bridge or tunnel across the Hudson near the Tappan Zee. This has brought down the ire of the Tappan Zee Preservation Coalition against such a monstrous scenic intrusion on this beautiful stretch of the Hudson. They advocate return of passenger service on the West Shore Railroad line to a connection in North Jersey, either with the restored ferry service at Weehawken or a transfer to the rail tunnel to Penn Station. However, over recent years Conrail's freight traffic on the West Shore has grown to such a level that it will be necessary almost to triple the size of the existing single track (once four- and two-track) line to accommodate restored commuter service. Meanwhile, the entire region, and especially the Tappan Zee Bridge, is choking with motor traffic, which hardly induces existing firms to keep their headquarters in the area or new ones to move in. One possible solution might be to continue the New Jersey WatersEdge light rail rapid transit system north from Weehawken Ferry over the old Northern Railroad of New Jersey alignment to the Nyack area, which would not conflict with Conrail freight. Also, the old Erie Main Line should be rebuilt from Harriman to Middletown via Monroe and Goshen to serve the new development in southern Orange County. Those trains would continue to PATH and ferry connections at Hoboken over lines controlled by Jersey Transit. A spur of this Erie line could serve Stewart field and connect it with Manhattan and Northern New Jersey. An entire era of folly must be reversed if there is to be any real economic future for the mid-Hudson region.

The most promising development during this period has been the redevelopment of passenger ferry services and commuter boats. We will not review all the various routes that have been tried – many not proving feasible – but will list the most important of the many that have proven successful.

The real hero of this redevelopment is Arthur Imperatore, Sr., the trucking magnate who acquired the former New York Central rail yards along the Weehawken waterfront for redevelopment. He remembered the West Shore ferries of his own youth, and, like John Stevens a century earlier, realized that ferries to Manhattan were the key to the development of his land. In 1986 his ARCORP Corporation developed a ferry operation from Port Imperial, on the site of the old West Shore Terminal, to West 38th Street and Whitehall Street in Manhattan, using small high-speed passenger boats. The service proved immensely popular and he developed feeder mini-bus lines both in Manhattan and in New Jersey, which were included in the price of the ferry ticket. He also built large parking fields at Weehawken and is presently awaiting development of commuter and light rail services to his planned palatial ferry terminal at Weehawken. (Local roads and parking lots are presently at saturation and this is needed to support more boat service.) He has also acquired control of the Hoboken Terminal to Battery Park City. This restored ferry service started in 1989 under the sponsorship of the Port Authority. He operates lines from West 38th Street to Lincoln Harbor in South Weehawken and to Liberty State Park, and from Battery Park City to Exchange Place, Jersey City, Liberty State Park, as well as a tourist operation to Tarrytown, New York, in conjunction with Historic Hudson Preservation tours to Sunnyside, Upper Phillips Manor, and Kykuit. He also operates ferries on the East River from East 34th Street and is contemplating upriver service to Nyack and downbay to Sandy Hook Park. All operations are now run by his new corporation, New York Waterway. With inauguration of a planned new line from Hoboken Terminal to West 38th Street, New York Waterway will have successfully replicated the basic service pattern of Hudson River ferries in the classic era of the railroad ferries. All this builds upon the experience of operators starting with John Stevens and Robert Fulton, described in our early chapters. A good thing is a good thing forever.

Other independent operators have established successful lines from lower Manhattan to LaGuardia Airport, Rockaway, Newark Airport, Elizabethport, Bayonne, Brooklyn, Atlantic Highlands, Highlands, and Keyport. The downbay lines are hydrafoil catamarans cruising up to 35 mph.

Less successful than the ferry services have been the excursion boats on the Hudson. A great tradition came to an end on Labor Day, September 4, 1989, when the Day Line ship *M. V. Dayliner* made her final round-trip cruise between Manhattan and Poughkeepsie, closing out a service begun in 1840 and predecessor lines operated by Robert Fulton in 1807 with the *Clermont*. This leaves no regularly scheduled large-ship excursion service on the Hudson. Thus the Hudson, birthplace of steamboating, is ironically almost the only major river in the world without such service! The *Dayliner* was subsequently jumboized and converted into the largest floating dinner/convention boat in New York. She was not economically successful in this service and in 1995 she was converted into a gambling ship for service on Lake Michigan out of northern Indiana ports. The writer has acted as consultant for several firms seeking to build new vessels for Hudson River service. Despite the fact that naval architects and marine economists have come up with affordable designs and promising economic projections for such service, and various lenders have agreed to loans for the greater part of the cost of such a ship (about $7 million), equity investors have remained shy of the venture—often citing the probable ethnic distribution of the projected patronage as their reason for not wanting to get involved, even though this simply reflects the overall ethnic distribution of the entire metropolitan area, in which they do not hesitate to make other major investments. The situation is irrational, and a public disgrace. It leaves a gaping hole in the New York tourism package.

Fortunately, the smaller lines running shorter trips remain well and largely profitable. Circle Line at Manhattan offers many other trips besides around Manhattan. The historic *Commander* of Hudson Highlands Cruises operates from Haverstraw, Peekskill, and West Point; the *Rip Van Winkle* of Hudson River Cruises operates from Rondout; and Dutch Apple Cruises operate from Albany up to Troy and Waterford and down to New Baltimore, providing an opportunity to cruise through several locks and into the Erie Canal. New York Waterways offers service from Manhattan and Weehawken to Tarrytown. Many ferries are also available for off-hour charter.

Dinner cruise boats have become popular all along the Hudson, ranging from diminutive stern-wheelers offering simple fare at modest prices upriver to luxurious floating gourmet ships based in New York City and New Jersey.

Occasionally a coastal cruise boat will schedule a passage up the river or a cruise for up to a week, visiting important tourist landings. However, attempts to raise capital for a ship of this nature, specifically designed for the Hudson, have proven unsuccessful and such services on the Hudson remain sporadic.

Returning to the railroad scene, some major changes have taken place. The Delaware & Hudson is now a wholly owned subsidiary of the Canadian Pacific Railway—their gateway to U.S. ports. The Susquehanna Railroad of the D. O. Corporation has stretched out to become a "little giant"! With recent acquisition of the New York, Chicago & St. Louis (Nickel Plate Line) from Norfolk Southern, they now operate between New Jersey and the Midwest, thus fulfilling the old dream of the pioneer New York & Oswego Midland and New Jersey Midland systems. They carry a great deal of container traffic on what are known as "stack trains." Since abandonment of their tunnel and branch from Little Ferry to Edgewater on the Hudson, they now terminate inland at North Bergen, N.J. and have to truck their containers over the public road from their rail head to the docks at Port Newark and Elizabethport — an unsatisfactory situation. They are presently seeking direct all-rail access to the major marine terminals. There is also a possibility of restoration of commuter trains on portions of their lines in New Jersey and Orange County, N.Y., with a terminal at Hoboken.

Conrail is consolidating operations on the West Shore and improving access connections in New Jersey and, because of increased traffic, beginning to rebuild multiple track up toward Albany to accommodate the increased traffic. This is fine in itself, but creates problems for restoration of passenger services. We have already discussed conditions on their Erie Line, which still handles some freight both for Conrail and for Susquehanna via trackage rights. The Poughkeepsie Bridge and connecting lines remain out of service. As the bridge itself is a National Engineering Landmark, its future is relatively assured, but it is really only usable as a railroad bridge and someday it will probably be rehabilitated for such use. Since this book was written, title has passed through several private owners.

On the East Shore line, long distance passenger service above Poughkeepsie is provided by Amtrak and local passenger service below there to Grand Central Terminal by MetroNorth Commuter Railroad. The entire line is served by Conrail for freight. The Spuyten Duyvil Drawbridge has been rebuilt and the Manhattan West Side Line of the old New York Central, beneath Riverside Drive, has been restored to passenger service. All Amtrak trains now serve Pennsylvania Station via this line rather than going to Grand Central, which is now limited to commuter services.

In New Jersey the electrification of the New York & Long Branch has been extended from Matawan to Long Branch, with plans to extend it to the end of the line at Bay Head. Re-electrification of the former Lackawanna Railroad lines to alternating current and completion of several new track connections in New Jersey, has now made it possible for all Lackawanna and North Jersey Shore trains to terminate either at Penn Station or Hoboken Terminal, thus, with the restored ferries, providing much greater flexibility and convenience. The service quality of all local commuter trains has greatly improved since last writing.

A light rail rapid transit line, known as WatersEdge Light Rail, is presently under construction in New Jersey from Bayonne to Jersey City and Hoboken, and ultimately to Weehawken and Ridgefield Park, over former freight lines. This will greatly facilitate development of the waterfront and interconnections between various commuter rail lines, Amtrak, PATH, and ferry services.

At present a task force entitled Access To The Region's Core has been jointly implemented by the Port Authority, Metropolitan Transportation Authority, and New Jersey Transit to study improvements, among them various subway extensions and possibly a new combined freight and passenger rail tunnel beneath the Hudson at about 63rd Street in Manhattan. It would have a West Side station near Lincoln Center. Passenger trains could access unused space in Grand Central Terminal directly from New Jersey. Freight traffic could move directly from New Jersey to Long Island and Southern New England without use of car floats or costly detours to the Castleton Bridge near Albany. Truck traffic in the metropolitan area would be greatly alleviated. The project would cost about $2.5 billion and would emulate the engineering of the English Channel tunnel.

Among miscellaneous riverfront topics, the New Jersey Science Museum has opened at Liberty State Park. Restoration of the Immigration Station at Ellis Island has also been completed. The historic Hoboken Ferry Terminal is finally undergoing thorough restoration. The former Day Line passenger vessel *Chauncey M. Depew,* moored for many years in the

Hackensack River at Secaucus as the Aratusa Supper Club, was struck broadside by a tug and sank, and the wreck has been removed. However, the ferryboat *Binghamton* remains at Edgewater, N.J. as a popular restaurant.

Residents of the New Jersey Hudson waterfront are going to court to seek an injunction against what they call the "Stealth Highway." They claim that the Port Authority and New Jersey State Highway Department are planning to build a major arterial highway from the Bayonne Bridge to the George Washington Bridge at Fort Lee without holding the legally required hearings on environmental impact. The furor over this is being covered in the *New York Times*. Certainly such a road, while very convenient to many, would completely destroy the character of many communities.

Battery Park City and the World Financial Center have been completed in Manhattan between West Street and the old pierhead line. They incorporate many office and residential buildings and such features as a Crystal Palace–type glass atrium overlooking the river, with palm trees and fountains, where concerts are held daily; a large yacht basin; a new ferry terminal; and an elegant waterfront promenade with benches and decorative lighting standards overlooking the mouth of the Hudson into the Upper Bay—an outstanding location. Unfortunately it is built on filled land and is thus vulnerable to earthquakes, unlike the adjacent World Trade Center which is built on bedrock.

At Yonkers, Scenic Hudson has successfully fought planned construction of six 38-story apartment buildings along the waterfront which would have destroyed views of the Hudson and the Palisades for most of inland Yonkers. A more modest and acceptable alternative plan has been followed. The Public Dock and Railroad Station at Yonkers have also been restored.

In the mid-1980s there was much talk of tapping the Hudson at Chelsea for drinking water for New York City. This would have affected the Hudson's salinity and bio-system tremendously and lowered the quality of New York City's drinking water. Scenic Hudson, under the leadership of Alexander Zagoreos, sponsored a series of seminars at the Museum of Natural History, leading to a massive alternative water conservation program which is proving very effective. However, this proposal can always come up again and proves that the river is always under threat.

Despite the stagnant economy, the pace of change remains rapid along the Hudson. It is necessary to direct this change in desirable directions and to maintain vigilance.

As I conclude what has been a twenty-year writing project and look back upon forty years of active participation in environmental and transportation matters, teaching, and museum work, I would like to offer a very brief wish-list for the Hudson:

1. Get a fast and comfortable day excursion boat back on the Hudson—preferably an authentic steam-powered sidewheeler of moderate size, similar to the old *Albany* of the Day Line.
2. Re-establish inexpensive excursion services for young people, elderly, disabled, and lower-income people in general to serve the Palisades, Piermont/Hook Mountain, Rockland Lake Landing, and Bear Mountain State Park.
3. Build the necessary new rail tunnel to alleviate the entire region's traffic problems. Have faith in Greater New York.
4. Fiscally penalize towns that close the riverfront to nonresidents. The river belongs to everybody.

Finally, I would wish that everyone will come to know, love, and enjoy the Hudson.

37 Millennium Report

This is my first opportunity since our last revision in 1996 to bring the ongoing saga of the Hudson River up to date. Since then, the economy has turned around and we have experienced "boom times," albeit unevenly distributed. The resulting resurgence of development is putting renewed pressures on open areas and roads and is pushing up property values, forcing out many longtime residents as a new elite discovers the delights of the Hudson Valley. The river itself—even views of it—has become far less accessible. New "trophy" homes, for instance, have cut off views of the Tappan Zee, Haverstraw Bay, and even the Manhattan skyline from New Jersey. There is still no excursion service on the river and no promise of commercial or governmental funding to re-establish such service. Ferry services continue to expand, but their high speed, lack of comfort, high prices, and their routes and schedules make them ill-suited for sightseeing and tourism. Unless you own your own boat, you are effectively shut off from enjoying the Hudson from the water. Even the views from the railroad are being cut off by ailanthus trees—ill-smelling shrubs imported from Asia, but sacred to environmentalists.

It helps to be rich if you want to enjoy the Valley. The inns and restaurants are reaching a sublime five-star standard, priced accordingly. One gastronomic palace near West Point has reached ethereal heights of splendor with a prix-fixe menu priced at $80.00 per person (sorry—no credit cards), "one of the great bargains in the Hudson Valley." The writer greatly enjoys dining at this establishment—on someone else's check!

The Hudson is again under siege from industry. A very large coal-burning power plant is planned for Athens, near the outlet of Murderer's Creek. The West Shore Railroad will greatly benefit from the revenues from one-hundred-car coal trains from Wyoming and Montana; meanwhile, there is no more track space for commuter trains to relieve local congestion. The scenic and historic nature of this area near Olana Castle was no impediment to this monument to progress.

Speaking of railroads, in 1999 Conrail was broken up into two major parts. The giant Norfolk Southern (NS) System acquired 58 percent of Conrail's Northeast mileage. In the Hudson Valley/Catskill region their main impact is acquisition of rights over the old Erie line from Buffalo to Jersey City through New York's "Southern Tier." This somewhat impacts New Jersey Transit and Metro North commuter services west of the Hudson. The principle targets are the deep-water berths at Elizabethport, Port Newark, and Bayonne. The other 42 percent of Conrail was acquired by CSX Transportation Corporation, an amalgam based on the former Baltimore & Ohio, Chesapeake & Ohio, and several major southern lines. CSX has acquired ownership and/or operating rights east of Buffalo over the former New York Central to Selkirk and thence to Boston over the former Boston & Albany. They also operate south from the Albany/Selkirk terminal area to New York City—with a connection to the Long Island Railroad—over the former Hudson River Railroad along the eastern shore of the Hudson. This line is also used by Amtrak and Metro North for passengers and by Canadian Pacific (CP) for freight. On the west side of the river, CSX uses the former West Shore Railroad to terminals at Ridgefield Park, Port Newark, and points south. The West Shore is now a major link in CSX's main Florida-to-New England freight route. Complete double-tracking is under construction between New Jersey and Selkirk to accommodate mile-and-a-half-long freight trains on frequent schedules. To complete the stew, CSX and NS have jointly acquired the formerly independent New York, Susquehanna & Western Railway, serving northern New Jersey, as a ''relief line.'' So much for any easy restoration of commuter and other passenger services.

Local highways and vehicular river crossings are jammed to capacity—and beyond. Thruway Authority engineers tell us that the Tappan Zee Bridge, opened in 1955, is not only jammed to capacity but is collapsing and must be replaced. There is talk of adding light rail or heavy rail to any new bridge—or, possibly, tunnels, which would help restore the view of the Tappan Zee. But at present, all is acrimonious argumentation.

On a positive note, Amtrak has improved track between Poughkeepsie and Albany/Rensselaer to 110-mph standards and is planning to implement two-hour schedules between New York and Albany. A large and beautiful new station and transportation center, with bus platforms and auto parking, is nearing completion at Rensselaer. There are plans for trains from there to Troy, Saratoga, and into Vermont both via Whitehall and via Bennington and Manchester to Rutland and Burlington, largely restoring the old Rutland Railroad services.

North of Albany, the former Delaware & Hudson has been acquired by the St. Lawrence & Atlantic Division of Canadian Pacific. Amtrak's premier daytime passenger train between New York, Albany, and Montreal, the *Adirondack*, has been luxuriously refurbished and offers what is now being called one the world's most scenic all-day train trips. Amtrak's *Ethan Allen* services on the D & H to Vermont via Whitehall are proving to be exceptionally popular; additional trains are being added to the schedule. The former D & H North Creek branch, along the rugged and ''untamed'' section of the Hudson River between Saratoga and North Creek, is now being operated by the independent North Hudson Railroad, which operates excursion passenger and freight service.

Far to the south, in New Jersey, restoration of the historic Hoboken Terminal has been completed, returning it to its Belle Epoque grandeur and beauty. It is a smaller equivalent of the recently restored Grand Central Station in Manhattan. There are also plans for a new Penn Station in Manhattan, utilizing the splendid adjacent Central Post Office building. The building of additional rail tunnels beneath the Hudson seems likely, but the details will take time to work out. Meanwhile, the rapidly growing ferry system, led largely by New York Waterway, is handling rapidly increasing traffic. The reader is referred to the updated list of Hudson River ferry routes on page 306. These largely serve the gigantic new waterfront residential and office developments in Bayonne, Jersey City, Hoboken, Weehawken, Guttenberg, North Bergen, Edgewater, and Manhattan. In Hudson County, New Jersey, the new Hudson Bergen Light Rail system has opened its initial seven-mile segment between Bayonne and Exchange Place, Jersey City. By 2002, the line will reach Hoboken; eventually, the line is planned to extend to Ridgefield Park and possibly even to Nyack. Ferries and light rail are the only workable solutions to the traffic nightmare created by extensive development in this area. New ferry routes are planned further upriver between Haverstraw and Ossining and between Tivoli and Saugerties. Farther south, along the New Jersey shore of Sandy Hook Bay, electrification of New Jersey Transit's New York & Long Branch line has been extended from Mattawan to Long Branch. Express Navigation has changed its name to Seasstreak and implemented luxury super-high-speed ferries between Manhattan and the Atlantic Highlands area.

In 1999 the Hudson was designated "An American Heritage River" by the federal government. The first Hudson River Navigator appointed to this program was J. Eric Scherer, who is supposed to help obtain all kinds of good "federal funds" for Hudson River improvement projects. We shall see. General Electric remains reluctant to clean up the PCBs, and many more Hudson River fish have been declared unsafe for human consumption. In the first week of March of this year the Indian Point nuclear power plant had an accidental emission of radioactive steam, leading to renewed protests and agitation for its closing and removal. It might be safer to simply seal if off and leave it in place rather than attempt to find a new dumping ground for the radioactive material. However, by June the operators were claiming that all is well and were seeking permission to resume operations. The fact that his old facility is built adjacent to the Ramapo Fault line, near a major metropolitan area, appears to be only a minor consideration.

On June 2, 2000, a groundbreaking ceremony was held at Beacon, New York, for the DIA center for the arts, a major new art museum in the former International Paper Company box printing plant. This will be America's largest modern art museum.

Kingston Point Park and Catskill Point Park are both being restored to their former beauty and Albany's waterfront Corning Preserve is in the process of beautification. Much attractive commercial and residential redevelopment continues in Brooklyn, Manhattan, and along the New Jersey waterfront. However, if the present plans for re-industrialization of the Hudson succeed, it might not be long before the renewed effluvia returned to the river will emit aromas offending the delicate nostrils of the down-river luxury apartment gentry, thus bringing about a massive collapse of waterfront residential property values. Then the residents can decide whether they prefer increased dividends or outdoor amenities in their back yards.

The Hudson Valley has always been a warpath and battleground. First, its was the Delawares vs. the Iroquois; next, the French vs. the Indians. Then the English vs. the Dutch and later the English vs. the French. Later, it was sloops vs. steamboats and then steamboats vs. railroads. Now we bring you industrialization vs. civilization. The Hudson is a great theater, and the show never ends.

SELECTED BIBLIOGRAPHY

Although a few rare books are cited in the text, the books listed below are all reasonably accessible to the student. I have listed current reprints where available rather than scarce first editions, except in cases where the originals are cited in the text.

Adams, Arthur G. *The Catskills: An Illustrated Historical Guide with Gazetteer.* New York: Fordham University Press, 1990.

Adams, Arthur G., with Roger Coco, and Harriet and Leon R. Greenman. *Guide to the Catskills With Trail Guide and Maps.* New York: Walking News, Inc., 1975.

Adams, Arthur G. *The Hudson River in Literature, An Anthology and History.* Albany: State University of New York Press, 1981. (Revised edition 1988. Fordham University Press, Bronx, NY.)

Adams, Arthur G. *The Hudson River Guidebook.* New York: Fordham University Press, 1996.

Bailey, Rosalie Fellows. *Pre-Revolutionary Dutch Houses and Families In Northern New Jersey and Southern New York.* New York: Dover Publications, Inc., 1968.

Baxter, Raymond J. and Arthur G. Adams. *Railroad Ferries of the Hudson.* Lind Publications, Woodcliff Lake, NJ, 1987. (Revised edition 1999. Fordham University Press, Bronx, NY.)

Beebe, Lucius. *20th Century, the Greatest Train in the World.* Berkeley, California: Howell-North, 1962.

Beebe, William. *Report on the Eleventh Expedition the Department of Tropical Research of the New York Geological Society.* New York: *NY Geological Society,* 1928.

Best, Gerald M. *The Ulster & Delaware-Railroad Through the Catskills.* San Marino, Ca: Golden West Books, 1972.

Boyle, Robert H. *The Hudson River: A Natural and Unnatural History.* New York: W. W. Norton & Company, Inc., 1969.

Bruce, Wallace. *The Hudson By Daylight.* New York: Bryant Literary Union, 1901 & 1907. Reprinted by Walking News, Inc., New York, 1982.

Bruce, Wallace. *The Long Drama.* Printed in *The Centennial Celebration and Washington Monument at Newburgh, N.Y.: Report of the Joint Select Committee.* Washington: Government Printing Office, 1889.

Bryant, William Cullen. *A Scene on the Banks of the Hudson.* In *The Hudson River in Literature,* by Arthur G. Adams. New York: Fordham University Press, 1988.

Bryant, William Cullen. *Catterskill Falls.* In *The Hudson River in Literature,* by Arthur G. Adams. Albany: State University of New York Press, 1981.

Bryant, William Cullen, Ed., *Picturesque America.* New York: D. Appleton, 1872.

Burroughs, John. *Our River.* Article in Scribner's Magazine, New York, 1880.

Cawley, James and Margaret. *Exploring the Little Rivers of New Jersey.* New Brunswick, N.J.: Rutgers University Press, 1961.

Cole, David. *History of Rockland County.* New York: J. B. Beers & Co., 1884.

Cole, Thomas. *The Wild.* In *The Hudson River in Literature,* by Arthur G. Adams. New York: Fordham University Press, 1988.

Cooper, James Fenimore. *Leatherstocking Edition of Complete Novels.* New York: G. P. Putnam Sons. Undated Limited Edition. His following novels contain material pertinent to the Hudson River: *Ashore and Afloat; The Chain-bearer; Home as Found; Homeward Bound; The Last of the Mohicans; The Pioneers; The Red-Skins; The Spy; Satanstoe; Water-Witch.*

Dayton, Fred Erving. *Steamboat Days.* New York: Frederick A. Stokes Company, 1925.

De Lisser, R. Lionel. *Picturesque Catskills-Greene County.* Northampton, Massachusetts: Picturesque Publishing Company, 1894.

De Lisser, R. Lionel. *Picturesque Ulster.* Woodstock, New York: Twine's Catskill Bookshop, 1968. Originally published in eight numbered parts, Kingston, New York, 1896 to 1905.

Downing, Andrew Jackson. *The Architecture of Country Houses.* New York: Dover Publications, 1969. Originally published New York: D. Appleton & Company, 1850.

Drake, Joseph Rodman. *The Culprit Fay and Other Poems.* New York: George Dearborn, 1835. *The Culprit Fay* is also included in *The Hudson River in Literature,* by Arthur G. Adams. New York: Fordham University Press, 1988.

Elting, Irving. *Dutch Village Communities on the Hudson River.* Baltimore: Johns Hopkins University, 1886. Reprinted New York: Johnson Reprint Corporation, 1973.

Evers, Alf. *The Catskills: From Wilderness to Woodstock.* Garden City, New York: Doubleday & Company, Inc. 1972.

Flexner, James Thomas. *That Wilder Image: The Painting of America's Native School from Thomas Cole to Winslow Homer.* Boston, 1962.

The Four Track Series. Periodical Published by the New York Central Railroad, New York. Published c1880-c1930 on irregular basis.

Gekle, William F. *A Hudson Riverbook.* Poughkeepsie, New York: Wyvern House, 1978.

Haines, Henry S. *Efficient Railway Operation.* New York: The Macmillan Company, 1919.

Hamlin, Talbot. *Greek Revival Architecture In America.* New York: Dover Publications, Inc. 1964. Original edition: Oxford University Press, 1944.

Hardy, A. C. *American Ship Types.* New York: D. Van Nostrand Company, Inc., 1927.

Harper's School Geography. Anonymous. New York: Harper & Brothers, 1888.

Helmer, William F. *O. & W.: The Long Life and Slow Death of the New York, Ontario & Western Ry.* Berkeley, California: Howell-North, 1959.

Helmer, William F. *Rip Van Winkle Railroads.* Berkeley, California: Howell-North Books, 1970.

Hilton, George W. *The Night Boat.* Berkeley, California: Howell-North Books, 1968.

Hilton, George W. *The Staten Island Ferry.* Berkeley, California: Howell-North Books, 1964.

Hine, Charles Gilbert. *The Old Mine Road.* New Brunswick, N.J.: Rutgers University Press, 1963. Original edition 1909.

Howat, John K. *The Hudson River and Its Painters.* New York: Penguin Books, 1978. First published The Viking Press, 1972.

Howell, William Thompson. *The Hudson Highlands.* New York: Walking News, Inc., 1982.

The Hudson—Scenes Remembered. Poughkeepsie, N.Y.: Antique Print Association, 1975.

Hungerford, Edward. *Men of Erie.* New York: Random House, 1946.

In The Hudson Highlands. New York: Publication Committee of the New York Chapter of the Appalachian Mountain Club, 1945. Re-issued by Walking News, Inc., New York, 1979.

Irving, Washington. *Autobiography. The Works of Washington Irving.* Fulton Edition. New York: Century Company, 1909.

Bracebridge Hall. The Works of Washington Irving. Fulton Edition. New York: Century Company, 1909. Includes the Hudson River tales: *Wolfert Webber, or Golden Dreams,* and *Dolph Heyliger.*

A History of New York—From the Beginning of the World to the End of the Dutch Dynasty, by Diedrich Knickerbocker. The Kinderhook Edition of *The Works of Washington Irving.* New York: G. P. Putnam's Sons, 1880.

The Sketch Book of Geoffrey Crayon, Gent. Included in *The Works of Washington Irving.* Kinderhook Edition. New York: G. P. Putnam's Sons, 1880. Includes the Hudson River tales: *Rip Van Winkle,* and *The Legend of Sleepy Hollow.*

NOTE: The above extracts are also available in *The Hudson River in Literature—An Anthology and History,* by Arthur G. Adams. Albany: State University of New York Press, 1981.—Rev. 1988 Fordham University Press.

Keller, Allan. *Life Along the Hudson.* Tarrytown, N.Y.: Sleepy Hollow Restorations, 1976. Rev. 1997 Fordham University Press.

Kobbe, Gustav. *Jersey Coast and Pines,* (1885) Reissue, New York: Walking News, Inc., 1982.

Longstreth, Morris T. *The Catskills.* New York: The Century Co., 1918.

Lossing, Benson J. *Field Book of the American Revolution.* New York: Harper & Brothers, 1852.

Lossing, Benson J. *The Hudson: From Wilderness to the Sea.* Troy, N.Y.: H. L. Nims & Co., 1866.

Lyon, Peter. *To Hell In A Day Coach: An Exasperated Look At American Railroads.* Philadelphia: J. B. Lippincott Company, 1968.

McCabe, John B. *Hiking With History in the Hudson Highlands.* New York: Carlton Press, Inc., 1977.

Mack, Arthur C. *The Palisades of the Hudson* (1909) Reissue, New York: Walking News, Inc., 1982.

Maybee, Carleton. *Listen to the Whistle: An Anecdotal History of the Wallkill Valley Railroad in Ulster and Orange Counties, New York.* Fleischmanns: Purple Mountain Press, 1995.

Miers, Earl Schenck. *Where the Raritan Flows.* New Brunswick, N.J.: Rutgers University Press, 1964.

Morris, George Pope. *Poems by George P. Morris.* New York: Charles Scribner, 1853.

Morrison, John Harrison. *History of American Steam Navigation.* New York: W. F. Sametz, 1903.

New York Walk Book. New York-New Jersey Trail Conference and The American Geographical Society. Garden City, N.Y.: Doubleday-Natural History Press, 1971.

Nutting, Wallace. *New York Beautiful.* Garden City, N.Y.: Garden City Publishing Co., Inc., 1936. Original edition New York: Dodd Mead and Company, Inc., 1927.

Oechsner, Carl. *Ossining, New York.* Croton-On-Hudson, N.Y.: North River Press, 1975.

Paulding, James Kirke. *New Mirror For Travellers; and Guide To The Springs.* New York: G. & C. Carvill, 1828.

Paulding, James Kirke. *The Dutchman's Fireside—A Tale.* New York: J. & J. Harper, 1831.

Reynolds, Helen Wilkinson. *Dutch Houses in the Hudson Valley Before 1776.* New York: Dover Publications, 1965. Originally published in 1929 by Payson and Clarke, Ltd. for the Holland Society of New York.

Rifkind, Carole, and Levine, Carol. *Mansions, Mills and Main Streets.* New York: Schocken Books, 1975.

Ringwald, Donald C. *Hudson River Day Line: The Story of a Great American Steamboat Company.* Berkeley, California: Howell-North Books, 1965. — Rev. 1990 Fordham University Press.

Shaughnessy, Jim. *Delaware & Hudson.* Berkeley, California: Howell-North Books, 1967.

Steuding, Bob. *Rondout: A Hudson River Port.* Fleischmanns: Purple Mountain Press, 1995.

Storm King Pumped Storage. Washington: U.S. Government Printing Office, 1966.

Swanberg, W. A. *Jim Fisk: The Career of an Improbably Rascal.* New York: Charles Scribner's Sons, 1959.

Van De Water, Frederic F. *Lake Champlain and Lake George.* New York: The Bobbs-Merrill Company, 1946.

Van Zandt, Roland. *The Catskill Mountain House.* New Brunswick, N.J.: Rutgers University Press, 1966.

Van Zandt, Roland. *Chronicles of the Hudson: Three Centuries of Travellers' Accounts.* New Brunswick, N.J.: Rutgers University Press, 1971.

Wakefield, Manville B. *Coal Boats to Tidewater.* South Fallsburg, N.Y.: Steingart Associates, 1965.

Wakefield, Manville B. *To The Mountains By Rail.* Grahamsville, N.Y.: Wakefair Press, 1970.

Whitman, Walt. *Mannahatta.* Included in *An American Anthology* by Edmund Clarence Stedman. Cambridge, Mass.: Houghton Mifflin Company—The Riverside Press, 1900. *Crossing Brooklyn Ferry.* Included in *American Poetry and Prose,* Norman Foerster, Ed. New York: Houghton, Mifflin Company, 1947.

Whitson, Skip. *The Hudson River One Hundred Years Ago.* Albuquerque, N.M.: Sun Publishing Company, 1975.

Whitson, Skip. *New York City 100 Years Ago.* Albuquerque, N.M.: Sun Publishing Company, 1976.

Whitson, Skip. *Old Long Island.* Albuquerque, N.M.: Sun Publishing Company, 1976.

Willis, Nathaniel Parker. *American Scenery.* London: George Virtue, 1836.

Willis, Nathaniel Parker. *Out-Doors at Idlewild; or, the Shaping of a Home on the Banks of the Hudson.* New York: Charles Scribner, 1855.

Willis, Nathaniel Parker. *Rural Letters.* Auburn, N.Y.: Alden, Beardsley & Co. 1853.

Wilstach, Paul. *Hudson River Landings.* Port Washington, N.Y.: Ira J. Friedman, Inc. 1969. Original edition: New York: The Bobbs-Merrill Company, 1933.

Wyckoff, Jerome. *Rock Scenery of the Hudson Highlands and Palisades.* Glen Falls, N.Y.: Adirondack Mountain Club, 1971.

HUDSON RIVER FERRY ROUTES

1) Sarles Rope Ferry (1800-193?)
2) Powers-Briggs Rope Ferry (1800 193?)
3) Bemis Heights Rope Ferry (c1750-c1866)
4) Ashley's Ferry (Troy) (c1700-c1860)
5) Hitchcock's Ferry (Troy-Albany) (c1916)
6) Albany-Bath (North Ferry) (1831-1904)
7) South Ferry (Albany-Greenbush) (1684-c1880)
8) Primitive Ferries Albany to Crawlier First mentioned c1637.
9) Albany-Greenbush (Railroad Ferry) (1836-c1880)
10) Coxsackie-Nutten Hook (1800-1938)
11) Athens-Hudson (1778-1947)
12) Catskill-Hudson (c1800-1935)
13) Catskill-Greendale (1851-1935)
14) Saugerties-Tivoli (1800-1842; 1851-1924; 1931-1938)
15) Kip Ferry (Kipsbergen, near Rhinecliff). c1702
16) Kingston-Rhinecliff (1752–1943; 1946–1957)
17) Rondout-Sleightsburg (Skillypot Chain Ferry) (1870-1922)
18) Poughkeepsie-Highland (New Paltz Landing) (1793-1941)
19) Milton Ferry (c1760-c1865)
20) Hampton Ferry (New Hamburg-Cedarcliff) Very early, dates unknown.
21) Wappingers Falls-Newburgh (c1880-c1940)
22) Newburgh-Beacon (Quassaick-Fishkill) (1743-1963)
23) Newburgh-Fishkill Railroad Car Ferry (1872-1902)
24) Fishkill-New Windsor (Military Ferry during Revolution)
25) Cornwall-Cold Spring-West Point-Peekskill Passenger Ferry (c1850-1918)
26) Cornwall-Storm King Depot (1850-1892)
27) Cold Spring-West Point (c1700-still operating) (U.S. Army)
28) West Point-Constitution Island (c1775-still operating) (Army)
29) West Point-Garrison (Phillipstown) (c1680-1928—Commercial) (U.S. Army ferry still operated)
30) Peekskill-Jones Point (Caldwell's) (1800-c1900)
31) Peekskill-Haverstraw (1835-c1900)
32) Kings Ferry (Verplanck's Point-Tomkins Cove/Stony Point) (c1700-c1800) (Revived 1922-1924)
33) Verplanck's Point-Haverstraw (1837-c1900)
34) Crugers-Grassy Point (sporadic service during 19th century)
35) Crugers-Haverstraw (c1852-c1900)
36) Haverstraw-Ossining (early 20th century)
37) Ossining-Rockland Lake Landing (Slaughter's Landing) (1835-c1860)
38) Tarrytown-Nyack (1834-1941-autos, 1956-passengers)
39) Piermont-Irvington (1841-1861) (1932-c1941)
40) Piermont-Manhattan (Erie Railroad) (c1850-1868)
41) Dobbs Ferry-Sneden's Landing (Paramus) 1698-1944
42) Yonkers-Alpine (early operation c1700-Patroon's Ferry)(1876-1882; 1885-1895; 1923-1956)
43) Dyckman Street-Englewood Cliffs (1915-1942; 1948-1951)
44) Englewood Cliffs-Manhattan—Downtown (1860-1884)
45) Burdetts Ferry (Fort Lee-Carmansville) (c1658-c1800)
46) Fort Lee-Canal Street Manhattan (1832-c1910)
47) Fort Lee-Manhattanville (1880-1896)
48) Edgewater-125th Street (Public Service-Electric Ferry) (1888-1950)
49) Edgewater-Flushing Bay (World's Fair) (1964)
50) Bull's Ferry (Shadyside-Spring Street) (c1700-1909)
51) Guttenberg-Spring Street (1832-1909)
52) Guttenberg-42nd Street (West New York) (West Shore-New York Central) (1902-1922)
53) Weehawken-42nd Street (Colonial 1700-1834)
54) Weehawken-42nd Street (Slough's Meadow) (Private 1859-1872)
55) Weehawken-42nd Street (Slough's Meadow) (Railroad 1872-1902)
56) Weehawken Terminal-42nd Street (West Shore) (1884-1959)
57) Weehawken Terminal-Jay Street (West Shore) 1885-1892)

57A) Weehawken-Port Imperial-W. 38th Street (c1986-operational)

57B) Weehawken-Port Imperial-Whitehall Street (c1988-operational)

58) Weehawken Terminal-W 13th St. (West Shore) (1892)

59) Weehawken Terminal-Franklin St. (West Shore) (1893-1909)

60) Weehawken Terminal-Desbrosses St. (West Shore) (1909-1930)

61) Weehawken Terminal-Cortlandt St. (West Shore) (1930-1959)

62) Weehawken-W 23rd St. (Undercliff) (Electric Ferry) (Baldwin Avenue) (1926-1943)

62A) Weehawken (Lincoln Harbor) Whitehall Street (1989-

63) De Klyn's Ferry (Hoboken-Spring Street) (1796-c1806)

64) 14th Street Hoboken-14th St. Manhattan (1886-1903)

65) 14th Street Hoboken-23rd St. (1903-1942) (Lackawanna Railroad)

65A) 13th Street Hoboken-38th Street Manhattan (New York Waterway) (start 2000)

65B) 13th Street Hoboken-Battery Park City (New York Waterway) (start 2000)

66) Hoboken-Barclay St. (1774-1967) (Hoboken Ferry Co.-Lackawanna)

67) Hoboken-Murray Street (1817-1819)

68) Hoboken-Vesey Street (1811-1817)

69) Hoboken-Spring Street (1813-1836)

70) Hoboken-Hulbert Street (1822)

71) Hoboken-Canal Street (c1823-1836)

72) Hoboken-Christopher Street (1836-1955) (Lackawanna)

73) Hoboken-14th Street (Hoboken Ferry Co.-Lackawanna) (1886-1903)

74) Hoboken-23rd Street (Lackawanna) (1903-1942)

74A) Hoboken-Cortlandt Street (North Cove) (1989-

75) Budd's Ferry (Harsimus) (c1802) (Restored c1988) (Newport City)

76) Pavonia Ferry (Jersey City-Chambers Street) (c1733) (Erie 1861-1959)

77) Pavonia Ave.-23rd Street (Erie) (1869-1942)

78) Newark Avenue-Duane Street (Erie RR Steamers *New Haven* and *Erie,* run in service of Paterson & Hudson River RR (1851-1861)

79) Paulus Hook Ferry (Exchange Place Jersey City-Cortlandt Street) Colonial 1764-1811; Stevens 1811-1814; Fulton 1814-1853; Pennsylvania Railroad 1853-1949). (Direct Line c1988)

80) Exchange Place-Desbrosses Street (1862-1930)

81) Exchange Place-W. 23rd Street) (1897-1910) (Pennsylvania)

82) Exchange Place-W. 34th Street (1880-1883)

83) Exchange Place-Fulton Street Brooklyn (PRR-Annex Ferry) (1877-1910)

84) Exchange Place-Atlantic Avenue, Brooklyn (Pennsylvania) (1929-1935)

85) Bay Street, Jersey City-Manhattan (Pennsylvania) (c1890s)

85A) Jersey City, Morris Basin-Pier 11, Wall Street (New York Waterway catamaran service) (start 2000)

86) Communipaw Ferry (Colonial) (1661-1786)

87) Communipaw Ferry (Central RR NJ) Liberty Street (1864-1967)

88) Communipaw Ferry (Central RR NJ) Clarkson Street (1876-1877)

89) Communipaw Ferry (Central RR NJ) W. 23rd (1905-1941)

90) Communipaw Ferry (B & O RR - Royal Blue Route) Whitehall Street (1897-1905)

91) Communipaw Ferry - Battery - (Circle Line) (c1975-now operating)

92) Ellis Island-Whitehall Street (U. S. Government) (1892-1954)

93) Ellis Island-Battery (Circle Line) (1975-currently operational)

94) Black Tom (National Docks) Morris Pesin Dr.-Liberty Island and Battery (1975-still operational)

95) Caven Point (Port Liberté)-Manhattan (c1988-operational)

96) Elizabethport-Bergen Point-Pier 2 North River Manhattan (Central RR NJ) (c1814-c1885) Steamers *Red Jacket, Chancellor, Kill Von Kull,* and double-ender *Central*

97) Elizabeth Port, Bergen Point, Wall Street East River (Direct Line) (c1986-operational)

98) Bedloes Island (Liberty Island)-Battery (1886-still operational)

99) Bedloes Island-Liberty State Park-Communipaw (Circle Line-1975-operational)

100) Governors Island-Whitehall Street (U. S. Government) (1637-operational)

101) Manhattan-Brooklyn (East River). Various lines to different streets. Most important line in recent years to Fulton Street and to Atlantic Avenue. (1642-1942) Attempted revival c 1987, from South Street Seaport.

102) Wall Street Manhattan-Atlantic Highlands Area (Direct Line) Various lines to Sandy Hook Bay points (1986-operational)

103) Whitehall Street Manhattan-St. George, Staten Island (1712-operational)

104) Brooklyn 39th Street-St. George, Staten Island (1924–1946)

105) Brooklyn 69th Street-St. George, Staten Island (Brooklyn & Richmond Ferry Co.) (1912–1939)

106) Brooklyn 69th Street-St. George, Staten Island (Electric Ferries) (1939–1954); (City of New York) (1954–1964)
107) Port Richmond, Staten Island-Bergen Point, Bayonne (1695–1961)
108) Howland Hook, Staten Island-Elizabethport (1850–1961)
109) Linoleumville, Staten Island-Carteret, NJ (1764–1960) (New Blazing Star) (Double-enders 1916–1929)
110) Tottenville, Staten Island-Perth Amboy, NJ (1659–1963)

PARTIAL FERRY VESSEL ROSTERS OF RECENT TIMES

For a more complete listing, see Raymond J. Baxter and Arthur G. Adams, *Railroad Ferries of the Hudson* (New York: Fordham University Press, 1999).

TABLE 1 — *NEWBURGH-BEACON FERRY*

Name of Vessel	Power	Propulsion	Length	Breadth	Depth	Built	Place
Dutchess	Steam	Screw	135'	56'	14'	1910	Newburgh*
Orange	Steam	Screw	135'	56'	14'	1914	Newburgh*
Beacon	Steam	Screw	145'	40'	16'	1921	Groton**

*Marvell Shipyard, Newburgh, N.Y.
**Groton, Connecticut

TABLE 2 — *YONKERS-ALPINE FERRY*

Paunpeck	Steam	Sidewheel	197'	35'	13'	1882	Newburgh
*F. R. Pierson**	Steam	Sidewheel	197'	35'	13'	1885	Newburgh
John J. Walsh	Diesel	Screw	147'	38'	14'	1937	Brooklyn
Weehawk	Diesel	Screw	146'	37'	13'	1926	Camden, NJ

*F. R. Pierson, built as *Musconetcong* for Hoboken Ferry Co.-DL&W RR *Paunpeck* originally built for Hoboken Ferry Co.-DL&W RR.

Gross Tons:
F. R. Pierson	–	846
Paunpeck	–	850
Walsh	–	370
Weehawk	–	405

TABLE 8 — *ROCKAWAY BOAT LINES—BREEZY POINT FERRY*

C. Washington Coyler	screw	60x18x2	13 gt	1913	Morehead City, N.C.
Commander	screw	61x24x5	14 gt	1917	Morehead City, N.C.
Columbia	screw	75x20x5	13 gt	1919	Brooklyn

NOTE: All vessels foot-passengers only. All originally steam and now converted to diesel.

MAJOR RAILROAD PASSENGER AND FERRY TERMINALS ALONG THE HUDSON IN NEW JERSEY

TABLE 1: *WEEHAWKEN TERMINAL*
Served the following railroads:
1) West Shore Railroad
2) New York, Ontario & Western
3) North Hudson County Railway
4) Ulster & Delaware Railroad
5) Public Service Railway (Electric)
Ferries operated to:
1) West 42nd Street
2) Franklin Street
3) Jay Street
4) Desbrosses Street
5) North Cove—Cortlandt Street—Battery Park City
NOTE: Not all services operated simultaneously

TABLE 2: *LACKAWANNA TERMINAL HOBOKEN* (Still in service in 1983)
Served the following railroads:
1) Morris & Essex Railroad
2) Delaware, Lackawanna & Western Railroad
3) Erie Railroad
4) Erie-Lackawanna Railway
5) New Jersey & New York Railroad
6) Northern Railroad of New Jersey
7) North Hudson County Railway (Elevated line).
8) Public Service Railway (Elevated and electric surface).
9) Hoboken Ferry Company
Ferries operated to:
1) Barclay Street
2) Christopher Street
3) 14th Street
4) 23rd Street
5) North Cove—Cortlandt Street

TABLE 3: *ERIE PAVONIA AVENUE TERMINAL-JERSEY CITY*
Served the following railroads:
1) Erie Railroad
2) New Jersey Midland Railroad
3) New York, Susquehanna & Western Railroad
4) Northern Railroad of New Jersey
5) New Jersey & New York Railroad
6) New York & Greenwood Lake Railroad
Ferries operated to:
1) Chambers Street
2) 23rd Street

TABLE 4: *JERSEY CITY EXCHANGE PLACE TERMINAL*
Served the following railroads:
1) New Jersey Railroad & Transportation Company
2) Pennsylvania Railroad
3) New York & Long Branch Railroad
4) Lehigh Valley Railroad
5) New York, West Shore & Buffalo Railroad
6) Paterson & Hudson River Railroad
7) Morris & Essex Railroad
8) New York & Oswego Midland Railroad

9) Ridgefield Park Railroad

10) Jersey City & Albany Railroad

11) New Jersey Midland Railroad

12) New York, Susquehanna & Western Railroad

13) New York & Erie RR, and the Union RR used the same ferry slips, but a separate 6 ft. gauge terminal slightly to the north of the main terminal.

Ferries operated to:

1) Cortlandt Street

2) Desbrosses Street

3) West 23rd Street

4) Fulton Street Brooklyn

5) Atlantic Avenue Brooklyn

6) 34th Street

7) Battery Park City—World Financial Center

Served the following steamship lines:

1) Cunard Line—To Europe

2) Isthmethian Lines—Central America

3) Meseck Line—Rye Beach and Bridgeport

4) Wilson Line—Rye Beach and Hudson River points

5) Keansburg Steamboat Company—Battery, 69th Street Brooklyn, Atlantic Highlands, Keansburg, New Jersey

TABLE 5: *JERSEY CENTRAL COMMUNIPAW TERMINAL-JOHNSTON AVENUE*

Served the following railroads:

1) Central Railroad of New Jersey

2) Philadelphia & Reading Railway

3) Baltimore & Ohio Railroad

4) New York & Long Branch Railroad

5) Lehigh Valley Railroad

6) New York & Newark Railroad

Ferries operated to:

1) Liberty Street

2) Clarkson Street

3) Whitehall Street

4) West 23rd Street

Jersey Central Steamboats operated from West 41st Street, Manhattan, and the Battery to Sandy Hook, Atlantic Highlands, and Long Branch.

TABLE 6: *ORDER OF TERMINAL ABANDONMENTS*

1) Exchange Place—1995 Reopened

2) Weehawken—1986 Reopened

3) Erie-Pavonia

4) Jersey Central-Communipaw (Restored as visitor's center for Liberty State Park)

5) Hoboken Terminal—Renovated in 1980 for continued operation.

TABLE 7: *NEW JERSEY STATIONS OF HUDSON & MANHATTAN RAILROAD (PATH).*

1) Newark—Pennsylvania Station

2) Harrison

3) Journal Square - Jersey City

4) Henderson-Grove - Jersey City

5) Exchange Place - Jersey City

6) Pavonia Avenue - Erie Terminal - Jersey City

7) Hoboken - Lackawanna Terminal

Manhattan Terminals are at World Trade Center downtown and Herald Square (West 33rd Street and Broadway) uptown.

MANHATTAN NORTH RIVER PIER OCCUPANCY IN 1934

Pier #	Street	Tenant
A	Battery Pl.	Department of Docks & Ferries
1	Battery Pl.	Coney Island Service — Iron Steamboat Co.
2	Roosevelt St.	United Fruit Company
3	Morris St.	United Fruit Company
7		United Fruit Company
8	Rector St.	Lehigh Valley Railroad
9	Rector St.	United Fruit Company
10	Albany St.	Central RR of New Jersey
11	Cedar St.	Central RR of New Jersey
	Liberty St.	Central RR of New Jersey Ferry
	Cortlandt St.	Pennsylvania RR Ferry
	Cortlandt St.	West Shore RR Ferry
13	Fulton St.	Delaware, Lackawanna & Western RR
14	Vesey St.	New England Navigation (Fall River Line)
15	Vesey St.	New England Navigation (Fall River Line)
	Barclay St.	Lackawanna Ferry to Hoboken
16	Barclay St.	New York Central Railroad
17	Park Place	New York Central Railroad
18	Murray St.	Eastern Steamship Co.
19	Warren St.	Metropolitan Steamship Co. (Boston Line)
	Chambers St.	Erie Railroad Ferry to Pavonia
20	Chambers St.	Erie Railroad
21	Duane St.	Erie Railroad
22	Jay St.	West Shore RR and Baltimore & Ohio RR
23	Harrison St.	New York Central and N Y, Ontario & Western
24	Franklin St.	New York City
25	Moore St.	Eastern Steamship Co.
26	Beach St.	Eastern Steamship Co.
27	Hubert St.	Pennsylvania Railroad
28	Laight St.	Pennsylvania Railroad
29	Vestry St.	Pennsylvania Railroad
	Debrosses St.	Pennsylvania RR Ferry (abandoned)
32	Canal St.	North German Lloyd Line
34	Spring St.	Clyde Line
35	Vandam St.	Pier abandoned
36	Charlton St.	Clyde Mallory Lines
37	Charlton St.	Clyde Mallory Lines
38	King St.	Lehigh Valley Railroad
39	W. Houston St.	Central Railroad of New Jersey
40	Clarkson St.	New England Navigation Co.
41	Leroy St.	Delaware, Lackawanna & Western RR
42	Morton St.	Royal Mail Steam Packet Co.
43	Barrow St.	Hudson River Steamship Co.
	Christopher St.	Lackawanna Ferry to Hoboken
44	Christopher St.	Delaware, Lackwanna & Western RR
45	W. 10th St.	Italian Line
46	Perry St.	Savannah Line
48	W. 11th St.	Southern Pacific Railroad
49	Bank St.	Southern Pacific Railroad
50	Bethune St.	Southern Pacific Railroad
51	Jane St.	Morgan Line (SP RR affiliate)
52	Gansevoort St.	Hudson Navigation Co. (Albany Night Line)

Between Piers 52 at Gansevoort St. and 53 at Little West 12th St., there was land filled in west of West Street with several small streets running from W to E, bisected by two short streets running N to S, with three small, undesignated piers belonging to New York City along the western frontage. These small streets, naming them from south to north, were: Lawson Avenue; Grace Avenue; Thompson Avenue; Hewitt Avenue; Loew Avenue; and Bloomfield Avenue. There is no name shown on the short north and south streets or alleys.

From Pier 53, at Little West 12th Street, to Pier 62, at W 22nd St., was a set of large and unified piers used by transatlantic liners and known as the Chelsea Piers. They were joined by neo-classical continuous facade on the West Street frontage.

Pier #	Street	Tenant
53	Little W 12th St.	Cunard Line
54	W 13th St.	Cunard Line
56	W 14th St.	Cunard Line
57	W 15th St.	French Line
58	W 16th St.	Atlantic Transportation Co.
59	W 18th St.	White Star Line
60	W 19th St.	White Star Line
61	W 21st St.	White Star Line
62	W 22nd St.	American Leyland Line
	W 23rd St.	Central RR of New Jersey Ferry
	W 23rd St.	Lackawanna RR Ferry to Hoboken
	W 23rd St.	Erie Railroad Ferry to Pavonia
63	W 23rd St.	American & Cuban Steamship Co.
64	W 24th St.	Anchor Line
65	W 25th St.	Panama Steamship Co.
66	W 26th St.	Lehigh Valley Railroad
67	W 27th St.	Erie Railroad
68	W 28th St.	Delaware, Lackawanna & Western RR
69	W 29th St.	New York City
70	W 30th St.	New York City
71	W 31st St.	Cunard Line
72	W 32nd St.	New York Central RR
73	W 33rd St.	New York Central RR
74	W 34th St.	Furness Prince Lines
75	W 35th St.	New York City Fire Department
76	W 36th St.	New York Central RR
77	W 37th St.	Pennsylvania RR
78	W 38th St.	Pennsylvania RR
79	Abbatoir Pl.	New York City
80	W 40th St.	Central RR of New Jersey (Sandy Hook Boats)
81	W 41st St.	Hudson River Day Line
82	W 42nd St.	West Shore RR (New York Central)
	W 42nd St.	West Shore Ferry to Weehawken
83	W 43rd St.	West Shore Railroad
84	W 44th St.	United American Line
86	W 46th St.	United American Line
88	W 48th St.	New York City (Site of later liner piers)
89	W 49th St.	New York City (Site of later liner piers)
90	W 50th St.	New York City (Site of later liner piers)
91	W 51st St.	New York City (Site of later liner piers)
92	W 52nd St.	New York City (Site of later liner piers)
93	W 53rd St.	New York State Barge
94	W 54th St.	New York City
95	W 55th St.	Furness Withy Lines
96	W 56th St.	Italian Line
97	W 57th St.	Italian-American Line
98	W 58th St.	Interboro Rapid Transit Co.
99	W 59th St.	New York Central RR
102-B	W 62nd St.	NY Central RR Carfloat Bridge
103-D	W 63rd St.	NY Central RR Carfloat Bridge
104-E	W 64th St.	NY Central RR Carfloat Bridge
105-F	W 65th St.	NY Central RR Carfloat Bridge
106-G	W 66th St.	NY Central RR Carfloat Bridge

Pier #	Street	Tenant
108-H	W 70th St.	NY Central RR Carfloat Bridge
113	W 79th St.	New York City (Site of present Marina)
114	W 80th St.	New York City (Site of present Marina)
—	W 95th St.	Undesignated
—	W 96th St.	Undesignated
—	W 97th St.	Undesignated
—	W 98th St.	Undesignated
—	W 102nd St.	Undesignated
—	W 107th St.	Undesignated
—	W 108th St.	Undesignated
—	W 113th St.	Undesignated
—	W 116th St.	Undesignated
—	Tieman Place	Undesignated
—	St. Clair Pl.	Hudson River Day Line & Iron Steamboat Co.
—	W 125th St.	Ferry to Edgewater (Public Service)
—	W 131st St.	Manhattan Terminal Co.
—	W 132nd St.	Undesignated
—	W 133rd St.	Undesignated
—	W 134th St.	Undesignated
—	W 135th St.	Undesignated
—	W 138th St.	Undesignated
—	W 139th St.	Undesignated
—	W 150th St.	Undesignated
—	W 151st St.	Undesignated
—	W 152nd St.	Undesignated
—	W 154th St.	Undesignated
—	W 155th St.	Undesignated
—	W 156th St.	Undesignated
—	W 157th St.	Undesignated
—	W 158th St.	Undesignated
—	W 163rd St.	Undesignated
	Dyckman St.	Ferry to Englewood

NOTE: The reason for the many "Undesignated" piers above W 80th St. is that the City of New York was trying to consolidate parcels of land for the Riverside Park and Hudson River Expressway and free the area from commercial use. All these piers have since been removed, with the exception of a few around W 125th St.

By the end of the 2nd World War the major transatlantic liner activity had moved north from the Chelsea Piers to those between West 42nd and West 57th Streets—Site of the New York City Passenger Ship Terminal, opened in 1974 and operated by the Port Authority on behalf of the City of New York. The Cunard and White Star Lines merged and from the late 1940s till the early 1970s operated from their own piers on the site of the new 1974 terminal. It was here that the *"Queen Mary"* and *"Queen Elizabeth"* used to dock. The French Line also docked in this area, and their greatest ships were the *"Normandie"* (which burned here at the pier), *"Ile de France"* and *"France."* American Export Lines operated the *"Atlantic," "Independence"* and *"Constitution"* from pier 83. The United States Lines used to operate the *"America"* from Pier 62 at the Chelsea docks, but later moved operations uptown. The *"United States"* operated from the uptown piers. Piers 88 through 97 were used by the American Export Line, United States Line, Cunard Line, Swedish American Line, Italian Line, Home Lines, and Furness Burmuda Lines.

SOME FAMOUS HUDSON RIVER STEAMBOATS

Pioneer Period

North River Steam Boat of Clermont Built by Robert Fulton in 1807.
  First trip New York to Albany on August 17-19, 1807, in 28 hours and 45 minutes. 149 ft. long. Sidewheel.

Swallow 1836	Sidewheeler	225 ft.	Ran aground and on fire.
Issac Newton 1846	Sidewheeler	320 ft.	Palatial nightboat.
Alida 1847	Sidewheeler	249 ft.	Day boat.
New World 1848	Sidewheeler	352 ft.	Palatial nightboat.
Francis Skiddy 1951	Sidewheeler	312 ft.	Day boat.
St. John 1864	Sidewheeler	393 ft.	Palatial nightboat.
Dean Richmond 1865	Sidewheeler	348 ft.	Palatial nightboat.
Drew 1866	Sidewheeler	366 ft.	Palatial nightboat.

Modern Nightboats

Kaaterskill 1882	Sidewheeler	285 ft.	Catskill Evening Line.
Adirondack 1896	Sidewheeler	388 ft.	Albany Night Line.
Berkshire 1907	Sidewheeler	422 ft.	Albany Night Line. The largest.
C. W. Morse 1903	Sidewheeler	411 ft.	Albany Night Line.
Renamed *Fort Orange* in 1922.			
Trojan 1909	Sidewheeler	317 ft.	Albany & Troy Night Lines.

  Last nightboat on the River—operated until 1939. Renamed *New Yorker* in 1939.

Benjamin B. Odell 1911	Screw propeller	263 ft.	Central Hudson Line.

Modern Dayliners

Mary Powell 1861	Sidewheeler	288 ft.	Very fast. "Queen of the River."

  Originally built for Mary Powell Steamboat Co. of Kingston. Later operated for Hudson River Day Line.

New York 1887	Sidewheeler	335 ft.	Hudson River Day Line.
Albany 1880	Sidewheeler	314 ft.	Hudson River Day Line.
Hendrick Hudson 1906	Sidewheeler	379 ft.	Hudson River Day Line.
Robert Fulton 1909	Sidewheeler	337 ft.	Hudson River Day Line.
Washington Irving 1913	Sidewheeler	414 ft.	Hudson River Day Line.
DeWitt Clinton 1913	Twin Screw	320 ft.	Hudson River Day Line.
Chauncey M. Depew 1913	Single Screw	185 ft.	Hudson River Day Line.
Alexander Hamilton 1924	Sidewheeler	349 ft.	Hudson River Day Line.
Peter Stuyvesant 1927	Single Screw	269 ft.	Hudson River Day Line.
Dayliner 1971*	Twin Screw, Diesel	308 ft.	Hudson River Day Line.

  *In present day operation.

BRITISH SOVEREIGNS

1485-1509	Henry VII	Tudor	Catholic
1509-1547	Henry VIII	Tudor	Catholic/Protestant
1547-1553	Edward VI	Tudor	Protestant
1553-1558	Mary	Tudor	Catholic
	(Married to Phillip II of Spain)		
1558-1603	Elizabeth I	Tudor	Protestant
1603-1625	James I	Stuart	Protestant
1625-1649	Charles I	Stuart	Protestant
	(Beheaded by the Regicides)		
1649-1660	Oliver Cromwell	"Lord Protector"	Puritan Commonwealth
1660-1685	Charles II	Stuart	Protestant (Restoration)
1685-1688	James II	Stuart	Catholic
	"Glorious Revolution" of 1688		
1688-1702	William III and	House of Orange	Protestant
1689-1694	Mary (1689-1694)	Dutch	
1702-1714	Anne		Protestant
1714-1727	George I	House of Hanover	Protestant
1727-1760	George II	House of Hanover	Protestant
1760-1820	George III	House of Hanover	Protestant
1820-1830	George IV	House of Hanover	Protestant
1830-1837	William IV	House of Hanover	Protestant
1837-1901	Victoria	House of Hanover	Protestant
	(Married Prince Albert of Saxe-Coburg-Gotha (d1861)		
		House of Wettin	Protestant
1901-1910	Edward VII	House of Wettin	Protestant
1910-1936	George V	House of Wettin	Protestant
1936	Edward VIII	House of Wettin	Protestant
	(Abdicated to marry Wallis Warfield Simpson, an American divorcee. Became Duke of Windsor)		
1936-1952	George VI	House of Wettin	Protestant
		(anglicized to Windsor)	
1952-	Elizabeth II	House of Windsor	Protestant
	(Married Philip Mountbatten, Duke of Edinburgh)		
	(Son Charles Philip Arthur George, born 1948), now Prince		
	of Wales).		

PRESIDENTS OF THE UNITED STATES

George Washington	Federalist	1789-1797
John Adams	Federalist	1797-1801
Thomas Jefferson	Republican	1801-1809
James Madison	Republican	1809-1817
James Monroe	Republican	1817-1825
John Quincy Adams	Republican	1825-1829
Andrew Jackson	Democrat	1829-1837
Martin Van Buren	Democrat	1837-1841
William Henry Harrison	Whig	1841
John Tyler	Democrat	1841-1845
James K. Polk	Democrat	1845-1849
Zachary Taylor	Whig	1849-1850
Millard Filmore	Whig	1850-1853
Franklin Pierce	Democrat	1853-1857
James Buchanan	Democrat	1857-1861
Abraham Lincoln	Republic	1861-1865
Andrew Johnson	Republican	1865-1869
Ulysses S. Grant	Republican	1869-1877
Rutherford B. Hayes	Republican	1877-1881
James A. Garfield	Republican	1881
Chester A. Arthur	Republican	1881-1885
Grover Cleveland	Democrat	1885-1889
Benjamin Harrison	Republican	1889-1893
Grover Cleveland	Democrat	1893-1897
William McKinley	Republican	1897-1901
Theodore Roosevelt	Republican	1901-1909
William Howard Taft	Republican	1909-1913
Woodrow Wilson	Democrat	1913-1921
Warren G. Harding	Republican	1921-1923
Calvin Coolidge	Republican	1923-1929
Herbert C. Hoover	Republican	1929-1933
Franklin D. Roosevelt	Democrat	1933-1945
Harry S. Truman	Democrat	1945-1953
Dwight D. Eisenhower	Republican	1953-1961
John F. Kennedy	Democrat	1961-1963
Lyndon B. Johnson	Democrat	1963-1969
Richard M. Nixon	Republican	1969-1974
Gerald R. Ford	Republican	1974-1977
Jimmy Carter	Democrat	1977-1981
Ronald Reagan	Republican	1981-1989
George Bush	Republican	1989-1993
Bill Clinton	Democrat	1993-

GOVERNORS OF NEW YORK

First Dutch Period

Adriaen Jorissen Tienpoint, Director	1623-1624
Cornelis Jacobsen Mey, Director	1624-1625
Willem Verhulst, Director	1625-1626
Peter Minuit, Director General	1626-1632
Bastiaen Jansen Krol, Director General	1632-1633
Wouter Van Twiller, Director General	1633-1638
Willem Kieft, Director General	1638-1647
Peter Stuyvesant, Director General	1647-1664

First English Period

Richard Nicolls, Governor	1664-1668
Francis Lovelace, Governor	1668-1673

Second Dutch Period

Cornelis Evertsen, Council of War	1673
Anthony Colve, Governor General	1673-1674

Second English Period

Edmund Andros, Governor	1674-1677
Anthony Brockholls, Lt. Governor	1677-1678
Sir Edmund Andros, Governor	1678-1681
Anthony Brockholls, Governor	1681-1682
Thomas Dongan, Governor	1682-1688
Sir Edmund Andros, Governor	1688
Francis Nicholson, Lt. Governor	1688-1689
Jacob Leisler, Lt. Governor	1689-1690
Henry Sloughter, Governor	1691
Richard Ingoldesby, Commander In Chief	1691-1692
Colonel Benjamin Fletcher, Governor	1692-1697
Richard Coote, 1st Earl of Bellomont, Governor	1697-1701
John Nanfan, Lt. Governor	1701
Viscount Edward Hyde, Lord Cornbury, Earl of Clarendon, Governor	1702-1708
John Lovelace, 4th Baron Lovelace, Governor	1708-1709
Peter Schuyler, President of the Council	1709
Richard Ingoldesby, Lt. Governor	1709-1710
Gerardus Beekman, President of the Council	1710
Robert Hunter, Governor	1710-1719
Peter Schuyler, President of the Council	1719-1720
William Burnet, Governor	1720-1728
John Montgomerie, Governor	1728-1731
Rip Van Dam, President of the Council	1731-1732
William Cosby, Governor	1732-1736
George Clarke, Lt. Governor and President of Council	1736-1743
George Clinton, Governor	1743-1753
Sir Danvers Osborne, Governor (suicide)	1753
James De Lancey, Lt. Governor	1753-1755
Sir Charles Hardy, Governor	1755-1757
James De Lancey, Lt. Governor	1757-1760

Cadwallader Colden, Lt. Governor, President of Council		1760-1761
Robert Monckton, Governor		1761
Cadwallader Colden, Lt. Governor		1761-1762
Robert Monckton, Governor		1762-1763
Cadwallader Colden, Lt. Governor		1763-1765
Sir Henry Moore, Governor		1765-1769
Cadwallader Colden, Lt. Governor		1769-1770
John Murray, 4th Earl of Dunmore, Governor		1770-1771
William Tryon, Governor		1771-1774
Cadwallader Colden, Lt. Governor		1774-1775
William Tryon, Governor		1775-1777
William Tryon, Governor (British Usage)		1777-1780
James Robertson (British Usage)		1780-1783

Governors of the State

George Clinton		1777-1795
John Jay		1795-1801
George Clinton	Democratic-Republican	1801-1804
Morgan Lewis	Democratic-Republican	1804-1807
Daniel D. Tompkins	Democratic-Republican	1807-1817
John Taylor (Acting Governor)	Democratic-Republican	1817
De Witt Clinton	Democratic-Republican	1817-1823
Joseph C. Yates	Democratic-Republican	1823-1825
De Witt Clinton	Democratic-Republican	1825-1828
Nathaniel Pitcher (Acting Governor)	Democratic-Republican	1828
Martin Van Buren	Democrat	1829
Enos T. Throop (Acting)	Democrat	1829-1831
Enos T. Throop	Democrat	1831-1833
William L. Marcy	Democrat	1833-1839
William H. Seward	Whig	1839-1843
William C. Bouck	Democrat	1843-1845
Silas Wright	Democrat	1845-1847
John Young	Whig	1847-1849
Hamilton Fish	Whig	1849-1851
Washington Hunt	Democrat	1851-1853
Horatio Seymour	Democrat	1853-1855
Myron H. Clark	Whig	1855-1857
John A. King	Republican	1857-1859
Edwin D. Morgan	Republican	1859-1863
Horatio Seymour	Democrat	1863-1865
Reuben E. Fenton	Republican	1865-1869
John T. Hoffman	Democrat	1869-1873
John Adams Dix	Republican	1873-1875
Samuel J. Tilden	Democrat	1875-1877
Lucius Robinson	Democrat	1877-1880
Alonzo B. Cornell	Republican	1880-1883
Grover Cleveland	Democrat	1883-1885
David Bennett Hill	Democrat (Acting)	1885
David Bennett Hill	Democrat	1886-1892
Roswell P. Flower	Democrat	1892-1895
Levi P. Morton	Republican	1895-1897
Frank S. Black	Republican	1897-1899
Theodore Roosevelt	Republican	1899-1901
Benjamin B. Odell, Jr.	Republican	1901-1905
Frank W. Higgins	Republican	1905-1907
Charles Evans Hughes	Republican	1907-1910
Horace White (Acting)	Republican	1910
John Alden Dix	Democrat	1911-1913
William Sulzer	Democrat	1913

Martin H. Glynn	Democrat	1913-1915
Charles S. Whitman	Republican	1915-1919
Alfred E. Smith	Democrat	1919-1921
Nathan L. Miller	Republican	1921-1923
Alfred E. Smith	Democrat	1923-1929
Franklin D. Roosevelt	Democrat	1929-1933
Herbert H. Lehman	Democrat	1933-1942
Charles Poletti (Acting)	Democrat	1942
Thomas Edmund Dewey	Republican	1943-1954
Averell Harriman	Democrat	1955-1958
Nelson Rockefeller	Republican	1958-1973
Malcolm Wilson	Republican	1973–1974
Hugh Carey	Republican	1975–1982
Mario Cuomo	Democrat	1982–1994
George Pataki	Republican	1994–

THOSE CONFUSING CLINTONS

1) George Clinton - British Colonial Governor of New York from 1743 to 1753

2) Sir Henry Clinton (1738-1795) British general in American Revolution. Fought against James and George Clinton at Forts Clinton and Montgomery in Highlands. Son of George Clinton, the British Governor.

3) George Clinton (1739-1812) Born at Little Britain, N.Y., near Newburgh. First Governor of New York State (1777-1795). He also served a second term (1801-1804). Later Vice President of the United States. Acted as a General in The Revolution.

4) James Clinton (1733-1812) Older brother of George Clinton, the first American Governor of New York. General in both the French & Indian and Revolutionary Wars. Helped defend Fort Clinton, in the Highlands, against the British General Sir Henry Clinton. Father of De Witt Clinton.

5) De Witt Clinton (1796-1828) Born at New Windsor, N.Y. Son of James Clinton, and nephew of George Clinton. Served as Governor of New York State for two terms (1817-1823, 1825-1828). Father of the Erie Canal. The first steam locomotive on the Mohawk & Hudson Railroad was named in his honor.

POPULATION GROWTH OF NEW YORK STATE

1664	10,000 est.
1756	96,756
1800	589,051
1810	959,049
1820	1,372,812
1830	1,918,608
1840	2,428,921
1850	3,097,394
1860	3,880,735
1870	4,382,759
1880	5,082,871
1890	6,003,174
1900	7,268,894
1910	9,113,614
1920	10,385,227
1930	12,588,066
1940	13,379,662
1950	14,830,192
1960	16,782,304
1970	18,241,266
1980	18,190,740
1990	17,990,455

COUNTIES ALONG THE HUDSON RIVER

1681	The Shires of Counties Act passed.	
1683	The following counties were erected:	
	Albany	Named for title of Duke of Albany & York, later James II
	Dutchess	Named for his wife
	Kings	Named for King Charles II
	New York	Named for title of Duke of Albany & York - The Proprietor
	Orange	Named for William, Prince of Orange
	Richmond	Named for Duke of Richmond, son of Charles II
	Queens	Named for Catherine of Braganza, wife of Charles II
	Suffolk	Named for English county of same name
	Ulster	Named for Duke of York's earldom in Ireland
	Westchester	Named after Chester in England
1682	Bergen	In East Jersey - Dutch for "hilly." Included present day Hudson County.
1683	Monmouth	In East Jersey - Named for Duke of Monmouth
1683	Middlesex	East Jersey - Named for county in England
1683	Essex	East Jersey - Named for county in England
1784	Washington	Named for George Washington—Taken from Tryon, which was taken from Albany in 1772, but which no longer exists. It was named for Governor William Tryon of New York.
1786	Columbia	Named in honor of Christopher Columbus. From Albany.
1791	Rensselaer	Named in honor of early Patroons. Taken from Albany.
1791	Saratoga	Indian "sah-rah-ka" or "side hill." Taken from Albany.
1798	Rockland	"Rocky land." Taken from Orange.
1800	Greene	Named for General Nathaniel Greene. Taken from Albany and Ulster.
1812	Putnam	Named for General Israel Putnam. Taken from Dutchess.
1813	Warren	Named for General Joseph Warren, killed at Battle of Bunker Hill. Taken from Washington.
1840	Hudson	In New Jersey. Named in honor of Henry Hudson and the Hudson River. Taken from Bergen.
1914	Bronx	Named for early settler Jonas Bronck. Taken from New York.

PRESENT AREAS OF COUNTIES IN SQUARE MILES

Albany	531	
Dutchess	816	
Kings	71	(Brooklyn)
New York	22	(Manhattan)
Orange	829	
Queens	108	
Richmond	57	(Staten Island)
Suffolk	922	
Ulster	1143	
Westchester	435	
Washington	837	
Columbia	643	
Rensselaer	665	
Saratoga	814	
Rockland	178	
Greene	653	
Putnam	235	
Warren	883	
Bronx	41	

General Index

Vessel Index

I — Ferry Boats
II — River, Bay, and Sound Steamboats
III — All other types of ship

I. Ferry Boats

II. River, Bay, and Sound Steamboats

III. All other types of ships